THE PUBLIC
ADMINISTRATION
THEORY PRIMER

THE PUBLIC ADMINISTRATION THEORY PRIMER

SECOND EDITION

H. George Frederickson
University of Kansas

Kevin B. Smith
University of Nebraska

Christopher W. Larimer
University of Northern Iowa

Michael J. Licari
University of Northern Iowa

WESTVIEW
PRESS

A MEMBER OF THE PERSEUS BOOKS GROUP

Westview Press was founded in 1975 in Boulder, Colorado, by notable publisher and intellectual Fred Praeger. Westview Press continues to publish scholarly titles and high-quality undergraduate- and graduate-level textbooks in core social science disciplines. With books developed, written, and edited with the needs of serious nonfiction readers, professors, and students in mind, Westview Press honors its long history of publishing books that matter.

Every effort has been made to secure required permissions for all text, images, maps, and other art reprinted in this volume.

Westview Press books are available at special discounts for bulk purchases in the United States by corporations, institutions, and other organizations. For more information, please contact the Special Markets Department at the Perseus Books Group, 2300 Chestnut Street, Suite 200, Philadelphia, PA 19103, or call (800) 810-4145, ext. 5000, or e-mail special.markets@perseusbooks.com.

Library of Congress Cataloging-in-Publication Data
  The public administration theory primer / H. George Frederickson . . . [et al.].—
2nd ed.
    p. cm.
  Includes bibliographical references and index.
  ISBN 978-0-8133-4576-5 (pbk. : alk. paper)—ISBN 978-0-8133-4577-2
(e-book) 1. Public administration—United States. I. Frederickson, H. George.
  JF1351.F734 2012
  351.73—dc23
                                                    2011035509

10 9 8 7 6 5 4 3 2 1

CONTENTS

PREFACE

The first edition of *The Public Administration Theory Primer* sought to address a problem faced sooner or later by all students, scholars, and practitioners of public administration. In order to make sense of what we study or practice we need some structure or framework to understand decisions, outcomes, causes, and the like; in other words, we need a theory. The big problem in the field of public administration is not that we lack theory; the problem is one of surfeit rather than deficit. The big challenge is ordering, synthesizing, and making sense of multiple theoretical and empirical perspectives. The first edition of the primer was explicitly aimed at meeting that challenge.

Since its publication in 2003, *The Public Administration Theory Primer* has been adopted by scores of instructors, cited in hundreds of scholarly articles, and served as a comprehensive survey of the field for thousands of students and academics. Though it continued to serve as a standard reference and text, events inside and outside the academy left the first edition increasingly dated. There have been numerous new developments and contributions in public administration theory since its publication; changes in government and management practices have created new demands for different types of theories; and some of the concepts and models given extensive coverage in the original edition have either passed from favor or been superceded by subsequent work.

This second edition of *The Primer* retains the original's thematic focus and general organization, but is extensively updated to include the latest directions and developments. These include the rise of reporting as a means to hold bureaucracy accountable (see Chapter 2), the continuing evolution of the "hollow state" or "shadow bureaucracy" and the rise of network theory (see Chapter 5), new psychological/biological behavioral research with big implications for decision theory and, especially, rational choice (see Chapters 7 and 8). The contributions of nearly a decade's worth of new research is woven into all the chapters, some of which has altered our conclusions about the health and robustness of some popular conceptual frameworks (see Chapter 10).

Many deserve thanks for making the second edition of *The Primer* possible. We appreciate the hard work, faith in the project, and patience in seeing it through to fruition of Anthony Wahl, our editor at Westview. We also have a long list of debts to many others whose contributions through two editions should not go unmentioned. These include Ken Meier, Leisha DeHart-Davis, and Tom Catlaw. We thank our colleagues at the Department of Public Administration of the University of Kansas, the Department of Political Science at the University of Nebraska, and the Department of Political Science at the University of Northern Iowa for encouraging and supportive environments in which to work. We thank Dwight Waldo for his inspiration. Above all we thank our spouses, Mary Frederickson, Kelly Smith, Danielle Larimer, and Kirsten Licari, for their unflagging and loving support.

1

Introduction:
The Possibilities of Theory

Why Do We Need Theory in Public Administration?

All the great human events in history were probably achieved by what we today would call public administration. Organization and management *practices* in collective or public settings are certainly as old as civilization, and significant changes in those practices tend to accompany historical shifts in mass-scale social organization and operation.[1] For example, the transition from feudal society to the extended nation-state was made possible by the centralization of policy, on the one hand, and the decentralization of policy implementation, on the other (Tout 1937; Ellul 1955; Chrimes 1952). The colonial era would be described the same way, but on a worldwide scale (Gladden 1972). There are splendid comparisons of British, French, Portuguese, Dutch, and Belgian approaches to issues of colonial centralization and decentralization, the management of courts, and the organization and management of navies and armies (Gladden 1972, 323–333). Extensive archaeological research indicates that early Armenian civilizations were built on rather elaborate forms of administration (Von Hagen 1962; Prescott 1908; Mason 1957; Morley 1956). In China, the Sung dynasty (A.D. 960–1279) "maintained substantially the traditional Chinese system of government and administration. The Emperor, who was supreme, was advised and assisted by a Council of State whose members, varying from five to nine, supervised individually the several organs of Administration, which were grouped under (1) the Secretariat-Chancellery, (2) the Finance Commission, and (3) the Bureau of Military Affairs" (Gladden 1972, 191; Yutang 1947; Loewe 1966; Balazs 1964; Weber 1947).

In these and countless other examples, the elemental features of public administration permeated social development; indeed, it is argued that civilization *requires* the elemental features of public administration (Waldo 1946, 1956; Wildavsky

1987; Douglas and Wildavsky 1982). Following Max Weber, the elemental features of public administration include (1) some basis of formal authority with claims to obedience; (2) intentionally established laws and rules, which apply to all; (3) specific spheres of individual competence, which include task differentiation, specialization, expertise, and/or professionalization; (4) the organization of persons into groups or categories according to specialization; (5) coordination by hierarchy; (6) continuity through rules and records; (7) the organization as distinct from the persons holding positions or offices in it; and (8) the development of particular and specific organizational technologies (Weber 1952). Virtually all considerations of the great epochs of human history have found the building blocks of organization and management (Gladden 1972). The *practices* of public administration are, then, as old as civilization and essential to the development of civilization.

Although the practice of public administration is very old, the formal study of public administration and the elaboration of public administration theory are very new. As a separate self-conscious or self-aware academic and intellectual thing— a body of knowledge, a field of professional practice, an academic subject, a form of politics, a social construction of reality—public administration is young. When measured from the *Federalist*, public administration is more than 225 years old, more than 22 decades, more than 7 generations. When measured from the publication of Woodrow Wilson's founding essay (1887/1941), public administration is more than 125 years old, more than 12 decades, more than 3 generations. As a separate and self-conscious collection of concepts, ideas, reforms, courses and degrees, and professed answers to public problems, public administration is a young adult.

In his encyclopedic description of what we know about public administration, James Q. Wilson claims to have little interest in theory and expresses the opinion that theory has little to offer to an understanding of bureaucracy:

> I wish that this book could be set forth in a way that proved, or at least illustrated, a simple, elegant, comprehensive theory of bureaucratic behavior. I have come to have grave doubts that anything worth calling "organization theory" will ever exist. Theories will exist, but they will usually be so abstract or general as to explain rather little. Interesting explanations will exist, some even supported with facts, but these will be partial, place- and time-bound insights. Many scholars disagree with me. More power to them. (1989, xi–xii)

If contemporary understandings of public administration are merely recitations of facts derived from research—letting the facts speak for themselves—can public administration theory be taken seriously?

One purpose of this book is to answer this question with a firm *yes*. Despite Wilson's disclaimer, theory is the bedrock of understanding public administration.

Indeed, in many ways Wilson's own work is a profoundly important theoretical contribution.

There is no theorist more clever than the scholar claiming to have no theory. Simply to arrange the facts, describe the research findings, and claim no theory may appear to be safe. But theory of some kind will have guided the selection of which facts to present, how to order those facts, and how to interpret them. All theories have weaknesses, and denying theory while doing theory has the big advantage of not having to defend those weaknesses. Denying theory while doing theory has other advantages as well. It helps to avoid the stereotypes of, say, decision theorists or rational choice theorists. To claim to be atheoretical skirts the truth-in-labeling test. Without acknowledging a theory or expressing an interest in a theory, the scholar can attempt to avoid labels and stereotypes. These are all compelling reasons to avoid theoretical boxes and categories; but these reasons do not diminish the centrality of theory in all of public administration.

Can theory be important in a field as applied, practical, and interdisciplinary as public administration? This book answers this question with another firm *yes*. We believe it is self-evident that a need exists for greater conceptual clarity and theoretical reliability in the treatment of public administration. It is always tempting in an applied field to fall back on common sense and wisdom as sufficient to the task of implementing public policy. In fact, common sense and wisdom are necessary for carrying out effective policy, but they are not sufficient, especially when common sense and wisdom are poorly defined or not defined at all. Deep thinking is also helpful, but insufficient. The certainties derived from the deep thought of one generation are often poor guides for succeeding generations. For example, it is presently accepted almost universally that public bureaucracies are slow, cumbersome, self-serving, and inefficient—the common sense or wisdom of our day. We act on that common sense by deregulating, downsizing, contracting out, privatizing, encouraging bureaucratic risk taking and innovation, and loosening controls on government purchasing and bidding. In the 1930s, when the United States was in a deep economic depression, an opposite type of common sense prevailed. Based on *that* common sense, we depended on centralized government to solve common problems. We are now rapidly moving away from dependence on centralized government, and common sense and conventional wisdom appear to guide these trends.

In the past forty years, public administration has developed more systematic patterns of inquiry about the substance of public organization behavior, public management, and public policy implementation. This work has contributed to an increasing reliability in understanding public administration. The work of public organizations has been examined with improved conceptual, methodological, and theoretical forms of analysis. These forms of analysis seek to create knowledge that is retraceable, cumulative, and, at least at some level, replicable. These forms of analysis aspire to be *scientific*, using the word "scientific" here to mean a kind of formal rationality by which the insights and discoveries of one generation form the foundation for the inquiries of the next generation. Knowledge, then, becomes collective and cumulative. This is not to suggest that the social world, of which public administration is a part, is as amenable to formal scientific applications as is the physical world. It is not. But it is to suggest that the art and science of public administration should be just that—art and science. The science and art of policy administration is definable, describable, replicable, and cumulative.

A further purpose of this book is to describe in some detail several theories and analytic approaches that contribute to what we know about public administration. We also aim to describe areas of public administration theorizing that are underdeveloped. If we can accept that each approach to the subject of public administration is guided, at least in some rudimentary way, by a theory or set of theories, the questions are these: Which theories or approaches are the most promising, the most influential? Which are the most important now and likely to be the most important in the future? What phenomena in public administration and governance are not yet adequately described or explained? One particular area that is in need of greater study is the "shadow bureaucracy"—the extensive network of private and nonprofit enterprises that exist to carry out public programs. The purpose of this book is to set out a detailed description of the authors' selection of key theories in contemporary public administration in the hope of improving the reliability of our knowledge and our understanding of public administration.

No claim is made here for only one theory of public administration. Because the field is both interdisciplinary and applied, a single theory derived from a contributing discipline, such as the market model from economics, may be informative and useful. But much of public administration cannot be described, explained, or accounted for by using the market model. Each of the other theories described in this book informs our understanding of public administration and public policy. No theory standing alone is capable of accounting for the complexity of the field. Taken together, however, the theories significantly contribute to what we know and understand public administration to be.

The Uses of Theory

Consider this policy arena: With the destructive power of hurricanes, tornados, floods, tsunamis, and wildfires, the critical nature of public administration is self-evident. Is public administration in the form of the disaster prevention and management system (Army Corp of Engineers, Federal Emergency Management Agency, Forest Service, Coast Guard) doing the best it can with a "wicked problem" (Rittel and Webber 1973)? Will better public leadership and management help (Kettl 2007)? How valuable and efficient is planning when natural disasters are so infrequent in any one location? How can better coordination with nonprofit and charitable organizations such as the Red Cross help? Will stricter regulations about where and how people may build houses and businesses help? How much responsibility do government agencies have for rescuing people who have ignored orders to evacuate?

Before we can seriously consider these public policy and public administration issues, a certain reliability of understanding will be helpful. How do we comprehend the issues and order the facts? How does our understanding, thus derived, guide policy and action? The themes set out in the remaining chapters of this book promise to improve our understanding of public administration and suggest, therefore, how it can be strengthened. When a good theory is based on reliable and replicable knowledge, nothing is more practical. What is the best theory or mix of theories to inform our policy decisions and policy implementation in crime and lawlessness? What could be more practical than the answer to that question? That answer would be especially useful and practical if the theory or theories were based on the observation of specific events *and* on observations and accumulations of patterns, experiences, and occurrences that, taken together, suggest a way to ameliorate the problem.

How can theory be useful? The validity or usefulness of any theory depends on its capacity to *describe*, to *explain*, and to *predict*.

A theory, to be useful, should accurately describe or depict a real-world event or phenomenon. Most theories do this at some level of abstraction. Most important public administration phenomena are complex, and therefore description is an abstract representation of phenomena. All descriptions require that the analyst decide which elements in a complex phenomenon to emphasize. All descriptions are distortions of reality and are relative to the circumstances prevailing at the time of the description. Descriptions are often like a still photo or a series of still photos—and often fuzzy photos at that. Description is less often like a videotape. In the same way that motion photography is an advancement on still photography, our descriptive technologies in public administration are still relatively primitive still photos.

Because of the limitations of descriptions, a useful theory will explain the phenomenon being described. Explanation can account for the known distortions of reality embedded in description. Explanation can also account for why the analyst sees some factors in an event or phenomenon as more important than others. A description asks what happened or what is happening, but even the best description of what is happening may fail to answer these equally important questions: Why did this happen, or why is this happening? Explanation may not sharpen the fuzzy photo of a description but, as Ansel Adams demonstrated with his black-and-white still photography, there is an important difference between *seeing* a picture and *understanding* a picture. In public administration, the descriptive features of theory help us see; the explanatory features of theory help us understand.

If theory helps us to see and understand public administration phenomena, should theory, therefore, help us to predict? Yes. Consider Herbert Kaufman's (1969) theory of cyclical change from a professionally based and neutrally competent public administration to a politically responsive and partisan public administration. Kaufman's theory contains strong predictive properties. Although less specific to public administration, Albert Hirschman's theory (1982) of change in the social and political world is similar and equally as useful.

The tendency is to expect too much of prediction in theory. Because public administration is practical and applied, some seek a theory that, if followed, will achieve a predictable result. Prediction should be interpreted largely to account for patterns, probabilities, and likely outcomes, not specific results flowing inexorably from the application of a particular theory. When prediction is loosely defined to account for a range of situations over time, its capacity can be impressive.

An expectation of description, explanation, and prediction from theory in public administration places this book rather firmly in the positivist tradition; however, it is recognized and understood that not all events follow foreseeable patterns. There are randomness and chaos, particularly at the microlevel or in one event or a small group of events. But in a multitude of ways, we daily see, recognize, understand, and bet on predictable patterns of collective human behavior. Broad, macrolevel patterns of individual and collective behavior in public administration can be seen, described with considerable reliability, and understood at a level that allows for reliable prediction. Aaron Wildavsky's work (1984) on budgeting is illustrative. Michael Cohen and James G. March's (1986) description of universities as organizations is another example. Herbert Simon's bounded rationality is powerfully predictive (1947/1997).

In public administration theory, issues of precision versus generality are important. Greater precision and specificity in the description and explanation of a public administration phenomenon are always purchased at the price of generalization. The more a theory is precise or, as is presently popular to say, contingent, the more the power to account for a broad pattern of events, and therefore to predict a range of like phenomena, is reduced. The problem is that big theory, grand overarching theory, is usually made so general by simplifications and assumptions as to render it unable to explain anything but the most obvious occurrences. Systems theory comes to mind; so do simplified applications of market economics to public administration. The richness, texture, and substance of events and phenomena can be lost in big theory. Precise theory, on the other hand, can be so rich and contextual as to be bereft of generalizing potential. Because the contemporary use of case studies, examples of best practices, and single analyses of particular policies illustrates the weaknesses of precise theory in supporting generalizations, this book will dwell on eight theories that have qualities of both precision and empirical richness *and* qualities of generalization.

It is appropriate to turn now to what is meant here by *theory* as that word applies to public administration. At a loose and almost casual level, theory is simply an orientation, framework, technique, or approach. For example, without referring to a particular theory, one might write that there is a theory (or there are theories) of life cycles in organizations. Or one might refer to a personal opinion as a theory. Theory is not used here in this relaxed form. Theory, in the more formal meanings of the term, has the following three meanings. *First*, in the natural and physical sciences, theory means a rigorous testing of predictive theorems or hypotheses using observable and comparable data. These hypotheses, once tested and verified, form the basis of theories, assertions, or representations of reality. Theory in the natural or physical sciences can claim considerable accuracy in representing reality because the classification of order in the physical world is advanced, as are capacities to recognize and measure natural phenomena. Theory, thus derived, often serves as a highly reliable guide for action. In the social world, of which public administration is a part, the problems of recognizing patterns, designing categories, and measuring and comparing phenomena are much greater. Therefore, the aims of theory in public administration are different (and, some would say, lower).

Second, theory in the social sciences and in public administration means the ordering of factual material (history, events, cases, stories, measures of opinion, observation) so as to present evidence through definitions, concepts, and metaphors that promote understanding. To be sure, this understanding is, at least in part, subjective, because it was constructed by the theorist. This theory is based on the rigorous and intuitive observation of social behavior, organizational behavior, institutional dynamics, political systems and behavior, patterns of communication, and culture. We will argue here that theory derived from such observation is basic to *all* action in public administration. Most of this action is not formally and explicitly acknowledged as driven by a particular theory. Public administration decisions and action are, nevertheless, based on fundamental assumptions about social behavior, patterns of human cooperation, incentives for action, and the like. Because of this, one of the primary tasks of theory in public administration is to make explicit and describe the assumptions that guide action and to develop the categories, concepts, definitions, and metaphors that foster an understanding of those assumptions.

Third, in public administration the meaning of theory is normative—theories of what ought to be. These theories form the bridges among public administration, political science, and philosophy. Dwight Waldo (1946) taught us that all theories of public administration are also theories of politics. Public administration practice is a busy and untidy world in which costs and benefits, all normatively based in nature and effort, are allocated among citizens through the authority of the state. Theories of public administration guide the authoritative allocation of public goods. Once again, the task of the theorist is often to discover theory that accounts for or describes observable regularities in behavior *and* to evaluate the normative implications of such behavior. It is often true that public administration theorists use a mix of the second and third definitions of theory.

The meaning of theory in public administration is more than just a question of how rigorous the measurement and how precise the observation are. Theory is classified by the form, degree, or nature of its elaboration. For example, some theory simply presents methodological questions such as the debate over so-called best practices research (Overman and Boyd 1994). Other theory uses deduction and the synthesis of research findings in developing hypotheses to guide future research. The Theibot Thesis and much of rational choice theory are good examples of this kind of theory. According to surveys of articles in leading public administration journals, this is the most common form of theory presentation in the field (Cleary 1992; Adams and White 1994; Forrester and Watson 1994; White and Adams 1994). Other theory is derived from the specific field-testing of a particular hypothesis or cluster of hypotheses. The empirical test of the Theibot Thesis is a good example of this form of elaboration (Lowery, Lyons, and DeHoog 1992; Lyons and Lowery 1989). Theory also may vary by scope, some theory being broad and presuming to account for, say, all public organizations, and other theory being narrow to account for, say, law enforcement organizations. Furthermore, theory in public administration can differ depending on whether the subject is generally organizational, operational, managerial, or generally policy-specific.

Finally, in public administration there is a special test of theory—how useful is it? Because of this test, the degree of measuring rigor and precision and the level of elaboration in a theory may be less important than the question of usefulness. Good or useful theory presumes to organize and classify data in such a way as to screen facts and then focus on only the most important. The test of a theory's usefulness is often its criteria in selecting and classifying facts, and if these are accurate, the theory will enhance understanding, guide research, and powerfully describe, explain, and predict.

Is a Useful and Reliable
Public Administration Theory Possible?

In the 1960s, at the time of the so-called behavioral revolution in political science, there were essentially two positions regarding the prospects for a rigorous empirically based theory or set of theories to explain political behavior. Although political behavior is not exactly the same thing as public administration, the parallels, particularly with regard to theory development, are strong. In public administration, there were, and some would say still are, essentially the same two positions regarding empirically based theory.

These two positions were the classical, or traditional, and the scientific, or behavioral. The essence of the traditional position is that public administration involves purposes and authority in a way physical science does not. In the social world, facts can be measured, but they are transitory. Furthermore, in issues of collective human purposes, wisdom, intuition, and judgment are of surpassing importance, but they are difficult to measure and classify. Therefore, many elements of public administration are essentially subjective.

The traditional position also argues that proponents of the behavioral position, to the extent they confine themselves to analysis of those things that can be verified by known measurement techniques, deny themselves some of the most important tools presently available for coming to grips with the substance of public administration. By denying the importance of intuitive guesses, judgment, and wisdom, theorists working exclusively from the scientific and behavioral perspectives can make themselves remote from all that is important in public administration. This argument is especially strong when it comes to issues of ethics and morality in policy and public management. Traditionalists argue that by being more scientific, public administration shies away from the big questions of right and wrong. The tidy models of the behavioral theorist, they argue, can lend a specious air of authority to such work.

By contrast, the behaviorists' argument takes the positivist position that collective human behavior exhibits enough order to justify a rigorous search, measurement, classification, and depiction of that order. This can be done either by separating facts from values—logical positivism—and theorizing about the facts or by explicitly dealing with the value implications of factually derived theory. The behaviorists' position claims that simplifying models based on explicit assumptions furthers the development of experimentation and reliable findings. Besides, if there is disagreement regarding the theorists' assumptions, theory in the long run will be the better for it. As for issues of ethics, morality, wisdom, and other fuzzy concepts, the behaviorist position is that such variables are not beyond the reach of empirically derived theory.

Weber (1952) was a social scientist in the positivist tradition who argued that human behavior, particularly bureaucratic behavior, exhibits observable and describable patterns that can be scientifically verified. But he also argued that social reality is composed of the ideas and beliefs of social actors. The task of social science must therefore be the interpretation of action in terms of subjective meaning. Today, a fully developed theory of interpretive social science (Weber 1952; Winch 1995) argues that in the social context humans act intentionally according to shared ideas and beliefs and shared meanings associated with those ideas and beliefs. This argument has evolved to the widely supported view that reality is socially constructed; indeed, it is further suggested that it is useful to think of organizations as shared meanings or understandings (Weick 1979). Interpretative social science can include interpretations of the past (history), interpretations of events (case studies), and interpretations of decisions and actions by participant observations.

Some argue that interpretive social science and positivist, or behavioral, social science are competitive and irreconcilable (Winch 1995). But it is our view, and the dominant perspective in contemporary social theory (MacIntyre 1984), that there can be theory that describes empirically observed regularities in the social world as well as interpretations of those regularities.

Today, the traditional and behavioral positions in public administration are in many ways reconciled. Both positions are essentially right in that they acknowledge the importance of observation and categorization and the central place of theory as the appropriate means to express reality and guide action. Public administration theory derived from historical analyses, institutional study, and philosophy is now understood to be as legitimate as public administration theory derived from statistical analysis and mathematical models. Fuzzy phenomena such as leadership and the "principles of public administration" are now the subjects of empirical analysis and theory-building (Behn 1991; Hood and Jackson 1991).

The reconciliation of traditional and behavioral public administration reflects this perspective: "Science is not a substitute for insight, and methodological rigor is not a substitute for wisdom. Research that is merely rigorous may well be routine, mechanical, trivial, and of little theoretical or policy value. However, . . . in the absence of such rigorous and controlled analysis even the most operational data are of little value" (Singer 1966, 15).

Even with this reconciliation, theory-building in public administration is influenced by tastes and fashions. There is always the law of the instrument: When the theorist has a methodological or conceptual hammer, everything begins to look like a nail. In the policy schools, the case method has taken on some aspects of a hammer; the market model and mathematical conclusions so derived have been applied to a lot of nails lately. Nevertheless, despite examples of methodological and theoretical excesses, public administration theory has never been healthier than at present.

From the traditionalist and behavioralist positions of thirty years ago, public administration has evolved to a field enjoying a considerable theoretical richness. A single dominant theory, an intellectual hegemony, would have impoverished the field. Instead, there are several strong and important theories and many important theorists, a condition befitting a field as applied and interdisciplinary as public administration.

Finally, we come to the uses or purposes to which theory in public administration may be put. There are countless examples of public administration theory applied to less than wholesome purposes; the program-planning-budgeting systems devised to make it appear that the United States was winning the war in Vietnam comes to mind. The willingness of the field to embrace and rationalize cutback management without being forthright about a resulting diminution in organizational capacity is another example. Our predictive capacities are limited, and even when we can predict, predictions sometimes run counter to the public administration wisdom of the day. What, for example, would we predict about the long-range effects of the currently popular idea of reducing governmental purchasing and bidding regulations? A sensible prediction would be that reduction in excessive regulation will increase efficiency. But too much deregulation in this area will in the long run almost certainly result in greater corruption. It was corruption, after all, that caused many of the regulations to be adopted in the first place (Frederickson 1999a).

Although we cannot control the uses to which public administration theory will be put, public administrators can often influence the use of theory. It should be the aim of good public administration scholarship to arm public administrators with the most reliable available theory. Biology cannot control medicine, and physics cannot control engineering. But modern medicine wouldn't amount to much without biological research and theory, and engineering is deeply dependent on physics for its theory. Researchers and theory builders in public administration must meet the ultimate and most difficult challenge to public administration theory: They must do their best to provide reliable theory, always with the hope that public officials will use that theory to make democratic government as effective as possible. Albert Einstein was once asked, "Why is it that when the mind of man has stretched as far as to discover the structure of the atom we have been unable to devise the political means to keep the atom from destroying us?" He replied, "That is simple, my friend, it is because politics is more difficult than physics" (Herz 1962, 214n). Even though politics is more difficult than physics, politics in the past fifty years has managed, so far, to keep atomic energy from destroying us; indeed, atomic energy has in many ways become a boon to humankind. The question is whether politics can continue to bend atomic energy to worthy purposes even though such bending is difficult.

Insofar as theories of public administration are also theories of politics, the application of public administration theory is always difficult, particularly in the context of democratic government. Public administration theory is increasingly sophisticated and reliable, and thereby it holds some promise of continuing to make important contributions to the day-to-day effectiveness of democratic government.

Some Contemporary Theories of Public Administration

It is not the purpose of this book to describe an all-encompassing view of public administration reality or even to present a comprehensive survey of theories on the subject. The succeeding chapters present particular theories or families of theories that, in the authors' judgment, have contributed significantly to the body of knowledge in public administration, have the potential to make such contributions, or have important heuristic value. The selection of theories omits some important theoretical areas (game theory, administrative law, theories of ethics, network theory). It nonetheless includes a wide enough variety of public administration theory to illuminate the possibilities and limitations of contemporary theorizing in the field.

The selection of theories and models, subtheories, concepts, research findings, and individual theorists included in each theory or family of theories in the following chapters may elicit disagreement, even sharp disagreement. Public administration is not a tidy field, and no two theorists would presume to tidy it up in the same way. The authors can only hope that the following ordering of public administration knowledge and theory will stimulate debate and the subsequent refinement of theoretical categories. It was often difficult to place the work of particular theorists in particular chapters. For example, modern network theorists such as H. Brinton Milward and Laurence O'Toole might disagree with the inclusion of network theory as part of the general body of bureaucratic politics theory and prefer to think of network theory as important enough to merit a separate and freestanding treatment. It will also be evident that network theory can be as easily grouped with governance theory as with theories of bureaucratic politics. There are obviously areas of overlap and duplication between and among the eight theories we have selected. Although we attempt to point out the most important, overlap and duplication are part of a much larger point. Each theory, or family of theories, connects with the other seven. That connection is what makes public administration a field, a separate self-conscious body of knowledge. Part of doing theory is to disaggregate the subject and examine the parts in detail; but an equally important part of doing theory is to put together again.

Chapter 2 considers theories of political control over bureaucracy. From the beginning of the field, a fundamental debate has questioned the appropriate range of discretion for bureaucrats in a democratic polity. Contemporary research on this subject has contributed to the development of political control theory. Chapter 3 treats the subject of bureaucracy as theories of bureaucratic politics, a lively and popular body of theory that particularly reflects the contributions and influence of political science. Chapter 4 takes up the subject of the houses in which public administration happens, the formal and informal organizational structures of organizations. Over the past thirty years, this body of theory has changed dramatically—from organization theory to institutional theory. Chapter 5 changes the analysis from the houses of public administration to the management of work in those houses. Management theory is a body of work that is not only rather old, as in scientific management, but is also very new, as in contemporary theories of leadership and Total Quality Management, or is still being developed, as in recent descriptions of shadow bureaucracy and the hollow state. Chapter 6 is a discussion of postpositivist and postmodern public administration theory. This body of theory is most heavily influenced by contemporary sociology and by trends in philosophy. Of the theories considered herein, postmodern theory is the most normative. Chapter 7 is a consideration of decision and action theory. This body of theory is a primary bridge to other, similar fields, such as planning, business administration, and operations research. Chapter 8 is a treatment of rational choice theory, an influential perspective on public administration particularly reflecting the colonization of the social sciences and public administration by economics. Chapter 9 takes up the newest theoretical perspective in public administration: governance, including the trend toward the hollowing out of the state. The eight chapters set out the essential details of each of these theories, suggesting that each is an important part of public administration. The final chapter puts these parts together and attempts to describe and to understand public administration theory in its entirety.

Notes

1. The "public" in public administration is to be broadly defined here. Public is used in its pregovernmental meaning to include governments and nonprofit, not-for-profit, nongovernmental, parastatal, and other organizations having a clear public purpose other than what is generally understood to be commerce or business. See Frederickson 1997b.

2

Theories of Political Control of Bureaucracy

Introduction: What Are Theories of Control of Bureaucracy?

Control-of-bureaucracy theory is an approach to public administration theory particularly associated with matters of compliance or responsiveness. This question is central to the control-of-bureaucracy theory: Does the bureaucracy comply with the law or with the preferences of lawmakers or elected executives? To answer this question, control-of-bureaucracy theorists accept some form of the politics-administration (or policy-administration) dichotomy. Sometimes the dichotomy is described and accepted explicitly; other times it is simply assumed. But the logic of political control-of-bureaucracy theory is difficult, if not impossible, without assuming significant distinctions between political and administrative phenomena in democratic government.

The politics-administration dichotomy traces to the origins of modern public administration. When the American founding documents were formulated, the dichotomy was in the separation of legislative and executive powers, with Alexander Hamilton arguing for an energetic president able to control the day-to-day operation of government and Thomas Jefferson arguing for an elected legislature exercising direct and heavy control over the president (Rohr 1986; Kettl 1993a). At the state and local levels of American government, the politics-administration dichotomy was also played out through legislative (the city council) and executive (the mayor) powers. All fifty states have a separation of powers structure, and until the twentieth century, so did almost all cities.

At all levels of American federalism, the separation of powers was altered by the emergence of a merit-appointed professional and permanent civil service.

When the civil service was in the early stages, Woodrow Wilson (1887/1941) set out the most formal and rigid version of the dichotomy by arguing in his seminal essay on modern public administration that politics should not meddle in administration and administration should not meddle in politics. The dichotomy was broadly accepted in American public administration until the mid-1900s, when Dwight Waldo (1946) and Herbert Simon (1947/1997) challenged the dichotomy, each for different reasons. To Waldo, all administrative acts were political at a fundamental level. To Simon, it was difficult empirically to unbundle politics from administration, and vice versa. So from the 1950s through the 1970s the received wisdom was that there was no dichotomy. Then in the 1980s, the dichotomy reemerged and is now alive and well and found in control-of-bureaucracy theory.

The significance of control-of-bureaucracy theory is that it provides for the analysis of public administration by making distinctions between political and administrative acts or actions and/or between political and administrative actors. These distinctions are especially useful analytically because they provide for the parsing of variables on the basis of politics (usually independent variables) and administration (usually dependent variables).

We come, then, to the second important assumption in the control-of-bureaucracy theory: In democratic self-government, elected officials, including legislators and executives (presidents, governors, mayors), should control the decisions and actions of appointed (usually civil service) officials. In American political science, the form and character of political control over bureaucracy are a long-standing debate about what ought to be the proper range of discretion given bureaucracies and bureaucrats (Finer 1941; Frederich 1940). In modern times, this debate is best characterized, on the one hand, by the Theodore Lowi (1979) argument that we need a juridical democracy in which laws and regulations are so precise and so limiting that they deny bureaucracies latitude in carrying out the law and, on the other hand, the Charles Goodsell (1983) argument that a wide bureaucratic discretion is essential to achieve effective and humane fulfillment of the law. Donald Kettl captures these differences well and puts them in historic context:

> Different approaches to the study of administration usually come from one of two conflicting traditions in American politics—and each tradition leads to a very different perspective on the role of administration in American democracy. Some students of administration come to the subject with a fundamentally Hamiltonian bent. Like Alexander Hamilton, they seek a vigorous state vested with a strong administrative apparatus. Other students of administration, however, are fundamentally Madisonians. Like Madison, they see in a delicate balance of power the best protection against tyranny. The competition of political

interests, in their view, lessens the risk that bureaucracy can abuse individual liberty. (1993a, 407)

The control-of-bureaucracy theory draws deeply from the Madisonian well of distrust of administrative power. Many control-of-bureaucracy theorists are from those parts of American political science that are essentially Madisonian. Economists and theories of economics have colonized political science and tend also to be Madisonian. By comparison, traditional and self-aware public administration, with its emphasis on management, expertise, and professionalism, tends to be rather Hamiltonian in cast and perspective (Kettl 1993a).

Listing some contemporary book titles in public administration is one interesting way to illustrate the control-of-bureaucracy theory's modern popularity:

Breaking Through Bureaucracy by Michael Barzelay (1992)
Holding Government Bureaucracies Accountable by Bernard Rosen (1989)
Controlling Bureaucracies by Judith Gruber (1987)
Taming the Bureaucracy by William Gormley (1989)
Facing the Bureaucracy: Living and Dying in a Public Agency by Gerald Garvey (1992)
Public Administration: Balancing Power and Accountability by Jerome McKinney and Lawrence Howard (1998)
Controlling the Bureaucracy: The Theory and Practice of Institutional Constraints by William West (1995)
Bureaucracy: What Government Agencies Do and Why They Do It by James Q. Wilson (1989)

There is little question that bureaucracy and the issues concerning the control of bureaucracy are presently central to modern public administration theory. Because the politics-administration dichotomy is the primary assumption in the control-of-bureaucracy theory, the next section defines and describes the logic of bureaucratic control using the dichotomy. This is followed by an attempt to answer the theoretical and empirical question of whether bureaucracies and bureaucrats are responsive to their elected masters. Are they "out of control"? That will be followed by a consideration of the principal-agent approach to the control-of-bureaucracy theory.

The Difference Between Politics and Administration

The simple representation of the differences between policy and administration, following James Q. Wilson (1887/1989) and Frank Goodnow (1900), would look like this (Figure 2.1):

FIGURE 2.1   TRADITIONAL REPRESENTATION OF THE
DIFFERENCES BETWEEN POLITICS AND ADMINISTRATION

GOALS   MEANS

POLICY	ADMINISTRATION

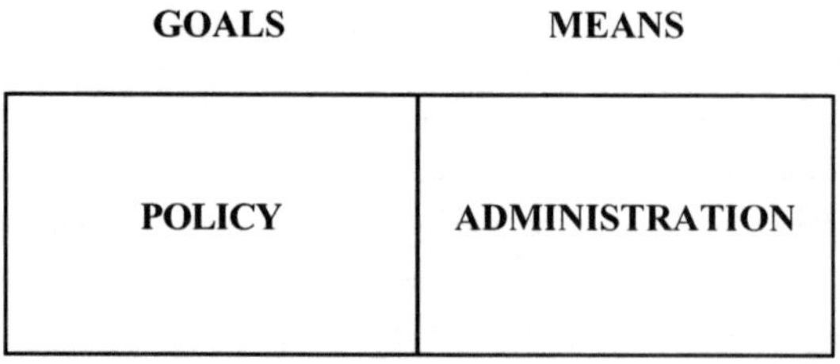

This representation of the differences between policy and administration begs
the question of the level of precision, specificity, and detail in policy, on the one
hand, and the level of discretion in administration, on the other. In the reform
era and the early decades of public administration, it was probably assumed that
administration entailed a generous range of discretion that held open the doors
for technical expertise and administrative efficiency. And it was further assumed
that the line between policy/politics and administration was a "firewall." The empirical critique of the differences between policy and administration could be represented this way (Figure 2.2):

FIGURE 2.2   EMPIRICALLY VALID REPRESENTATION OF THE
DIFFERENCES BETWEEN POLITICS AND ADMINISTRATION

GOALS   MEANS

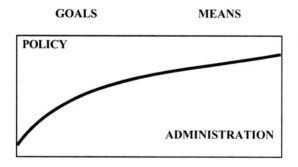

Empirically, this model is more nearly accurate, the evidence being that bureaucrats are often engaged in policy agenda-setting and policymaking (Kingdon
1995; Bardach 1977) and that elected officials are often engaged in what would
ordinarily be described as management or administration (Gilmour and Halley
1994).

This model does display clearly that there is in a general sense political control
over bureaucracy. But it also indicates that this control is limited and contingent
and that there may be as much bureaucratic control over policy as there is political

control of administration. Such a general model serves the useful purpose of graphically representing theory, but like all models (verbal, mathematical, graphic), it does not account for or explain the details or nuances in a particular pattern of political-bureaucratic interaction. Many individual studies of policy implementation and bureaucratic control do provide such details (Gilmour and Halley 1994).

One of the most interesting theoretical advances in control-of-bureaucracy theory comes from the study of the American council-manager form of city government. There has long been the premise in council-manager government that there is and should be a clear distinction between the popularly elected city council and its responsibility to set law and policy, on the one hand, and the role of the professional city manager the council employs to lead the bureaucracy and carry out policy, on the other. Because of the conceptual firewall between politics and administration, in theory this form of local government is close to the ideal-type dichotomy depicted in Figure 2.1; it is certainly closer to that ideal type than other forms of American local government, state governments, or the national government. The council-manager form of local government is also especially useful to study because of its relative simplicity: The elected officials or politicians are all in one body, the council, and the bureaucrats and technicians are all working for the manager, who is a professional rather than a politician. All other forms of American government have elected legislators (city council, county commission, state legislature, federal legislature) *and* an elected executive. The bureaucracy in these forms has, at least by implication, two political masters or principals—legislative and executive. The council-manager form of government is, then, because of its relative simplicity, ideally suited to the study of theories of control of bureaucracy.

James H. Svara (1994) has made extensive studies of cities employing the council-manager form and of relations between elected city councils and professional city managers. His research indicates that there are four models of relations between elected officials and administrators as follows (Figure 2.3).

In each figure, the heavy line marks the boundary between the spheres of elected officials and appointed officials. All the space above the heavy line is the responsibility of *elected officials*; below the line, the responsibility of *administrators*.

The policy-administration dichotomy model set out in Figure 2.3a resembles that in Figure 2.1 and represents the traditions of municipal reform and the classic council-manager form of local government. It also fairly describes the early theory of Wilson and Goodnow as well as the logical positivism of Herbert Simon and his distinctions between facts (administration) and values (policy). The problem is that the model lacks a strong and consistent empirical warrant even in the study of council-manager government, where one would expect to find a firewall between politics and administration.

Svara's "mixture in policy" model set out in Figure 2.3b represents the influence of behaviorists David Easton (1965), Robert Dahl (1947), Wallace Sayer (1958),

FIGURE 2.3   FOUR MODELS OF THE RELATIONSHIP
BETWEEN POLITICS AND ADMINISTRATION

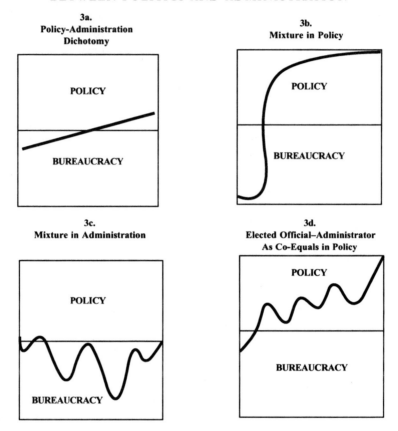

and others who defined politics and administration as the distribution of values, costs, and benefits. Politicians and bureaucrats both participate in this process of distribution, and in it administrators have extensive opportunities to "set policy-initiating proposals, exercising discretion, writing budgets, and determining the delivery of services—and through implementation they shape policy formulated by elected officials" (Svara 1994, 5). The upper arc of the curved line represents the vast expanse of bureaucratic power in policymaking, or, put another way, the absence of political control in bureaucracy. The lower portion of the curved line indicates the incursion of politics into various limited matters of administration, a form of control over bureaucracy particularly associated with the delivery of a particular service, the letting of certain purchase or capital construction contracts, or the making of certain administrative appointments. The mixture in policy model of council-manager government has a considerable empirical warrant and fairly represents the common pattern of bureaucratic control in the classic council-manager city setting (Frederickson, Johnson, and Wood 2004).

Figure 2.3c is described by Svara as the "mixture in administration" model and illustrates essentially the opposite of the mixture in policy model shown in Figure 2.3b. The relationships represented here show deep probes by elected city council members into the day-to-day conduct of government administration. Some describe this as micromanagement and express concern over political meddling and the possible return of local political corruption, which the municipal reform movement sought to stamp out (Newland 1994). Others describe the mixture in the administration model as legislative prerogatives reasserting themselves to curb the excesses of an uncontrolled bureaucracy or as a kind of political responsiveness (Bledsoe 1993). The mixture in the administration model would be an accurate empirical representation of council-manager-form cities that have a pliant and passive city manager and assertive full-time paid city council members elected by districts.

Figure 2.3d illustrates the "elected official–administrator as co-equal" model; this shares many of the characteristics of the mixture in policy model shown in Figure 2.3b. To Svara, this model represents the New Public Administration assertion (Frederickson 1980; Frederickson 1997b), the Blacksburg Manifesto argument (Wamsley and Wolf 1996), and the Charles Goodsell (1983) contention that public administrators have an inherent policy legitimacy and an ethical obligation to protect the interests of the underrepresented (sometimes called social equity), to act as agents for the citizens, and to administer city affairs according to the law, council directives, *and* bureaucratic standards of efficiency and fairness (Frederickson 1997b; Wamsley and Wolf 1996; Goodsell 1983). Svara's co-equal model (Figure 2.3d) accurately describes cities with councils that limit their work to setting policy and approving an annual budget and strong but fair city managers free to carry out policy and deliver services according to their standards of efficiency and fairness without involving the council. The co-equal model would best represent the absence of control over bureaucracy *or* the assumption, commonly found among city managers, that the requirements of political control are satisfied by passing statutes, setting standards, and passing a budget.

In using these models, Svara found there were empirical problems because "we are burdened with such imprecise definitions of the central concepts that distinctions between office and function are difficult to make. One cannot conclude . . . that the only distinction between 'policy' and 'administrative' decisions is who makes them. It is essential to the task at hand to discriminate precisely among functions in the governmental process without presuming who discharges them" (1994, 8). Svara then sets out the four-part model shown here as Figure 2.4, Parsing the Dichotomy, which uses four, rather than two, categories of governmental activity and describes illustrative tasks for political officials and bureaucrats in each category.

FIGURE 2.4   PARSING THE DICHOTOMY:
DIMENSIONS OF GOVERNMENTAL PROCESSES

Illustrative Tasks for Council	Council's Sphere	Illustrative Tasks for Administrators
Determine purpose, scope of services, tax level, constitutional issues.	**Mission**	Advise (what city "can" do may influence what it "should" do), analyze conditions and trends.
Pass ordinances, approve new projects and programs, ratify budget.	**Policy**	Make recommendations on all decisions, formulate budget, determine service distribution formulae.
Make implementation decisions such as site selection, handling complaints, and overseeing administration.	**Administration**	Establish practices and procedures and make decisions for implementing policy.
Suggest management changes to manager, review organizational performance in manager's appraisal.	**Management**	Control the human, material, and informational resources of organization to support policy and administrative functions.

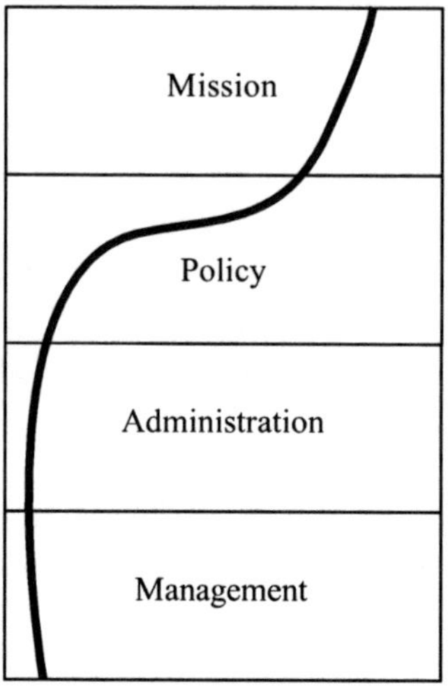

To this he again sketches the curved line, which best represents the most commonly found pattern of relationship between politics and administration.

Manager's Sphere

Using the four-part model, he then arrays the findings of his field research in four separate representations of the four-part model, shown here as Figure 2.5. In the four boxes in Figure 2.5, the dotted line represents the solid line shown in Figure 2.4. Some cities are best described as having a strong manager, shown in box 2.5a. The most notable finding here is that the manager's space for action is greater in all four functions of government. This could be described as the corporate, or board of directors, model, in which policy is heavily defined by the manager and the council merely approves or makes legitimate that policy. The council grants the manager and the bureaucracy broad and essentially complete discretion in the daily affairs of city government. The opposite of this is found in the council-dominant model set out in box 2.5b, which illustrates a wide space of council involvement at all four levels. This could also be called a council control-of-bureaucracy model. The important point in the strong-manager and council-dominant models is the across-the-board character of power and influence. The council incursion pattern shown in 2.5c describes a council that probes more deeply in all areas than in the typical model, yet is not consistently assertive in all

FIGURE 2.5   DERIVATIONS FROM TYPICAL DIVISION

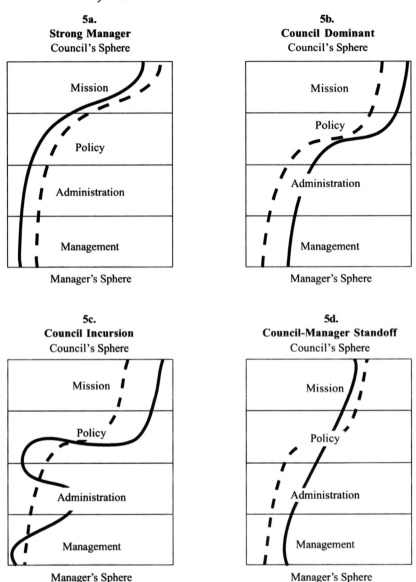

5a.
Strong Manager
Council's Sphere

Mission

Policy

Administration

Management

Manager's Sphere

5b.
Council Dominant
Council's Sphere

Mission

Policy

Administration

Management

Manager's Sphere

5c.
Council Incursion
Council's Sphere

Mission

Policy

Administration

Management

Manager's Sphere

5d.
Council-Manager Standoff
Council's Sphere

Mission

Policy

Administration

Management

Manager's Sphere

areas. The incursive council makes administrators wary of offering any proposals concerning mission and is unpredictable in its reactions to policy recommendations from staff. It accepts many recommendations but in some cases undercuts extensive staff preparation and sets off to make its own policy decision. The council probes persistently but somewhat haphazardly into administrative matters and dabbles in management (Svara 1994, 56).

Thus the boundary line is "ragged" in this situation. Box 2.5d illustrates a standoff between an assertive manager and an equally assertive council. Each checks and contains the other without the council's taking complete control or the manager's getting what is believed to be deserved administrative discretion.

These models capture and illustrate some of the rich variation found in managerial and bureaucratic responses to political control in council-manager-form cities. Other research indicates that the structure of council-manager cities is changing. At one time, most council members in council-manager cities were elected at-large; now they are elected by district. It used to be, too, that councils were strictly part-time and made up of usually white, male business leaders; now council members are increasingly full-time, increasingly paid, are more often female, are more often persons of color, have staff assigned to them, have working spaces in city hall, and have access to city vehicles and that modern symbol of real power: the cell phone (Renner and DeSantis 1993; Bledsoe 1993).

Mayors in council-manager-form cities were once primarily ceremonial, merely the senior member of the council. Now they are increasingly directly elected as mayor, are paid, work full-time, have staff, and so forth. Council-manager cities that have made these structural changes are called "adapted cities" and clearly have moved toward greater political control of the city bureaucracy (Frederickson, Johnson, and Wood, 2003).

In researching this issue, Greg J. Protasel (1994) found that council-manager-form cities that are now "adapted cities" seldom abandon the council-manager form. But council-manager cities that are not adapted are more likely to abandon the model in favor of the strong-mayor model. This is, following Protasel, because of the leadership gap illustrated in Figure 2.6. The figure, which uses the Svara four-part functional description of city governmental activities turned on its side, describes functions that are exclusive to the council or the manager, functions that are shared, *and* a gap in leadership. When cities fill that gap by adapting, they tend to retain the council-manager form. When they leave a leadership vacuum or the manager attempts to fill it, more likely abandonment of the council-manager form will be considered.

It is evident from the study of the council-manager form of city government that the use of policy and administration as units of analysis does illuminate the theory of public administration. Further, theories addressing the political control of bureaucracy can easily be tested by using political and administrative variables. This suggests that, although the simple policy-administration dichotomy is without empirical support, a nuanced conception of policy and politics, on the one hand, and administration, on the other, does account for or explain variations among organizations or cities as to the degree of political control of bureaucracy, as well as some of the character or quality of that control or its absence.

FIGURE 2.6   THE LEADERSHIP
IN THE COUNCIL-MANAGER PLAN

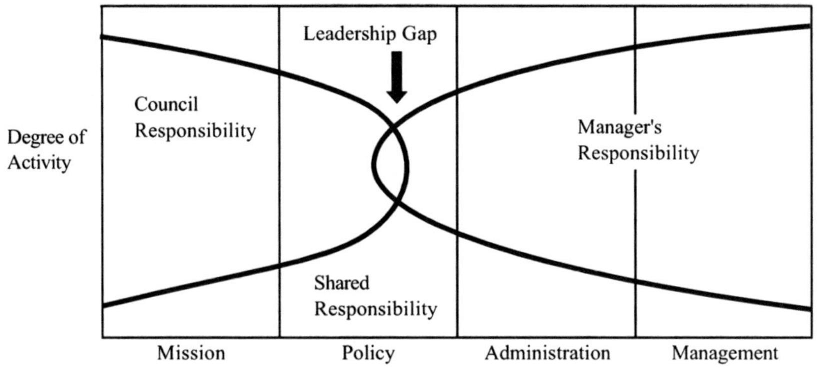

Are Bureaucracies Out of Control?

We turn now to the more complex forms of democratic government and to the theories that purport to explain or account for the roles and behavior of bureaucracy, particularly as those roles and behavior are or are not controlled by elected officials.

One group of theories concerning the control of bureaucracy could be described as *theories of bureaucratic capture.* This theory traces primarily to studies of the federal government, particularly to studies of the regulatory process and the independent regulatory commissions. In one form of this theory, the industries regulated or licensed (airlines, railroads, telephones, etc., at the national level; electric, gas, and other utilities at the state level; and general retail business at the local level) come, through time, to heavily influence or even to control their regulators (Huntington 1952). Under these circumstances, the regulators are sometimes referred to as "having gone native." Another version of capture theory is that the bureaucratic process is dominated by a triumvirate of policy actors: an interest group, a congressional committee charged with the oversight of a particular agency, and a government agency (Wood and Waterman 1994). Originally, this was a variant of theories of pluralism, commonly known as "iron triangles" and later as "issue networks" (Heclo 1978). A third version of capture theory suggests that policy elites control bureaucracies (Selznick 1949). It is assumed, correctly, that legislatures have passed enabling legislation that created the regulatory agencies and through the delegation of rule making, and even adjudicatory powers, have given those bureaucracies wide discretion in regulating entire fields of business, such as transportation or stock markets. Capture theorists argue that the actual functioning of these agencies was outside of the control of the president (governor, mayor), and Congress (state legislature, city council). Therefore, capture theorists sometimes refer to the connections among the regulated industry, the regulatory agency, and the relevant legislative committee as "policy subsystems" beyond presidential and congressional control.

The interesting thing about capture theories is that they suggest that there is *too much political control* of bureaucracy rather than not enough. As we will see, this is an argument almost exactly the opposite of the more common contemporary theories that political control of bureaucracy is rather limited.

How do theories of bureaucratic capture hold up empirically? Not especially well. As Wood and Waterman put it:

> The deregulation movement of the 1970s challenged one of theory's basic premises, namely, that the regulatory agencies serve the interests of the regulated clientele, not the public interest. The theory could not stand up to the empirical test. . . . In one industry after another, regulatory agencies aggressively promoted deregulation. Had the deregulation movement been confined to one or two agencies, it might easily have been dismissed as a mere exception to a larger rule. But the deregulation movement was broadly based, involving numerous agencies and regulated industries. (1994, 19–20)

It could be added that the federal government's experience with deregulation has, in a general way, been repeated by American state and local governments.

If regulated industries had captured the public agencies charged with regulating them, and this capture had resulted in particular favorable circumstances for those industries, it would be assumed that the industries, ceteris paribus, would have fought to retain regulation and that the public agencies held prisoner by them would have fought to retain regulation. That did not happen.

What did happen was the very popular executive and legislative politics of deregulation. It turns out that the policy subsystems that were presumed to have captured bureaucracies were permeable, especially to the influence of elected officials—political principals. As a result, modern variants on capture theory account for such external political influences as described in the work of Hugh Heclo (1978), and John Kingdon (1995). These newer variants have much softer assumptions about bureaucratic capture by interest groups or regulated industries and are much more likely to reflect arguments about "overhead democracy" as an approach to the political control of bureaucracy (e.g., Ringquist 1995; Wood 1993).

A local government cousin of theories of bureaucratic capture are theories of client responsiveness. In these theories, it is assumed that jurisdictions establish institutions such as police departments, welfare agencies, and schools. Elected political leaders set policy and establish budgets and use some form of merit-based civil service system to employ the large groups of bureaucrats who must carry out the work—ordinarily direct service to such clients as schoolchildren, the poor, victims of crime, or those suspected of violating the law. Ordinarily, those who directly serve clients are professionals or semiprofessionals, such as schoolteachers, social workers, or police officers—all having a distinct client-serving orientation. Indeed, the training and education of these professionals put a much greater emphasis on how to serve client needs than on how to respond to political principals or policy directives. It is often true that these bureaucrats see themselves as professionals providing a direct service and ordinarily do not see themselves, at least primarily, as public officials or public servants (Gruber 1987). These bureaucrats greatly value autonomy and the widest possible range of discretion in responding to client needs (Lipsky 1980; Gruber 1987). They "work for their clients" more than they "work for the mayor, the city council, the school board, or the county commission." It could be said, then, they these bureaucrats are "captured" by their clients, although there are those who would caution us against conflating "capture" with client responsiveness in these situations (Meier 1997).

Client responsiveness theory is essentially traditional public administration theory emphasizing agency effectiveness and the instrumental values of efficiency, economy, and equity (Frederickson 1997b). To what extent does this theory have an empirical warrant?

First, the seminal research on client responsiveness theory was done by Michael Lipsky in his classic *Street-Level Bureaucracy: Dilemmas of the Individual in Public Services* (1980). Its findings are now a part of the public administration intellectual furniture:

1. Resources are chronically inadequate.
2. The demand for services tends to increase to meet the supply.
3. Goal expectations for agencies tend to be ambiguous, vague, or conflicting.
4. Performance oriented toward goal achievement tends to be difficult, if not impossible, to measure.
5. Clients are typically nonvoluntary; partly as a result, clients for the most part do not serve as a primary bureaucratic reference group.
6. Street-level bureaucrats usually have at least some latitude or discretion in providing their services.
7. Under conditions of scarce resources and high demand, bureaucrats ration services.
8. To bring greater predictability to the resource stream, street-level bureaucrats husband such worker resources as time and energy.
9. They control clients by the maintenance of distance, autonomy, expertise, and symbols, thereby reducing the consequences of uncertainty.
10. Street-level bureaucrats are often alienated from their work and exhibit forms of psychic withdrawal.
11. Street-level bureaucrats tend to be middle class and to ration their services based on middle-class values such as work, thrift, and the like.

Lipsky's findings seem to indicate that street-level bureaucrats are not so much captured by their clients as they are faced with daunting social tasks and limited resources. In their forms of client responsiveness are they, then, also responsive to their political and policy masters? Lipsky suggests that unless and until goals are made clearer and performance measures tied to clearer and more precise goals, street-level bureaucracy will stay about the same. There is little doubt that the responsibility for ambiguous, vague, and conflicting goals belongs to elected officials. The question, then, is not one of whether there is or should be greater political control of bureaucracy; the question is the assumed political direction or policy content in that control. Lipsky's findings indicate that resource scarcity coupled with vague and conflicting goals will produce bureaucrats who cope by exercising some form of control over their work. Does this mean they are out of control? No. Schools, welfare agencies, and police departments are generally doing what the law and what public policy call for—at least to the extent in which that law and policy are clear.

Second, Judith Gruber's (1987) research paints a rather less flattering picture of bureaucratic actions and attitudes toward political control. Drawing from James D. Thompson's (1967) theory that bureaucrats seek to buffer themselves from outside forces; from Anthony Downs's (1967) theory that bureaucracies prefer the status quo and resist change; and from Robert K. Merton's (1957) theory that bureaucrats resist change, Gruber, who based her research on interviews in a mayor-form city in the upper East Coast, finds bureaucrats to be self-serving and resistant to controls. She finds that bureaucrats "have a significant latitude of action, and they like it that way" (1987, 92); "prefer outside actors who have very little power" (94); do not welcome either city council or mayoral influence in departmental affairs (92–96); and find citizen influence somewhat more welcome (96).

But these bureaucrats believe in democratic government and in political and policy control over their work, although they tend to define the legitimate range of these controls rather narrowly, limiting it to winning elections, passing statutes, making policy, and approving budgets. Bureaucrats tend to be suspicious of elected officials who move beyond these forms of control and attempt to get into what they define as the legitimate role of administration—which is broadly defined to include a wide range of what Gruber sees as policy. These public officials are insulated from the political affairs of the city and tend to take their advice from one another. But, as Lipsky found, bureaucrats work in a world of constraints—rules and regulations that proscribe their actions, limited resources, and pressure for services. Finally, Gruber found bureaucrats to be greatly influenced in their actions and opinions by their professional associations and by the technology of their work and that they resist political intervention that runs counter to these influences. When this happens, political or policy intervention, according to these bureaucrats, tends to be for the political self-interest of elected officials.

FIGURE 2.7   POLITICAL AND ADMINISTRATIVE VALUES

	Politics		Administration
ACTIVITY	Game		Problem solving
PLAYERS	Representatives		Experts
PIECES	Interests/Symbols	C I T Y	Information, Money, People, Things
		M A N A	
CURRENCY	Power	G E	Knowledge
CONVERSATION	What do you hear?	R	What do you know?
DYNAMICS	Conflict, Compromise, and Change		Harmony, Cooperation, and Continuity

One could dismiss Gruber as being rather too Jeffersonian, but she has likely painted a relatively accurate portrayal of the attitudes of upper-level bureaucrats. But this does not mean that public administrators are out of control or cannot be controlled. It does mean that elected officials and upper-level public administrators often hold different values and beliefs about democratic government and about organizational effectiveness. John Nalbandian (1995), a city mayor *and* a professor of public administration, sets out these contrasting values this way (Figure 2.7).

At the city level, following Nalbandian, Svara, Timothy Bledsoe, and others, elected officials and bureaucrats clearly have different values. Their views of their roles and activities differ, as do their tools and conversations. Although there may not be a literal politics-administration dichotomy, there certainly is a dichotomy of values. Elected officials and political analysts might regard the city bureaucracy as out of control. It isn't. It isn't out of control, but it is influenced by values that are, at times, different from ordinary political values.

The evidence indicates that street-level bureaucrats have some discretion in policy implementation as well as considerable influence in policymaking. In recent research on schools, Kenneth Meier, Joseph Stewart Jr., and Robert England compared three hypotheses regarding the direction of policy discretion by public administrators:

The *underclass hypothesis* contends that political systems are biased in the distribution of policy outputs, that poor and minority residents receive a less than equal share of city services. The *elections hypothesis* views politics as a way either to counter the class bias of urban government or to reinforce it. The elections hypothesis suggests that political elites will distribute urban services to benefit their political supporters. The *bureaucratic decision rules hypothesis* . . . holds that government services are allocated according to rules formulated in the bureaucracy. (1991, 156)

Most of the research on urban service delivery tends to reject the underclass hypothesis and the elections hypothesis and to support the bureaucratic decision rules hypothesis, and the Lipsky and Gruber findings just described would be typical of that research. Meier, Stewart, and England, however, found that school bureaucracies tend to be more politically responsive than previous research would indicate and that bureaucratic decision rules are less influential than was previously thought; in other words, school bureaucracies tend to be politically responsive.

The direction of the political control of bureaucracy was tested in a National Science Foundation–funded study done by Steven Maynard-Moody, Michael Musheno, and Marisa Kelly (1995). They were particularly interested in the decision norms (similar to decision rules) of street-level bureaucrats and in questions of justice and fairness. Using a form of story analysis, they tested these hypotheses:

1. Street-level bureaucrats are more likely to use justice norms to resolve dilemmas when three organizational conditions are present:
   a. The street-level bureaucrat feels he or she has the control to resolve a dilemma,
   b. he or she operates in a work culture that encourages the exercise of discretion by street-level bureaucrats, and
   c. the local work culture promotes a vision of clients compatible with the way street-level bureaucrats identify with their clients.
2. Street-level bureaucrats operating within a local work culture that encourages the use of discretion will use various coping strategies to approximate just outcomes when their identification with clients is strong but conflicts with those evident in the local work culture or is incompatible with available resources.
3. Street-level bureaucrats operating within an environment that discourages discretion and that places constraints on their abilities to control a situation may use coping strategies to meet the demands of their jobs, but not to orchestrate outcomes compatible with their norms of justice. They will cope with injustice by ignoring its presence.
4. Street-level bureaucrats working in different organizations within the same policy area will demonstrate different patterns of resolving justice dilemmas because of differences in local work and identity cultures.

The Maynard-Moody, Musheno, and Kelly argument is that with grants of adequate discretion, bureaucracies will tend toward fairness and justice. This supports the "social equity" normative standards for public administrators argued by H. George Frederickson (1997b).

We return to the question of whether capture theory, particularly the capture of bureaucracy by interest groups or clients, has an empirical warrant. The answer is mostly no. In the extent to which laws, regulations, and budgets support clients and client interests, and bureaucrats carry out those laws and regulations and serve those clients by using their appropriations, then, capture theory is salient. But this is usually interest groups' and/or clients' capture of *politics*, not of bureaucracy. At the national level, where issues of political control of bureaucracy are far more complicated, the James Q. Wilson (1989) synthesis is especially helpful:

> Congress has always micromanaged the federal bureaucracy, but the form of that micromanagement has changed from seeking favors for political supporters (there is still a good bit of this) to devising elaborate, detailed rules for bureaucracy, engaging in close oversight, and demanding information. (242)
>
> Agencies with tasks that are hard to specify and difficult to evaluate and that are imbedded in conflict-ridden political environments can barely be controlled by legislatures at all, except by multiplying the procedural constraints that the agencies are supposed to observe. (250–251)

An interesting illustration of the contingent effects of context and task is found in the research of Terry Moe (1989). He studied such controversial agencies as the Consumer Product Safety Commission, the Occupational Safety and Health Administration, and the Environmental Protection Agency. Business interest groups strongly oppose both the objectives and the activities of these bureaucracies and are not shy in pressuring Congress to either dismantle or change them. Congress finds the repeal of the enabling legislation for these agencies to be politically untenable, so it uses a different approach: "Opposing groups are dedicated to crippling the bureaucracy and gaining control over its decisions, and they will pressure for fragmented authority, labyrinthine procedures, mechanisms for political intervention, and other structures that subvert the bureaucracy's performance and open it to attack" (1989, 216).

At the state and national levels, one of the complicating factors in control-of-bureaucracy theories is divided government. In the ordinary theory of public administration, there is the executive assumption—public administration is part of an executive branch headed by an elected governor or president. When the governor or president is in one party and the legislature (or one house of the legislature) is controlled by the other party, who is to have control? In orthodox public administration theory, as well as in virtually every proposal for reform, the elected executive is understood to be at the top of the control hierarchy. Robert Gilmour and Alexis Halley, based on a careful observation of Congress, several presidents, and the federal bureaucracy in ten specific case studies, suggest that the "co-management" of bureaucracy is a more apt empirical description. If this is so, developing an empirically testable control-of-bureaucracy theory is made much more complex. They suggest the following:

> The cases collectively suggest that the term congressional co-management of policy implementation and program execution characterizes the transition from a congressional reliance on post-audit oversight of executive branch performance to pre-audit congressional program controls and direct congressional participation with the executive in the full scope of policy and program development and implementation. The cases show a "congressional co-manager" intervening directly in the details of policy development and management rather than enacting vague, wide-ranging, sweeping statutes to change fundamental policy directions. The cases also suggest that congressional co-management is as much a result of actions in the executive branch as it is a result of actions in the legislative branch. (1994, 335)

Based on this observation and on their case studies, they present the following hypotheses:

EFFECTS ON POLICY AND PROGRAMS

1. "Congressional intervention has prompted or forced changes in program priorities, directions, the speed of program implementation, and the visibility of programs on the executive policy agenda." (352)
2. "Congressional intervention has had intended effects on substantive policy outcomes and other effects that were neither intended nor anticipated." (353)
3. "Congressional intervention has operated to keep both branches focused on narrowly defined, short-run programs and has inclined to continue existing programs while submerging hard questions about alternatives or large policy issues." (354)

EFFECTS ON CONGRESSIONAL OVERSIGHT

1. "The Congress observed in these ten case studies was not a gadfly. Once particular committees, members, and staffs were involved in the details of implementation, they tended to stay involved until the situation changed or until safeguards were in place to assure that desired progress would continue." (355)
2. "Congress has created a new network of agencies, commissions, staffs, and other entities to conduct oversight functions, thereby supplementing some

committees and subcommittees in their oversight roles. Congress also places great reliance on the investigatory and oversight roles of its own support agencies." (356)

3. "The influence, expertise, and commitment of members of Congress and their staffs were critical to sustaining detailed congressional involvement." (356)

EFFECTS ON EXECUTIVE MANAGEMENT

1. "Congressional initiatives both strengthened and burdened the hands of agency administrators, sometimes one more than the other. The burden came in the form of the added workload of new requirements and the erosion of the long-term capacity to manage. The strength came in the form of 'an added stick' in dealing with the Office of Management and Budget and the regulated community and in forceful incentives to comply with statutory mandates and to avoid public censure." (358)

2. "Congressional initiatives changed the structure of governmental activities and functions. This shift is characterized by the creation of an array of commissions, boards, and specially designated offices within and between both branches." (358)

Gilmour and Halley (1994) observed five styles of congressional co-management. The strategic-leader style is associated with strengthening departmental management in directions favored by Congress. The Department of Defense is a good example.

Congress may approach co-management as a consulting partner, and foreign aid is illustrative: Congressional concessions for human rights, abortion, and the like are built into foreign aid decisions, as are high levels of financial support for favored countries such as Israel.

Congress may co-manage as if it were a superintendent by issuing mandates including management procedure, schedules, and other details ordinarily left to public administrators. In many respects, policy is implemented by the Department of Agriculture as if Congress were the "supermarket of agriculture."

Congress may be a combative opponent by using a kind of zero-sum logic, particularly when bureaucracy makes mistakes. The recent case of the failure of the Forest Service–controlled burning program and the problem of untrimmed and overgrown forests near towns is illustrative. Congress is simply bringing back grants of discretionary authority once held by the Forest Service.

Finally, Congress can be a passive observer. At certain times the association between Congress and the CIA and the FBI is illustrative, although recently Congress has been much less passive.

The evidence for these forms of congressional co-management is compelling. Taken altogether, they seem to indicate that there are many forms of political control over bureaucracy at the federal level and that such control is extensive. It does not appear that bureaucracy is out of control. If anything, the range of bureaucratic discretion appears narrow. Gilmour and Halley do a splendid job of detailing the characteristics of congressional co-management, but they have less to offer those interested in the effects of co-management on the bureaucracy. Gilmour and Halley do make this point:

> Congressional co-management has both improved and blurred the clarity of executive accountability for results. Increased accountability was documented in the form of new independent entities to check on the performance of the executive and more frequent or more extensive reporting requirements. Complicated lines of authority, responsibility, and accountability were more frequently observed, especially in domestic policy where an emerging congressional "parabureaucracy" significantly affects interbranch relations and executive capacity.
>
> As a matter of general complaint among some executive branch officials and other observers, Congress's members and their staffs have insinuated themselves inappropriately and unaccountably into administrative management. Although the anecdotal evidence to support such assertions is enormous, they are not given much weight by the ten cases investigated for this study. (1994, 368)

The clearest evidence of how individual bureaucrats respond to the problems of divided government and co-management is in the splendid research of Marissa Martino Golden (1992). Using a modified version of Albert O. Hirschman's concepts (1970) of bureaucratic exit, voice, and loyalty, she studied bureaucrats in the Civil Rights Division of the Department of Justice and in the National Highway Transportation Safety Administration (NHTSA) of the Department of Transportation during the administration of a Republican president, Ronald Reagan, and a Democratic Congress. It is important to remember that the Reagan administration was particularly antibureaucratic, advocated a strong policy departure from the status quo, and was in a decided ideological disagreement with congressional leaders as well as strong policy advocates in the bureaucracy.

The assumption that bureaucrats either cooperate or resist, Golden argues, is too simplistic. She determined that promoting or inhibiting bureaucratic resistance depended upon the bureaucrat's careerist ideology, the dominant agency profession (law, engineering), the agency's esprit, the agency's history, and the confidence of the careerists. In the Civil Rights Division, she found a long-standing ideology of support for the rights of racial minorities and women, a dominant profession (law), and a deep bureaucratic commitment to enforcing the civil rights laws. In the face of the Reagan administration's attempts to dismantle the division or force it not to enforce these laws, Golden found the widespread use of voice in several forms: a war of memos between career attorneys and political appointees, some use of leaks and sabotage, and very little cooperative action. There was a good bit of exit, some of it so-called creative resignation, to make a point. But exit was not taken lightly, and bureaucrats carefully weighed the tradeoff between exit and the consequent loss of voice. There was loyalty, sometimes mixed with withdrawal or neglect. Often voice and loyalty worked together, namely, the bureaucrat who stays on in part because of the desire to be an influential policy voice.

At the NHTSA, the issue was air bags. Congress and the NHTSA wanted them, but the automobile industry and the Reagan administration did not. A rule calling for air bags was in place at the beginning of the Reagan administration. The rule was first rescinded, then overruled by the Supreme Court, and then taken "up" to the level of Transportation Secretary Elizabeth Dole and out of the hands of NHTSA. Golden found some use of voice in attempts to influence policy, but much less than at the Civil Rights Division. There were some leaks to interest groups and Congress by career bureaucrats, but virtually no exit. There was a good bit of loyalty and steady policy implementation following presidential leadership, as well as a good bit of passive behavior and neglect.

Overall, the bureaucrats in the Civil Rights Division, when compared with those at NHTSA, were more ideological, shared a common esprit de corps, tended to be in the same profession, and had a long history of court successes. And, too, they had generally good career alternatives. In short, bureaucratic responses to political control under conditions of divided government depend on at least these factors.

Agency Theory

This chapter closes with a review of the most popular contemporary theory of political control of bureaucracy: principal-agent theory or, more simply, agency theory. This new framework has been widely applied to studies in the influence of principals, particularly Congress and the president, and agents, namely, the civil service. The initial premise in this theory was that bureaucracies are either out of control or at least very difficult to control. This premise is taken primarily from the early economic analyses of bureaucracy by Gordon Tullock (1965), Anthony Downs (1967), and William Niskanen (1971), all of whom regarded the bureaucracy as if it were a maximizing or self-seeking individual or firm in a market. In this premise, the bureaucracy hoards information (information asymmetry), seeks autonomy, and shirks.

Using both empirical field research primarily with quantifiable data and deductive math modeling, agency theorists have tested the range and form of legislative and executive control over bureaucracy. Almost all this research is conducted on the national government. In their review of the findings, Dan Wood and Richard

Waterman (1994) state that agency theory is explicit in its assumption of the logic of the politics-administration dichotomy. The assumption, of course, is that the relationship between elected leaders (principals) and civil servants or bureaucrats (agents) is hierarchical and could be understood as a series of contracts or transactions between a buyer of services and a provider of services. In the public context, the elected "buyer" attempts to shape the service to his or her preferences by laws, regulations, executive orders, appropriations, hearings, and all manner of co-management. The bureaucratic "seller" of services is a mixture of professional education and expertise, responds to laws and constitutions, and attempts to serve its clients. Agency theory is an especially useful way to understand the relationship among time, politics, and bureaucracy. Legislators wishing to move bureaucracies toward their favored positions are controlled by past coalitions and the legislation resulting from those coalitions. According to Wood and Waterman, "Agency theory posits a process of interaction between principals and agents that is dynamic, evolving through time. Throughout this process, bureaucracies have distinct informational and expertise advantages over politicians. They understand the policy and the organizational procedures required to implement it. As a result, they have both the opportunity and incentive to manipulate politicians and processes for political gain" (1994, 23).

One important mechanism to control bureaucracy, which can perhaps be called the modern form of accountability, is the use of reporting to hold bureaucracies accountable for their performance. This creates a "distinctly subordinate and responsive role" for the agents (Dubnick 2005, 386). Thus, performance and accountability to political principles become tightly linked, and reporting thus enhances the power of the principal over the agent. The move toward the use of organizational report cards, particularly by the federal government since 2001, is symptomatic of this form of accountability. Organizational report cards are useful for establishing and maintaining control, as they provide data about many agents simultaneously and in standardized formats to principals who are interested in assessing performance (Gormley and Weimer 1999). They also serve to reduce the information advantage typically enjoyed by bureaucracy over elected officials. The use of reporting as a control mechanism became well known when George W. Bush's administration instituted the Program Assessment Rating Tool (PART), which the Office of Management and Budget used to hold other government agencies accountable for success. As an example of how the tool was used, poor PART scores in the Commerce Department resulted in the consolidation of the Community Development Block Grant program and the Economic Development Assistance program.

As reporting and program evaluation have increased in sophistication, tension has arisen between principals and agents. William Gormley and Steven Balla (2008) point out that because performance evaluation is intimately connected to accountability, agents subject to rigorous reporting expectations may lose the freedom to use their expertise to be innovative in the way they address the issues for which they are responsible. This can make it difficult for street-level bureaucrats to provide effective service. The popular example of this situation is the concern over how the No Child Left Behind Act would create incentives for teachers to simply "teach to the test" so that their classes and schools would look good on standardized federal performance reports.

Although reporting is an important method of controlling bureaucracy, the observation by Wood and Waterman (1994) that agencies still hold advantages in the areas of information and expertise still holds. Coupled with the fact that organizational report cards and program evaluation can never provide a full picture of bureaucratic performance, the principal-agent relationship is still nuanced and complex (Gormley and Balla 2008; Palumbo 1987).

Furthermore, Maynard-Moody and Musheno (2009) reveal that the set of relationships among citizens, agents, and the state is more complex than previously thought, which makes controlling bureaucracy more difficult. These findings are consistent with others, who agree that street-level discretion reduces the chances of control over those street-level workers (Brehm and Gates 1997). Maynard-Moody and Musheno find, for example, that, although we should acknowledge the difficulties of street-level work and tolerate some discretion in decisionmaking, we must not forget that street-level bureaucrats are indeed agents of the state. This creates, they argue, an unresolvable tension between the expectations of principal-agent theory and the relationships between citizens and street-level agents.

Nevertheless, in their review of findings based on agency theory, Wood and Waterman (1994) indicate the following:

1. Bureaucratic responsiveness to political control is the norm rather than the exception. A wide range of contingent factors, such as time, presidential and congressional agreement, and many others, influence the degree of bureaucratic responsiveness.
2. Political control mechanisms are important, especially presidential appointments, congressional appropriations power, hearings, and congressional staff effectiveness.
3. Organization matters. Agencies in executive or cabinet departments are more responsive, whereas independent agencies are less so.
4. Presidential statements are influential, as are the statements of senior congressional leaders.

How do bureaucracies respond to political control? In their review of agency theory research of federal agencies, Wood and Waterman conclude that there are dynamic bidirectional relationships in which legislators signal preferences to bureaucrats and bureaucrats signal preferences to legislators:

Some would argue that such two-way power relations are evidence of political dysfunction, given that bureaucracies are nonelected institutions. However, we suggest that the opposite is true. It is healthy for bureaucracy to use its information advantages to better inform principals on either policy matters or the nature of the bureaucratic process. Furthermore, bureaucratic resistance to duly elected politicians may actually sometimes be more consistent with democracy and public preferences than bureaucratic responsiveness may be. Citizens and many groups strongly opposed the de-regulation of the environment advocated by the Reagan administration, and the bureaucracy served as a check on presidential power. (1994, 126)

In carrying out policy, a bureaucracy is caught between past majority political coalitions and their laws and policies and current majority political coalitions *and* their preferences. This is further complicated by the co-management phenomenon; in fact, bureaucracies face multiple competing principals. In one principal-agent hierarchy, Congress is presumed to control; in another, the president. The combination of time and multiple competing principles makes bureaucratic adaptiveness essential. In the main, federal bureaucracies have adapted. The speed, direction, and tone of that adaptation are contingent.

Despite the rather negative rhetoric in some agency theory—phrases such as "agency deception," "bureaucratic shirking," and "agency information hoarding"—the general findings of this research make useful contributions to public administration theory.

In reconciling theories of bureaucracy with democratic theory, bureaucracies sometimes resist the control of principals. Environmental Protection Agency (EPA) administrator Anne Burford was directly involved in

illegal activities by actually encouraging hazardous waste operators to violate the Resource Conservation and Recovery Act of 1979. However, the EPA's resistance to the Reagan administration started much earlier than the . . . violations. Thus, as a matter of fact bureaucracies resist change that runs counter to public or organizational interests whether it contradicts legal mandates or not.

Thus, bureaucracies perform an integrative function for U.S. democracy. They blend demands from past democratic coalitions with those from current democratic coalitions to produce a policy output at a consistent level. (Wood and Waterman 1994, 145)

Conclusions

Theories of political control of bureaucracy are central to any sophisticated understanding of public administration. They are abundant in their variety and are tested using the full range of methodological techniques. Such theories are as old as Woodrow Wilson's writings and as new as agency theory.

It continues to be fashionable to say that there is no politics-administration dichotomy, as if such a statement conveyed a special insight. As theories of political control of bureaucracy indicate, to unbundle politics and administration is a key to understanding how politics controls bureaucracy and how bureaucracy influences politics and policy. Therefore, it is wrongheaded to approach the subject of public administration on the assumption that politics and administration are more or less the same thing. The preceding review indicates that the many and richly varied forms of politics and policy and the equally varied forms of public administration can, when put into the same equation, advance the development of verifiable theory.

After his retirement, Dwight Waldo was interviewed by two of his students, Brack Brown and Richard J. Stillman Jr. The portion of this interview having to do with the separation of powers and the politics-administration dichotomy is particularly interesting, given that Waldo, perhaps more than anyone else, contributed to the received wisdom that there is no such dichotomy:

STILLMAN: You've also indicated a similar difficulty with our understanding of the separation of powers. Why have advances been slow here as well? Is there any way out of this quandary that you deem promising?

WALDO: I suppose your next question will be, "What is the nature of reality?" What can I say to this subject in a few minutes? Well, I offer a few observations that I judge relevant.

First, the separation of powers is there—prominently and, for our purposes, permanently. The complicated scheme of separating and sharing powers and functions is built into the Constitution, and in more than two centuries the Constitution has been built into our national life. We have no alternative but to work with and/or around the tripartite separation.

Second, the politics-administration formula, perspective, approach, dichotomy—pick your own noun—was an attempt on the part of public administration to work with and/or around the separation of powers. It foundered, by common consent, but for various alleged reasons: It was empirically untrue to what happens and is impossible to operationalize; it was presumptuous if not impious, putting profane hands on a sacred scheme; it concealed ethical problems and encouraged illegal action. So, formally or ostensibly, we put the dichotomy aside. But at the same time, it lingers, both as an idea and as a practice. And I don't judge the lingering as simple inertia, a cultural lag. The twofold schema has too much going for it in logic and usefulness simply to disappear. We *do*, commonsensically, decide and execute, set policy and administer. (1986, 153)

Theories of political control of bureaucracy are, in sum, among the most empirically robust and theoretically elegant in public administration.

3

Theories of Bureaucratic Politics

Introduction: What Are Theories of Bureaucratic Politics?

Theories of bureaucratic politics seek to explain the policymaking role of administration and bureaucracy. Such frameworks typically reject the politics-administration dichotomy underpinning theories of bureaucratic control, viewing this division as an analytical convenience that imposes too steep a cost on theoretical development. Specifically, the price of making theory more tractable by separating administration from politics is held to be a willful ignorance of the central role of bureaucracy within the polity's power structure.

Since bureaucracies and bureaucrats routinely engage in political behavior, the need to account theoretically for the bureaucracy's political role is justified. Politics is generically defined as the authoritative allocation of values, or the process of deciding "who gets what, when and how" (Easton 1965; Lasswell 1936). Numerous studies confirm that bureaucracies and bureaucrats routinely allocate values and decide who gets what, that bureaucracies logically engage in "politics of the first order" (Meier 1993, 7). Theories of bureaucratic politics therefore begin by accepting what has long been empirically observed; that is, in practice, administration is not a technical and value-neutral activity separable from politics. Administration *is* politics (Waldo 1948).

Accordingly, theories of bureaucratic politics seek to breach the orthodox divide between administration and politics and attempt to drag the former into a systematic accounting with the latter. That traditional theoretical frameworks account poorly for bureaucracy's obvious and repeatedly observed political role has long been recognized. Even scholars traditionally credited with describing and supporting the politics-administration divide were well aware of the political role the bureaucracy plays, and the rigidity of the division accepted as their legacy has been described as a caricature of their arguments. Woodrow Wilson and Frank Goodnow, who both wrote at a time when public bureaucracies were ripe with

41

patronage, incompetence, and even outright corruption, were well aware that politics and administration represented a synthesis rather than two neatly separable portions of the public policy enterprise (Lynn 2001). Other prominent public administration scholars argued during the first half of the twentieth century that administrative theory had to account for politics, both in recognition of bureaucracy's real-world role and as a necessary element to building better explanatory frameworks within the discipline.

Among the most prominent of these was John Gaus (1931). He observed that federal agencies not only carried out clearly understood directives from Congress but also independently shaped those directives and exercised discretionary policymaking authority while translating the vague intentions of statutes into specific government actions. Bureaucracy obviously wields political power. This being so, those who sought to understand public agencies could not simply carve off administration from politics and leave the complexities of the latter to political theorists. If bureaucracies were helping to determine the will of the state, they were inescapably political institutions, and Gaus argued that administrative theory ignored this fact at its peril. Most famously, in the final sentence of an essay in *Public Administration Review*, he threw down an implied gauntlet to those who would fashion a theory of administration: "A theory of public administration means in our time a theory of politics also" (1950, 168). Gaus thus succinctly summarized the purpose of theories of bureaucratic politics.

As the broader intellectual history of political theory makes clear, this is a difficult objective, and for more than half a century students of public administration have had mixed success in meeting Gaus's challenge. The issues raised here are more complex than those at the heart of the theories of bureaucratic control. The goal is not to locate the dividing line between politics and administration because no such line exists, nor is it to ascertain how bureaucracies can be made accountable to their democratic masters, although this is a question of some importance to theories of bureaucratic politics. Questions of political power are the central focus:

- To what extent do administrative processes, as opposed to democratic processes, determine public policy?
- Who controls or influences the exercise of bureaucratic power?
- What is the role of bureaucracy in representing and advancing the goals of particular clientele groups or organized interests?
- To what extent do elective institutions and elected officials seek to shape and control administration as a means to advance their own political interests?
- What is the source of bureaucratic power?
- How does the important political role of nonelected institutions based in hierarchy and authority square with the fundamental values of democracy?

If anything has been learned by the efforts expended on developing theories of bureaucratic politics, it is that such questions have no easy answers.

Nevertheless, numerous studies have confirmed the need for systematic frameworks accounting for the political role of the bureaucracy. Several responses to this need have provided important insights into the political role of the bureaucracy, and in doing so, significantly expanded our understanding of public administration.

Administrative Theory as Political Theory

The seminal work that justified the need for a theory of bureaucratic politics is Dwight Waldo's *The Administrative State* (1948). Waldo did not construct a theory of bureaucratic politics in this book, but here and in later writings he made two critical contributions that have supported all subsequent efforts to do so. First, he undertook a devastating critique of the extant research literature. He argued that public administration scholarship revolved around a core set of beliefs that cumulatively served to constrain theoretical development. Key among these were the beliefs that efficiency and democracy were compatible and that the work of government could be cleanly divided into separate realms of decision and execution. These beliefs led public administration scholars to champion efficiency as the central goal of public agencies, to develop a "science" of administration to maximize that efficiency, and to ignore the political ramifications of these beliefs and the prescriptions they implied.

Second, and probably more important, Waldo argued that administrative scholarship was itself driven by a particular philosophy of politics. A good portion of *The Administrative State* is devoted to examining the scholarly public administration literature through the lens of five key issues in political philosophy: (1) the nature of the Good Life, or a vision of what the "good society" should look like; (2) the criteria of action, or the procedures for determining how collective decisions should be made; (3) the question of who should rule; (4) the question of how the powers of the state should be divided and apportioned; and (5) the question of centralization versus decentralization, or the relative merits of a unitary state versus a federal system.

Waldo concluded that public administration scholarship was anchored by well-developed responses to all of these issues. Like theorists from Machiavelli to Marx, public administration scholars had a vision of what the "good society" looks like: It is industrial, urban, and centrally planned; it has no poverty, no corruption, and no extremes of wealth. Science is its ideal, and waste and inefficiency are its enemy. These same scholars also had a clear preference for the criteria of action: A scientific analysis of the facts should decide what should be done. Public administration orthodoxy espoused particularly firm beliefs about who should rule:

"The assertion that there is a field of expertise which has, or should have, a place in and claim upon the exercise of modern governmental functions—this is a fundamental postulate of the public administration movement" (1948, 89–90). Technocrats blessed with the requisite competence and expertise were public administration's equivalents of the Guardians in Plato's *Republic*. On the particularly American issues of the separation of powers and centralization versus decentralization, Waldo argued that the preferences of administration scholarship were equally clear: Administration scholars were hostile to the tripartite partition of power in the American system and sought to increase the power of the executive at the expense of the judiciary and the legislature. They were also in favor of a centralized state. They placed their faith in the competence of a professional administrator, who, given the requisite power and authority, could tackle the obstacles standing before the realization of the good life.

If administration scholarship advanced such a distinct and definable political philosophy (some might say ideology), it raised an immediate and formidable intellectual obstacle to attempts at conceptually dividing politics and administration: How could students of administration claim that politics was largely external to their interests when their intellectual history revealed such a systematic value-based philosophy of government? Waldo pointed out that administration is frequently claimed to be at the core of modern democratic government, and that this claim helps justify the entire discipline of public administration. If this claim has merit, it implies that democratic theory must deal with administration, and that administrative theory must deal with democratic politics. As a practical matter of explaining the operation and role of administration in government, not to mention as a point of intellectual honesty, students of administration cannot deal with the problems of politics by assuming them away.

Waldo argued that administrative scholarship's failure to incorporate politics explicitly into its theoretical development was a product of its early cultural and intellectual environment. While recognizing the impossibility of cleanly dating the beginning of public administration scholarship as a self-conscious body of thought, Waldo took as his starting point writers such as Woodrow Wilson, Frank Goodnow, and Frederick W. Taylor, namely, influential management, administration, and organization theorists who wrote near the turn of the twentieth century. The work of these scholars reflected not only the dominant cultural values of their time but also the contemporary problems in administration they sought to address. Cultural values led them to accept science as the surest path to knowledge and commerce as the central activity of society. The central problems they sought to address consisted of an unappetizing stew of inefficiency marinating in political cronyism and seasoned with graft.

One of the outcomes of these contextual forces was that, from the beginning, students of administration adopted efficiency as their guiding principle. The term was vaguely defined, though "efficient administration" clearly meant "good administration." When administration scholars operationalized the concept, they mainly seemed to be talking about an input-output ratio, the most output for the least input being the implied objective (Waldo 1948, 201–202). A "good" decision or administrative act was thus one that maximized outputs for a given set of inputs. As Waldo pointed out, this is a concept fundamental to businesses operating in capitalistic markets, but it is not nearly so important to democratic government. Equity, consensus, or the satisfaction of particular interests is frequently the criterion for action in democratic processes, and none of these criteria are necessarily efficient; indeed, they are often inescapably inefficient.

Yet, as administration scholars accepted efficiency as their central principle, they also accepted democracy—a notoriously *inefficient* basis of organization—as the central principle of the American political system. This presented a problem in developing administrative theory. The formative era of administrative scholarship, with its focus on the scientific method, its guiding principle of efficiency, and its position in the shadow of business, meant that it developed in a decidedly undemocratic context. Not only was democracy not synonymous with efficiency and various other business and scientific practices incorporated into public administration orthodoxy, but also it was quite possibly hostile to them (Waldo 1952, 85). How could the principle central to the American political system be squared with the forces driving the theoretical development of public administration as a discipline?

Waldo argued that the founders of public administration solved the conundrum by accepting democracy as the guiding principle of the American political system, but keeping it external to their professional interests through the politics-administration dichotomy. By separating the work of government into two distinct operations and limiting their attention to the "nonpolitical" element, administration scholars were free to push for centralized power in the executive branch, to prescribe hierarchical and authoritarian bureaucracies as the basis for organizing public agencies, and to call for passing greater responsibilities to the technocrat. As long as these reforms increased efficiency in administration, and administration was kept separate from politics, theoretically the discipline did not have to square the contradictions these arguments presented to the egalitarian ideals of democracy.

As Waldo was careful to point out, the founders of public administration were not ideologically opposed to democracy. They were progressive reformers who embraced the romantic ideal of democracy as the "best" or "proper" form of government. The reality they faced at the time, however, was a public administration characterized by disorganization, amateurism, and dishonesty. Nineteenth-century reforms springing from the presidency of Andrew Jackson had dispersed and factionalized the power of government. Elected officials multiplied, the legislature took precedence over the executive, and government agencies were staffed through the spoils system. If administration were the core of government, the net result of these reforms created a serious problem for democracy in the United States at the turn of the twentieth century: a public administration shot through with incompetence, ripe for corruption. For public administration to gain competency and efficiency, it would have to cleanse itself of politics and learn the lessons of science and business. Good administration (and thus good government) could best be promoted by centralizing and concentrating power; by running agencies according to sound, scientific management principles; by making technical competence the criterion for civil service employment; and by shielding these technical experts from whatever winds happened to be stirring the dust in the political arena.

Waldo thus viewed the political philosophy inherent in public administration scholarship not as an attempt to usurp democracy, but as a necessary corrective to save it. As Waldo put it, "Democracy if it were to survive, could not afford to ignore the lessons of centralization, hierarchy, and discipline. Put bluntly, it was the maxim 'Autocracy during hours is the price of democracy after hours'" (1952, 87). Theoretically, the undemocratic elements of administrative orthodoxy—its emphasis on efficiency, hierarchy, and authority—could be seen in the service of democracy as long as the politics-administration orthodoxy held. An efficient and expertly run administrative apparatus insulated from politics and under the authority of a powerful executive would increase accountability and promote effective, competently run public programs and policies. If things did not work, everyone would know whom to blame and why, and the representative institutions of democracy could act accordingly.

The problem, as numerous scholars have pointed out, was that the politics-administration dichotomy did not hold. As Waldo meticulously detailed in his literature review, there was ample evidence that bureaucracies pushed some values over others, that bureaucracies acted as power brokers among competing special interests, and that lawmakers were increasingly reliant on and influenced by the expertise and opinions of administrators. Administrative theory simply could not ignore these realities and continue to usefully shape the direction of the discipline. At a minimum, Waldo argued, the concept of democracy and all its messy implications had to be brought back into administrative theory. Administrative scholars had to recognize that their central principle—efficiency—was not value neutral, and that its uneasy relationship with democratic principles had to be recognized (Waldo 1952, 90).

Waldo suggested that continued attempts to create a science of administration would result in theoretical dead ends because "science" was, in effect, a code word for preserving the core principle of efficiency, a signal for another attempt to inoculate administration against politics. In an essay in the *American Political Science Review*, Waldo singled out Herbert Simon's argument separating questions of administration into issues dealing with fact and issues dealing with values. Simon's enormously influential *Administrative Behavior* (1947/1997) had essentially demolished the extant research seeking to define and promulgate the "principles" or "laws" of a science of administration. Yet Simon sought to save the possibility of that science. He argued that it was conceivable if it limited its attention to decisions centered on facts (statements that can be tested to assess whether they are true or false) as opposed to values (statements that are validated by human fiat). Decisions of fact were central to the administrative realm, Simon argued, and could be scientifically guided toward the overall goal of efficiency. Waldo said that Simon was simply recasting the problem by substituting a logical division of politics and administration for an institutional division, and was doing so to preserve the central principle of orthodox administrative theory, namely, efficiency.

Efficiency could not remain the discipline's talisman against politics, Waldo argued, because administration *is* political. In Waldo's perspective, efficiency itself is a political claim. For example, how does one assess the efficiency of, say, a library, or the Department of Defense? If efficiency is defined as an input-output ratio, one has a choice of inputs and outputs to assess efficiency in both instances, although none is the unassailably objective "factual" option. As choosing among these options unavoidably involves values not just facts, efficiency can hardly be value neutral (Stone 2002, 65). If public administration insisted that its orthodox principles were politically neutral, Waldo argued, it would never be rid of the theoretical straitjacket it used to restrain itself from the world of politics. Waldo's argument bought a tart response from Simon (1952b), but even as Simon went on the offensive, there were signs that Waldo's point had sunk deep into the discipline. Published concurrently with Simon's essay was another by an equally prominent scholar—Peter Drucker (1952)—who wholeheartedly agreed with Waldo's assessment of the fundamentally political character of large-scale organizations, and suggested that, if anything, Waldo had not pushed his arguments far enough (see Simon 1952a for the complete essay on this point).

Waldo argued that at the heart of the problem with administrative theory is a version of the problem James Madison struggled with in *Federalist No. 10*: How do you preserve individual liberty without destroying the freedoms that make it possible? For Madison, it was the dilemma of constructing a government strong enough to protect individual liberty without making it vulnerable to the forces that would crush the liberties of others for their own selfish interests. For Waldo, "The central problem of democratic administrative theory, as of all democratic theory, is how to reconcile democracy . . . with the demands of authority" (1952, 102). How do we construct a theory that accommodates the hierarchical and authoritarian nature of the bureaucracy, the foundation of the modern administrative state and a seemingly necessary component of contemporary government, with the seemingly contradictory egalitarian, inefficient ideals of democracy? Waldo bestowed this grand and sweeping question upon the discipline rather than provide its answer, but the question is surely enough to justify the need to meld administrative theory with political theory, to motivate the search for a theory of bureaucratic politics.

Allison's Paradigm of Bureaucratic Politics

In the two decades following the publication of *The Administrative State* (Waldo 1948), an embryonic theory of bureaucratic politics began to emerge from a series of studies examining decisionmaking in the executive branch. The significant claim generated by these studies was that government decisions were products of bargaining and negotiation among interested political actors. As these studies focused on the executive branch, the central player in these bargaining frameworks was the president. The president, however, was argued to have little unilateral decisionmaking power; he had to accommodate the interests of the various institutional factions in the executive branch. Bureaucracies and bureaucrats, in short, played high-level politics, and usually played the game very well.

These studies were discursive rather than explicitly theoretical, but the parallels between them and the contemporary work on game theory—a highly formalized and mathematical approach to explaining behavior—are unmistakable. The loose bargaining framework adopted by this research quickly proved a useful way to organize empirical research and produced many of the raw materials for a more comprehensive theory. The best-known studies of this early bureaucratic politics literature include Samuel Huntington's *The Common Defense* (1961), Warner Schilling's 1962 essay on the politics of national defense, and, most famously, Richard Neustadt's *Presidential Power* (1960). Bureaucracies and executive branch officials were not portrayed here as neutral agents of implementation, but as active participants in determining the will of the state. These studies steadily built a case for a general theory of bureaucratic politics centered on bargaining games in the executive branch.

The first serious comprehensive attempt to produce such a framework was undertaken by Graham Allison in his book *Essence of Decision* (1971), and further refined by Allison and Morton Halperin (1972). Allison's immediate focus in *Essence of Decision* was explaining why the governments of the United States and the Soviet Union did what they did during the Cuban missile crisis. With a nuclear exchange at stake, these were policies of particular importance, but Allison was aiming well beyond the confines of one case study. Essentially, he posed a broad question that cut to the heart of bureaucratic politics: Why do governments do what they do? In other words, how is policy made, and who determines or influences it? To provide general answers to these questions, Allison articulated three theoretical models.

The first was the rational actor model (what Allison termed "Model I," or the classical model). Model I proposes that government decisions can be understood by viewing them as the product of a single actor in strategic pursuit of his own self-interest. The second model is the organizational process paradigm, or Model II, which argues that numerous actors are involved in decisionmaking, and decisionmaking processes are highly structured through standard operating procedures (SOPs). When a problem occurs, Model I assumes that the government will identify the potential responses to that problem, assesses the consequences of those actions, and choose the action that maximizes benefits and minimizes costs. In contrast, Model II assumes that the government will rely on organizational routines instead of a rational cost-benefit calculus to make that decision. Rather than search for all potential responses, the various components of government will act according to SOPs that, in effect, say, "When X happens, do Y."

The seminal contribution of Allison (1971) and Allison and Halperin (1972) to the bureaucratic politics literature came in the articulation of an alternative to Models I and II. Model III, or the bureaucratic politics paradigm, explains government actions as the product of bargaining and compromise among the various organizational elements of the executive branch. Allison's model of bureaucratic politics is constructed from four basic propositions. (1) The executive branch is composed of numerous organizations and individuals having divergent objectives and agendas. Any given issue will attract the attention and involvement of a set of these actors, who bring to that issue their divergent interests and motivations. (2) No preponderant individual or organization exists; in other words, no one actor in the executive branch is able to act unilaterally. The president might be the most powerful actor on a given issue, but he will not be the only actor, and his influence will be limited. (3) The final decision is a "political resultant"; in other words, what the government decides to do is the outcome of bargaining and compromise, the product of a political process. (4) There is a difference between making policy and carrying it out. Once an action is decided upon, the task of implementing that decision is handed over to others who must also make decisions about the specific actions to take. Those decisions are in turn shaped by the operating procedures and interests of the implementers (Rosati 1981).

With these as a starting point, a policy analyst's attention is immediately focused on power and politics within and among executive branch bureaucracies. Within the confines of the executive branch, Allison's model combines and makes little distinction between politics and administration, and in doing so seems to answer the challenge laid down by Gaus. In studying bureaucracy, as Allison put it, "the name of the game is politics: bargaining along regularized circuits among players positioned hierarchically within the government. Government behavior can thus be understood . . . as a result of these bargaining games" (1971, 144). Model III sees the components of the executive branch as semiautonomous organizations that do not act in unison on a series of single strategic issues, but act on a variety of issues according to their own conceptions of national, organizational, and individual goals. Instead of making policy and implementation decisions according to rational self-interest, or according to the dictates of SOPs, government actors decide on the basis of the "pulling and hauling" that is politics.

From its general premises, Model III systematically goes about explaining specific policies by seeking the answers to a few basic questions. (1) Who plays? In other words, what agencies or individuals have an important stake in a given issue, and whose behavior can have an important effect on government decisions and actions concerning that issue? (2) What determines each player's stand? This question stems from Allison's proposition that "where you stand depends on where you sit." Different agencies and individuals will have different perceptions of an issue and divergent preferences on what should be done based on their objectives, values, and sense of mission. (3) How are players' stands aggregated to yield governmental decisions and actions? Once it has been determined who are involved in a given issue and what their interests and objectives are, the challenge is to assess how these actors bargain to protect and advance their preferences. This means determining the relative influence of the players. Model III assumes that bargaining is highly structured and that "action channels" or "rules of the game" shape the process of decisionmaking and distribute power among players (Allison and Halperin 1972).

Allison's model of bureaucratic politics has had a significant impact on how bureaucracies are studied. It was not just a series of propositions formulated to explain one study, but rather a workable theory for understanding the policymaking role of bureaucracy. As such, the contribution of Model III to the theoretical development of public administration scholarship is hard to underestimate. Yet, although Allison undoubtedly reduced the paucity of theoretical substance in the field, Model III has had mixed success as a general framework for the study of bureaucratic politics. Model III is predicated on a series of intuitively appealing assumptions: Government actions are the product of bargaining among the organizational components of the executive branch, these actors have their own parochial interests, and their ability to translate those interests into policy is determined by their role in decisionmaking. These assumptions logically lead to testable propositions: Policy outcomes will reflect the parochial interests involved in the bargaining game, they also will reflect the relative power of the players involved in the game, and the power of the players will be determined by the "action channels," or regularized processes, used to structure decisionmaking. Unfortunately, subsequent scholarship has raised doubts about the empirical validity of these hypotheses and the conceptual structure that supports them (Rosati 1981; Rhodes 1994; Bendor and Hammond 1992).

Politics, Power, and Organization

Ironically, one of the implications of other work on bureaucratic politics is that Allison's Model III was, if anything, too limited in scope rather than too ambitious. In particular, Allison's framework left important organizational issues underdeveloped, and, like the majority of the studies the framework sought to synthesize, it was almost exclusively focused on the executive branch. As some scholars were to make clear, bureaucratic politics is not confined to bargaining games within the executive branch; it is a fundamental component of a broad power structure that includes Congress, the courts, organized interest groups, intergovernmental relationships, and the public at large. The nature and context of this power structure, and the role and relative influence of bureaucracies within it, are heavily dependent upon organizational issues. How bureaucracies are organized has been persuasively argued to play an important role in determining how power is distributed among various actors within the political system and in explaining how bureaucracies influence policymaking.

There are two key organizational dimensions to bureaucratic politics theory. The first deals with behavior. The primary goal here is to explain why bureaucrats and bureaucracies do what they do. The general presumption is that bureaucracies pursue important public missions and make numerous policy decisions, yet have only vague guidance from statutes. If legislatures, the institutions formally responsible for the goals of public agencies, only partially account for what bureaucracies do and why they do it, what explains the rest? The second deals with institutional structure and the distribution of power. The primary goal here is to understand how a bureaucracy's formal lines of authority, its relationship to other institutions, and the programs and policies placed within its jurisdiction all combine to determine the relative political influence of a broad range of political actors.

Explanations for the political behavior of bureaucracy and bureaucrats have deep roots in the organization theory literature. For example, Robert K. Merton (1957) argued that institutions structured as classic bureaucracies shape the personalities of the people who work for them. A bureaucratic environment, Merton argued, pressures people to conform to expected patterns of behavior—to follow rules, to be methodical and detailed. Given these pressures, bureaucracies will often substitute rules for ends, and they will adhere to SOPs even when those procedures clearly interfere with the organization's main mission. William Whyte Jr. echoed a similar theme in his work *The Organization Man* (1956). Whyte's research detailed the willingness of managers in US corporations to adopt the goals of the organizations they worked for as their own, to subsume their personalities into the larger organizational environment of their employment. Similar arguments about the pathologies of bureaucratic behavior have resurfaced more recently in such influential works as David Osborne and Ted Gaebler's *Reinventing Government* (1992).

If organizational structure shapes the behavior of particular institutions and the individuals within them, this has broad implications for those seeking to explain the policymaking role of bureaucracy. If bureaucrats make decisions that authoritatively allocate values, and organizational environment helps determine how those decisions are made, then organizational theory holds the potential to explain a good deal of how and why bureaucracy fulfills its political role.

One of the key contributions of organizational behavior scholarship to bureaucratic politics theory is James Q. Wilson's classic, *Bureaucracy: What Government Agencies Do and Why They Do It* (1989). Wilson posed a similar question to Allison, though it was more focused toward administrative matters. Instead of asking why governments do what they do, Wilson asked why bureaucracies do what they do. Wilson argued that bureaucrats have discretion in their decisionmaking, and that a complex set of factors determine how that discretion is exercised: "When bureaucrats are free to choose a course of action their choices will reflect the full array of incentives operating on them: some will reflect the need to manage a workload; others will reflect the expectations of workplace peers and professional colleagues elsewhere; still others may reflect their own convictions. And some will reflect the needs of clients" (1989, 88). Before Wilson's contribution, numerous scholars had argued that discretion in decisionmaking, in effect, made bureaucrats into policymakers, and bureaucracies into political actors. Wilson's work provided a richly detailed study of how and why this discretion was exercised to produce government action.

Wilson took a disparate set of examples to develop his argument (he started with the German army of World War II, prison systems in Michigan and Texas, and a public school in Atlanta). Some of the agencies were successful, some of them were not, and the performance of some bureaucracies went from good to bad, or vice versa. Wilson sought to explain what separated the successful agencies from the not so successful, and to understand variation in bureaucratic performance. In pursuit of this objective, he covered so much intellectual territory that it is difficult to provide a meaningful synopsis of the entire work. Key elements in his analysis, however, should convey some sense of the main arguments.

Wilson began with the presumption that the behavior of bureaucrats and bureaucracies was purposive; that is, it was motivated by some goal or objective. He rejected the argument that the goals driving bureaucratic behavior were wholly, or even largely, determined by legislatures. Wilson noted that bureaucratic missions encapsulated in law tend to be vague (the goal of the Department of State, for example, is to "promote the long-range security and well-being of the nation"). Fuzzy exhortations to "do the right thing" are politically appealing, but they provide no hint of the specific actions a bureaucracy is expected to undertake. In Wilson's terms, these goals do not define "operator tasks," meaning they do not tell the frontline workers of a bureaucracy what they should be doing. These workers, whom Wilson termed the "operators," are those whose work actually justifies the existence of a given organization—for example, teachers in a school, patrol officers in a law enforcement agency, or soldiers in an army (1989, 33–34).

As goals are vague (or even contradictory), bureaucracies cannot simply deploy their expertise to determine the best way of achieving the ends of policy. Something other than the product of the "politics" end of the politics-administration dichotomy must drive the behavior of bureaucrats and bureaucracies. What is it? What determines the behavior of the cop on the beat, the teacher in the classroom, the private on the front lines? Wilson proposed several potential answers: situational imperatives (the day-to-day events operators must to respond to), peer expectations, professional values, and ideology. He also argued that rules could also substitute for goals. When goals are vague, following established procedures and "going by the book" provide operators with a guide to low-risk behavior. Wilson also argued that most large organizations, and certainly many public agencies, have their own particular personalities. They have persistent, patterned ways of thinking about the purposes of the organization and the best means to achieve those purposes. Combined, these patterns constitute organizational culture, and they serve to socialize organizational novitiates into the "way things are done around here" (1989, 91–93).

Wilson was not just interested in identifying the behavioral motivations of operators; he also identified two other kinds of bureaucrats: managers (people who coordinate the work of operators to achieve organizational goals) and executives (people responsible for maintaining their organizations). He also identified systematic elements to the behavior of each level and how they interact with each other. For example, he argued that managers of public agencies have a different set of constraints upon their behavior than managers in private firms. At a most basic level, managers must have a clear sense of an organization's mission if they are to coordinate the work of operators toward that end, and executives must be capable of defending that mission and of supporting their organization's pursuit of a given objective. In the public sector, even these most basic elements of administration are complex because public organizations cannot control their broadly defined missions, nor can they unilaterally control other critical elements of management—revenues, personnel, and the means of production.

Wilson concluded that successful bureaucracies are those in which executives have created a clear sense of mission, identified the tasks that must be achieved to fulfill that mission, distributed authority within the organization according to those tasks, and provided subordinates (particularly operators) with enough autonomy to achieve the task at hand (1989, 365)—a fairly tall order given the complex environment of public agencies. Wilson's argument suggests that agencies given clear objectives and high levels of autonomy are more likely to be successful in achieving those objectives. Yet, as Wilson acknowledged, it is difficult to see how clear objectives can be routinely manufactured as an end product of a democratic process. If the administrative arm of government is given greater levels of autonomy, and if clearer goals are not forthcoming from the democratic institutions of government, the likely result is the transfer of increasing amounts of policymaking power to the bureaucracy. In its call for clearer missions and less centralization in public bureaucracy, Wilson's argument is ultimately prescriptive. Reorganization through deregulation, however, turns out to be an extension of bureaucratic politics rather than a way to channel it toward universally desired ends. Organization helps determine not only how bureaucracies and bureaucrats behave but also how power and influence are distributed among the various actors in the political system.

Government organization, or, more accurately, reorganization, is a subject near and dear to the discipline of public administration and a perennial feature of American politics. For virtually the length of the twentieth century, and continuing into the twenty-first, critics have argued that the central problem of government is poor management. In other words, the basic problem with government is administrative: It is ineffectively organized and inefficiently run. The orthodox response of public administration scholarship to this problem is to impose the politics-administration dichotomy, and on the administrative side, to organize government agencies by functional responsibility, put them into a logical hierarchy with one another, and clearly assign authority and responsibility within these hierarchies. In various guises through various administrations, such efforts were repeatedly made long after Waldo, Gaus, and others had pointed out that the conceptual foundation that supported such efforts was untenable. All these efforts at reorganization largely failed to meet their objectives when they ran into political difficulties.

In recent decades, the orthodox solutions have increasingly been abandoned for a "new" organizational paradigm that seeks to bring economy and efficiency to government by adopting market-oriented management practices. The "reinvention" movement of the Clinton administration, for example, sought to eliminate hierarchy, to put "customers" first, and to prize performance over accountability. Yet the reinvention movement also ran into political obstacles. Regardless of whether it is an orthodox call for centralization and reliance on the competence of the technocrat or a less traditional appeal for decentralization and reliance on market-based processes, the purported objective is the same: to improve the effectiveness and efficiency of government through reorganization.

Students of the organizational connections to bureaucratic politics argue that the reason government reorganization is never far from the public agenda, and the reason it never achieves its supposed goals, is because the organization of the government's administrative arm has little to do with economy or efficiency. Organization of the government's administrative arm is about power and politics. One of the most astute proponents of this argument is Harold Seidman, whose *Politics, Position, and Power: The Dynamics of Federal Organization* was immediately recognized as a landmark in the study of bureaucratic politics when it was first published in 1970 (it has since gone through several editions). Seidman's central argument was this: The institutional location and environment of a policy or program and the organizational structure, process, and procedures that govern it help determine the distribution of power and influence within the polity. This includes the distribution of power among executive branch bureaucracies, but also encompasses the balance of power among the three branches of the federal government, between the federal government and state and local governments, and between the government and organized interest groups. As Allison, Richard Neustadt, and others have demonstrated, bureaucratic politics within the executive branch almost certainly affected policy. Scholars such as Seidman suggested that bureaucracies—their organization, staffs, authority, and responsibilities—were involved in and often the focus of much broader and more intense political games.

Seidman supported his argument by examining the well-known organizational eccentricities of the executive branch through a political rather than an administrative lens. From the perspective of public administration orthodoxy, many elements of the executive branch are perversely designed. There are overlapping jurisdictions, unclear lines of authority, programs assigned to agencies with little regard to the functional priorities of the organization, and agencies built on a variety of organizational blueprints using a bewildering variety of organizational processes and procedures. To a public administration analyst steeped in the inviolability of the politics-administration dichotomy and prizing efficiency as a guiding principle, this makes little sense.

But it makes perfect sense from a political point of view. For example, five federal agencies regulate banks, savings and loans, and credit unions. Why the duplication? Why put up with the consumption of extra resources, the inevitable turf wars, and the confusion over regulatory authority? Administrative orthodoxy would call for consolidating regulation of depository agencies under one federal agency. Yet the banking industry has successfully resisted all efforts to achieve such administrative concentration. Why? Seidman argued that the duplication allows commercial banks to pick their regulators according to the activity they engage in. Duplication, in short, shifts power from the regulators to the regulated, and the banking industry has had enough influence in Congress to keep the "eccentric" administration of banking regulations. It is not particularly efficient or effective, but it is a politically desirable (or at least acceptable) way to regulate depository agencies (Seidman 1998, 14).

Looking at federal agencies through a political lens also offers numerous other insights into why programs and policies succeed or fail. A key determinant of a program's success or failure is where it gets assigned. Programs and policies will be neglected if they are assigned to an agency that considers them peripheral to its primary mission (a phenomenon also observed by Wilson). The National Oceanic and Atmospheric Administration (NOAA), for example, considers science its primary mission. When resources become scarce, the nonscience programs the NOAA administers (nautical and aeronautical charting, for example) are the first to suffer (Seidman 1998, 16). Such assignment and organizational issues determine not only the success or failure of the program but also the balance of political power. A program assigned to an executive department will be subject to different lines of authority and accountability than a program assigned to an independent agency, a government corporation, or any one of the other bewildering variety of organizational arrangements in the federal bureaucracy. Institutional type thus helps determine how power and influence over a given program are distributed among the executive, the legislature, various organizational components within each branch, and organized interest groups.

Accordingly, we should expect Congress to be intensely interested in the organizational makeup of the executive branch and deeply involved in questions of administration. Indeed, Seidman argued that one of the central reasons for the "eccentric" organizational makeup of the executive branch is the jockeying for political power among the various elements of the legislative branch. Congressional committees have historically operated as highly autonomous minilegislatures that routinely struggle for jurisdictional supremacy over policies or programs. In 1966, for example, two agencies were created to administer highway safety: the National Highway Safety Agency and the National Traffic Agency. Both agencies were headed by one appointee. In other words, structurally built into the administration of highway safety programs and policies are duplication, confused lines of authority, and many other management and organization issues that would tend to promote inefficiency. This makes sense if administration is viewed as inexorably intertwined with politics rather than separable from it. The reason for two agencies rather than one was a simple matter of intrachamber politics: Two Senate committees wanted to confirm the agency head, and the creation of two agencies achieved this purely political goal. The organizational and administrative "problems" of the executive branch are thus often "nothing but mirror images of jurisdictional conflicts within the Congress" (Seidman 1998, 27).

The bureaucracy is politically important not only to the president and to Congress but also to a broad range of organized interests. Seidman pointed out that the public bureaucracy has a parallel private bureaucracy—businesses that perform contract work for the government—heavily invested in the status quo. Contracting with a private firm to perform various public functions has its advantages. Private companies, for example, are subject to lower levels of oversight and accountability, which gives them an operational flexibility public agencies frequently lack. Using private companies also helps reduce the number of civil servants on the public payroll, an important consideration for presidents dealing with the size of the public bureaucracy, always a politically sensitive issue. The downside to these arrangements is the loss of accountability and the high resistance of private firms to changes in the public bureaucracy because their livelihoods are dependent upon preserving the status quo (Seidman 1998, 15).

Networks and Bureaucratic Politics

This fact that bureaucratic politics extends beyond the bureaucracy itself was highlighted by Laurence O'Toole (1997b) in his admonition to take networks seriously. For public administration, networks can be thought of as a set of organizations that are interdependent, that is, they share goals, interests, resources, or values. These interdependencies tie together not just public bureaucracies within, between, and among differing political jurisdictions, but private and nonprofit agencies as well, in the process creating new forms of organizational and management practices that are employed to achieve collective or public ends. O'Toole (1997a) argued that networked administration is not only common, but also increasingly important, for five main reasons. First, "wicked" policy problems require the mobilization of a variety of actors, both inside and outside government. Such problems are the result of multiple causes, and typically span more than one jurisdiction. A single agency will not be able to address these problems without help, from actors both inside and outside of government and from across levels of government. Second, political demands for limited government, but without reductions in demands for action, give rise to networks that include nonstate actors through contracting. As shown in Chapter 5, the implication of contracting is something we are only beginning to understand. Third, the need for bureaucracy to be responsive to the public naturally leads to the inclusion of citizen and industry groups in decisionmaking. Networks may indeed increase accountability to the public, but, as will be discussed, it is unclear if they always produce the democratic effects we expect. Fourth, as sophisticated program evaluations have revealed indirect or second-order effects of policies, implementation networks have been established to reflect those relationships. Fifth, O'Toole (1997b) noted that many mandates have multiple layers that essentially require program management to become networked. Here, he used the example of transportation program managers needing to account for the rights of disabled people.

O'Toole's (1997a) networked bureaucratic world raises important questions regarding our understanding of bureaucratic politics, governance, and accountability. Do these networks threaten democracy or enhance it? Should expectations of accountability and oversight be changed as the result of acknowledging that so many actors are involved in bureaucratic decisions? How do agencies wield political power in these networks? Some recent research has identified a "dark side" of networks—that network managers respond to elements of the network that are more politically influential, and thus the result is that networks may actually exacerbate already present inequality (O'Toole and Meier 2004). This raises important and disturbing questions about the nature and implications of the political power in networked administration. Other concerns, as addressed in Chapter 5, involve the "hollowing out" of the state.

The need to understand a networked bureaucracy is obvious, but it is unclear if we have made much theoretical headway since the mid-1990s. Most literature has focused on how to manage networked systems, rather than on implications for politics and governance (O'Toole and Meier 2004). O'Toole and Meier argue that networks should be treated as political institutions, since their establishment is often for political reasons (to perhaps avoid having to deal directly with a controversial issue), and always has political implications. Decisions to contract or privatize functions of government are inherently political, as they involve decisions to shift the locus of state power, and certainly represent choices to move public resources to other network members, including private companies or not-for-profit organizations. Yet beyond the call by O'Toole and Meier to focus on these political implications, the field has not yet produced the necessary work. Scott Robinson (2006), for example, argues we lack the conceptual tools to understand the governance implications of different types of networks and how political context shapes their creation, membership, goals, and outcomes. Given the explosive growth of networked administration and its poorly understood implications for public policy and effect on democratic values, there can hardly be a better example of the practical and critical need for theory development, not just in the realm of bureaucratic politics, but also in the general field of public administration.

Given the highly political nature of bureaucracy that Seidman, O'Toole, and others have described, efforts to make the administrative arm of government more effective and efficient persistently fail because the real objectives of bureaucracy have nothing to do with efficiency and better management practices. Power is really at stake in reorganization, and this is the reason the president, Congress, and other political actors take such an intense interest in administration. Reorganization has become such a perennial part of politics that it is increasingly pursued for its own sake—a political objective with no underlying administrative strategy whatsoever. During the 1990s, for example, House Republicans proposed abolishing the Departments of Education, Energy, Commerce, and Housing and Urban Development. The 1996 Republican presidential nominee, Bob Dole, also campaigned on a promise of eliminating the Internal Revenue Service. These proposals were largely calculated to make political profits from popular negative stereotypes of the bureaucracy and made no real sense from an administrative point of view. No one made serious proposals for the wholesale elimination of programs, no one had a strategic plan to reassign these programs, and no one made any real argument that the end result would be more effective and efficient government. The whole point seemed to be to attack the administrative infrastructure in the belief that smaller government was better government. Yet if there were to be no wholesale elimination of public programs, government would not get smaller, just more confused, and, in all likelihood, increasingly privatized (Seidman 1998, 110).

Such political games with the bureaucracy are not the sole province of Republicans. The Clinton/Gore administration played a particularly cynical game in its reinvention efforts, repeatedly publicizing the shrinking federal payroll. The quarter-million federal positions eliminated by the reinvention movement were mostly supervisors, personnel specialists, budget analysts, accountants, auditors, and the like. These people primarily oversaw third-party operations, namely, the private contractors the government increasingly uses to carry out public programs and policies. Contract employees who indirectly do the public's business vastly outnumber employees in the federal civil service, and reinvention shrank these numbers not at all. If anything, the cuts in the federal payroll made it much more difficult to hold third-party contractors accountable (Seidman 1998, 112–113).

Neither Wilson's nor Seidman's arguments constitute fully developed theoretical frameworks, and Wilson (1989, xi) explicitly raised doubts about whether a comprehensive theory of organizational behavior was even possible. Yet Wilson and Seidman both provide a series of empirically testable propositions that are characteristic of theoretical frameworks. From Wilson comes a rich set of hypotheses, which can be confirmed by observing bureaucratic behavior, about everything from professional norms to the substitution of rules for goals. Seidman's work points analysts toward the high political stakes surrounding organization and administration, and, in doing so, makes sense of the "eccentricities" that defied the expectations of traditional theoretical frameworks. Combined, both make it easier to understand why bureaucracies are the way they are, and why they do the things they do.

Although Seidman's work and Wilson's work are discursive rather than theoretical, more explicitly theoretical efforts from organization literature seek to explain at least some elements of the political behavior bureaucracies indulge in. John Kingdon's *Agendas, Alternatives, and Public Policies* (1995), for example, attempts to explain why government addresses some problems while ignoring others. Kingdon's analysis shows that government agencies have an important role in shaping the public agenda, not so much in determining agenda priorities but in acting as key members of "policy communities." These communities consist of actors who, through their specialized interests in particular policies and the density of their interconnections and common interests, can decide the fate of policy proposals. A fragmented community (for example, one in which agencies have conflicting goals on a particular issue) dissipates support for a policy proposal and severely limits its potential for success (Kingdon, 1995, 116–144). Although organizational context is shown here to play an important role in shaping the political role of bureaucracy, that role is not the primary focus of the theory.

The bottom line is that organization theory has provided an important lens for works such as Wilson's and Seidman's, signaled the importance of the growing phenomenon of networked administration, and in doing so has given ample justification for pursuing comprehensive explanations of the political role of bureaucracy. As yet, however, organization theory has not provided that comprehensive explanation.

Representative Bureaucracy

The theory of representative bureaucracy is perhaps the most explicit attempt to address the central problem of democratic administrative theory raised by Waldo (1952, 102): How can a theory that embraces the hierarchical and authoritarian nature of bureaucracy be reconciled with the seemingly contradictory egalitarian and ultimately inefficient values of democracy? The work of scholars such as Waldo, Allison, Wilson, and Seidman strongly suggests that bureaucracies are political policymaking institutions. Yet if bureaucracies are powerful policy actors engaged in "politics of the first order," they are also largely insulated from the ballot box and only partially held accountable to elected officials (Meier 1993, 7; Mosher 1982). This contradiction between bureaucracies making policy and basic democratic values raises one of the most important challenges for public administration theory: "How does one square a permanent [and, we would add, powerful] civil service—which neither the people by their vote nor their representatives by their appointments can readily replace—with the principle of government 'by the people'?" (Mosher 1982, 7). Any democratic theory of administration, Waldo suggested, must be capable of answering this question.

The theory of representative bureaucracy focuses on finding a way to legitimate the bureaucracy's political power in the context of democratic values. The central tenet of the theory is that a bureaucracy reflecting the diversity of the community it serves is more likely to respond to the interests of all groups in making policy decisions (Krislov 1974; Selden 1997). If bureaucracies are sensitive to such a diversity of interests, and these interests are represented in bureaucratic decisions and behavior, the argument is that bureaucracy itself can be considered a representative institution. If bureaucracy is a representative institution, its long-recognized political role can be accommodated with such basic democratic values as majority rule, minority rights, and equal representation.

The notion of legitimating bureaucratic power by treating bureaucracy as a representative institution was formally introduced by J. Donald Kingsley in *Rep-*

resentative Bureaucracy (1944). Kingsley's work, a study of the British public service, advanced the argument that the civil service should reflect the characteristics of the ruling social class. To carry out its role effectively within the polity, Kingsley argued, the civil service has to be sympathetic to the concerns and values of the dominant political group. These shared values connect the exercise of discretionary authority on the part of the bureaucrat to the will of the democratic state. Although Kingsley coined the term "representative bureaucracy," the basic idea he articulates is quite old. In the United States, the spoils system instituted during the nineteenth century resulted in a civil service that was dominated by major party loyalists (Meier 1975). Such a bureaucracy can be viewed as an extension of the majority party, and therefore of the preferences expressed at the ballot box. Such patronage systems, of course, also invite just the sort of problems that prompted scholars such as Goodnow and Wilson to seek some division between politics and administration: technical incompetence, favoritism in administrative decisionmaking, and outright corruption.

More contemporary advocates of representative bureaucracy reject patronage or spoils systems as an appropriate model for a representative bureaucracy for exactly these reasons. Instead, most accept the need for organizational arrangements as prescribed by administrative orthodoxy, namely, public agencies based on the Weberian rational-legal bureaucracy (Selden 1997). In contrast to the spoils system, the latter is seen as conferring various benefits, among them efficiency, making merit the basis of public-sector employment, and strengthening the role of technical expertise in decisionmaking (Meier 1993). Although this means accepting arguments from orthodox administrative theory, advocates of representative bureaucracy reject the notion of a politics-administration dichotomy. The theoretical and empirical lessons from the likes of Gaus, Waldo, Allison, Seidman, Wilson, and numerous others simply make it impossible to ignore or assume away the political role of the bureaucracy.

The theory of representative bureaucracy thus begins with the assumption that there are good reasons for public agencies to be organized the way they are (i.e., undemocratically) and that these undemocratic agencies exercise considerable political power. As Kenneth Meier puts it, "The theory of representative bureaucracy begins by recognizing the realities of politics. In a complex polity such as the United States, not all aspects of policy decisions are resolved in the 'political' branches of government" (1975, 527). The basis of bureaucratic power is assumed to derive from the discretionary decisionmaking authority that, as a practical matter, has to be granted to them because not all implementation and enforcement scenarios can be conceived of and accounted for in statutes. Elected officials may have numerous tools at their disposal to restrict bureaucratic power, but strong forces place practical limits on the use of these tools. Public support of programs or agency objectives, the information advantage bureaucrats often hold over elected officials because of their technical expertise, and simple political expediency all work to limit the constraints placed on bureaucratic power.

Perhaps the best-known argument that individual bureaucrats have an unavoidable policymaking role is Michael Lipsky's *Street-Level Bureaucracy: Dilemmas of the Individual in Public Services* (1980). Lipsky's central premise is that street-level bureaucrats—policemen, teachers, and the like—routinely have to make decisions that are not dictated by the mission of the organizations they work for, or the rules they are supposed to enforce. Street-level bureaucrats thus make policy as a result of their behavior. For example, no matter what the law says the speed limit is, in practice it is determined by the individual traffic cop. The discretion to make such on-the-spot decisions, which in effect are policy decisions, is going to be considerable, even for bureaucrats working within a dense tangle of rules designed to guide their behavior. It is simply a fact of political life that nonelected individuals, protected by civil service mechanisms and working for hierarchical (even authoritarian) bureaucracies, wield significant policymaking power in democratic polities. Given this, a key challenge for administrative theory is to account for this fact in the context of democratic values (Selden 1997, 13–26).

In meeting this challenge, those who advocate the theory of representative bureaucracy begin by seeking an answer to the same question posed by Wilson: Why do bureaucrats do what they do? Specifically, the focus is on explaining the behavior of bureaucrats when they exercise discretionary authority. Generally, it is assumed that bureaucrats are rational actors in the sense that they pursue self-interested goals when faced with discretionary choices. Proponents of representative bureaucracy argue that the goals driving behavior are supplied by the individual values of the decisionmaker. Thus, "if the administrative apparatus makes political decisions, and if bureaucracy as a whole has the same values as the American people as a whole, then the decisions made by the bureaucracy will be similar to the decisions made if the entire American public passed on the issues. . . . If values are similar, rational decisions made so as to maximize these values will also be similar" (Meier 1975, 528). This suggests that bureaucratic power can be harnessed to diverse and representative social interests even though the orthodox organizational arrangements of public administration are insulated from the basic processes and values of democracy. If the ranks of the civil service reflect the diverse interests and values of society, bureaucracy becomes a representative "fourth branch of government" with a legitimate basis for exercising power in a democratic system.

The first scholars to formulate and apply the basic arguments of representative bureaucracy in the United States were David Levitan (1946) and Norton Long (1952). Long adopted the most extreme stance, arguing that the national legislature, which was heavily tilted toward the upper strata of society, did not represent a variety of important national interests. Instead, "these interests receive more effective and more responsible representation through administrative channels"

(1952, 808). Long's claim was that the bureaucracy had more of a democratic character than the legislature because the ranks of the federal civil service were much more reflective of the American public. That diversity was reflected in administrative decisions, even as narrower interests dominated the decisionmaking of Congress. The normative claim was that the bureaucracy actually made up for the representative deficiencies of the legislature.

Although subsequent scholars have generally made less radical normative claims than Long, the two key questions driving Long's work have remained the basic focus of work on representative bureaucracy: (1) Do public agencies broadly represent the interests and values of the American public? (2) Are these interests and values reflected in the policy actions of bureaucracy? The first of these questions deals with the concept of "passive representation," or the extent to which the bureaucracy reflects the composition of society. Kingsley (1944) suggested that socioeconomic class should be the basic yardstick for comparing the composition of the civil service with that of the public. Kingsley's study, however, was focused on the British civil service. In the United States, Samuel Krislov (1974) argued that a more appropriate basis of comparison is race, ethnicity, and sex. These factors are assumed to be a key source of socialization, and thus of values. A large portion of empirical research on representative bureaucracy in the United States is thus devoted to examining the extent to which bureaucracy reflects the basic demographic composition of society. The general finding of this research is that minorities and women are proportionally represented in bureaucracy as a whole, but are underrepresented in the upper levels of bureaucratic hierarchies (Selden 1997, 45).

The second question deals with the concept of "active representation," or the relationship between passive representation and policy outputs or outcomes. Again, it was Krislov who made the key contribution to shaping scholarly thought on this issue. He argued that the demographic composition of the bureaucracy provides only indirect evidence of the representative nature of bureaucracy. The social profile of any given bureaucrat—race, sex, education, and so forth—provides only a limited indication of that bureaucrat's ability to advance the interests of these demographic groups. It is not enough, in other words, to find that women and minorities are roughly proportionally represented in the ranks of the civil service. Any serious claim that bureaucracy is a representative institution requires evidence that passive representation translates into active representation, that the more women and minorities join the civil service, the more the policy outputs of bureaucracies represent the broad interests of women and minorities.

Considering its importance to the theory of representative bureaucracy, it is not surprising that there has been a growing body of empirical work on this latter issue. Studies by Kenneth Meier and various colleagues (Meier, Stewart, and England 1989; Meier and Stewart 1992; Meier, Wrinkle, and Polinard 1999) have consistently found that minority representation in the civil service is related to policy outputs that favor the minority group. These studies have exclusively focused on education and the effects of minority representation on policy outputs (the research examined the impact of minority representation in teaching, on administrative and school board positions concerning school policies, and on outputs that affected minorities). Some research outside education has produced more mixed results (Hindera 1993a, 1993b; Selden 1997). However, much other research indicates that the conditions found by Meier and his colleagues do exist for other agency types as well as for representation for women (Keiser, Wilkins, Meier, and Holland 2002; Meier and Nicholson-Crotty 2006; Lim 2006; Wilkins and Keiser 2006).

A further development in the literature is to incorporate the concept of symbolic representation, which, unlike active representation, works cognitively on the public. Thus, when bureaucrats share the identification, experience, and characteristics of a portion of the public, that audience will perceive the actions of those bureaucrats as legitimate, even if the bureaucrats are not purposefully representing that group. Nick Theobald and Donald Haider-Markel (2009), by examining citizen attitudes about actions by police officers, show that actions by bureaucrats are more likely to be perceived as legitimate if citizens and bureaucrats share demographic characteristics. If this holds across agencies, it suggests that citizen attitudes about bureaucrats and policy implementation can be changed without actions on the part of bureaucrats that are expressly designed to represent certain groups (active representation). Furthermore, they argue that methods used by those studying representative bureaucracy have relied on aggregate data, which makes it difficult to know if their findings demonstrate active or symbolic representation. Considering the implications for democratic governance, it is important to clarify this question.

The key to representative bureaucracy's attempt to build a bridge between orthodox public administration theory and democratic theory thus still rests to no small extent on the ability of future empirical studies to support the theory's central hypothesis that passive representation will lead to active representation. Although the literature has expanded greatly since 2000, the issues raised by Theobald and Haider-Markel imply the more individual-level empirical work is needed.

Conclusions

It is probably fair to say that public administration scholarship has been more successful in demonstrating the need for theories of bureaucratic politics than in actually producing those frameworks. It has been more than half a century since scholars such as Waldo and Gaus exposed the rickety foundations of the politics-administration dichotomy and made a convincing brief that administrative theory had to share common ground with political theory. Since then, numerous studies have empirically confirmed the political role of the bureaucracy. Some of these, including those of Wilson and Seidman, center on a series of empirically testable propositions. Even if the works themselves are explicitly discursive, they contain the basic materials for constructing theory. To date, however, that construction project remains incomplete.

Allison's Model III and the theory of representative bureaucracy represent two of the better known and most widely employed bureaucratic politics frameworks. Although it is hard to underestimate Allison's contribution, it clearly falls short of a generally applicable theoretical framework. Allison's Model III is likely to continue to find gainful employment in structuring administrative studies, but evidence has steadily mounted that it is overambitious in scope and underperforming in practice. Although having a considerably older lineage than Model III, the theory of representative bureaucracy in one sense remains curiously underemployed. The basic model is parsimonious, and its predictive hypotheses are intuitively easy to grasp. Simply stated, the theory argues that a civil service reflecting the diverse interests and values of the community it serves will take those interests into account when exercising its discretionary authority. The validity of the theory is tied to the hypothesis that passive representation will lead to active representation. Even if we acknowledge the difficulties in operationalizing such tests, there are but a handful of published studies squarely aimed at empirically assessing this claim, and these have produced mixed and contradictory results.

Does the relative lack of success in producing widely applicable bureaucratic politics frameworks mean the effort to do so should be reassessed? The progenitors of the bureaucratic politics movement would surely answer no, for the simple reason that the most important characteristic of public administration is its political nature, and we ignore this at our peril. Long once wrote that "there is no more forlorn spectacle in the administrative world than an agency and a program possessed of statutory life, armed with executive orders, sustained in the courts, yet stricken with paralysis and deprived of power. An object of contempt to its enemies and of despair to its friends" (1949, 257).

Long's point was that the ability of a public agency to get things done was not dependent upon the responsibilities and authority granted to it by statute. The decentralized nature of the American system meant a program's success or failure was tied to the political muscle of the bureaucracy it was entrusted to. As Long succinctly put it, "The lifeblood of administration is power. Its attainment, maintenance, increase, dissipation, and loss are subjects the practitioner and student can ill afford to neglect" (1949, 257). Long argued that ignoring the political role of the bureaucracy robs administrative theory of a crucial connection to the real world and consigns any number of the prescriptive conclusions of scholarly work to failure.

Scholars such as Long, Gaus, and Waldo argue that, like it or not, bureaucracy is a political institution and that any useful theoretical framework has to recognize and account for this simple fact of political life. Public administration theory, in other words, must also be political theory. Theories of bureaucratic politics are designed with this objective in mind, and pursuit of this goal remains a profitable activity for students of public administration.

4

Public Institutional Theory

Like all complex subjects, public organizations are more easily understood after being unbundled, examined part by part, and reassembled for an assessment of their whole condition. The two essential parts to the modern study of public organizations are

1. the organization and management of contained and bounded public institutions, now generally comprehended by institutional theory, and
2. interinstitutional, interjurisdictional, and third-party couplings and linkages, now generally comprehended by network theory or governance theory, the subject of Chapter 9.

This chapter takes up the first of these parts, and in doing so further unbundles the subject. It is common to include both management and organization in considerations of the study of public organizations (Rainey 1997; Denhardt 1993; Moore 1995; Gortner, Mahler, and Nicholson 1997). Because we believe it useful to consider the study of administrative behavior and the management of public organizations as a subject separable from the study of public institutions, we have uncoupled them and deal with theories of public management in Chapter 5.

Institutional Theory

The golden age of public administration hegemony disintegrated in the 1950s. In the first decades of the twenty-first century, a New Public Administration hegemony based on a broadly accepted institutionalism is emerging. Institutionalism is not a theory in the formal sense; it is instead the framework, the language, and the set of assumptions that hold and guide empirical research and theory-building in much of public administration. It begins with an argument about the salience of collective action as a basis for understanding political and social institutions, including formal political and bureaucratic organizations. This is a challenge to political science, which sees institutions primarily as the framework for rational individual choice and emphasizes conflicting interests and competition. Institutions are affected by their social, economic, and political context, but they also powerfully affect that context: "Political democracy depends not only on economic and social contributions but also on the design of political institutions" (March and Olsen 1984, 738). The importance of the design of institutions on their behavior and on their political outcomes has been amply demonstrated (Lijphart 1984; Weaver and Rockman 1993).

The development of post-Weberian organization theory traces to the 1960s and the work of James Thompson, Herbert Simon, James G. March, Anthony Downs, William Buchanan, Gordon Tullock, Vincent Ostrom, and others. Vantages of organization theory from sociology, market theory from economics, theories of democratic control of bureaucracies from political science, and, perhaps above all, theories of bounded rationality all mixed, clashed, and combined in the interdisciplinary and cross-disciplinary considerations of complex organizations. By the 1980s, marked particularly by March and Johan Olsen's *Rediscovering Institutions* (1989), post-Weberian interdisciplinary organization theory came to be generally described as institutional theory. Because bureaucracy was never really lost, claims by March and Olsen to have rediscovered institutions may have been a bit bold, but these scholars nevertheless made institutional studies distinctive: distinct from organization theory but importantly informed by it; distinct from rational choice theory but importantly informed by it; and distinct from traditional public administration rooted in the reform era but importantly informed by it. In our time, institutional theory is the critical intersection at which the vantages of the disciplines meet in their attention to complex organizations. Institutions thus considered include states and other governmental jurisdictions and subjurisdictions, parliaments, bureaucracies, shadow and contract bureaucracies, nongovernmental organizations, universities, and corporations or private companies having clear and distinct public purposes. The point is, modern institutional theory is not limited to the study of government bureaucracies and as a result has moved well beyond the traditional study of jurisdictional public administration.

The perspective and tone of institutionalism in public administration were set in 1989 with the publication of the foundation documents, James Q. Wilson's *Bureaucracy: What Government Agencies Do and Why They Do It* and March and Olsen's *Rediscovering Institutions*. These authors point to the limitations of economics and market logic as theory that accounts for institutional behavior, and instead build their theories on the consideration of structure, particularly hierarchy, and individual and group behavior in institutional contexts; on the interaction of individuals and organizations and their wider political, social, and economic contexts; and on the influence of professional and cultural norms on institutional behavior patterns and institutional longevity and productivity. Much of the leading scholarship in public administration in the 1990s fits generally into the categories and concepts set out by Wilson, March, and Olsen.

Today we are all institutionalists. It is easy to defend this claim because we subscribe to the "big tent theory of institutions." Under the institutional theory big tent are scholars studying institutions from at least the following conceptual frameworks:

1. Structural theory, including the study of Westminster, presidential, and hybrid national forms and the associations between those forms and bureaucratic functioning (Weaver and Rockman 1993; Lijphart 1984; Peters and Pierre 1998)

2. Organizational design theory, which includes work on centralization, decentralization, devolution, and other structural variations, all in the "institutions matter" tradition (Hood and Jackson 1991)

3. Democratic control-of-bureaucracy theory, including accountability scholarship, principal-agent scholarship, and working, shirking, moral hazard, rent-seeking, and associated political economy scholarship (Behn 2000; Romzek and Dubnick 1987; Romzek and Ingraham 2000; Brehm and Gates 1997; Moe 1980, 1990; March and Olsen 1995)

4. The bureaucratic or administrative behavior perspective (as distinct from the managerial behavior perspective) (March and Simon 1993; March and Olsen 1989, 1995)

5. Managerial or new public management scholarship, both in the United States and abroad (Barzelay 1992; Kernaghan, Marson, and Borins 2000)

6. Performance, outcomes, program evaluation, and results perspectives (Forsythe 2001; Peters 2000; deLeon and deLeon 2002; O'Toole 2000)

7. Politics of bureaucracy theory (Fesler and Kettl 1996; Aberbach and Rockman 2000; Meier 1994; Tullock 1965)

8. Privatization, contracting out, and nonprofit organizations analysis (Light 1999; Kettl 1993b; Handler 1996; Kelleher and Yackee 2009)

9. Institutionalism, working primarily from the political economies and rational choice perspectives (Eggertsson 1990; Furubotn and Richter 1984, 1993; Downs 1967; Tullock 1965; Moe 1980, 1990; Bendor, Moe, and Shotts 2001)

Institutional scholars working from these several perspectives use the full range of social science methodologies as well as assumption-based deductive modeling. Since 1990, this scholarship has become more iterative, layered, and cumulative. More importantly, scholars now working from one or more of these perspectives are much better informed than in the past regarding the work of others who study institutions from their own perspective and from that of others.

There are many splendid examples of cumulative institutional scholarship, such as the LaPorte et al. series on high-reliability systems; the Milward and Provan series on the hollow state and contract regimes; the Meier et al. series on policy outcomes in education structures; the series by the Ostroms and others on the commons; empirical testing of the Theibout fragmentation thesis; the series on the diffusion of institutional innovation; and the long series of work on garbage can theory and the recent to-and-fro on that subject. There are many other examples, and all are good signs for the development of institutional theory. In this chapter, we review several of these bodies of work to illustrate the scope and characteristics of contemporary institutional theory.

Post-Weberian bureaucratic study is more scientific and rigorous, more nuanced, and much stronger theoretically than ever before. To be sure, there are institutionalists working from particular perspectives who claim the theoretical high ground and, in doing so, suggest that those working from other perspectives have less to contribute to institutional theory or that their perspective *is* institutional theory. And then there are the fads and fashions in perspectives and methodology: Academic journals, scholarly presses, and boards of editors attempt to judge these claims and sort through submitted research manuscripts for the best scholarship. Such is the nature of scholars and scholarship.

In the context of the fragmented and disarticulated state, institutional theory is especially salient (Frederickson 1999a). For example, in the so-called hollow state, with its extended contract and subcontract regimes, the characteristics of loose or tight interinstitutional coupling are as important as the bureaucratic features of each of the coupled institutions (Milward and Provan 2000b). Probably many more persons do "public" work by or through contracts than there are persons in the formal jurisdiction of bureaucracies. The institutional structures and behavior of these "shadow bureaucracies" are at the center of modern institutional theory and could be described as institutional theory's response to the fragmented and disarticulated state (Light 1999).

Institution theory captures and comprehends the rather long series of scholarship on coproduction, multiple stakeholders, public-private partnerships, privatization and contracting, and the increasingly fuzzy distinctions between things public and things private. Institutional theory has the particularly useful capacity to describe favorably the linkages, networks, and couplings of institutions coping with fragmentation, disarticulation, asymmetry between public problems and public jurisdictions, and high interdependence.

The Basic Idea

In simplified form, institutionalism sees organizations as bounded social constructs of rules, roles, norms, and the expectations that constrain individual and group choice and behavior. March and Olsen describe institutions as "the beliefs, paradigms, codes, cultures, and knowledge that support rules and routines," a description that differs little from classic organization theory (1989, 22). But institutionalism also includes core ideas about contemporary public administration: results, performance, outcomes, and purposefulness—concepts of less interest to organization theorists (Powell and DiMaggio 1991). Institutionalism, then, could be said to account for how institutions behave and how they perform (Lynn 1996). Institutionalism also combines the structural or organizational elements of institutions and their managerial and leadership characteristics (Wilson 1989; Rainey and Steinbauer 1999). Finally, institutionalism is not limited to formal governmental organizations, a large blind spot for earlier public administration scholars. Institutionalism includes empirical and theoretical considerations concerning the full range of so-called third-sector organization and fully recognizes the fuzzy distinctions between public and private institutions (Kettl 1988, 1993b; Salamon 1989; Light 1999).

Institutionalism assumes that policy preferences are neither exogenous nor stable but are molded through collective experience, institutions, education, and, particularly, professions. Institutionalism further assumes the centrality of leadership, management, and professionalism. It comprehends theory development all the way from the supervision of street-level bureaucrats to the transformational leadership of entire institutions (Smith and Lipsky 1993; Maynard-Moody and Musheno 2003).

Institutionalism recognizes the salience of action or choice and defines choice as expressions of expectations of consequences (March and Olsen 1984). In the modern world of productivity, performance, and outcomes measurement, institutionalism reminds us that institutions and those associated with them shape meanings, rely on symbols, and seek an interpretive order that obscures the objectivity of outcomes.

Institutionalism is particularly useful in the disarticulated state because its assumptions do not rest primarily on sovereignty and authority; they rest instead on the patterns of politics, order, and shared meaning found in governmental as well as nongovernmental institutions (Frederickson 1999a).

Finally, institutionalism lends itself to forms of modeling based on simplifying assumptions of rational self-interest or competitive markets. Some of the most advanced thinking in contemporary public administration is being done by formal modelers using assumptions of cooperation, order, principals and agents, hierarchy, institutional responses to contextual influences, networks, and governance— all essentially institutional assumptions (Hammond 1986, 1993; Hammond and Knott 1999; Lynn, Heinrich, and Hill 1999). We believe this theory-building will have a strong and lasting influence on the quality of public management scholarship because it fits fairly with that body of theory based on the logic of rational choice. The reason is simple—the simplifying assumptions and experiments used by national choice theorists can inform those elements of institutional theory based on the classic empirical and methodological canons of social science.

March and Olsen (1995) assert that most institutionalists work from a few key ideas:

First, institutions are understood to be a formal bounded framework of rules, roles, and identities (North 1990; Shepsle and Weingast 1987; Shepsle 1989).

Second, within the formal frameworks, "preferences are inconsistent, changing and at least partly endogenous, formed within political institutions" (March and Olsen 1995, 29). Alternate structural arrangements and institutional processes of socialization and cooptation shape preferences (Wildavsky 1987). Institutions "shape the definitions of alternatives and influence the perception and the construction of the reality within which action takes place" (March and Olsen 1995, 29).

Third, institutional theory emphasizes the logic of appropriateness based on institutional structures, roles, and identities. The logic of appropriateness is based on the assumption that institutional life is "organized by sets of shared memories and practices that come to be taken as given" (March and Olsen 1995, 30). Institutional structures are organized according to socially constructed rules and practices that are formally assumed and supported.

Fourth, the logic of appropriateness is based on matched patterns of roles, rules, practices, and structures, on the one hand, and a situation, on the other (Burns and Flam 1987). Appropriateness, then, is influenced by laws and constitutions and other authenticated expressions of collective preferences. But appropriateness is also influenced by emotions, uncertainties, and cognitive limitations. Appropriateness not only is applicable to routine decision problems but also comprehends ill-defined and novel situations, such as "civil unrest, demands for comprehensive redistribution of political power and welfare" (March and Olsen 1995, 32).

Fifth, one group of institutional theorists give importance to the idea of community and the common good. Among these institutionalists, effective public institutions are thought to be unlikely, if not impossible, if citizens are concerned only with self-interest. Therefore, these institutionalists tend to reject exchange theories that emphasize incentives, cost-benefit assumptions, and the assumption that the common good can be understood as the aggregation of self-interests (Mansbridge 1980).

Sixth, another group of institutional theorists who work from the rational choice perspective tend to use deductive assumption-based models and computer simulations (Moe 1980, 1990; Shepsle 1989; Shepsle and Weingast 1987; Bendor, Moe, and Shotts 2001; Furubotn and Richter 1993).

Seventh, some institutionalists tend to focus on order, and particularly on structures that impose order. Others do not find order in the rational reasoning of relationships between means and ends or in a notion of an efficient history in which exogenous forces shape the policy outcomes of political institutions (March and Olsen 1984). Instead, they find institutional order in historical processes that do not have equilibria, take extended periods of time, lead to nonunique equilibria, or result in unique but suboptimal outcomes. Theoretical attention to the inefficiencies of history involves a greater concern for the ways in which institutions learn from their experience; the possibilities that learning will produce adjustments that are slower or faster; and a concern for conditions under which the sequential branches of history turn back upon each other and the conditions under which they diverge. Such institutional perspectives involve characterizing the role of standard operating procedures, professions, and expertise in storing and recalling history. In seeking an understanding of endogenous order, that order shaped and influenced by roles, rules, and incentives, many institutionalists give considerable weight to both normative and symbolic order—the influence of languages, rituals, ceremonies, and symbols (March and Olsen 1984; Goodsell 1988; Frederickson 1997b).

With this simplified introduction to institutional theory, we now turn to its several forms and applications. First, we consider distinctions between organizations and institutions and the implications those distinctions have for organizational and institutional theory. We then turn to the simplest form of organizational structure, the hierarchy and its many variations. This is followed by a consideration of nonhierarchical approaches to institutional theory. Then we turn to several well-established parts of institutional theory: comparative institutional forms, fragmented and consolidated systems, garbage cans and rent seeking, and the diffusion of institutional innovation.

From Organizations to Institutions

In the classic study of public administration, organization theory is the body of knowledge to which scholars turn to understand the structures and relationships between structures and outcomes. Most modern organization theory is based on the study of firms, and what we know about structures tends to come from that literature. Many of the same variables—centralization-decentralization, costs, productivity, and hierarchy—are as applicable to the study of organizations in the public sector as to private firms. But there are important differences between the public and private sectors, and these are reflected in the differences between organization theory and institutional theory. Because of the possible confusion and ambiguity associated with the two terms, it is helpful to describe briefly their differences and similarities.

The term "institution" is used here to include public organizations that stand in a special relationship to the people they serve. They can invoke the authority of the state and can, thereby, enforce their decisions. Public organizations can claim legitimacy because of what they presumably contribute to a larger, often indivisible, and difficult-to-measure public interest. Such organizations, particularly at the level of the national state or its subdivisions, often have deep cultural identities associated with language, ethnicity, religion, custom, and geography. Public organizations are often infused with values such as citizenship and patriotism and identities such as Mexican or Canadian—values and identities well beyond the technical capacities and missions of such organizations (Frederickson 1997b).

Institution, particularly in the anthropological sense, also means broadly agreed-upon customs, practices, and allegiances. Marriage is an institution of this sort, as are the law, private ownership, private enterprise, taxation, and public education. Cultural institutions thus defined are very often *established*, as they are in the local school, as a public institution embodying the broader institutional culture. Applications of modern institutional theory in public administration tend to combine these two understandings of institutions, as in descriptions of institutions as socially constructed bounded collectivities (Weick 1979; March and Olsen 1989). Relying on economist Frank B. Knight, Norman Uphoff describes public institutions as "complexes of norms and behaviors that persist over time by serving collectively valued purposes" (1994, 202).

We come then to this understanding of organizations and institutions. Organizations, particularly those in the private sector, are bounded structures of recognized and accepted roles, but they are not ordinarily thought of as institutions, with the possible exception of the New York Yankees. Institutions that are also organizations, found primarily in the public sector, include the US Supreme Court, the Internal Revenue Service, the University of Kansas, the City of Boston, and the Commonwealth of Massachusetts. Interest groups, such as the National Rifle Association, the United Auto Workers, and the American Association of Retired Persons, are important organizations that certainly reflect the collective values of their members and capably influence public policy; but they are not, as the word is used here, institutions. Their purposes are to link to and influence public institutions. Public institutions codify and legitimize broadly based cultural institutions, such as marriage, which requires a government license, or collective bargaining, which is practiced in the context of public law and administration.

Because much of organization theory and institutional theory can be found in sociology (and to some extent in business schools), it is not surprising that the primary work on the distinctions between the two is done by a sociologist. W. Richard Scott, the eminent Stanford sociologist, is the author of the definitive work on the subject, *Institutions and Organizations* (1995). In highly sociological language, he defines institutions as "cognitive, normative, and regulatory structures and activities that provide stability and meaning to social behavior. Institutions are transported by various carriers—cultures, structures, and routines—and they operate at multiple levels of jurisdiction" (33). There are, Scott contends, three pillars of institutions: regulative, normative, and cognitive (35–62). The regulative pillar of institutions includes common elements of organization theory such as rules, laws, sanctions, a distinct inclination toward performance or results, a workforce defined by experience, forms of coercion, routines resting on protocols, standard operating procedures, governance systems, and systems allocating power and its exercise. Public administration embodies one especially important feature of Scott's regulative pillar: the constitutional and legal basis of authority and power. Virtually all the features of Scott's regulative pillar are essentially the same as those in modern organization theory, and particularly the applications of that theory found in public administration (Rainey 1997; Denhardt 1993; Gortner, Mahler, and Nicholson 1997).

Scott's normative pillar of institutions includes the logic of appropriateness as against rational goal-driven choice making, social expectations and obligations based on these expectations, patterns of certification and accreditation, and an emphasis on conformity and the performance of duty. Especially important to public administration are values and legitimacy of the public service in carrying out the democratic moral order, or, put another way, democratic regime values. Virtually all aspects of Scott's normative pillar of institutional theory would be easily recognized by students of public administration.

Scott's cognitive pillar of institutional theory includes patterns of behavior based on established categories and routines, patterns of institutional adaptation, innovation based on mimicking, a decided tendency toward institutional isomorphism, and tendencies to risk-aversion and orthodoxy. The legitimacy of cognitive patterns in public administration traces to broad-based political and even cultural support. Again, there appears to be little significant distinction between organization theory, as that phrase is generally understood in public administration, and Scott's conception of the cognitive aspects of institutional theory.

The bigger point here is that in public administration as well as in other applications of modern organization theory such as business or education administration, organization theory has become institutional theory. The differences have to do with the comparative emphasis on formal structure and on management in organization theory, the emphasis in institutional theory on patterns of collective behavior that are better understood as exogenous to the formal organization, and on patterns of interaction between institutions and their broader social, economic, and political contexts.

Hierarchy

The distinction between organizations and institutions brings us to the subject of hierarchy. Second only to bureaucracy as a subject of theoretical and managerial criticism, hierarchy is usually thought to be something that needs to be scrapped and replaced with better forms of organizing. Based on his observations of large-scale American business firms, Elliott Jaques made the following comment:

> Thirty-five years of research have convinced me that managerial hierarchy is the most efficient, the hardiest, and in fact the most natural structure ever devised for large organizations. Properly structured, hierarchy can release energy and creativity, rationalize productivity, and actually improve morale. Moreover, I think most managers know this intuitively and have only lacked a workable structure and a decent intellectual justification for what they have always known could work and work well. (1990, 127)

The explanation for the persistence of hierarchy and why the search for alternatives to it have proved fruitless is, first, that work is organized by task, and tasks are increasingly complex and tend to separate into discrete categories of increasing complexity; and, second, the mental work of management increases in complexity and also separates into discrete categories. A well-functioning hierarchy structures people in a way that meets these organizational needs: to add value to work moving through the organization; to identify and fix accountability at each stage; to place people of necessary competence at each organizational level; and to build a general consensus and acceptance of the unequal segmentation of work and the necessity for it (Jaques 1990).

The complexity of tasks increases as one goes higher in an organization's hierarchy, but the complexity of mental tasks increases even more. Experience, knowledge, mental stamina, and judgment are required at the apex of the hierarchy because of the need to see the big picture; to anticipate changing technology, among other changes; and to manage the organization's boundaries.

So the picture comes together. Managerial hierarchy, or layering, is the only effective organizational form for deploying people and tasks at complementary levels, where people can do the tasks assigned to them, where the people in any given layer can add value to the work of those in the layer below them, and, finally, where this stratification of management strikes everyone as necessary and welcome (Jaques 1990).

Long out of fashion in the study of public management, for even the most elemental understanding of hierarchy, is the necessity of turning to business administration. Doubtless the taproot of contemporary theoretical perspectives on formal organizational structure and design, and particularly on hierarchy, is found in the work by James D. Thompson (1967) and applied by Henry Mintzberg (1979, 1992). However unfashionable the traditional organizational chart may be in public administration, Mintzberg's famous elliptical parsing has become the standard for the visual images of hierarchy and the language used to describe those images. More importantly, in the private and public sectors these visual images and this language form the basis of testable hypotheses having to do with organizational structure and design.

Translating the categories of work from those commonly found in industry, such as sales and marketing, to categories commonly found in the public sector, such as legislative liaison and contract management, is relatively simple; and so is the adaptation of Mintzberg's model to the wide range of public sector institutions, namely, police departments, state departments of social services, the US Department of Agriculture.

Thompson argued that "uncertainty appears to be the fundamental problem for complex organizations, and coping with uncertainty, is the essence of the administrative process" (1967, 159). To protect itself from contextual buffeting, the organization will tend to seal off its technical and operating core through the standardizing of work processes (lots of rules), planning, stockpiling, professional gate keeping, training, the rationing of services, and so forth. Some organizations, particularly in the public sector, dominate their environments because they are the only legitimate source of service, the US Department of Defense being an example.

If uncertainty is the dominant contextual problem for institutions, interdependence is the primary internal problem. Among organization theorists, the concept of coupling is most commonly used to explain patterns of interdependence. Tasks and flows of work can be coupled in three ways: sequentially, by pooling, or reciprocally; and in all these, forms may be loosely or tightly coupled. Perhaps the best illustrations of these concepts as they are applied in the public sector are the extended series of research on high-reliability systems by Todd R. LaPorte and his colleagues (LaPorte and Consolini 1991); Martin Landau's work (1991) on redundant systems; Cohen and March's work (1986) on large research universities as loosely coupled systems; March and Olsen's work (1986) on garbage cans; the H. Brinton Milward series (1996) on the hollow state and the application of contract regimes; and Donald Chisholm's consideration (1995) of problem solving and organizational design.

The vast range and variety of hierarchies lend themselves to categories. *Simple hierarchical structures* are associated with smaller and newer organizations that emphasize direct supervision, centralization, and the strategic apex. Many nonprofit organizations under contract to the public sector tend in the direction of simple structures of this type. *Machine bureaucracies* tend to be older and larger hierarchies in which work standardization is critical. In such hierarchies, as illustrated by the US Postal Service, the technostructure is especially influential. *Professional bureaucracies* standardize work according to skills rather than the work, tend to be decentralized and loosely coupled, emphasize training and education, and often deal with complex problems. In professional bureaucracies, the operating core is especially influential, universities being the obvious example. The *divisionalized bureaucracy* is commonly found in contexts in which outputs need to be standardized but the need for services vary. State divisions of social services are examples, and so is the Internal Revenue Service. Middle management tends to be influential in such hierarchies. An *adhocracy* is the least formally organized hierarchy; it tends to emphasize mutual adjustment and to engage in team projects, to use matrix forms, and to mix centralization and decentralization. Role clarity, sharp divisions of labor, chains of command, and standardization are weak in adhocracies, but the search for innovation is strong. Computer software companies and the generalized R&D organizational format typify adhocracies, which have become the ideal modern structure emphasizing limited rules, flexible time, entrepreneurial management, and customer service. In the public sector, the NASA Manned Space Flight Center is often used as an illustration of adhocracy.

Any large-scale organization is likely to exhibit elements of each of these forms, and effective managers tend to understand the linkages between alternative structural choices and likely results. They know that structure matters, which often explains the tendency of management to push reorganization. When that happens, Mintzberg (1979, 1992), basing his study on private firms, suggests that the several components of hierarchy will tend to pull in particular directions. The strategic apex will pull in the direction of centralization and standardization. Middle management will tend to balkanize and protect turf. The technostructure will join the strategic apex in a pull to standardize. The support system will be inclined to collaborate and network. Finally, the operating core will see a powerful pull to professionalize. The public-sector push to contract out and to privatize does appear to run counter to the argument that the strategic apex will tend to centralization and standardization. Although there is almost always resistance at the operating core to contracting out, political pressure to downsize and save money by doing so would appear to run counter to centralization. But contracts are always replete with standards, and the contracting process may imply moving elements of control away from middle management to the strategic apex, where politically appointed persons are most influential. In contract regimes, the support staff's instinct to collaborate and network would appear to support contracting on the assumption that contractors are new partners and that elements of institutional structure and management can essentially be exported and hidden (Light 1999).

Indeed, even though networked bureaucracy has garnered much attention, and some think the trend is toward horizontal government (O'Toole 1997b; Kettl 2002), others such as Carolyn J. Hill and Laurence E. Lynn Jr. (2005) argue conversely. Hill and Lynn contend that rather than supplanting hierarchical government, networked or horizontal governing is being added in order to improve governance in an otherwise hierarchical system. Networks are important and should be taken seriously, but they perhaps are not replacing traditional structures of public administration. As we point out later, in Chapter 9, and as Hill and Lynn point out, hierarchy is quite necessary owing to how appropriations, constitutional authority, and jurisdiction work in the American political system. It is no surprise, then, that William West (1997) cautions us about rational choice theories concerning bureaucratic structure and political control. West points out that, among other flaws, a key limitation of such theories is that agencies have discretion over choosing courses of action in program implementation. For example, agencies may choose adjudication over rulemaking in order to avoid the influence of citizen or industry groups. In other words, agencies have options that insulate them from other participants in a network.

Alternatives to Hierarchy

Although it may be acknowledged that formal structure and hierarchy, defined broadly, are central to any understanding of institutions and are here to stay (March and Olsen 1989), the theoretical and methodological fashions of the day have tended toward transaction cost analysis, information asymmetry, principal-agent theory, and models of rational choice. Indeed, a leading symposium on the new institutionalism in public administration approached the subject primarily from the vantage of rational choice theory (Ferris and Tang 1993). In that symposium, Elinor Ostrom, Larry Schroeder, and Susan Wayne (1993) evaluated the successes of polycentric institutional arrangements for sustaining rural infrastructure in developing countries. Robert Stein (1993), using data from the International City/County Management Association (ICMA), analyzed alternative structural arrangements for city services in the United States and concluded that the real theoretical issue is not whether alternative services are provided by government or by private companies, but whether governments have effectively matched their service responsibilities and appropriate methods of service delivery. Jack Knott (1993) grouped public and private organizations according to how standardized their work was, the level of information asymmetry, the level of contextual political consensus and stability, and the level of internal cohesion, categories not unlike Mintzberg's, and concluded that management in private firms and management in public institutions have essentially the same basic problem: trust between principals and agents. Finally, as an illustration of the institutional perspective's broad methodological appeal, Thomas Hammond (1993) compared the processes and institutional arrangements of national states, baseball tournaments, bureaucratic hierarchies, and the organization of books in libraries to build a formal model of hierarchy. Having set out his formal model, Hammond concluded:

Every institution processes information so as to perceive and define problems, and every institution's decisionmakers choose among the available options to address these problems. The act of comparison lies at the heart of these two activities— problem perception and definition involve the comparison of some pieces of information with others, while choice involves the comparison of one option with another—and the argument in this essay has been that institutional rules creating hierarchies have a substantial impact on the nature of these comparisons. (1993, 143)

Much of institutional theory is based on the study of the most common characteristics found in public institutions and the logic and reasoning that flows from that study. Central to this logic and reasoning are concepts of bounded rationality, incremental adaptation, mixed scanning, loose coupling, trial and error, resource scarcity, political intervention and micromanagement, and illusory measures of performance. These concepts are highly useful in explicating and understanding ordinary public institutions. There is, however, a very different category of public institutions: the high-reliability systems. The best examples include commercial air travel; the provision of electricity, gas, and cable television services; and the operation of nuclear power plants, aircraft carriers, and submarines.

High-Reliability Systems

Tucked away in the recesses of public administration research and theory is a little storehouse of useful information about these high-reliability systems. The scholarly work of Martin Landau, Todd LaPorte, Paula Consolini, David Sills, Louise Comfort, Joseph Morone and Edward Woodhouse, Charles Perrow, James Reason, and Karl Weick has contributed to this storehouse. To summarize and simplify, here is what we know about high-reliability systems and why they work:

First, the physical technologies (radar, nuclear generating plants, and so forth) of these systems are tightly coupled, meaning that an important breakdown anywhere along the production process may cause the entire system to fail.

Second, this tight coupling is characterized by fixed and relatively rigid standard operating procedures, or procedure protocols, that do not ordinarily vary. This means that administrative discretion is sharply reduced.

Third, humans operating at any point in the production process of high-reliability systems require extensive technological training and constant retraining.

Fourth, such systems are ordinarily funded to a level that will guarantee high efficiency, or, to put it differently, efficiency is much more important than economy in the world of high reliability.

Fifth, such systems are highly redundant, there being two, three, or even four backup, or redundant, systems ready to take over should the primary systems fail. One thinks immediately of the redundancy that saved the Apollo 13 space mission.

Sixth, these systems are highly networked, meaning that many organizations are in the production chain. Consider, for example, air travel, which involves at least the following in a tightly coupled network: the Federal Aviation Administration; air traffic controllers; local airport managers; commercial airline companies, including pilots, flight attendants, and so forth; and airline manufacturers, airline maintenance companies, and fuel suppliers.

Seventh, these systems are composed of a marvelous mix of governmental, nongovernmental, and commercial organizations, the very definition of high-functioning public-private partnerships.

Eighth, when the systems are working properly, error reporting is encouraged and not punished. Indeed, initiatives to identify flaws in procedures and protocols and thereby avoid failure are rewarded.

Ninth, ordinarily such systems are rather hierarchical, both within the system and within the organization making up the system. But at times of peak load and emergencies, one finds rule switching by which officials move away from hierarchy and procedures to seek the expertise or experience that might account for or explain an anomaly and suggest possible nonroutine solutions. One thinks again of the Apollo 13 space mission (LaPorte and Consolini 1991).

These failure-free systems reveal how remarkably effective modern public and private organizations can be if they have adequate resources and are well managed. To be sure, failure-free systems are the subject of intense public scrutiny because of the visibility of failures, however rare.

There will be failures, and there will be accidents. Simple probability demonstrates that this is so (Perrow 1999). But every day we all enjoy the modern miracles of high-reliability systems. And, interestingly, when they fail, it is usually because of human fallibility.

It is difficult to imagine modern life without high-reliability systems. When they work perfectly, nothing appears to happen; in fact, everything happens properly.

Low-Reliability Systems and Their Improvement

As envisioned by LaPorte, high-reliability systems are quite rare (Bourrier 2011). Most systems or organizations simply do not exist in an environment where failure results in total catastrophe. As a result, trial and error is not only acceptable, but is also perhaps the best way to cope with potential risk (Wildavsky 1988). It is easy to understand how an unwillingness to take risks can paralyze an organization. The result is the paradox that in order to seek safety or improved effectiveness, an organization must accept a certain level of risk—it must tolerate at least some danger or mistakes. The trial and error process is needed because of the inability to rationally make decisions in the face of limited information, time constraints, and insufficient monetary and personnel resources. Consequently, the literature surrounding this has given us familiar concepts of decisionmaking such as "muddling through" (Lindblom 1959, 1979) and incrementalism (Wildavsky 1984). Owing to the fact that most of our organizations and systems are not high reliability, the literature has tended to focus on agencies and systems that are error-tolerant and that have goals that are difficult to measure (March and Olsen 1995). Such theories acknowledge that, although effectiveness is a goal, agencies anticipate and accept some degree of failure (Frederickson and LaPorte 2002).

The prospect, however, of using the literature on high-reliability systems to understand how to improve the performance of other agencies is tempting. H. George Frederickson and LaPorte (2002) argue that according to the typical view, reliability is increased either by maintaining bureaucratic order as traditionally understood in public administration or by rejecting that notion through purposeful redundancy. To shift away from these traditional understandings, Frederickson and LaPorte assert that one needs then to examine the operations of high-reliability organizations so as to be able to model their internal and external attributes.

An important caveat to all of this is the fact that errors are still possible, even as we learn more about high-reliability organizations. "False positives" occur when an organization expends resources to counter a nonexistent threat; "false negatives" occur when an organization disregards unlikely risks until a catastrophe happens. Balancing these risks is difficult (Kettl 2007), but since a false negative produces disaster, agencies and politicians will be biased toward preventing those. This increases the costs of administration, because minimizing this form of error will increase the number of false positives; therefore, efforts to minimize risk, even in high-reliability organizations, come at some cost.

An additional issue is what Frederickson and LaPorte (2002) term "the problem of rationality." As false negatives are avoided over time, there will be increased pressure to reduce administrative costs (incurred as the result of committing false positives). Kettl (2007) terms this "punctuated backsliding," in which a catastrophe places attention on avoiding further false negatives, but then vigilance—and funding—diminishes over time. Given that one of the key attributes of high-reliability organizations is adequate funding, this is a serious problem.

Additionally, improving agency performance often hinges upon more than the attributes (identified previously) of high-reliability organizations. For example, some programs have essentially an indefinite time horizon. Agencies in charge of monitoring nuclear waste, closed mines, or water resources must be able to do so for generations (LaPorte and Keller 1996). Not only do these issues demand high-reliability systems, but they also demand institutional constancy. As a result, true high-reliability organizations will probably remain rare. Although low-reliability organizations can be improved through the study of the high-reliability systems, there is some danger in treating them as high-reliable organizations. Performance simply will not match expectations. Karl Weick, Kathleen Sutcliffe, and David Obstfeld (2008) note that where efforts at improvements through Total Quality Management have failed, it is likely due to insufficient decisionmaking infrastructure (the sixth through ninth items in the previous section). One might also consider here the manner in which the No Child Left Behind Act treated local schools. Public schools are perhaps the antithesis of high-reliability organizations, yet the act treated them as if they could function—and be held accountable—as such.

Comparing Institutional Forms

The association between the institutional structures or designs of institutions and the policy and administrative outcomes of those institutions is an important and long-standing subject in political science. Some of the scholarly work on this subject is based on the study of the national state as a political jurisdiction, work that is generally well known (Lijphart 1984; Weaver and Rockman 1993). Less well known, but in many ways more empirically and theoretically significant, has been the study of the relationship between institutional structures and designs and the policy outcomes in American cities. At the level of the nation-state, institutional and constitutional designs differ in how they unify or divide government. Governments can be divided in various ways, including the formal separation of powers such as we see in the United States as well as in each of the fifty states, split partisan control of the executive and the legislative branches, and split partisan control between the legislative chambers. Partisan gridlock is the contemporary description of divided government. As a general descriptor, presidential-form government is divided government with checks and balances. Parliamentary-form national government is unified.

In the 1950s, political scientists were generally of the view that parliamentary structures were more unified than presidential structures and, therefore, improved the prospects for both political party effectiveness and generalized public policy efficiency (American Political Science Association 1950; Ranney 1954). In more recent times, scholars have considered divided government (Jacobson 1990; Fiorina 1996) and the implications of divided government (Mayhew 1991). This research draws the general conclusion that divided government, particularly split partisan control, is bad for public policy because it structurally allows for veto, empowers interest groups, frustrates effective policy development, and diminishes the prospects for effective policy implementation (Frederickson 1997a). David McKay, basing his findings on his studies of the American national government, writes that "DG (divided government) is almost universally perceived as a bad thing; among other sins, it allegedly undermines coherent and cohesive policymaking by removing the vital institutional connective tissue provided by common party control. DG has been invoked, therefore, as the cause of a number of problems, including the budget deficit, difficulties associated with the presidential appointment and treaty-making powers, and a general inability to produce effective domestic policy" (1994, 525).

David Mayhew (1991) and Morris Fiorina (1996) argue that divided governments are as likely as unified governments to produce important legislation because the credibility of legislation is increased when enacted under divided rather than unified governments. The problems, of course, are in carrying out policy under the conditions of divided government, and here the arguments run the other way. Divided government makes it considerably more difficult to carry out public policy effectively (Heclo 1977).

Both interpretations agree that structure matters. They disagree only about how it matters. But national states are hard to compare. American cities are much easier to compare, and they exhibit many of the same institutional design characteristics as national states.

In the progressive era, the municipal reform movement was a remarkably successful incremental process of institutional redesign for the purpose of changing the allocation of power and policy outcomes of American cities. In the late 1800s, the structure of almost all American cities was based on the separation-of-powers and checks-and-balances model used at the state and national levels. Political parties were as important in cities as they were at the state and national levels. Mayors were strong and sometimes fairly described as bosses. City employment was based largely on patronage, and widespread corruption was associated primarily with either skimming contracts or taking kickbacks from city contractors and vendors.

Reallocating power and changing institutional behavior were accomplished by changing the institutional rules and altering institutional roles. Nonpartisan elections replaced partisan elections. Civil service systems replaced patronage. Strong bid and purchase controls were adopted. The election of city council members changed from districts to at large. And an entirely new form of city government was invented, a form based not on the separation of powers but on the corporate model. In this model, the "board," or city council, was small, was elected at large, and comprised volunteers who stood for election as part of their civic duty rather than as part of building political careers. This new form of city council passed ordinances, set policy, established a city budget, and then passed the day-to-day work of the city on to a professional: the city manager. Thus was born a new profession and a cadre of educated and trained professionals dedicated to efficient and clean city government (Adrian 1955).

Fast-forward one hundred years and the results of redesigning the structure of city government are, by any measure, impressive. More than half of American cities use the council-manager form of government, which is similar to the parliamentary form of national government. Virtually all cities are operated on a day-to-day basis by merit-appointed civil servants. Serious corruption, such as fraud and kickbacks, is rare and tends to be associated with old-line "unreformed" mayor-council-form cities. Political parties are relatively unimportant at the city level in American politics, and mayors are, as a generalization, much less powerful and visible than they once were. Not only is professional city management powerful in council-manager form government, but also many mayor-council-form governments on separation-of-powers statutory platforms now have "chief administrative officers" who serve as the functional equivalent of city managers. There is little doubt that redesigning city rules and altering the roles of city officials were important in changing the behavior of cities and their policy outcomes (Frederickson, Johnson, and Wood 2003).

System Fragmentation

Institutional theory is also informed by the long-standing empirical, conceptual, and normative debate over the Tiebout Thesis, according to which multiple small jurisdictions in a metropolitan area aid marketlike individual choice, competition, and public service efficiency both in separate jurisdictions and in entire metropolitan areas (Tiebout 1956; Ostrom, Tiebout, and Warren 1961). Although often framed as a rational choice debate versus a nonrational choice debate, for institutional theory purposes this is a systems fragmentation versus a consolidated systems argument, with its attendant hypotheses and empirical tests.

At the outset, the theoretical question has to do with the unit of analysis. Fragmentation theory uses the individual or the family as the appropriate unit of analysis and the aggregation of individual and family choices as measures of rational preferences and institutional effectiveness. And, too, fragmentation theorists tend to use the logic of individual bureaucratic preferences to explain institutional choices (Niskanen 1971; Downs 1967; Ostrom 1973). Likewise, consolidated systems theorists use individual, family, and bureaucratic preference as units of analysis, but they also use overall measures of whole system effectiveness (Lowery and Lyons 1989; Lowery, Lyons, and DeHoog 1992; Rusk 1995; Stephens and Wikstrom 2000).

David Lowery, a leading critic of the Tiebout Thesis, neatly summarizes the consolidated systems theorists' critique of fragmentation theory by the straightforward testing of these three hypotheses:

1. Racial and income segregation will be greater in fragmented settings than in consolidated settings (2000, 63).
2. Fragmentation results in a spatial mismatch in which the poor and minorities are isolated in jurisdictions with limited fiscal capacity and a significant

demand for expenditures, but wealthy whites escape to enclaves with limited needs and a generous fiscal capacity (65).

3. Consolidated (limited or complete) systems are more likely to have policies that minimize sorting by race and income and maximize redistribution and generalized economic growth (68).

Basing his conclusions on his own work and the work of others, Lowery (2000) marshals considerable empirical verification for these hypotheses. Fragmentation theorists, for their part, marshal evidence and logic to reject the hypotheses (Ostrom 1973). But theorists from both vantages agree that relative levels of system fragmentation or consolidation matter a great deal in institutional functioning, in the just and equitable distribution of public service and life opportunities, and in citizens' preferences and involvement, although they sharply disagree about how.

Garbage Cans and Rent Seeking

Among the best-known elements of institutional theory is the logic of the garbage can. In the garbage can one finds order, but this order is neither sequential nor consequential and turns much of the rational logic of decision theory on its head. Order may not be sequential because the relationship between means and ends is often temporal; that is to say, public problems, public institutions, and opportunities for choices mingle in nonlinear ways as independent, exogenous streams flowing through a system (Cohen, March, and Olsen 1972; March and Olsen 1989; Weick 1979). Public problems in the garbage can seek solutions; at the same time, public institutions may be attracted to particular problems. Problems, solutions, and decisionmakers are temporal phenomena simultaneously available and can form a temporal order. "A computer is not just a solution to a problem in payroll management, discovered when needed. It is an answer actively looking for a question. Despite the dictum that you cannot find the answer until you have formulated the question well, you often do not know what the public policy question is until you know the answer" (March and Olsen 1989, 13). In the absence of structural constraints, simultaneity, not means-ends sequences, determines the linkages between problems and solutions and between institutional answers and questions.

Perhaps the best-known public-sector empirical application of the garbage can is found in the work of John W. Kingdon. In *Agendas, Alternatives, and Public Policies* (1995), he describes shifting alliances, poorly understood technologies, changing perceptions, and an unclear mix of means and ends that could only be explained as temporal sorting, or simultaneity. The evident disorderliness of institutional simultaneity suggests the inadequacy of theoretical explanations ordinarily used to attempt to understand institutions.

In much of the history of public administration, we have also assumed orderly relationships between public problems and their solutions, and we have assumed that these were means-ends consequential relationships. From the garbage can perspective, elements of consequential arguments and rhetoric appear in institutional decision processes, but so do observable patterns of problem-solution simultaneity. Rather than *the* answer to a particular public policy question, in the garbage can an *appropriate* answer is most likely (March and Olsen 1995).

From this logic, it has been determined that patterns of institutional reform and reorganization are ad hoc, guided by a kind of pragmatic simultaneity (Seidman 1980; Szanton 1981; Salamon 1989; Meier 1980). In a similar way, patterns of public policymaking are patchwork (Skowronek 1982), opportunistic pragmatism (Johnson 1976), and "putting square pegs into round holes" (Radin 2000). Much of the language of public policy and administration is consequential, a rhetoric of performance, results, program evaluation, and outcomes. Institutional practices, however, tend in the direction of seeking the understanding of preferred outcomes through limited available data as well as searching for institutional arrangements that link institutional capacities and problems needing attention.

In an entirely different language and from a starkly different conceptual vantage, one finds the garbage can's sibling, and her name is rent seeking. Borrowed from economics and applied to public policy studies, rents are the description of a market having multiple firms (institutions) and the differences between their total costs and their total incomes (rents are not to be confused with profits; economists are fussy about this). These rents can be thought of as a surplus in a completely efficient public sector. (Pareto optimal efficiency is understood as the allocation of public goods so that at least one person is made better off without everyone else being made worse off.) The set of prices and quantities (goods or services) that produces the greatest social surplus is thought to be the most efficient (Weimer and Vining 1989). The problem, of course, is that from the narrow perspective of efficiency, markets and nonmarkets (public institutions) "fail" because of a long list of problems, such as monopolies, information asymmetry, and adverse selection.

For public-sector institutions, there are other problems; these primarily have to do with institutional structural factors that may be *inefficient*, such as unequal opportunities, the voting paradox (what does a mandate mean?), preference intensity, the disproportionate influence of organized interests, district-based geographic constituencies, limited decisionmaker time horizons, problems measuring and valuing public outputs, professional preferences in the bureaucracy and civil service protection, and highly fragmented authority. In this nonmarket context we find several forms of rent seeking. Of the hundreds of examples, here are a few: agriculture crop subsidies and price supports, tariffs protecting domestic firms, professions restricting entry, monopoly regulation of utilities, price caps, and tax loopholes (Buchanan, Tollison, and Tullock 1980). Of course, the longest-standing and best-known example of the garbage can and rent seeking is the pork barrel allocation of funds through the United States Army Corps of Engineers for domestic harbor and river dredging and management (Mazmanian and Neinaber 1979). In the logic of rent seeking, the annual congressional pork barrel allocations to the Army Corps of Engineers (not to mention dozens of other forms of pork barrel, including all leading American research universities) would be described as falling far short of efficient, and the methodological tools used in public policy analysis assist in the measurement of such rent seeking inefficiency. But from the vantage of the garbage can, there is both a recognition of the inherent inefficiency in such arrangements and a conceptual description of March and Simon's rule of appropriateness.

"Actions are chosen by recognizing a situation as being familiar, frequently encountered, type, and matching the recognized situation to a set of rules" (March and Simon 1993, 8). Appropriateness refers to a match of behavior to a situation. The match may be based on experience, expert knowledge, or intuition; if so, it is often called "recognition" to emphasize the cognitive process of pairing problem-solving action correctly to a problem situation (March and Simon 1993, 8–13). The match may be based on role expectations, normative definitions of a role without significant attribution of moral virtue, or problem-solving correctness to the resulting behavior (Sarbin and Allen 1968, 550). The match may also carry with it a "connotation of essence, so that appropriate attitudes, behaviors, feelings, or preferences for a citizen, official, or farmer are those that are essential to being a citizen, official, or farmer—essential not in the instrumental sense of being necessary to perform a task or socially expected, nor in the sense of being an arbitrary definitional convention, but in the sense that without which one cannot claim to be a proper citizen, official, or farmer" (March and Olsen 1995, 30–31).

The observant reader will have noted that we include garbage can theory and elements of rational (means-ends) choice theory under the big institutional theory tent, although rational choice theory is the subject of Chapter 8. More dedicated adherents to rational choice theory would likely disagree with this grouping. The primary difference between garbage can theory and rational choice theory has to do with methodology and the matter of conceptual parsimony. The original application of garbage can theory in political science, by March and Olsen (1984), was based on an extensive assumption-based cognitive simulation model that logically verified a garbage can relationship between means and ends, problems and solutions, questions and answers. Their model was recently reconsidered and the simulation redone by Jonathan Bendor, Terry Moe, and Kenneth Shotts, who claim the results discredit the simulation and the theory upon which it is based:

This is ironic. The informal theory of the garbage can is famous for depicting a world that is much more complex than that described by classical theories of organizational choice. The latter's tidy image of goal specification, alternative generation, evaluation, and choice is replaced by a complex swirl of problems looking for solutions, solutions looking for problems, participants wandering around looking for work, and all three searching for choice opportunities. Yet, the simulation depicts almost none of this and in fact creates a world of remarkable order. (2001, 182)

Rational choice theorists much prefer carefully specified assumptions, particularly assumptions of bounded rationality and the parsimonious use of a limited number of variables in computer simulations. Most of the research scholarship on principal-agent theory, the prisoner's dilemma, and the tragedy of the commons is based on these methodological and conceptual preferences. Johan Olsen, in response to the claims that the March and Olsen presentation of garbage can theory goes to this point, argues:

The comments by Bendor, Moe, and Shotts are unlikely to improve our understanding of political organizations and institutions. They misrepresent the garbage can and the new institutionalism, and their unsuccessful example of how these ideas can be "rescued" is hardly promising. By building on a narrow concept of what is valuable political science, and by assuming away interesting challenges, they cut themselves off from some of the key issues that have occupied political scientists. Their own program is without substantive political content. They do not tell us which political phenomena they want to understand, and their separation of politics from its institutional and historical context makes it difficult to discuss which basic assumptions are most likely to be helpful—those they suggest or those of the garbage can or institutional perspectives. In sum, they indicate an unpromising route and point research in the wrong direction. (2001, 196–197)

Lost in this methodological and conceptual argument is the bigger point that both approaches attempt scientific understanding of public institutions. Under the institutional big tent, the rational choice theorists tend to see themselves in the center ring. Garbage can theorists tend to be less preoccupied with a place in the center ring, but they strongly assert the methodological and scientific validity of their theory and how they have tested it.

The Diffusion of Innovation

The study of the diffusion of institutional innovation (change) is a core body of research in institutional theory. The Progressive Movement in the first fifty years of the twentieth century spread many important organizational and policy innovations, including the council-manager form of city government, the short ballot, the secret ballot, merit systems in government, workers' compensation laws, aid to the blind and deaf, and minimum wage laws. Edgar McCoy (1940) measured state policy innovations between 1869 and 1931, including old age pensions, women's suffrage, and workers' compensation, and ranked the states according to whether they were early or late adopters. Using maps, he found the centers of these innovations were in New York, California, Wisconsin, and Michigan, and he traced the paths of diffusion in concentric circles from those centers. Paths of diffusion were influenced by state variations in transportation and communication capacities, wealth, and urbanization. From this grew the McCoy Innovation Index, which even now explains regional patterns of innovation diffusion.

Long before the federal government took on widespread regulatory and social responsibility roles, the states were busy with the diffusion of innovation to include railroad regulation, health regulation, and labor regulation. Back in 1883, Albert Shaw, writing about the Illinois legislature, said that laws were emulated verbatim from one state to another, and he argued that statutes were the same throughout a group of neighboring states. New York, Michigan, Ohio, Minnesota, Wisconsin, and Illinois have been identified by historian William Brock as the taproots of the expansion of state social responsibility.

Herbert Jacob's *Silent Revolution: The Transformation of Divorce Law in the United States* (1988) explains the rapid diffusion of no-fault divorce laws. New York and California adopted this concept in 1966 and 1970, respectively; by 1974, forty-five states had followed suit; and in 1985, the lone holdout (South Dakota) joined in. Jacob found no evidence that the idea was propagated by the usual sources: social movements or interest groups, policy networks, bureaucrats, the governor or legislators. Because no-fault divorce was noncontroversial, was cost free, and had been successfully adopted by other states, it spread rather easily. Moving beyond his case study, Jacob argues that many other laws spread in a similar fashion.

Evidence suggests a contagion process. Peter K. Eisinger (1989), in the most extensive study to date, reports that business location incentive programs (mostly tax abatements) increased from 840 in 1966 to 1,213 in 1985. The average number of programs per state doubled in the twenty-year time period. Surely this rapid spread of location incentives did not happen because state governments independently reached the same conclusion about their desirability.

Paul Peterson and Mark Rom in *Welfare Magnets* (1990) illuminate the debate over whether states will "rush to the bottom" in support of putting pressure on welfare, to avoid becoming welfare magnets. In a careful statistical analysis of welfare benefit levels, poverty rates, and state-level explanatory variables, Peterson and Rom find that low-income persons move in response to benefit levels (and to employment opportunities). They also find that state policymakers are sensitive to the size of the low-income population and to the possibility of welfare migration, and they reduce benefits accordingly. States with high benefit levels, such as Wisconsin, cut benefits by the period's end. This action produces a convergence effect that pushes benefit levels downward.

Richard Nathan (1993) observes that states have often undertaken liberal initiatives when the national government is captured by conservatives; later, when liberals capture Washington, they bring along policies that have already been tested at the state level. Noting that state initiatives in the 1920s were the models for federal New Deal programs in the 1930s, Nathan finds it unsurprising that the same thing happened in the 1980s: Conservatives controlled Washington, and liberals turned to the states. This is part of an equilibrating tendency in our federal system wherein interests not satisfied at one level turn to another. This tendency counters the centralizing trend that most observers see in American federalism and lends credence to James Madison's claim that "opposite and rival" interests could be accommodated in a federal system.

It is a safe estimate that at least half of American cities with populations between 25,000 and 200,000 have exactly the same dog leash laws. This is not because Ann Arbor and Beverly Hills have the same problems with dogs; it is because dog leash laws and most other laws were taken from model city laws. These laws were put together and distributed by the National League of Cities and the National Civic League. Indeed, there is a possibility that Beverly Hills and Frankfurt, Germany, have the same dog leash laws owing to the handiwork of the International Union of Local Officials and their model laws publications.

Doubtless, the ultimate study is Everett M. Rogers's *Diffusion of Innovations* (1995). Rogers, in a synthesis of thousands of studies of change, has found that innovations or reforms spread in diffusions, which exhibit a common pattern—the S-curve. At first the adoption of change or reform is slow, with experimentation, trial and error, and the challenges of being the guinea pig. Once a few others adopt reform successfully, there tends to be a steep climb in adoption, followed by a leveling off. When institutional change reaches the leveling-off stage (it may include most other similar institutions, but innovations are seldom judged to have been successfully spread if they involve fewer than half the cases), further investments in seeking additional adopters are usually wasted.

"Diffusion refers to the spread of something within a social system" (Strang and Soule 1998, 266). This spread is from a source to one or more adopters and can include the spread of types of behavior, technology, beliefs, and, most important for our purposes, structure. Diffusions in social systems happen in surprisingly predictable ways, a very good example being the spread of structural changes among American cities.

Although Rogers and others who have studied diffusion tend to focus their interests on what they describe as innovation, the patterns of change and reform in the structures of American cities exhibit virtually all the features found in the S-curve theory of innovation diffusion. The municipal reform movement began slowly late in the nineteenth and early in the twentieth centuries. By the 1920s, municipal reform was a well-known set of ideas and a widely shared ideology, particularly among opinion leaders; it spread steadily from the 1920s through the 1940s, resulting in the almost universal adoption of municipal civil service personnel systems, bid and contract controls, the short ballot, the secret ballot, and the systematic elimination of political party designations for those standing for city office. And, of course, the council-manager form of government grew steadily during this period, particularly in the Midwest, the South, and the West. The new cities in the great American suburban diaspora almost all adopted the council-manager form. By the mid-1960s, the municipal reform movement was running out of gas and a new set of ideas was steadily emerging, the so-called reform-of-the-reform, or the postreform movement. This movement, too, can be seen as an S-curve, and it appears to be in the midst of a steep climb, one that will no doubt level off in the years to come (Frederickson, Johnson and Wood, 2003).

Patterns of diffusion (some are more comfortable simply calling diffusion "change"; those who favor a particular diffusion tend to call it a reform or an innovation) are explained by a series of attendant hypotheses.

First, there is an association between the presence of a perceived crisis and the propensity to adopt a change (Rogers 1995; Strang and Soule 1998). At the height of the municipal reform era, the problems associated with graft and corruption in American cities were described or characterized as crises or disasters (Flentje 1993). The fat boss mayor evoked in the political cartoons of the day had a surprising capacity to further the interests of reformers. The greater the real or perceived institutional crisis or problem, the greater the prospects for institutional change.

Second, the compatibility between the purposes of a change or reform and the dominant values in a social system is important. This easily explains the almost universal adoption of the council-manager form of government in homogeneous American suburbs. The employment of a professional manager, a merit-based civil service, and a part-time city council made up of members elected at large all fit comfortably with the dominant values of middle-class families able to commute by car to their jobs and thus escape the problems of the inner city. Starting in the 1960s, the demographics of many American cities changed, and with those changing demographics came different values and concerns on the part of those now living in those cities. Most council-manager cities now have identifiable political leadership in the form of a directly elected mayor subject to some form of direct political accountability. In addition, the majority of council members in council-manager cities are now elected by district, enhancing the specific neighborhood responsiveness of city councils (Frederickson and Johnson 2001).

Third, spatial proximity is important. The spatial proximity of midwestern and western cities, for example, explains why these cities were early adopters of many of the features of municipal reform. The Northeast, by comparison, saw fewer examples of "reformed cities," and there has been somewhat less diffusion of municipal reform there.

Fourth, "the mass media play a crucial role in amplifying and editing the diffusion of collective action" (Strang and Soule 1998, 270). The media tend to focus on problems and things going wrong, and such a relentless focus influences public opinion, lending itself to the general view that something needs to be done or that things need to be fixed. Crime and drugs are associated with getting tough on crime, which results in sentencing guidelines, three strikes and you're out, and the currently popular "broken-windows" concept that well-maintained urban areas will lead to reduced crime. When there is a snowstorm and the city is slow to plow the streets, the media report and amplify the matter and elected officials are held responsible. Logically, these officials will look for ways to "solve the problems," and often the solutions are structural, these days in the direction of changing the city structure to give the mayor more power. The contemporary media tend to be as enthusiastic about strengthening the mayor's role as they were about weakening it seventy-five years ago. The most widely read publication in American local government is *Governing Magazine*. It has run several major stories about "The Lure of the Strong Mayor" and the importance of mayoral leadership in modern American cities. The media have played a central role in today's reforms and in those of the past seventy-five years.

Fifth, change agents are often the carriers of change, the agents of diffusion. "The professions and occupational communities form an allied source of new practice" (Strang and Soule 1998, 271). These communities of experts provide the venues for discussions, conferences, e-mail correspondence, newsletters, and magazines. Many mayors are active in the National Municipal League (NML) and are influenced by opinion leaders active in NML as well as the literature and other services of NML. City managers are active in the ICMA and are also influenced by ICMA opinion leaders and the ICMA publications. Many top consulting firms, such as the Innovations Group, are change agents influential in suggesting changes. It would be unusual in the extreme for a consulting firm to review a city and to conclude that everything is fine and nothing needs to be changed.

Sixth, closely associated with the media and with diffusion change agents is the matter of fashion setting. "Today, the management fashion industry is very big business. While the theorization and hyping of organization action has always been fundamental in managing, a strong trend toward the externalization of organizational analysis is apparent. The consultant, the guru, the management scholar populations are on the rise, as are the output of the business press and the sales of business books" (Strang and Soule 1998, 278). In a thorough review of the movement of social policy, Christopher Hood and Michael Jackson (1991) found that neither analysis nor rational reasoning moves policy. Instead, just as Aristotle argued, individuals and the institutions they inhabit are moved by rhetoric; by the power of narratives, stories, examples; and by arguments that win in the context of circumstances that people understand. Like fashion, preferred "doctrines" change over time and tend to move in S-curve patterns. Doctrines can and do move across institutions by contagion, mimicry, and the bandwagon effect, often with little connection to data, analysis, or informed historical understanding (Strang and Soule 1998).

Seventh, both individuals and institutions tend to change so as to acquire prestige, status and social standing, perhaps the most interesting and unique factor. "Models of management diffuse from central firms to the larger business community as they prove their utility in responding to new politico-economic conditions. Haverman shows that deregulation led thrifts to follow large, financially profitable thrifts into new markets" (Strang and Soule 1998, 275). This led to disastrous investments in Mexico. Midsized firms use the accounting firms used by large well-known companies in seeking the legitimacy that those firms might carry. Universities mimic Ivy League and other prestigious schools and justify the changes by pointing to similar changes at the prestigious universities. In the era of prizes, report cards, and rankings, the pressure to mimic prestigious institutions is increased. Cities prepare for years to apply to receive an All-American City designation given by the National Civic League. Cities also conform to a set of preestablished criteria to receive a favorable report card grade in the *Governing Magazine* evaluations of city effectiveness. Cities compete for the Harvard Innovation Awards, each claiming that the change it made was especially significant, productive, or equitable. Corporations and public agencies compete for the government-sponsored Balderidge Awards, which include highly questionable criteria such as benchmarking (benchmarking is actually copying the innovations of others rather than being innovative oneself).

One aspect of diffusion theory is particularly interesting. Paul DiMaggio and Walter Powell (1983), in their research of the diffusion of innovation in American businesses, found what Max Weber long ago called "the iron cage." In his brilliant early descriptions of bureaucracy, Weber argued that in the modern world the organizational and managerial characteristics of bureaucracy are so universal and compelling that these bureaucracies can become iron cages that are hard to change. DiMaggio and Powell found "iron cages of isomorphism" in corporate America in which firms were influenced by crisis, proximity, prestige, and the other forces of diffusion and, over time, came increasingly to resemble one another. Institutions, they found, will borrow from, copy, or mimic the technology, management style, and structural qualities of other institutions perceived to have either greater success or greater prestige. Therefore, in the iron cage of isomorphism, institutions increasingly begin to resemble each other or to homogenize.

DiMaggio and Powell also found little association between the propensity of firms to change or adapt, on the one hand, and their productivity, on the other. Research on the patterns of structural change in American cities and the results of those changes runs counter to DiMaggio and Powell's claim that there is little or no association between the propensity to change and outcomes or results. The history of structural changes associated with the American municipal reform movement and the results of that reform indicate that a diffusion of municipal-reform-driven changes to American cities did result in significantly altered behavior in cities (Frederickson, Johnson, and Wood 2003).

Conclusions

The biggest and easiest criticism of institutional theory is essentially the same as the critique of organization theory. Both lack parsimony, and both include dozens of variables, dozens of hypotheses, and a singular lack of a simplifying core premise such as the rational pursuit of self-interest. These criticisms also carry with them methodological preferences and biases, particularly having to do with competing views of social science. Undoubtedly, those parts of modern institutional theory that trace to the evolution of public-sector applications of organization theory are more than a little vulnerable to these criticisms. Concepts such as sense making and appropriateness are fuzzy and subject to wide-ranging interpretations. Field-based empirical testing of these concepts has tended to be observational, interpretative, case based, and qualitative—falling short of the methodological rigor to which many in the social sciences aspire. At the core of the dustup between Bendor, Moe, and Shotts and their rational choice critique of garbage can theory and March and Olsen and their defense of it are the issues of theory parsimony and methodology. Both views go even deeper to issues concerning the philosophy of science and competing views about how to do social science.

It is our view that modern institutional theory is past this debate, and the big tent conception of institutional theory covers both perspectives. Rational choice scholars applying principal-agent logic to information asymmetry and transaction costs in matters of public policy are doing institutional theory. So, too, are scholars doing interpretive thick descriptions of the same public policy matters. Both are studying public institutions and developing institutional theory.

Because of the vastness of institutional theory, it is fairly subject to the criticism that it lacks a center of gravity, a simplifying assumption. This is a valid criticism, but should not cause us to lose sight of institutional theory's very real accomplishments and possibilities. The possibilities and limitations of institutional theory are in some ways a microcosm of the development of public management theory itself. There is a growing theoretical structure, a commonly accepted set of definitions and agreed-upon premises, an elaborate if somewhat opaque vocabulary, and an increasingly iterative and cumulative body of knowledge. Above all, institutional theory highlights the unique properties and characteristics of public institutions and their problems and promises.

5

Theories of Public Management

Introduction: Developments in Public Management Theory

Although changing tastes have had some influence on all fields of theory and application, no approach to public administration has been more subject to the fads of the day than management. The birth of the modern field coincided with the popularity of the scientific management of Frederick W. Taylor, the application of time-and-motion studies to public activities, and the relentless search for the one best way. Like the "Total Quality Management" of the 1980s and today's logic of continuous improvement, scientific management was borrowed from business administration early in the twentieth century and applied to public administration and government.

Through time, in government much of what was understood to be scientific management separated itself from the more general subject of management, particularly the management of the staff functions, budgeting, and personnel, and became the taproot of the modern field of operations research. Half engineering and half business administration, operations research is a highly successful application of mathematics and computing power to classic business management issues such as scheduling, pricing, quality control, efficiency in production processes, and the delivery, warehousing, and inventory of products. Operations research is equally important in the public sector, particularly in public organizations for which such techniques are useful: the planning and development of weapons systems; highway and transportation systems; water and waste management systems; nuclear-power-generating systems; air traffic control systems; and large-scale data management tasks such as the tax returns and records of the Internal Revenue Service and the management of the Social Security, Medicare, and Medicaid systems.

In contemporary theory, the applications of operations research theory is most often found in settings described as tightly coupled systems in which machines, equipment, or technology is coupled with human management. The theoretical literature on high-reliability systems, covered in Chapter 4, is also often an application of operations research and concepts of scientific management (LaPorte and Consolini 1991).

Of the early features of American public administration—a merit-based civil service, the separation of administration from politics, the "principles" of administration, administration as part of executive government, and the application of scientific management—it can be plausibly argued that both the theory and the logic of scientific management have been the most influential and enduring. Scientific management theory and logic are so persuasive in many important parts of government and the public sector that they are simply assumed, understood, and therefore usually invisible to the ordinary citizen; they are evident only when a system built on such theory and logic breaks down. When an airplane falls out of the sky, a child dies of e-coli bacteria, or a soldier dies from "friendly fire," the citizens and their elected leaders "see" complex public systems built and operated on the assumptions of scientific management. When the people "see" an airplane fall out of the sky, they often fail to see that at 5:00 P.M. on any workday afternoon in the United States, more than 300,000 people are hurtling safely through the skies at five hundred miles per hour. By any reckoning, this is a scientific management miracle combining technology, private enterprise, and government control and management. Yet all agree that as air travel increases, these systems must be made even safer (Perrow 1999; Frederickson and LaPorte 2002). However one describes it—the one best way, Total Quality Management (TQM), the high-performance organization, or continuous improvement—the legacy of scientific management is ubiquitous.

In the early years of modern self-conscious public administration, scientific management theory and application were most often found in the field of public works, then a close cousin of public administration. Indeed, until the 1960s the American Society of Public Administrators, the American Public Works Association, and the International City/County Management Association (ICMA) shared the same headquarters building on the campus of the University of Chicago. Leonard White's original text (1929) contains a chapter on public works administration, and many of the early ICMA publications had to do with public works. Gradually, the two fields drifted apart, engineers identifying with public works and comfortable with scientific management techniques, public administrators identifying with the staff functions of government, such as budgeting and personnel administration and seemingly more interested in the arts of management. In the academy and in the literature—textbooks and journals—public works and public administration, with just a few exceptions, are now almost entirely separate (Felbinger and Whitehead 1991a, 1991b). In practice, however, every county has a department of public works; every county has extensive data management systems for property assessment; every state has elaborate social service data management systems as well as highway and other transportation systems; and the national government has engineering and systems operations research specialists of many types. In practice, then, scientific management is still very much a part of public administration.

Scientific management theory, in its original Taylorist sense and its modern TQM sense, is generally in the family of decision theory. The purposes and characteristics of decision theory are essentially problem definition and problem solving—how to control air traffic, how to operate an efficient sanitary sewer and treatment system. Sophisticated decision theoretic models deal with goal ambiguity, resource limitations, incomplete information, and satisficing. We cover these topics in Chapter 7. Management theory may have elements of problem solving, but it is ordinarily understood to have to do with the study and description of directing ongoing routine activities in purposeful organizations.

With the separation of public works from public administration and Herbert Simon's assault on "the principles" in the 1950s, and the emphasis on policy analysis and policymaking in the 1980s and 1990s, the subject of management lost cachet and fell off the public administration radar screen. A few blips lingered. In the 1960s and 1970s, there was some interest in generic administration, meaning essentially that management is management wherever practiced; several generic schools of business and public administration were established on the strength of this logic (Cornell, California at Irvine, California at Riverside, Ohio State, Missouri at Columbia and Kansas City, Brigham Young University, Yale) (Litchfield 1956). Most generic schools have now been discontinued or have evolved small separate and essentially autonomous departments of public administration in large business schools. The generic schools had virtually no effect on actual public administration practices or theories.

The 1960s and 1970s saw some interest—particularly in the New Public Administration—in theories of democratic administration, including flat hierarchies, worker self-management, project management, matrix organizations, and the elimination of competition as an incentive for work (Marini 1971; Frederickson 1980). These theories have had some effect on practices and are commonly found in contemporary "good public management" models.

The social equity theory found in the New Public Administration of the 1960s and 1970s has also had a long shelf life. It came along at a time of high concern for fairness in the workplace, equal employment opportunities, affirmative action, and comparable worth. Many of these concepts became statutory, organizations and procedure to adopt these values appeared, and social equity is now widely practiced. In their assessment of the effects of the social equity aspects in New Public Administration, Jay Shafritz and E. W. Russell (1997) write this:

From the 1970s to the present day [public administration scholars] have produced an endless stream of conference papers and scholarly articles urging public administrators to show a greater sensitivity to the forces of change, the needs of clients, and the problem of social equity in service delivery. This has had a positive effect in that now the ethical and equitable treatment of citizens by administrators is at the forefront of concerns in public agencies. Reinforced by changing public attitudes, the reinventing government movement and civil rights laws, the new public administration has triumphed after a quarter century. Now it is unthinkable (as well as illegal), for example, to deny someone welfare benefits because of their race or a job opportunity because of their sex. Social equity today does not have to be so much fought for by young radicals as administrated by managers of all ages. (1997, 451)

From the 1950s through the 1970s, with the exception of a continuing interest in budgeting and personnel staff functions, the arguments of the New Public Administration, and a brief interest in "management by objective," academic public administration had little to say regarding management in the practice of public administration. Beginning in the mid-1980s, the subject of management returned to public administration with a vengeance, in theory and in practice.

It being understood that the most rigorous applications of management theory in public administration are found in operations research and public works, and that these applications are best described as decision-theoretic, we now turn to modern theories of public management. Unlike decision theory, these theories are not primarily problem solving, but are instead descriptive of management behavior or function as prescriptive guides for management improvement in the ongoing routine work of organizations.

It is common in public administration theory to combine the subjects of management and organization and to treat them either as linked or as the same thing. This custom has led to some conceptual and theoretical confusion. For example, decentralization is often described as a management phenomenon, although it is generally agreed that many, if not most, aspects of centralization and decentralization are organizational or structural phenomena. To reduce this confusion and to sharpen the theoretical point, we have unbundled management and organization theory and treat them separately. Public management is taken to mean the formal and informal processes of guiding human interaction toward public organizational objectives. The units of analysis are processes of interaction between managers and workers and the effects of management behavior on workers and work outcomes. The purpose of this chapter is to describe and evaluate theory, either empirically or deductively derived, that accounts for or explains public management behavior.

Theories of public organization, by contrast, have to do with the design and evolution of the structural arrangements for the conduct of public administration and with descriptions or theories of the behavior of organizations as the unit of analysis. Although separating management and organization for conceptual and theoretical refinement has its advantages, we do not contend here that management and organization are distinct in an empirical sense. They are not. Management almost always occurs in the context of organization, and organization is seldom effective without management. Therefore, in the closing chapter, management and organization are bundled back together, as they are in the empirical world, and theories of their relationship are presented.

The following discussion describes theories of public management in four categories. First, and most important, is traditional public management theory, thrust forward. Second is the current popularity of leadership as public management. Third is the theory derived from the longer-standing practice of conducting public management by contract. Fourth are theories of governance that explain important features of public management.

Traditional Management Theory Thrust Forward

Traditional management theory has its origins with Frederick W. Taylor and his influential *The Principles of Scientific Management*, which was published originally in 1911 and is still in print (2010). His subject was business, particularly the shop. His purpose was to move from rules of thumb, customs and traditions, and ad hoc approaches to business management toward a body of scientific principles. His principles were based on precise measurements of work processes, as well as outcomes; on the scientific selection of workers; on the optimal placement of workers in describable work roles; on the division and sequencing of work processes to enhance productivity; and on the cooperation of workers in achieving the organizational objective. The application of these principles, Taylor believed, would lead managers and workers to the one best way.

As business innovations often do, these concepts soon colonized government. They became a central part of the Progressive Era and the movement to reform government, and they were highly influential in the development of civil service systems in government at all levels. The widespread use of tests for hiring and promotion, position descriptions, and employee evaluations are all reflections of scientific management. Indeed, one could argue that modern-day testing generally—for progress in school, for admission to universities and graduate schools, and for professional standing in law, medicine, accounting, teaching, and so forth—are also contemporary manifestations of the logic of scientific management. The desire for certitude, to measure precisely and thus order and categorize the world properly and thereby make sense of it, is doubtless as strong today as it was at the nadir of scientific management.

Luther Gulick (1937), one of the founders of modern public administration, embraced the orthodoxy of scientific management, applied it to government, and introduced the most famous mnemonic in the field—POSDCORB, which represents his theory of the seven major functions of management:

- Planning
- Organizing
- Staffing
- Directing
- Coordinating
- Reporting
- Budgeting

Until the mid- to late 1950s, any treatment of management in public administration was essentially an elaboration of POSDCORB. Often combined with an essentially scalar, or hierarchical, theory of organization, these principles of management had a kind of commonsense quality that was appealing to practicing public administrators as well as to those studying the field or preparing for practice. Early criticisms of the principles said they were top-down, they were essentially prescriptive, and they underemphasized natural forms of cooperation—but they formed the core of the field. From the 1930s to the 1950s, important modifications and adaptations were made to the principles of scientific management. Chester Barnard (1938) identified and set out the acceptance theory of authority, which argues that authority does not depend as much on persons of authority or on persons having authority as it depends on the willingness of others to accept or comply with directions or commands. In classic theory, it was argued that policy, instructions, guidance, and authority flowed down the hierarchy, and communication (what we would now call feedback) flowed up. Barnard demonstrated that considerable power accumulated at the base of the hierarchy, and that theories of effective management needed to be modified to account for the culture of work in an organization, the preferences and attitudes of the workers, and the extent to which there was agreement between workers' needs and interests and management policy and direction. He described the "functions of the executive" as having less to do with the formal principles of administration and more to do with securing workers' cooperation through effective communication, through workers' participation in production decisions, and through a demonstrated concern for workers' interests. In a sense, then, authority is delegated upward rather than directed downward.

Another modification to the principles of scientific management came as the result of the Hawthorne studies. These describe the Hawthorne effect, which explains worker productivity as a function of observers' attention rather than physical or contextual factors. Subsequent interpretations of the Hawthorne effect suggest that mere attention by observers is too simplistic, and that workers saw in the experiments altered forms of supervision that they preferred and that caused productivity to increase (Greenwood and Wrege 1986). The Hawthorne experiments and the work of Barnard introduced a human relations approach that forever changed management theory. Classical principles of scientific management and formal hierarchical structure were challenged by the human relations school of management theory, a body of theory particularly influenced by Douglas McGregor (1960). McGregor's Theory X and Theory Y represented an especially important change in management theory. Here are the competing assumptions of Theory X and Theory Y:

THEORY X ASSUMPTIONS

1. The average person dislikes work and will try to avoid it.
2. Most people need to be coerced, controlled, directed, and threatened with punishment to get them to work toward organizational goals.
3. The average person wants to be directed, shuns responsibility, has little ambition, and seeks security above all.

THEORY Y ASSUMPTIONS

1. Most people do not inherently dislike work; the physical effort and the mental effort involved are as natural as play or rest.
2. People will exercise self-direction and self-control to reach goals to which they are committed; external control and the threat of punishment are not the only means for ensuring effort toward goals.
3. Commitment to goals is a function of the rewards available, particularly rewards that satisfy esteem and self-actualization needs.
4. When conditions are favorable, the average person learns not only to accept but also to seek responsibility.
5. Many people have the capacity to exercise a high degree of creativity and innovation in solving organizational problems.
6. The intellectual potential of most individuals is only partially used in most organizations.

Following these assumptions, Theory X managers emphasize elaborate controls and oversight, and they motivate by economic incentives. Theory Y managers seek to integrate individual and organizational goals and to emphasize latitude in performing tasks; they seek to make work interesting and thereby encourage creativity.

It is important to point out that the work of Chester Barnard, the Hawthorne experiments, and McGregor was behavioral, which is to say that it was based on field research. The earlier work of Taylor and others, though it was called scientific management, was less a result of nonsystematic observations and more a result of deductive logic.

One important and different approach to management theory in the evolution of public administration is the sociology of Max Weber (1952), who founded the formal study of the large-scale complex organizations he labeled "bureaucracy." Although he did his work in the late nineteenth and early twentieth centuries, it was not generally available to Americans until after World War II. Weber's purpose was to describe the salient characteristics of enduring large-scale organizations, which he labeled "ideal types," ideal meaning commonly found or generally characteristic. He was particularly interested in rationality, or collective goal-oriented behavior, as in the rational organization. He was opposed to the class distinctions characteristic of Europe in the early twentieth century and to the resulting nepotism and spoils. He argued that rational bureaucracy practices a specialization of labor. Jobs are broken down into routine, well-defined tasks so that workers can perfect those tasks and so that job applicants can be tested in specialized areas to meet formal qualifications. He described the formal rules, procedures, and record-keeping characteristics of bureaucracies as well as their scalar, or hierarchic, characteristics. The bureaucracy, he argued, is impersonal and rational because individual selection and promotion are strictly on the basis of merit, scientifically determined.

Weber's bureaucracy was more popular with academics than with practitioners, and it is a theory of management only in the sense that it describes what he identified as characteristics commonly found in large and complex organizations that have endured. The critique of Weber's work is well established. The ideal type bureaucracy tends to inertia, resists change, is mechanistic rather than humanistic, and is subject to goal displacement and to trained incapacity. Bureaucracy, in the present day, has become the object of a political derision that blames the problems of government on the people and organizations that operate public programs. And bureaucracy is an equally popular whipping boy for scholars and consultants who seek to make public programs more effective. Despite all this criticism, Weber is acknowledged to have developed one of the most empirically accurate and universal descriptions of the large-scale complex organization in its time, a description that is often accurate even today.

No criticism of the principles of public administration was so devastating as Simon's critique (1946)—dismissing them as proverbs. He demonstrated that the principles of public administration were contradictory, had little ability to be generalized as theory, and were fuzzy and imprecise. In the place of the principles of management, which he found theoretically wanting, he developed what has become decision theory. This theory has had a profound influence on public administration, most of it good. But the obliteration of the principles of management as a straw man was not essential to the presentation of decision theory and to its eventual importance. The principles of management were obliterated, nevertheless—at least in the theoretical sense.

From the late 1950s through the mid-1980s, little serious theoretical work was done on management in public administration. The subject gradually disappeared in the texts as well as in the pages of the *Public Administration Review*. The irony is, of course, that management continued to be the core of public administration practice. It is no wonder that during this period there was a growing distance between public administration scholarship and theory and public administration practice.

During this period, fortunately, a strong interest in management theory in sociology, social psychology, and business administration continued. Much of this work was in the so-called middle-range theories, particularly group theory, role theory, and communications theory. More recently, this past decade has seen a rebirth in interest in management in public administration, with the prolific work of those involved with the Texas Education Excellence Project. The contributions of this literature are reviewed later.

Further, a revitalization of scientific management has started, with new empirical attention to Simon's critique of Gulick's POSDCORB-derived management principles. Kenneth Meier and John Bohte (2000) offer and test a theory that links span of control (the number of subordinates managed by a single supervisor) to bureaucratic performance. Interestingly, Meier and Bohte conclude that both Simon and Gulick were right. Simon's critique that there is no single correct span of control was supported, but so was Gulick's principle that smaller spans of control are preferable when the authority has more information and skill than the subordinates. Meier and Bohte (2003) followed this study with another that examined diversification of function, stability, and space, which Gulick viewed as the three important determinants of span of control. Gulick's hypotheses were supported, but Meier and Bohte found that span of control needs to be thought of within the context of organizational hierarchy: What matters for span of control at one level of an organization may not matter at another. This research suggests that the insights and utility of Gulick's management principles are far from over.

Group Theory

Theories of groups are primarily theories of organization rather than theories of management, but group theory has important implications for public management. Most of these implications have to do with contrasting approaches to managerial control. In classic management theory, control is exercised by policy, rules, regulations, and oversight. In group theory, the effective group will develop shared goals and values, norms of behavior, customs, and traditions (Homans 1950; Shaw 1981). Effective management in the context of group theory nurtures, cultivates, and supports group goals and norms that are compatible with and supportive of

TABLE 5.1   COMPARING TRADITIONAL
AND GROUP THEORIES OF MANAGEMENT CONTROLS

Characteristics	Managerial Controls	Group Controls
Means of control	Policy, rules, regulation, and oversight	Shared goals, values, and traditions
Sources of control	Mainly external mechanisms	Mainly internal motivation
Position design	Narrow subtasks; doing rather than thinking	Whole task; doing and thinking
Definition of duties	Fixed	Flexible, contingent
Accountability	Usually individual	Often in the group
Structure	Tall; top-down	Flat; mutual layered influence
Power	Emphasis on legitimate authority	Emphasis on relevant information and expertise
Responsibility	Performing individual tasks	Performance of work unit or group
Rewards	Extrinsic	Intrinsic
Innovation	Less likely	More likely
Employee reaction to management	Compliance	Commitment

institutional purposes and missions. Table 5.1 is a comparison of traditional forms of managerial controls and forms of control based on group theory.

Most aspects of group theory are now embedded in the public management literature, and many public managers seek to develop the kinds of group goals, motivation, and commitments that support public institutional goals. John Di-

Iulio Jr.'s research (1994) on the characteristics and management of the Federal Bureau of Prisons (BOP) demonstrates the power of group theory in public administration. In attempting to account for the behavior of BOP employees, DiIulio found principal-agent theory and rational choice theory weak. He turned to a version of group theory sometimes called the strong-culture organization, mixed with theories of leadership, to explain employee behavior:

> Rational choice theories of bureaucracy are neither illuminating nor helpful. In effect, rational choice theorists of bureaucracy are half-baked Barnardians. With [Chester] Barnard, they understand that organizations are devices for fostering and sustaining cooperation among self-interested individuals who have disparate beliefs, dissimilar motivations, and conflicting goals. With him, they recognize that the individual is always the basic factor in organization, that the "functions of the executive" are to induce self-interested workers to cooperate in ways that foster, rather than frustrate, achievement of organizational goals, and that money and other tangible goodies are often potent inducements.
>
> But the rational choice theorists miss the other half of Barnard—and no small part of human nature to boot. They discount the importance of what Barnard termed the "moral factor." . . . More broadly, they discount the tug of social sentiments and relegate the efficacy of moral motivations to a limbo of lesser behavioral reality.
>
> In sum, rational choice theorists of bureaucracy underestimate the propensity of people to redefine their self-interest in terms of the preferences of leaders they respect, the well-being of co-workers they care about, and the survival and reputation of organizations they labor for. It may well be true that under most conditions, most bureaucrats, especially within government, follow narrow definitions of self-interest. But that is neither the whole story nor the most important part of the story of what public servants—corrections officers, fire fighters, police officers, public health workers, social workers, and others—do on a day-to-day basis. Even in the bowels of government agencies, there is more self-sacrifice, and less self-interest, than rational choice theory allows. For the principled agents of the BOP and other government bureaucracies Americans can and should be proud and thankful. (1994, 288–289)

Role Theory

Social psychologists tend to define all human organizations as role systems. In observing organizations in action, we see that what are actually organized are the acts of individuals in particular positions or offices. In role theory, each office or position is understood to be relational; that is, each office is defined in its relationship to others and to the organization as a whole, and often to the organization's purposes.

Persons in roles exhibit essential persisting features of behavior, such as the behavior of school superintendents, prison wardens, or data entry workers. Role theorists observe and measure the persisting patterns of behavior of persons in common roles; they especially study the relations between persons in particular roles, both inside and outside the organization. Each officeholder performs in a role set, a contextual set of relationships with others who hold particular role expectations toward the officeholder.

Perhaps the best-known study in role theory was in the public sector, a study of school superintendents (Gross, Mason, and McEachern 1958). Persons and groups in the superintendents' role set include other internal roles such as teachers, principals, and members of the school board, as well as significant external roles, such as parents, parent-teacher organizations, business groups and leaders, social and fraternal groups, the state office of education, and so forth. School superintendents behave according to perceived role expectations; in the best of circumstances, superintendents' perceived role expectations will be accurate and compatible so that they will know what others expect of them and perceive a general agreement in the role expectations of others. Regrettably, this rarely happens, and superintendents are caught, or perceive themselves caught, in competing role expectations, described in role theory as cognitive dissonance.

Role theorists have consistently demonstrated that role occupants, such as school superintendents, tend to misperceive the role expectations of others. Ordinarily, this misperception exaggerates the strength, duration, and specificity of the positions of others and results in excessive managerial caution and organizational inertia.

Of course, real observable role conflict does occur. When the school superintendents experience genuine unresolvable role conflict regarding hiring, promotion, salaries, and budget matters, they tend to have low job satisfaction and will probably change jobs. One key to success is the ability of some school superintendents not to exaggerate the expectations of others and to find compromises that reduce conflict.

Higher levels of management tend to be associated with multiple roles, and sometimes role overload. Managers, however, tend to find greater job satisfaction as roles increase. The more roles a manager takes on, the greater the tendency to seek generalized, overall solutions, programmed solutions, one-size-fits-all answers. The greater the number of roles, the greater the tendency to use authority and sanctions and to search for one generalizable efficiency—often a short-term efficiency at that.

Henry Mintzberg (1992) used the concept of roles to identify the three primary managerial roles, a set of categories now widely used in management theory for business but equally applicable to management in public administration. Managers in their interpersonal roles can act as figureheads performing primarily symbolic duties, as leaders building relationships with subordinates, or as liaisons emphasizing contacts at the edges of the organization. In their informational roles, managers act as monitors seeking useful information, as disseminators transmitting information internally, or as spokespersons transmitting information outside the organization. In their managerial roles, managers are as entrepreneurs initiating and encouraging innovation, as disturbance handlers, as resource allocators, or as negotiators. Based on personal characteristics and the needs of organizations at particular points of time, managers take on combinations of these role characteristics.

There are now three excellent public administration descriptions of several of these role combinations: Mark H. Moore's *Creating Public Value: Strategic Management in Government* (1995); John M. Bryson and Barbara Crosby's *Leadership for the Common Good: Tackling Public Problems in a Shared-Power World* (1992); and Barry Bozeman and Jeffrey D. Straussman's *Public Management Strategies: Guidelines for Managerial Effectiveness* (1991). Each develops for the public sector several of the same theories Mintzberg developed for business.

Communication Theory

Much of what is understood to be public management depends upon effective communication. Communication theory is a mix of cybernetics, linguistics, and social psychology. The language of communication theory resembles the language of systems theory: inputs, throughputs, outputs, feedback loops, entropy, homeostasis. Although communication is always individual or singular, communication theorists tend to regard the work group or the organization as their unit of analysis, and in doing so, they anthropomorphize the organization. Anthropomorphic thought promotes organizational guessing, organizational memory, organizational consciousness, organizational culture, organizational will, and, especially, organizational learning—all of which are based upon communication. This logic is particularly helpful in building a management theory of communication, now a considerable body of knowledge (Garnett 1992).

The theory of communication found in public administration argues that most downward communication, or communication with subordinates, emphasizes task directives and organizational policy and procedures. The communication of agency mission and performance is often neglected, the result being low morale, preoccupation with routine tasks, and indifference to agency performance (Garnett 1992). Public managers overestimate the power of communication through memoranda, e-mail, telephone, and other such channels, and they underestimate the power of direct communications through or by managerial action. The use of internal models of effectiveness or examples of organizational success is an effective means of organizational learning. Effective communication occurs when managers establish work standards through collective means and provide feedback on performance as measured against agreed-upon standards. Keeping channels clear for upward communication is a staple in communication theory, as is the importance of redundant, multiple, and overlapping communication channels downward, upward, and laterally (Garnett 1992).

Effective communication with other agencies and with agency publics is an enduring feature of managerial communication theory. Communication between organizations is most often associated with shared professional training perspectives and with regular training. In a metropolitan area, city public works directors, chiefs of police, fire chiefs, and city administrators often communicate both formally and informally with their counterparts; indeed, lateral communication networks are often robust and enduring. It is sometimes said that a city public works director will spend more time communicating with other city public works directors in a metropolitan area than with other agency heads in his or her own city government (Frederickson 1997a). Lateral communication and coordination in complex organizations are aided by assigning key people to so-called lynchpin responsibilities (Likert 1961, 1967).

Communication with external publics ordinarily involves segmenting publics and specifically designed procedures for communicating agency positions, performance, services, and so forth. Agency communication with an interest group would differ from its communication with a legislative body or committee, or an individual member of that body, for example. Effective agency communication with publics has as much to do with receiving as with sending signals, most agencies being much better at the latter than the former. Incoming messages are often highly filtered, agency managers receiving bits and pieces of information but often not understanding the full substance or meaning of signals sent by publics. Selective listening is a persistent problem in public organizations (Garnett 1992).

Evolution of Management Theory

The most significant progress in management theory from the 1950s through the 1970s was in developing and testing middle-range theories such as group, role, and communication theories. Most of this work has been in the study of business management rather than public management and has now fully migrated to our literature. The middle-range theories, particularly group, role, and communication theory, are now the guts of management theory in business and public administration.

The text by Simon, Donald Smithburg, and Victor Thompson published in 1950 was far ahead of its competition, then and now, mostly because it used middle-range theory generously. For a generation, this text was the source of most faculty lectures on theories of management in the public sector (Simon 1991). Most of the texts written in the 1970s, 1980s, and 1990s treat budgeting and personnel staff functions as if they were management, and most do not include a separate treatment of management theory, let alone the middle-range theories that contribute to it.

The most complete treatment of middle-range theories in public administration is found in the now-out-of-print *Administrative Organization* by John Pfiffner and Frank P. Sherwood (1960). In it, the authors set out the formal structures of public organizations and then use the concept of overlays to describe how organizations actually behave and managers actually function. Overlays describe modifying processes and conditions and how they influence behavior and outcomes. A public organization is, for example, understood to have an important "group overlay" that should inform managers of group behavior; indeed, an effective manager should have a rudimentary theory of groups to help with management decisions and action. There are also role overlays, communication overlays, problem-solving overlays, and, most important, power overlays. Pfiffner and Sherwood's book stands as the most complete midcentury treatment of management theory in public administration. That it was in print only from 1960 to 1967 is evidence of the general lack of interest in the subject of management in the scholarly public administration of that era.

The good news is that management theory is back. We start with this question: After fifty years, has the positivist decision-theory founded by Simon met the promise of a body of empirically verified theory? Christopher Hood and Michael Jackson (1991) argue that the results disappoint on three counts. First, the old principles of management—Simon's proverbs—persist and even flourish. Second, there is no commonly accepted or agreed-upon theory or paradigm of management in public administration based on decision theory. Third, the positivist administrative science of decision theory appears to have had little effect on the day-to-day practices of public management, and the language, arguments, and influence of the principles of management in public organizations remain surprisingly "proverbial." "It seems that Simon's attack on the proverbial approach to administration might never have existed, for all the practical influence it has had on administrative argument" (1991, 21).

Building on his earlier "science of muddling through" critique of decision theory, Charles Lindblom, with David K. Cohen (1979), found that "professional social inquiry" such as decision-science seldom influences either public policy or public administration. Instead, an interactive process of argument, debate, the use of ordinary knowledge, and a form of social or organizational learning is not only a more commonly found form of social problem solving; it is also safer and less inclined to large-scale risk or error. Along the same lines, Giandomenico Majone, in his brilliant *Evidence, Argument, and Persuasion in the Policy Process* (1989), demonstrates that the skills of policy analysis and the capacity to engage in public problem solving are forms of a dialectic not unlike the arguments or debates of generally informed participants. This dialectic is less like the authoritative findings of a scientist and more like the debate or argument of lawyers.

Finally, as a research methodology and an epistemology, positivism is now less universally accepted than it was at midcentury. In part, this is because it has not lived up to its promise. More importantly, positivism, particularly the logical positivism that distinguished between values and facts, often failed to account for values, norms, and traditional political philosophy, and sometimes didn't even acknowledge them. Nevertheless, positivism and the canons of social science methodology and epistemology tend to dominate academic perspectives regarding management theory in public administration. In the practices of public administration, however, positivism is less influential.

As a way to distinguish between public management principles that are scientifically verifiable and principles that are simply understood and accepted, Hood and Jackson suggest that the principles are better understood as *doctrines*; and as doctrines, they are powerfully influential in both debating and carrying out policy. These doctrines, following Hood and Jackson, have six recurring features: (1) They are ubiquitous, found wherever there are organizations; (2) they are based on "soft data" and "soft logic," often lacking key elements and assumptions; (3) they are a constantly shifting "received view" or "received wisdom," having more to do with metaphor, rhetoric, packaging, and presentation and less to do with objectively or conclusively demonstrating the scientific superiority of one view over another; (4) they are often contradictory; (5) they are unstable, the changing fads and fashions of taste makers; and (6) they tend to rotate—old ideas dressed in new clothes (1991, 17–18).

Unlike scientifically verifiable principles, these doctrines are accepted for reasons best explained not by hard data but by the analytic techniques associated with rhetoric. In rhetoric, one persuades or influences another by developing a linguistic solution to a problem, or by "naming" the problem in a way that elicits general agreement about a course of action. The use of metaphor is key because all institutions are so-called cognitive paradigms grounded in shared understandings and meanings. One thinks of the deeply contentious contemporary debate over abortion in the United States. During his candidacy for president, Bill Clinton stated, "I am personally against abortion. Abortion is, however, the law of the land, but it should be safe, and rare." By repeating that statement, he seemed to find a center position acceptable to most, though not to those at the extremes.

Rhetoric requires the generous use of ambiguity, the crafting of general positions that can be favorably viewed from a wide spectrum of public positions. Positions must be aligned with the general or greater good. Arguments are selective, which means that evidence supporting the arguments is used, whereas contrary evidence is not. For rhetoric to be successful, those who listen to it or witness it must be willing to suspend disbelief, just as one does when watching good theater (Hood and Jackson 1991). A doctrine such as "a government that works better and costs less" has a powerful rhetorical appeal, is a "solution" that matches contemporary values, is ambiguous, is supported by selected best practices, is identified with the greater good, and, it being evident that costing less is at best unlikely, requires one to suspend disbelief.

The problem, of course, is that a theory of management in public administration built on such an epistemology is decidedly out of phase with ordinary definitions of science. The "doctrines of management" model tested by the logic of rhetoric is at once postmodern and retrograde, an up-to-date version of Aristotle's description (1932) of linguistic solutions to social problems. From the perspective of those who actually practice policymaking and public administration, the logic of the doctrines of management is a close theoretical approximation of reality—certainly much closer than theories of rational choice or decisionmaking—but the latter have a much greater cachet in the academy.

The doctrines of administration can be described this way (this is a considerably adapted, much simplified and condensed version of doctrines found in Hood and Jackson [1991, 34–35]):

1. Doctrines of scale
   a. Large, intermediate, small
   b. Centralized, decentralized
2. Doctrines of service provision (how organized and managed)
   a. Direct governmental service
   b. Contracting out
   c. Privatization
3. Doctrines of service provision (citizen or client choices)
   a. Compel both costs and benefits
   b. Allow choices of either costs or benefits
4. Doctrines of specialization
   a. By characteristics of work
   b. By characteristics of clientele
   c. By location
   d. By process
   e. By purpose
5. Doctrines of Control
   a. By input—budget, staff size
   b. By process
   c. By competition
   d. By standards of professional practice
   e. By outputs
   f. By outcomes
   g. By direct political control
   h. By direct administrative control

6. Doctrines of discretion
    a. By law and regulation
    b. By professional latitude
    c. By deregulation
    d. By risk taking
7. Doctrines of employment
    a. Selected and promoted by merit
    b. Selected by representation of groups
    c. Selected by technical skills
    d. Selected by administration skills
    e. Selected by cultural skills
8. Doctrines of leadership
    a. Direct political leadership
    b. Direct administrative leadership
    c. Neutral competence/professional expertise
    d. Entrepreneurshipl/advocacy
9. Doctrines of purpose
    a. Carry out the law
    b. Maintain orderly and reliable institutions
    c. Facilitate change
    d. Add value

Another way to think about the doctrines of public management is to turn to the enduring questions of management: Under what circumstances are neutral competence and professional expertise more important than political responsiveness? What, on the other hand, are the circumstances under which political responsiveness is more important than neutral competence and professional expertise? What are the technological, geographic, and managerial issues that determine whether an organization should centralize or decentralize? What ought to be the criteria or standards for appointment and promotion in public employment? How much discretion should be allowed to street-level bureaucrats and their managers? These, and similar questions, summarized previously as doctrines, were addressed by the early principles and the contemporary doctrines. The questions are essentially the same, but the answers are very different. Table 5.2 compares the answers to these questions found in traditional and contemporary principles.

The influential modern literature on management in public administration powerfully illustrates how the principles are reemerging. Virtually all of it uses the logic of rhetoric, selective case-based empirical "evidence," and a kind of missionary zeal (Graham and Hays 1993; Rainey and Steinbauer 1999; Osborne and Gaebler 1992; Barzelay 1992; Cohen and Eimicke 1995). Very often missionaries,

TABLE 5.2   COMPARISONS OF TRADITIONAL
AND CONTEMPORARY PRINCIPLES OF MANAGEMENT
IN PUBLIC ADMINISTRATION

Doctrine	*Traditional Principles*	*Contemporary Principles*
Scale	Large—centralized	Small—decentralized
Service Provision	Direct government service	Contract out
	Compel costs and benefits	Choices in costs and benefits
Specialization	By characteristics of work	By characteristics of clientele
	By work processes and purpose	By location
Control	By professional practice standards	By competition
	By inputs (budgets, staff size)	By outcomes
	By outputs, processes	By administrative
	By administration	
Discretion	By laws, regulations	By deregulation
	By professional latitude	By risk taking
Employment	By merit, affirmative action, technical skill	Same
Leadership	Based on neutral competence	Based on entrepreneurial advocating
	Professional expertise	
Purpose	To carry out the law	To facilitate change
	To manage orderly and reliable institutions	To create public value

not to mention politicians, consultants, and academics, find their work easier if there is a devil, an evil empire, or a straw man. In public management theory, the devil is BUREAUCRACY. Preferred doctrines of public management are suggested as ways to "banish bureaucracy or to reinvent government: how the entrepreneurial spirit is transforming the public sector from schoolhouse to statehouse, city hall to the Pentagon" (Osborne and Gaebler 1992). These doctrines are argued, just as the principles were eighty years ago, on the observation of so-called best practices rather than on replicable social science (Osborne and Gaebler 1992; Cohen and Eimicke 1995). Nevertheless, the modern principles of entrepreneurial public management are now nearly a hegemony in the practices of public administration.

These doctrines have been given, or have taken, the name New Public Management (NPM) and are sometimes referred to as the "new managerialism." They have a particularly strong base in Western Europe, Australia, and New Zealand, as well as in the United States. The Organization for Economic Co-operation and Development is a particularly strong advocate of the New Public Management and encourages countries to adopt its principles. Although there is an extensive scholarly critique of NPM, it is a safe generalization that its principles have been widely accepted in the modern practice of public administration (Frederickson 1997b). Whether the application of these principles is better government, and particularly better government for whom, is subject to debate. No doubt the application of the early principles of management did result in cleaner, more efficient, and more professional government. But with that has come larger and more expensive government.

NPM is presently very influential in the practices of public administration. In a postmodern and rhetorical sense, the New Public Management can be explained and understood as presently acceptable doctrines of management. But the canons of social science demand a more precise identification of variables, more precision in the suggested association between variables, greater precision in measurement, and a greater replication of findings. Research using these techniques indicates that NPM principles can result in a selective and short-run increase in efficiency; are negatively associated with fairness, equity, or justice; seldom reduce costs; and have produced numerous innovative ways to accomplish public or collective purposes (Berry, Chackerian, and Wechsler 1995; DiIulio, Garvey, and Kettl 1993).

A particularly pointed empirical critique of NPM comes from Kenneth Meier and Laurence O'Toole (2009), who base their inferences on an extensive series of studies on public management produced by those involved with the Texas Education Excellence Project, which has recently been subsumed into the more encompassing Project for Equity, Representation, and Governance. The sum of this work allowed Meier and O'Toole to evaluate ten "proverbs" of NPM against the evidence from the project. Specifically, they find the following:

1. Contracting out is often not done for reasons of performance and efficiency, but rather to get rid of problems.
2. Lean and delayered organizations are vulnerable to external stress, such as budget cuts or other emergencies.
3. Good management is not necessarily good for everyone. The distributional consequences of management can affect some clientele more than others. If equity is a concern, this is a troubling finding.
4. Organizations that are stable can perform well and adapt to changes in their environment, and managerial flexibility is not a necessary component of change.
5. Organizations are not at the mercy of their political environments. Decisions to network are choices rather than functions of the environment. Fur-

ther, organizations need not even match their environment; networking can be effective in a hierarchical environment, and hierarchy can help in a networked environment.

6. Change-oriented managers are not necessarily better than conservative managers. Change-oriented management works best only when the political environment is stable. When the environment is less stable, a more conservative approach is more effective.

7. Skilled management can overcome some of the failures of political actors. When political institutions fail to represent citizens, agencies with skilled managers can still be successful.

8. Rather than good managers making all the difference, they make *some* difference. Managers cannot do everything, and even though good management matters, it can not be the "solvent for a wide range of economic and social ills" (Pollitt 1990, 1).

9. There is not necessarily a pattern to follow that will produce good management. Good managers consider their skills and the needs of their organizations, and then make decisions about what to do.

10. Good managers do not necessarily have to choose between competing goals. They take advantage of positive spillovers, and use training and incentives to simultaneously achieve goals that are normally thought to require tradeoffs.

Meier and O'Toole are not simply pointing out the limits of NPM; their argument is that to advance public management theory—and certainly to improve management practices—we need sustained, rigorous, empirical research. Improving the study of public management requires hard data rather than the repackaging of principles into doctrines and their sale under a new acronym.

Leadership as Public Management

The most interesting aspect of management's resurgence in public administration is the prominence of leadership as an energizing and legitimating idea. The sources of contemporary literature on leadership in public administration are found in the schools of public policy or policy study. Most were established in the 1970s at many of America's most prestigious universities, in several replacing or subsuming existing graduate programs in public administration. Together they formed the American Association for Policy Analysis, later changed to the American Association for Policy Analysis and Management, and established the *Journal of Policy Analysis and Management*, now in its sixteenth year. One part of the agreed-upon or understood methodology was the case study, preferably with participant observation, designed to escape "the dead hand of social science." Policy analysis, particularly the tools of microeconomics, was the second acceptable form of methodology. The approach is interdisciplinary, following Lasswell's description of the policy sciences.

In the early years, the scholarship emanating from the schools of policy study mostly consisted of cases and policy analysis, the most famous being Graham Allison's description (1971) of high policymaking as bureaucratic politics in the Cuban missile crisis. In the Allison perspective, bureaucratic politics means the mingling of outside informed experts, agency or departmental officials, and political (usually appointed rather than elected) officials to solve problems. Bureaucratic politics came to be a preferred way to theorize about the role of public managers in making policy, certainly preferable to theorizing about the day-to-day management of a bureau or an office. Bureaucrats, in high policy, are understood to be leaders, a very legitimating perspective.

Over time, the leadership approach to management has grown and is now in full flower. Leadership is among the leading topics in the hundreds of cases in the heavily used Kennedy School of Government Case Program. The study of management in the policy schools has come to be the study of what leaders do, rather than the study of management theories, in either the original or the contemporary form.

Robert D. Behn (1991) describes leadership as the key to improved performance in the Massachusetts Welfare, Training, and Employment Program. The quality of education in elementary schools can be found in leadership (Meier, Wrinkle, and Polinard 1999). What determines the quality of a prison? Leadership (DiIulio 1987). In the Terry L. Cooper and N. Dale Wright (1992) collection, the legendary role of Robert Moses and Austin Tobin in the development of the New York Port Authority is explored. The collection also contains impressive studies of William Ruckelshous (Dobel); Elmer Staats (Frederickson); C. Everett Koop (Bowman); Elsa Porter (Radin); Marie Ragghiaonti (Hejka-Ekins); Beverly Myers (Stivers); George Marshall and J. Edgar Hoover (Hart and Hart); and George P. Hartzog (Sherwood). Even Daryl Gates, the sheriff of Los Angeles County before the Rodney King incident in 1996, is presented as a leader (Moore 1995).

Distinctions between leadership and management are sometimes found, the most famous being the Warren Bennis couplet "The manager does things right; the leader does the right thing" (2003, 42). Bennis argues that there is too much management and not enough leadership, particularly in American business. Ronald Heifetz (1994) uses group theory and communication theory to formulate a particularly perceptive argument that leadership is helping groups and organizations do "adaptive work" and that it is particularly difficult to do that from positions of authority. There is not much convincing evidence that there is an important distinction between leadership and management, aside from labeling some things as leadership and therefore important, and other things as management and therefore less important.

In the bigger picture, the emphasis on leadership in public administration has doubtless been influenced by the general resurgence in the study of leadership in many fields and disciplines. The two best treatments of public management as leadership are Mark H. Moore's *Creating Public Value: Strategic Management in Government* (1995) and Heifitz's *Leadership Without Easy Answers* (1994). Neither of them relies on the principles of management, although Moore references much of the NPM literature. The characteristic or quality of leadership that Moore identifies after reviewing many of the case studies in the Harvard collection is

> a certain kind of consciousness: [leaders] are imaginative, purposeful, enterprising, and calculating. They focus on increasing the value of the organizations that lead to the broader society. In search of value, their minds range freely across the concrete circumstances of today seeking opportunities for tomorrow. Based on the potential they see, they calculate what to do: how to define their purposes, engage their political overseers and coproducers, and guide their organizations' operation. Then, most remarkable of all, they go ahead and do what their calculations suggest they should. (1995, 293)

These findings are a kind of leadership version of the best practices research found in the NPM literature, and like that research, they are grounded in direct observations that describe or account for singular events that are difficult to replicate. This is theory built on soft, qualitative findings, difficult to replicate and equally difficult as a body of knowledge or data from which one might draw defensible findings or conclusions. This research is unquestionably a series of fairly clear snapshots of what has happened and how it happened in individual cases, recognizing the biases of the camera operator.

Perhaps a better way to view this framework is taken from cultural anthropology, where it is assumed, first, that "reality" is a social construction rather than an objective thing or phenomenon that is the same for all observers; and, second, that organizations are a system of socially constructed and cognitively ordered meanings (Lynn 1996; Boisot 1986; Weick 1995). This form of knowledge is tacit, understood, often unspoken, but generally shared and accepted; it is also understood to be inherently vague, ambiguous, and uncertain, but is nevertheless often an important guide for behavior. "Codified knowledge, in contrast, is more impersonal, associated less with proper socialization or experience than with skill in abstract thinking or linear reasoning" (Lynn 1996, 112).

Laurence E. Lynn Jr. makes informative observations on this form of managerial theory:

> Some types of knowledge are easier to come by, because they are more linear and impersonal than others. Considerations of deference and trust do not intrude. We may call such knowledge "scientific" or "technocratic." Uncodified, undiffused

knowledge, e.g., the tacit, intuitive knowledge of a wise and experienced manager who communicates primarily in face-to-face forums and by the example of behavior, is difficult to master in any conventional sense because considerations other than the literal and the logical are involved. We may call such difficult-to-acquire mastery "artistic."

For codified, technocratic knowledge, the university course, the supervised workshop, and the problem set or other formal assignment, all emphasizing individual goal achievement, may be the most efficient approaches to learning. For tacit, artistic knowledge, mentorship, apprenticeship, and internship tending toward socialization—and perhaps prolonged on-the-job experience—are likely to be the most efficient ways to promote learning. Where both types of knowledge, or their subtle integration, are required for success, vicarious experience in simulated work situations featuring both social and intellectual demands—for example, case discussions requiring the application of a mix of analytic frameworks—may be the appropriate approach to learning. (1996, 113)

Managing by Contract

The contracting-out phenomenon goes by several names—government by proxy (Kettl 1993b); third-party government (Smith and Lipsky 1993; Salamon 1989); hollow government; the hollow state (Milward 1994, 1996; Milward and Provan 2000a); shadow government and the contracting regime (Kettl 1988; Egger 2006). Contracting out is also a theory of the control of bureaucracy and of organization theory. Here we will deal only with contemporary government contracting as a theory of management.

Contracting out is a key feature of the contemporary doctrines of management in public administration. Since the mid-1990s, a steadily increasing percentage of public activities has been carried out "indirectly" by contractors and for virtually every conceivable government function (Kettl 1993b). Most theories of management assume a contained or bounded institution with managerial responsibilities for directing the day-to-day internal functioning of the organization as well as responsibility for conducting boundary transactions that link the organization to other organizations and to its publics. The work of public administrators is increasingly not this kind of management; it is, instead, the management of contracts. Virtually all the capital functions of state and local governments have always been done by contract, primarily with architectural firms; building contractors; bridge builders; highway construction and maintenance firms; sewer, sanitation, water works, and systems companies; and dam builders. The US Defense Department has always contracted for airplanes, ships, tanks, guns, and war technology. Most of the work of the National Aeronautics and Space Administration and the

Department of Energy is done by contract. It is estimated that one-sixth of total federal spending (including entitlement) has gone to contractors (Milward 1994); this amount, as shown by federal spending figures, has been more than matched during the 2000s. The federal government has many more civilian employees on the "contract" payroll than on the actual civilian payroll (Frederickson 1997b). It has been shown that cuts in the federal workforce can result in an increase in the contract payroll (Light 1999).

With this background, we turn to issues of management theory, and ask these questions: Can government by contract be properly considered a form of management? What would be the salient feature of a management theory that assumed work is being done by contract?

Can government by contract be thought of as a form of public management? The answer is yes. Contract management is, however, different from traditional management in many significant ways and therefore requires a somewhat different theory. It is fashionable to use principal-agent theory to explain the contracting regime as an organizational scheme, and the theory is useful for that purpose. But principal-agent theory offers little to management theory, particularly when compared with traditional theory, which is based on the direct study of managerial behavior and managerial options in contract circumstances. The "findings" based on these observations would include those discussed in the following paragraphs.

First, the oldest and still one of the largest forms of contracting out is for capital construction and repair and maintenance purposes, particularly at the state and local levels of government. To be effective, such contracts must be highly precise regarding the quality of materials and workmanship, schedule, and the like. Contractors are ordinarily held to very tight specifications. The contracting government, particularly for large-scale contracts, ordinarily has an on-site project manager who often has czarlike powers and who carefully watches to see that the contractor complies with specifications. The contracting firm is usually organized and managed in the so-called project management style, which brings together several skills and technologies. Large contracting firms almost always use a matrix organizational form showing established skill-based departments that assign workers to projects (Davis and Laurence 1977). The critical point in the contract is the link between the government's project manager (principal) and the firm's project manager (agent). To be effective, a combination of extensive technological knowledge, trust, and toughness must be evident (Donahue 1989).

One of the best studies of contracting and privatization concludes that contracting works best when (1) what needs to be done can be clearly and precisely described for purposes of contract negotiation and compliance; (2) desired outcomes can readily and easily be measured or identified; (3) penalties are imposed for noncompliance with the contract; and (4) contractors may be discontinued or changed (Donahue 1989). Contracting for the construction and maintenance of buildings, highways, bridges, and other capital facilities tends to meet these criteria. As long as the four criteria are met, principal-agent theory can adequately explain management by contract. The reason for our skepticism about the value of principal-agent theory here is that these criteria are rarely met.

The key theoretical points here are the differences between a continuing permanent hierarchy and a contract. In the former, motivation, worker acceptance of directives, group behavior, role differentiation, and managerial style are all critically important. In the latter, these requirements are exported to the contracting firm, leaving government management to entail contract monitoring and oversight. In capital contracting for discrete projects, there are usually many qualified bidders, or, put another way, a genuine market and a capacity on the part of the government to get the best product at the best price (Rehfuss 1989).

Because of cost controls on government, fewer and fewer public employees become responsible for more and more contracts. This situation reduces contract management to paper shuffling and auditing (Kettl 1993b; Rehfuss 1989; Cigler 1990; DeHoog 1984). State and local governments have diminished the capacity for contract management and oversight and are gradually being hollowed out. The problem, then, is not the theory of management by contract so much as it is the application of the New Public Management concepts, and particularly contracting out, without providing for effective contract management.

Second, contracts for large-scale weapons systems, for airplanes, for space projects, and for research and development are another matter. Ordinarily, only a few qualified bidders are available, and it is in the government's interest to underwrite in some form the capabilities of the limited number of potential contractors. The idea of a market, therefore, is less applicable in this form of contracting because there is little competition. It is often difficult to know in advance the final cost of a contract. The government may specify a preferred result or outcome in a given period but fail to know precisely how that outcome will be achieved. It is possible to know in advance how to build a building or a bridge. It is possible to "know" that ways can be found to cure diseases, clean up toxic dumps, and destroy incoming missiles; but because we do not know *how* to do these things, governments contract with technically qualified organizations to attempt to find answers. This form of contracting is riskier and the results less predictable than contracting for capital projects.

The project management approach is the most commonly used theory of management for contracts of this sort (Cleary and Henry 1989). But as Donald F. Kettl (1993b) puts it, very often the government is not a "smart buyer." The capacity to be a smart buyer depends on the quality of the market. If the market has genuine competition, as happens when construction companies bid for capital projects, the government may have the capacity to be a smart buyer. When it is clear what the government wants and can easily determine the quality of those goods or services, the government can be a smart buyer. But when these conditions fail to materialize, as often happens, the government is faced with so-called market imperfections. Kettl, who bases his results on his splendid study of government contracting, sets out the following hypotheses about what happens when market imperfections increase:

1. Interdependence among buyers (government) and sellers (contractors) increases.
2. Boundaries between public and private are blurred, making it difficult to know what functions or activities are governmental or public.
3. The problem of absorbing uncertainties increases.
4. Buyers and sellers become more highly coupled, making their interests indistinguishable.
5. Conflicts of interest on the part of contractors reduce the quality and quantity of information they supply government.
6. Internal organizational cultures become more important than market incentives.
7. Organizational capacity for learning declines and the likelihood of instability increases. (1993b, 179–197)

For management theory, it appears that by contracting out, governments export some management issues, such as the day-to-day direction of activities, contacts with clients or customers, the organization of work, and the supervision and motivation of workers. Contracting redefines administrative discretion by delegating it to buyers. And contracting appears to decrease public management responsibility for orderly and reliable institutions and increase the long-range probability of instability. For management objectives, contracting does save money, but not primarily because of improved management. Contractors save money through greater flexibility with workers, including lower pay, fewer benefits, and more part-time work (Kettl 1993b).

Third, the social services have seen the most rapid growth in contracting, estimated to have grown from 25 percent to over 50 percent in the 1980s (Chi, Devlin, and Masterman 1989), and includes daycare centers, mental health services, foster care, drug and alcohol rehabilitation, adoption services, elderly services, job training, community development, Medicaid, and others. Contracting for social services moved from the periphery to the center of the welfare state when states were given greater latitude in service delivery and eligibility standards as part of welfare reform (National Commission for Employment Policy 1988). Most social services contracts are not put out for bid but are negotiated with one, usually continuing, provider. Contractors seldom change because the market is limited. Goals are hard to define, making it difficult to measure outcomes or performance. Rather than a market or a government monopoly, the contracting of social services is best understood as a negotiated network. The management doctrines and skills required to be effective in negotiated networks are treated in the next section on governance.

Nonprofit organizations are usually the contract agencies for social services. Compared to government hierarchies, nonprofits employ fewer professionals, recruit more volunteers, and hire more part-time and nonpermanent workers at lower salaries and benefits (Smith and Lipsky 1993). The top professionals in these nonprofit organizations have considerably higher incomes, however, than their counterparts in government hierarchies (Herzlinger and Krasker 1987). These professionals tend to find nonprofit settings particularly attractive because opportunities for wider discretion and greater commitment are more plentiful there than in government hierarchies (Majone 1984).

To counter the trend to deprofessionalize, governments have increasingly required contractors to employ qualified professionals, obtain the appropriate licenses, and be able to withstand facilities inspections and audits (Smith and Lipsky 1993). Still, most contracting social service agencies keep costs down by deprofessionalizing. Steven Smith and Michael Lipsky claim that "the restrictions on professional practice in all types of nonprofit agencies receiving government funds combined with low wages, job insecurity, and intractable social problems have made nonprofit agencies in general less attractive work environments for human service workers. Loyalty to the agency fades when there is no advantage to working in one place rather than another" (1993, 117). As a result, workers in nonprofit social service organizations have shown declining morale (Smith and Lipsky 1993).

Smith and Lipsky describe the tasks of nonprofit social service managers in several ways. *First*, there is the problem of cash flow. Governments are notoriously slow, feeble, and unpredictable in making reimbursements for services already rendered, seldom a problem in a government hierarchy. *Second*, nonprofit social service organizations usually have a board of directors that sets policy and hires the top executives. These boards may stay at the policy level and simply direct the way of the organization; but they may also be meddling micromanagers. *Third*, renegotiating the contract and bidding for new contracts are a nonprofit way of life. *Fourth*, governments contract out to hold down costs and to increase flexibility; nonprofits are constantly reconfiguring their structures, processes, and payrolls to squeeze out those savings and remain competitive bidders. *Fifth*, the "dance of contract renewal" is often protracted and political, requiring managers to devote large amounts of time to survival activities. In summary, compared to the hierarchical government social service director, the nonprofit manager is more concerned with survival, cash flow, and the politics of a board of directors. This nonprofit manager is almost always very entrepreneurial and shows a high tolerance for the tensions of contract renewal; this manager also enjoys much greater latitude in the management of the nonprofit organization than does the hierarchical government manager.

After an extensive study of four nonprofit mental health service providers under government contract, Keith Provan and H. Brinton Milward (1995) determined that a stable and continuing relationship with government funders contributed to higher performance. Network management was more effective when it was centralized and monopolistic. Resource-rich governments and their contractors were more effective than resource-starved governments. Finally, direct funding to a stable, centralized, monopolistic provider proved the most effective.

Having described these and other differences between contract management and ordinary public management, we close this section with a brief consideration of how government can be an effective and smart buyer. Following Kettl (1993b), it is essential to recognize that contract management is a growing and important form of public management. It has made for smaller government in the sense of there being fewer employees. But it has not made government a smart buyer. Indeed, a smart-buying government must have a somewhat different kind of bureaucracy, one with many more frontline bureaucrats trained, hired, and rewarded to do contract management. Midlevel bureaucrats must be trained in a contract-theoretic form of management. Elected officials, consultants, and academics should lower the rhetoric that has done so much to establish the NPM hegemony and the contract regime. Governments should avoid contracting for core government functions. Governments as well as public administration scholars and practitioners should recognize that the application of market methods in the public sector raises important new issues of governance, the subject to which we now turn.

Governance

Although governance is the subject of Chapter 9, here we take up several important implications of governance for management theory. The implications for governance of management by contract have only recently begun to be explored. Milward and Provan (2000a) showed that as of 2000 the effect of contracting on citizens' perceptions of the legitimacy of the government had not been addressed, nor had questions of how to govern networks. Although our knowledge has developed over the intervening years, the questions still remain. The answers will almost certainly center on how networks are managed, since the hollow state's main task is to "arrange networks rather than to carry out the traditional task of government, which is to manage hierarchies" (Milward and Provan 2000a, 362).

Note that this implies a need for theories of management to incorporate networks and contract management into our understanding of public administration. Our skepticism of the ability of principle-agency theory to adequately explain management by contract is now more clear: A hollow state is not engaged in that type of relationship. Indeed, as demonstrated by David Van Slyke (2007), agency theory assumptions need to be relaxed per Kathleen Eisenhardt's suggestion to account for the contextual elements of the relationship, such as the length of time the parties have been in contact and the level of conflict, in order to accurately explain contracting relationships. By comparing agency theory with stewardship theory as proposed by James H. Davis, Lex Donaldson, and F. David Schoorman (1997), Van Slyke shows that contracting relationships can change over time, as trust replaces some of the need for monitoring. Relationships that start out with an emphasis on control, per agency theory, can change to ones based on goal convergence. However, he also shows that there is room for the development of a hybrid approach that combines agency theory with stewardship, since reputation can be developed in a steward relationship, but then used as a reward to promote goal alignment, per agency theory.

One result of contracting that is important for governance is the increased influence of organized interests on agency decisionmaking (Kelleher and Yackee 2009). Simply put, contracts open a new way for organized interests to lobby public managers, which Christine Kelleher and Susan Webb Yackee identify as a "contract pathway." This pathway has implications for governance, since the pathway raises the issue of trade-offs between equity and responsiveness (Wilson 1989). Kelleher and Yackee also point out that contractors may be viewed in two ways: positively as partners or negatively as special interests. These concerns about governance and politics surrounding contracting—as opposed to just market efficiency—indicate broader factors at play beyond what is predicted by NPM. Amir Hefetz and Mildred Warner (2004) show that managers understand the importance of monitoring, but also see the need for responsiveness. Importantly, they point out that agencies also contract back in as a way of carrying out their duties of providing quality service in a responsive manner.

Contracting may also have perverse effects on policy outcomes. Janice Dias and Steven Maynard-Moody (2007) show that the firm monitoring structures often present in contracts can create conflicts between management and workers, and distort the incentives for behavior on the part of the contractor. Emphasis on short-term production over long-term goals, or on maximizing output while minimizing costs, can create policy failure, since contracts such as these simply ignore the importance of public management. The key here is that a focus on establishing a principal-agent relationship, traditionally understood to be necessary for successful contracting, can actually come at the expense of success, rather than enhancing it. Clearly, the usefulness of agency theory and New Public Management approaches is being increasingly questioned. We can conclude that, even though management by contract is not new and is here to stay, we are only just beginning to fully understand its implications for governance.

Our discussion on contracting out described the changed functions of the public manager in a contract regime. Contracting, however described, weakens a manager's capacity to manage directly by delegating management. In the abstract and theoretical sense, those who support contracting argue that contracting out should allow managers to focus on goal setting, performance standards, and policy framing—referred to in the popular literature as steering—and leave the contractor to do the rowing (Osborne and Gaebler 1992). But the evidence appears to run in the other direction. Contracting appears to export not only the details of day-to-day government work but also much of the capacity to direct or to control policy (Peters 2000; Rhodes 1994). Several approaches to effective contract management have already been set out. Nevertheless, insofar as contracting out is part of the governance perspective, it is difficult to escape the conclusion that contracting may result in short-run savings and efficiencies as well as reduce the capacity of public managers to manage.

In addition, of course, is the matter of accountability. All systems of proxy management decrease the clarity of accountability. In tranquil times, this may not be a problem; but when there is a crisis, a lack of clear accountability in a contract or a chain of contracts and subcontracts is often the subject of political inquiry.

Conclusions

At its origins and for the first fifty years of the field, management was at the core of public administration. Because management is what most public administration professionals do, theories of management fundamentally informed the practices of public administration. But at about midcentury, American public administration scholars lost interest in management theory and turned to theories of rational choice and decisionmaking, loosening much of the early close connection between theory and practice. During this period, the field of business administration, as well as social scientists in the so-called middle-range theories (group theory, role theory, communication theory), was busy developing management theory. Then, starting in the mid-1980s, the study of management in the public sector began to reappear, although in new theoretical clothing and speaking a new language.

One form of this theory, principal-agent theory, has been of particular interest to scholars seeking to build knowledge of organizational and managerial behavior in the public sector. Principal-agent theory has made an important contribution to our understanding of the political control of bureaucracy, the subject of Chapter 2; has generally demonstrated that political principals do control administrative agents; and has added to our knowledge of some of the nuances of political control and administrative responsiveness. But principal-agent theory appears to be less useful as a basis for management theory in the public sector.

A second contemporary form of management theory in public administration is the so-called New Public Management, or the new managerialism. Like earlier reforms, it is partly imported from business management. Some of the business management theories of the 1960s and 1970s colonized public administration, such as management by objective and Total Quality Management. And the work of the middle-range theories has been widely adopted in the reemergence of management theories in public administration. And like earlier reforms, the NPM has often been the work of consultants, journalists, and politicians rather than the work of scholars. The primary reason for this is methodological and theoretical.

Among scholars, the emphasis is upon building theory and the body of knowledge. This requires the formal identification of variables, some precision in their measurement, a formal articulation concerning the relationships between variables, field-testing of those relationships, and the replication of findings. Little of the work associated with the New Public Management would satisfy the canons of social science.

Many management theorists in the newer schools of public policy represent an important exception among scholars. One of their arguments was that their scholarship should contribute directly to solving public problems and to ensuring better government management, and that this scholarship should not be held down by the "dead hand of social science." Their work tends to consist of observation-based case studies, inductive logic, and a kind of informed presentation of suggestions for either policy improvement or better management. It is often said that "this may be good management, but it is not very good science." Put another way, modern concepts of public management work in practice, but not in theory.

There is little doubt that the NPM has reconnected theory to practice. At all levels of government, public managers are reinventing government, reengineering government, attempting to be entrepreneurial, attempting to better serve their customers, attempting to be more innovative, attempting to take risks, and attempting to add value. Although it may not be good science, at least in the positivist conception of social science, the New Public Management is influential. It has replaced the old principles of public administration with a new set of principles, or doctrines. These are the doctrines of contracting out, decentralizing, granting greater discretion to managers, increasing citizen or customer choices, deregulating, organizing so that there is competition, and determining effectiveness according to outcome measurement. In applying these doctrines, the public manager must be a leader and an entrepreneur and must practice governance. But this leader/entrepreneur is still a bureaucrat. The irony is, therefore, that, although the New Public Management would banish bureaucracy, in fact it replaces bad bureaucracy with good bureaucracy by calling the latter something else!

Hood and Jackson, as well as Majone, suggest that the theory of New Public Management is best understood not as positivist social science but as the logic of rhetoric. This logic views the organization, the agency, or the government bureau as a "cognitive paradigm" of shared meanings and agreed-upon understandings. Organizations are moved or changed by adjustments in meanings and understandings, usually brought about by changing patterns of rhetoric. In management theory, the New Public Management doctrines are the contemporary "winning arguments" concerning how to manage government agencies. These winning arguments have more to do with received wisdom, with shifting metaphors, and with presentation and packaging than with objective, scientifically verifiable evidence.

Finally, in the contemporary theory of management in public administration, three particularly important concepts/metaphors dominate: leadership, contracting out, and governance. The modern emphasis is upon strong, heroic, muscular leaders rather than neutrally competent technocrats. But assertive administrative leadership in a political world always presented dangers, both to the logic of democratic self-government and to long-run bureaucratic effectiveness. The modern emphasis is on contracting rather than on direct government service. But contracts are often ill managed, and serious questions of accountability persist. Governance is the modern theory of network management and has a considerable empirical warrant.

The theory of management that was part of the inception of public administration made important contributions to improving the effectiveness and honesty of government in the United States. Only time will tell if contemporary management theory will have as lasting and profound an effect.

6

Postmodern Theory

The other families of theory described and evaluated in *The Public Administration Theory Primer* generally accept as their basic thesis the positivist canons of empirical social science. In contrast, postmodern public administration theory is the antithesis of positivism and the logic of objective social science. Indeed, postmodern theory rejects many of the basic epistemological assumptions of behavioral social science, and for that reason we initially had difficulty locating a chapter on postmodern theory in this book. But because postmodern theory has influenced institutional theory and public management theory, and has many adherents in public administration, some more orthodox and passionate than others, we judged a chapter on this theory necessary and relevant. More importantly, the various streams of the theory that have now combined and flow together in the river of postmodern theory have obviously influenced other bodies of theory covered in these pages.

Organizational Humanism and Postpositivism

The concept, ideas, and arguments that we lump together as postmodern theory have an interesting provenance in modern public administration.[1] Although arbitrary, it could be said that what is now thought of as postmodern public administration theory had its origin in the pioneering work of Chester Barnard (1948) and his interpretation of the results of the Hawthorne experiments (Roethlisberger and Dickson 1939). In contrast to the emphasis on formal organizational structure and the principles of management in very early public administration, Barnard described organizations as highly social environments in which workers are as interested in recognition and psychological support as they are in salary and favorable working conditions. In such settings, the informal features of day-to-day organizational functioning are more important than a formal bureaucratic structure in terms of both workers' satisfaction and productivity. Barnard's concepts were later simplified and put into philosophical context by Douglas McGregor (1960).

Individuals in organizations, McGregor argued, are naturally inclined to work, to seek responsibility, to cooperate, to be productive, and to take pride in their work. Organizations, however, are structured and managed on the assumption that employees dislike work and if given the chance will be lazy and will shirk, and because of this, directions and production quotas are necessary. By the mid-1960s, the humanistic or organizational humanism perspective in public administration was emerging, based largely on the work of Barnard and McGregor.

In the late 1960s, generally associated with what came to be known as the New Public Administration, a group of theorists resistant to what they believed were exaggerated claims to scientific validity in public administration met at Syracuse University's Minnowbrook Conference Center in upstate New York. They were concerned with what they judged to be the misuse of data and facts to justify continuation of the war in Vietnam, and they believed that behavioral and objective public administration was relevant neither to pressing public issues such as war, poverty, and racism, nor to the organization and management of public institutions. From the Minnowbrook Conference and many subsequent gatherings emerged a set of concepts that challenged the orthodoxy of the day.[2] Among the concepts and assumptions that emerged from Minnowbrook and the so-called New Public Administration that are now core ideas in postmodern public administration are these:

1. Public administrators and public agencies are not and cannot be either neutral or objective.
2. Technology is often dehumanizing.
3. Bureaucratic hierarchy is often ineffective as an organizational strategy.
4. Bureaucracies tend toward goal displacement and survival.
5. Cooperation, consensus, and democratic administration are more likely than the simple exercise of administrative authority to result in organizational effectiveness.
6. Modern concepts of public administration must be built on postbehavioral and postpositivist logic—more democratic, more adaptable, more responsive to changing social, economic, and political circumstances. (Marini 1971)

Over the years following Minnowbrook, some of the more humanistically oriented participants continued meeting, usually in unstructured forums that functioned more like a loose network than an organization. These meetings evolved into what is now the Public Administration Theory Network, or PATnet, the group of scholars most particularly identified with postpositivism and now postmodern theory. Two books were especially important in this evolution, Thomas S. Kuhn's *The Structure of Scientific Revolutions* (1962) and Peter L. Berger and Thomas Luckmann's *The Social Construction of Reality* (1967). From Kuhn came the generally shared conviction among PATnet members and postpositivists that building an entirely New Public Administration paradigm was both possible and necessary. From Berger and Luckmann came the belief that such a paradigm would be built on the foundation of postpositivist sociology, particularly on the logic of the social construction of reality. Much of the literature and theorizing now found in *Administrative Theory and Praxis*, the PATnet journal, reflect this theoretical perspective toward public administration. This perspective is rather fully illustrated by the key propositions and paradigmatic claims in Michael M. Harmon's *Action Theory for Public Administration* (1981):

1. In public administration, regarded both as a branch of social science and as a category of social practice, *paradigms* are appropriately conceived as theories of values and knowledge whose purposes are to improve administrative practice and integrate types of theory.
2. Beliefs about human nature are central to the development of theories in public administration as well as all other branches of social science. In order to provide the foundation for developing and integrating epistemology with descriptive and normative theory, these beliefs should be ontologically grounded rather than selected for reasons of convenience.
3. The primary unit of analysis in social theory should be the face-to-face situation (or encounter) between two people, which is preferred over the individual and over more encompassing units of analysis such as the group, the nation-state, or the "system."
4. People are by nature active rather than passive, and social rather than atomistic. This means that people have a measure of autonomy in determining their actions, which are at the same time bound up in a social context. This social context is necessary not only for instrumental purposes but also for the definition of people's status as humans.
5. People's "active-social" nature implies an epistemology (i.e., ground rules for determining the validity of knowledge), which focuses on the study of subjective meanings that people attach to their own actions and the actions of others.
6. Description and explanation in social science should be primarily concerned with *action*, a concept that directs attention to the everyday meanings people give their actions.
7. The concept of action provides the basis for challenging the adequacy of social science theory, whose fundamental orientation is toward the observation and analysis of behavior.
8. The primary conceptual issues in the development of a theory of values for public administration are the relation of substance to process and of individual to collective values.

9. The primary value in the development of a normative theory for public administration is mutuality, which is the normative premise deriving from the face-to-face relations (encounters) between active-social selves.

10. Just as descriptive theory about larger collectivities is derivative of the encounter, so, too, should normative theory about those collectivities be derived from mutuality, the normative expression of the encounter. The idea of social justice is the logical extension of mutuality applied to social collectivities and should therefore be regarded as the normative premise underlying "aggregate" policy decisions made by and implemented through public organizations. (Harmon 1981, 4–5)

Applications of postpositivism to public administration were informed by phenomenology, the philosophical argument that reliable scientific inquiry cannot be based on external observation by outside researchers. The actions of persons in collective settings can be understood only from the standpoint of the actors themselves (Denhardt 1993). The phenomenological approach seeks to determine how actors interpret their circumstances, the meaning they attach to those circumstances, and the patterns of interpretation between actors in collective settings (Harmon and Mayer 1986). In this perspective, meaning and the interpretation of meaning are at the core of administrative behavior:

> The world of meaning becomes central to a phenomenologist and represents a critical break with the technique of the natural sciences. All consciousness is consciousness of something: we seek something, we hope for something, we remember something. Every act of consciousness, as we reflect on it, bestows on our world meaning to which we in turn give order. The human capacity to endure action with meaning sets the reality to be examined by the social scientist, quite apart from the reality of the natural scientist, and therefore, the methodology of the natural scientist cannot be copied by the social scientist. Rather, the social scientist must seek ways to understand the structure of consciousness, the world of meanings of the social actor. (Denhardt 1993, 189)

Adherents to the phenomenological approach to research and theory in public administration tend to be grouped into the interpretive theorists camp, represented by Michael Harmon, and the critical theorists camp, represented by Robert Denhardt and Ralph P. Hummel.

Interpretive or action theory was at the time a rather straightforward challenge to the rational decision theory of the day (Harmon 1989). As we describe in Chapter 7, in the decision-theoretic perspective, the decision is the focal point of understanding administration. Thinking precedes deciding, and deciding precedes action. Decision-theoretic logic is built on an assumption of instrumental rationality insofar as it is possible to calculate the relationship between means and ends. In their rules, decisionmakers will rationally seek efficiency in the direction of preferred objectives, determined by some measure of the extent to which goals are being achieved (Harmon and Mayer 1986, 123).

Although modified over the years by satisficing and bounded rationality, decision theory nevertheless understands the decision to be the key unit of analysis. The action theory alternative argues that patterned relationships among thinking, deciding, and doing assumed in decision theory are seldom found. Furthermore, the dichotomy between facts and values and the dichotomy between means and ends were dismissed long ago (Lindblom 1965). As accurate representations of reality, facts, and values, means and ends are seldom so easily separated as decision theory suggests.

Action theory, the interpretive theory alternative to decision theory, claims the following:

1. The epistemological distinction between values and facts, however useful it may be for instrumental purposes, reflects an artificial reconstruction of the process by which the social world is constituted, maintained, and contested. These social processes are characterized initially by the fusion of what we have come to call "values" and "facts." Thus, the fundamental differences between the action and the decision perspectives are explainable by their differing stances regarding the epistemological priority of distinction.

2. The possible existence of the transcendent moral good inheres in the process by which social life is constituted rather than, at least chiefly, in ends that are ostensibly informed by values. Ends, including purposes and interests, may be seen as derived from and contingent on social processes. "Moral" is therefore not a synonym for values or ends, but rather describes a quality that inheres in acting subjects who are engaged in social interaction.

3. Social processes are principally processes of collective sense making through which social "facts" are produced by negotiation. By extension, organizations are chiefly structured contexts for sense making and only secondarily decisionmaking arrangements.

4. Rather than thought preceding action (linked by decisions), thought and action are mutually constitutive and coextensive. Decisions are not objectively real but are objectifications of the ongoing flow of social process. Informally, decisions may be thought of as "stopped processes."

In the action-theoretic perspective, organizational purpose and values can only emerge from social processes based on interactive patterns of action and the values attached to them. Harmon points out that "the good does not reside in preconceived purpose as informed by abstract thinking about moral values. Rather it is a function of the nature and quality of social relations through which purposes change" (1989, 149). The good, and the extent to which that good is being organizationally furthered, is a process of conscious interpretation on the part of those in organizations. It is also a process whereby researchers seek to understand administrative behavior and interpret actions and their meanings.

As a separate and distinct approach to public administration theory, the interpretive/action theory concept had limited traction. The ideas and concept upon which interpretative action theory is based, however, became central to what eventually became postmodern public administration theory.

Also resting on a phenomenological foundation, critical theory in the postpositivist tradition is especially influenced by Jürgen Habermas (1970, 1971) and the distinction among instrumental, interpretative, and critical reasoning. Modern social theory, following Habermas, is "infused with instrumental reason, which leads to unreflexive use of technique in the control of social relationships" (Harmon and Mayer 1986, 320). Critical reasoning seeks to "emancipate" these in collective settings from asymmetric power relations primarily through authentic discourse. In our day, the notion of emancipation is described as the empowerment of workers. It is through authentic discourse that truth claims can be tested and refined in the search for "hermeneutic" (the study of the relationship among reason, language, and knowledge) truth. Denhardt's application of critical theory states that

> a critical theory of public organizations would examine the technical basis of bureaucratic domination and the ideological justifications for this condition, and would ask in what ways members and clients of public bureaucracies might better understand the resultant limitations placed on their actions and in turn develop new modes of administrative praxis.
>
> In contrast to the emphasis on order and regulation that we find in the mainstream literature in public administration, a critical approach would emphasize the conditions of power and dependence that characterize contemporary organizational life and the considerable potential for conflict and disorder that these conditions portend. Such an approach would enable us to rethink issues of organizational change in dialectical terms, as a consequence of competing forces operating in a linguistic context, and would thus permit a more dynamic understanding of organizational life. Moreover, such an approach would reveal certain contradictions inherent in hierarchical organizations. By specifying the ways in which current relationships of power and dependence result in alienation and estrangement, critical theory of public organizations would suggest more direct attempts to improve the quality of organizational life. (1993, 203–204)

Hummel's approach to critical theory is somewhat broader and bolder. "Generations of newcomers," he writes, have subscribed to this advice: Think critically about work. We can now question *structure.* Is top-down command really necessary? Is it effective? Can hierarchy be flattened? Can division of labor be eased?

We can question *culture.* Are efficiency and control the only values to be pursued by bureaucracies, public and private? What about human purpose beyond these?

We can question *psychology.* Do we need to accept the destruction of our self when we enter employment?

We can question bureaucracy's devaluation of *speech.* Surely top-down commands shouted at us in an atmosphere of fear are not the only tools for getting us to do the work.

Finally, there is *the political question.* For a while it seemed there was no alternative to the bureaucratic transformation of politics. Efficiency and control had become the standards to measure success even there. Lost was any sense of political imagination. (1994, 2–3)

Those associated with both the interpretative and critical approaches to post-positivist public administration have tended to also be part of a developmental training movement. Put very simply, through developmental training individuals and organizations can more nearly achieve their potential. Training, now often called organizational learning or the learning organization, enables the organization and the individuals in it to trust more, to listen, and to practice authentic communication (Argyris 1962; Argyris and Schon 1978; Golembiewski 1972). The purpose of this kind of organizational intervention is to unfreeze bureaucratic rigidity and empower workers to achieve their potential. Organizational interventionists of this type are thought to be educators, researchers, and change agents all at once (Denhardt 1993). Although it has had its ups and downs over the years, the organizational development movement is alive and well; in its modern form, interventionists are usually called consultants, and the quest for human potential through training and intervention has given way to best practices, benchmarking, mixed scorecards, and other more modern fashions in contemporary organizational development.

The paradigmatic claims of postpositivism are most evident when their logic is applied to theories of organization and management. As often happens with paradigmatic arguments, they are as much metaphor as they are models or paradigms, and this is particularly so in presentations of the postmodern paradigm of organization and management. Furthermore, those making paradigmatic arguments stylize, exaggerate, and make a straw man out of one paradigm to make more impressive the counterparadigm they favor. The postpositivist critique of the characteristics and practices of classic organization and management describes them as more hierarchical, mechanical, determinate, and simplified than they really are. David Clark's (1985) paradigmatic comparisons are especially useful because he not only arrays contrasting (although stylized) concepts but also evaluates what he regards to be the success of the postpositivist paradigm. Notable is his general conclusion that the classic organizational paradigm and the positivist objective scientific logic that supports it have had remarkable staying power.

Clark's assessment of the status of the postpositivist paradigm, although somewhat dated, is still essentially accurate. For theoretical purposes, it is useful, although simplistic, to contain the number of variables considered in the evaluation of a public institution. The parsimony and elegance of an explanatory theory can be powerful and useful. Theories that attempt to explain everything and to account for the possible influence of all variables have the advantages of so-called thick description found in larger case studies. But they have the disadvantages, too: They cannot convincingly account for the two or three most powerful forces influencing an organization or a policy; nor can they convincingly eliminate interesting possibilities that do not pan out. The embrace of complexity in the postpositivist argument is very closely connected to other facets of the argument—particularly indeterminance, mutual causality, and morphogenesis. All these facets of postpositivist thought negatively evaluate the tendency of public institutions to be stable, predictable, orderly, and reliable. The determinate order of bureaucracy and its tendency to resist easy change, particularly change that would be externally imposed by change agents or internally achieved by empowered workers, are long-standing bugaboos to postpositivists out to make public institutions better. At the same time, our general understanding of actual patterns of organizational change has been considerably advanced through the use of the postpositivist logic of change as a discontinuous meander that is far less rational than positivist theory would predict (March and Olsen 1989). Patterns of organizational change are clearly not linear, but postpositivist characterizations of classic institutional theory as describing linear change processes were inaccurate to start with. Finally, hierarchy, a fundamental organizational problem from the postpositivist perspective, turns out to have remarkable staying power. Hierarchy persists, we have learned, because hierarchical organizations provide highly valued order, stability, and predictability not only to those who are expecting services from public institutions but also to those who work in them (Jaques 1990). Despite all the proposed alternatives to hierarchy, and despite the "pathology" of hierarchy, we have not been able to invent an equally reliable way to divide work, coordinate that work, and fix responsibility for it.

Among most of its adherents, postpositivism is not thought to be primarily antipositivist. Table 6.1 provides a summary of organizational paradigms. Among postpositivists and organizational humanists, there are theoretical challenges to social science epistemology, and pronounced challenges to change-resistant public bureaucracies. Nevertheless, most postpositivists have generally accepted empiricism and the logic of the accumulation of knowledge. Postpositivists, it could be

TABLE 6.1 PROFILES OF NEW AND CLASSIC ORGANIZATIONAL PARADIGMS

Organizations Are:

Commentary

Simple   Complex

`|—— x ———|    |————————|`

Classic Paradigm
Not a difficult call; the boundaries of a
classical bureaucracy are clear; so in fact are
the elements; operating efficiently and
effectively ought to be imagined as
the sum of its parts; one of its charms
is that it simplifies the operation of a
large, complex organization; bureaucracy
ideally achieves permanence and generality.

New Paradigm
Clearly the transitional paradigm has
introduced greater complexity to the field of
organizational studies. The boundaries of
classical bureaucracies were opened by
inquirers concerned with external constraints
and influences. The theorist of the individual
(expectancy, needs) introduced added critical
personal variables. Contingency theory and
bounded rationality strive to account for
complexity not found in Weberian models
but the limit has been nearly reached; the
model cannot stand added weight.

Hierarchic   Heterarchic

`|——— x ———|    |————————|`

Classic Paradigm
This characteristic is asserted axiomatically
in the Weberian paradigm; hierarchy is
essential and unchanging; rules are written
and binding; human action is oriented to a
hierarchy of functions; there are
commanders and commands, leaders and
followers.

New Paradigm
Little movement; the basic hierarchy is
essential and unchanging. The modifications
deal more with style and substance, e.g.,
recognition that slavish adherence to
hierarchal imperatives is ineffective,
emphasis on techniques of participatory
decisionmaking and decentralization. The
bureaucratic paradigm can tolerate only
minimal manipulation of its concepts of
order.

(Table 6.1 continued from page 139)

Determinate	Indeterminate	**Classic Paradigm**

├────X────────┤   ├──────────────┤

Classic Paradigm
The Weberian adjectives noted earlier define the classic paradigm as determinate, e.g., precisely, unambiguously, clearly, shared. And Weber's reflections on the characteristics of a bureaucratic system included calculability; note from Weber, bureaucracy is superior in precision, in stability, in the stringency of its discipline, and its reliability (Parsons 1947, 337).

New Paradigm
An interesting struggle has occurred on this characteristic within the dominant paradigm. Can one argue reasonably that no change is discernable and still recognize contingency theory, situational leadership, bounded rationality? I think not. However, the values held by those who work within that paradigm suggest that precision, clarity, calculability, and reliability are still what the game is all about.

Linear causality   Mutual causality

├────X────────┤   ├──────────────┤

Classic Paradigm
The rational, sequential characteristic of the bureaucratic paradigm demands a distinction between cause and effect; managers are instructed not to think in circles; mutual causality suggests that such circularity may be the only route to improvement; a bureaucratic paradigm is a rational sequential paradigm.

New Paradigm
Guba (1985) commented in his paper that the movement in inquiry on this characteristic has been from a linear view to Cook and Campbell's activity theory. That roughly matches the change in organizational theory. Contemporary theorists recognize multiple causality and mutual causality, discuss feedback and feed-forward loops, but finally deal with the issue as a transitory limitation to our understanding of organizations—a form of bounded causality.

Assembled   Morphogenic

├────X────────┤   ├──────────────┤

Classic Paradigm
A morphogenetic metaphor for organizational change was unimagined in the bureaucratic paradigm; the spontaneous, unpredictable, and discontinuous nature of the change process challenges the basic

(Table 6.1 continued from previous page)

		rational structure of bureaucratic functioning; again calculability is undermined, traditional organizational planning modes are useless.

New Paradigm
Natural selection and associated evolutionary models have received sufficient attention by organizational theorists to argue that the morphogenetic metaphor for organizational change is more tolerable than other characteristics of the new paradigm. The stumbling block is the extent to which rational selection dominates the use of the metaphor. The conflict arises around the issue of calculability in planning for or anticipating organizational change.

Objective   Perspectival

Classic Paradigm
Weber believed that bureaucracy portrayed a natural order; such a belief assumes the notion that there is an objective reality to be discovered out there; as Parsons noted, Weber linked the methodology of science to the substantive problems of rational action—that linkage led him to a both positivist and bureaucratic position.

New Paradigm
Modifications in this characteristic are more apparent than real. No one denies the impact of human constructions of reality on organizational behavior, but the theorists, researchers, and practioners are solid in their faith in a discoverable, objective reality out there.

SOURCE: David L. Clark 1985: 66–67.

said, display a kind of postenlightenment pessimism because social science has not delivered as promised. The positivist notion that the social world is orderly, that this order can be understood, described, and explained, and that accumulated knowledge thus attained can form the basis of theory is, in the view of most post-positivists, simply wrong. One of the two leading treatments of postmodernist public administration puts it this way:

We are urging movement away from the idea that there is a reality "out there" that a value-free research can account for by formulating law-like generalizations whose veracity is observable, testable, and cumulative. We reject the notion that the "what is?" question can be addressed credibly only by objective observers, as the emphasis on natural science would prescribe. Merely asking one question rather than some other question betrays some measure of subjectivity. If disinterestedness were required, there would be no inquiry. We acknowledge that the positivist project and its methodology have some validity; but exclusive reliance on it occludes many phenomena available to human perception. (Fox and Miller 1995, 79)

Although pessimistic about objective social science, most postpositivists would not, however, be generally described as antistate or antigovernmental. That would change with the coming of postmodernism.

Postmodern Perspectives in Public Administration

To attempt to understand postmodern public administration, one must begin with the postmodern characterization of modernity or high modernity. Modernity is the Enlightenment rejection of premodernity, of myths, mysteries, and traditional powers based on heredity or ordination. The Age of Reason rejected a natural order that subjugated many in the name of royalty or deity, and replaced that natural order with systems of democratic self-determination, capitalism, socialism, and Marxism. Equally importantly, the Age of Reason rejected knowledge based on superstition or prophecy and replaced it with knowledge based on science. All modern academic disciplines and fields of science are rooted in the Enlightenment and in an epistemology based on the objective observation of phenomena and the description, either quantitatively or qualitatively, of phenomena. Modernist epistemology assumes discernible patterns of order in both the physical and the social worlds, and in the social world it assumes a positivist and rational association between means and ends. Modernism is the pursuit of knowledge through reason, and knowledge thus derived is simply assumed to be factual and therefore true.

To postmodernists, modern public administration based on Enlightenment logic is simply misguided. In the first place, facts can neither speak nor write and cannot, therefore, speak for themselves (Farmer 1995, 18). Facts represent propositions or hypotheses derived from observation. In the telling of facts, therefore, the observer is not only an active shaper of the message sent but also an active shaper of the likely image received. In the second place, "the view that social science is a matter of cumulative accretion of knowledge through the work of the human subject neutrally observing the action and interaction of the objects—letting the facts speak for themselves—is untenable. It is difficult to cling to the view that the mind is some kind of possessive receptor of outside activities such as impressions or ideas" (Farmer 1995, 18).

Because the observer of facts is the teller of those facts, for postmodernists the language of that telling is important. The social construction of reality is language based, and language is at the core of the postmodern argument. Therefore, postmodern public administration is all about semantics and, as postmodernists put it, *text*. "Hermeneutics (the study of relationship between reason, language and knowledge) concerns texts; it is concerned with interpreting, with specifying significance, with achieving intelligibility. Texts, in this case, can be written texts or texts in the form of social practices, institutions, or other arrangements, or activities" (Farmer 1995, 21).

As we study or textualize our subject, we engage in a pattern of reflexive interpretation, a process of description, either qualitatively or quantitatively, that interprets reality in the form of reflex or response between the subject and the one describing the subject. Thus it is argued that public administration theory is, in fact, the language of public administration (Farmer 1995). The reflective language paradigm is, following David John Farmer, "a process of playful and attuned dialogs with the underlying content of the language of public bureaucracy . . . an art that seeks to draw out and use the consequence of hermeneutic, reflexive and linguistic character of the way in what we should understand and create public administration phenomenon" (1995, 12).

Postmodernists describe modern life as hyperreality, a blurring of the real and the unreal. Postmodernists such as Jean Baudrillard claim that a fundamental break with the modern era has occurred recently. Mass media, information systems, and technology are new forms of control that change politics and life. Boundaries between information and entertainment are imploding, as are boundaries between images and politics. Indeed, society itself is imploding. Postmodernity is the process of destroying meaning. The ideals of truth, rationality, certainty, and coherence are over because, for Baudrillard, history has ended. Postmodernity is characteristic "of a universe where there are no more definitions possible. . . . It has all been done. The extreme limit of these possibilities has been reached. . . . All that remains is to play with the pieces. Playing with pieces—that is postmodernism" (Baudrillard, quoted in Farmer 1995, 6). To the postmodernist, Disneyland is neither more nor less real than Los Angeles and the other suburbs surrounding it. All are hyperreality and simulation (Baudrillard 1984).

Modernity is also characterized in postmodernity as particularly authoritarian and unjust. Much of postmodern language has to do with the abuse of governmental power, including bureaucratic power. As such, postmodern theory is an affront to orthodox public administration based on a rational, centralized structure necessary for control. Key subjects in the postmodern lexicon are colonialism, including corporate colonialism; social injustice; gender inequality; and the distribution of wealth between the developed and so-called third world. The irony is, of course, that the

Enlightenment brought what is now described as democratic government and, in the countries that practice it, what is now generally thought to be the highest level of human freedom, self-government, and well-being in history. Nevertheless, postmodernists are not wrong regarding poverty, injustice, and inequality.

Finally, modernity, in the postmodern perspective, is primarily concerned with objective knowledge and its development. Postmodernity is more concerned with values and the search for truth than in characterizations of knowledge. Farmer (1995) describes modernity as expressions of the *limits* of particularism, scientism, technologism, and enterprise.

Particularism

According to Farmer:

> The national particularism of American public administration does have profound disadvantages in terms of contraries and blind spots. A contrary was noted earlier between particularism and universalism. The urge for the less bounded and the focus on the more bounded are also contraries. Insofar as it is interpretationist, public administration has an interest in interpretations that are as little culture bound as possible. This interest in the intercultural is a facilitating insight. Without the intercultural interest, for instance, insightful questions can be overlooked. (1995, 55–56)

No doubt modern public administration is largely a twentieth-century American product, complete with many of the attendant cultural blinders. But specialists in comparative administration have long understood this, as regular reading of the journal *Administration and Society* would attest. Comparativists have long argued against the exportability of American public administration. Much of the impetus behind the so-called New Public Management (NPM), or new managerialism, comes from the Western European countries, Australia, and New Zealand (Considine and Painter 1997; Kernaghan, Marson, and Borins 2000). Modern public administration is less and less an expression of American particularism; indeed, two of the leading new journals in the field, *Governance* and *Public Management Review*, are European.

Particularism also has to do with the emphasis on government in public administration. H. George Frederickson argues for a conception that distinguishes *public* from *governmental*: "The public lives independently of the government, and government is only one of its manifestations." The term "public" has come to have such a narrow meaning in our time that "we think of public as pertaining to government and having to do with voting and the conduct of officials." An adequate theory of the public, according to Frederickson, should be based on the

Constitution, on an enhanced notion of citizenship, and on systems for responding to the interests of "both the collective public and the inchoate public, and on benevolence and love" (1991, 395).

Finally, particularism in postmodernity is overly preoccupied with efficiency, leadership, management, and organization. The current emphasis on performance measurement is illustrative of the functional nature of modernist public administration (Forsythe 2001). Especially interesting is that measures of performance seldom ask the fairness question, performance for whom? The postmodernist would insist on asking that question.

Scientism

It is everywhere evident that science has had a lot to do with developing contemporary public administration theory. Over the years, the scientific perspective in public administration has evolved from

1. Luther Gulick and Lyndon Urwick's *Papers on the Science of Administration* in 1937;
2. to Herbert Simon's *Administrative Behavior* in 1947;
3. to the development of the *Administrative Science Quarterly*, still arguably the most prestigious journal in either business or public administration;
4. to Charles Lindblom's use of the title "The Science of Muddling Through" to poke a bit of fun at science;
5. to modern scientific perspectives on the field represented by the rational choice modeling perspective described in Chapter 8;
6. to the decision-theoretic perspective described in Chapter 7.

In this work, the word "science" is used in different ways. Simon's *The Sciences of the Artificial* (1969) formed part of the basis of what is now described as artificial intelligence, although there are, of course, debates over the intelligence of artificial intelligence. Nevertheless, modern systems of communication, robotic manufacturing, contemporary air travel, and many forms of modern medical practice are all built on the scientific logic of artificial intelligence.

Science is also used more casually in public administration, simply as a word to lend importance to an idea or to cover a hypothesis or perspective with what are presumed to be the qualities of science. The simple fact that science is used in public administration in this way shows how important science is to all modern disciplines and academic fields. In the postmodernist perspective, scientific or positivist ideas "are privileged in the sense that, if derived in accordance with scientific procedures, they are considered to give greater assurance of truth" (Farmer 1995, 71). Subjective first-person understandings of public administration phenomena are not so privileged, nor is the application of intuition, value judgment, or imagination to public administration.

To the postmodernist, the scientific perspective is usually stylized, which is to say simplified and exaggerated for emphasis. For example, Farmer lists Donald N. McCloskey's "Ten Commandments of the Golden Rule of modernism in economic and other sciences" (1985). They are as follows:

1. Prediction and control is the point of science.
2. Only the observable implications (or predictions) of a theory matter to its truth.
3. Observability entails objective, reproducible experiments; mere questionnaires. Interrogating human subjects is useless because humans might lie.
4. If, and only if, an experimental implication of a theory proves false is the theory proved false.
5. Objectivity is to be treasured; subjective "observation" (introspection) is not scientific knowledge because the objective and subjective cannot be linked.
6. Kelvin's Dictum: "When you cannot express it in numbers, your knowledge is of a meager and unsatisfactory kind."
7. Introspection, metaphysical belief, aesthetics, and the like may well figure in the discovery of a hypothesis but cannot figure in its justification; justifications are timeless, and the surrounding community of science is irrelevant to their truth.
8. It is the business of methodology to demarcate scientific reasoning from nonscientific, positive from normative.
9. A scientific explanation of an event brings the event under a covering law.
10. Scientists—for instance, economic scientists—ought not to have anything to say as scientists about the oughts of value, whether of morality or art. (Farmer 1995, 72)

This characterization of science, aside from its straw man quality, has limited application to public administration primarily because the field never fully accepted scientism in the first place. Virtually all the aspects of the application of science to public administration were debated over fifty years ago by the two giants of the field at the time: Dwight Waldo and Herbert Simon. This debate is as meaningful now as it was then. Because this debate is also central to decision theory, a summary is found in Chapter 7.

Today, public administration is still science and art, facts and values, Hamilton and Jefferson, politics and administration, Simon and Waldo. Some call for a grand and overarching theory that "would bring the field together." For our tastes, public administration is now very much together in all its complexity, a complexity richly and forever informed by Simon and Waldo. Although a simplistic characterization, Simon's early work could be described as high modern public administration. Because Waldo's work always questioned the primacy of objective rational social science, Waldo might be thought of as the first public administration postmodernist, although he would strongly have resisted such a categorization.

Technologism

Public administration has always been associated with ways to organize and ways to manage. Defined in its broadest sense, this is the technology of public administration. Much of public organization and management is low tech, to be sure, but it is very often the management and organization of high-tech institutions (Farmer 1995, 89). The operations of high-reliability systems such as air traffic control, for example, combine high tech and low tech in what Farmer describes as sociotechnology. An excellent recent example of empirically supported public organization and management theory that would be described as sociotechnology is Hal Rainey and Paula Steinbauer's "galloping elephant" thesis (1999). Our best research on the organization and management of large complex institutions indicates that, using primarily traditional principles of public administration, these institutions are "galloping elephants" that are surprisingly effective and swift. In other words, low-tech public administration primarily founded on a generalized understanding of modern theory in all its forms works surprisingly well in practice. If this is so, empirical support is lacking in postmodern claims that a public administrative theory built on a modernist scientific epistemology doesn't work well.

All modern social systems tend to wish to find technological answers to social, economic, and political questions. A common contemporary argument, for example, is that the Internet should enhance a citizen's community and political involvement. Postmodernists rightly point out that the search for technological answers to social, economic, and political questions tends to be faddish. Postmodernists, like social observers generally, worry about the dehumanizing aspect of both low-tech bureaucratic functioning and high-tech systems, and they have evidence to support their worries. Consider as illustrative the Tuskegee venereal disease project in the United States or the Holocaust in Nazi Germany. Postmodernists are correct in their assertion that technology can blur moral and ethical lines. There could be no better modern example than the current debate over the use and possible misuse of our knowledge of the human genome.

It is fortunate that as a field there has been a long series of literature on matters of public ethics and morality. Just because new technology might enable public administrators to do things has never meant that public administration *should* do them. Public administration, when compared to other applied, interdisciplinary fields, such as planning, social work, business administration, or law, has always made a comparatively strong emphasis on values and ethics.

Enterprise

Few things are more predictable than the standard government reform calling for
the public sector to be more businesslike (Light 1999). And no one made more
sense of it than Gulick, who, having seen almost every twentieth-century reform,
wrote this:

> "Businesslike" is the next metaphor designed to take in the unsophisticated. The
> business universe at this point is designed to generate profits and power for the
> owners and top managers of economic enterprises on the basis of a very short
> time span. Since the nation state aims at a span of centuries and drives not for
> economic profits for the owners of capital but at the life, liberty and happiness of
> all its people, the fundamental drive should be not to be "businesslike" but to
> make business a little more "government like." It is desirable to be efficient in the
> honest business sense but not at the cost of the welfare of the people. (1984, 34)

Over the years, the rhetoric has changed. The 1990s reinventing government
initiative at all levels of government called for public administrators to be entrepreneurs and to break through bureaucracy by guiding the public sector in the
direction of being more customer oriented, an idea taken directly from the enterprise textbook (Osborne and Gaebler 1992). Reinventors would also improve
public administration by applying market concepts such as agency competition,
earning through special fees rather than generalized taxation, and the privatization
of public services. Initiatives to apply the logic of enterprise to public administration did not, however, go unchallenged (Kettl 1988; Goodsell 1983). Indeed, from
the beginning of the field there has been a consistent literature pointing out the
difference between government and enterprise and questioning the application of
business principles to public administration (Martin 1965; Marx 1946). Certainly
the concerns of postmodernists about applying business concepts to the public
sector, and particularly the assumption that the motivations of public officials can
be understood only as rational self-interest, are warranted; there has, however,
been an extensive critique of these ideas in the pages of the *Public Administration
Review* and other leading journals. The recent emphasis on the deregulation of
business and on privatization has also been critiqued (Frederickson 1999a). The
public administration critique concerning the application of business ideas holds
that business concepts seldom carry the day in the public sector. But there are
powerful political and economic forces generally supportive of applying business
concepts to public management. The greatest inroads into applying enterprise to
the public sector come from rational choice theory, a subject considered and critiqued in Chapter 8.

To sum up: From the postmodern perspective, criticisms of modernist public
administration include (1) its overreliance on the logic and epistemology of objec-

tive rational social science; (2) its implicit support for authoritarian, unfair, and unjust regimes; (3) its bias toward American particularism; (4) its too-great attachment to functional management and organization technologies; and (5) its willingness to be overly influenced by the capitalist logic of enterprise. Having reviewed the postmodern critique of modernist public administration, we now turn to the more difficult question: What, after all, is postmodern public administration?

Looking for Postmodern Public Administration Theory

The primary reason it is difficult to pin down a description of postmodern public administration theory or a serviceable definition of the postmodern perspective is this: One cannot, it is claimed, understand, judge, or evaluate postmodern public administration by using modernist criteria or standards (Farmer 1995, 144–145). When we are "involved with the assumptions of modernity and regard them as constituting 'common sense,' we fail to understand and justify the claims of postmodernity in terms of modernity" (145).

> Postmodern public administration should be understood as negating the core mind-set of modernity, as negating the assumptions that have underlain important thinking during the last five centuries. Postmodernity should be interpreted as denying the core pattern of ideas, the Weltanschauung [a generally accepted worldview or philosophy of life] that constitutes modernity; this denial would include denying the very process of having a Weltanschauung. It would deny that the central task is the picturing of the world, denying the value of grounding the subject's knowledge of the world in the subject. It would deny the view of nature and role of reason implicit in modernity's view of the centered subject. It would deny macrotheory, grand narratives, and macropolitics. It would deny the distinction between reality and appearance. Postmodernity's denial of modernity, as this list implies, is denial in a particular way. It would not permit a denial of modernity in the sense of a return to premodernity. According to postmodernists, we cannot return to the old gods, to the old society where the subject is embedded in a social role and a value context.
>
> These formulations are negativities. Modernity can yield convenient sets of propositions that invite examination in terms of the laws of logic. Postmodernity does not fit into this mold. . . . Part of the difficulty in comprehension can be understood if we examine what it would mean for postmodernity to be incoherent nonsense. To be incoherent and nonsensical, a postmodern view (or any other view) would have to fail to meet some set of criteria for coherence and sense; it would have to fall outside the pale of sense and coherence. This understanding fails if postmodernism is recognized as denying a distinction between sense and nonsense and between coherence and incoherence. It fails if postmodernism is recognized to go on to deny that this means nonsense exists; there is

only an intermingling of sense and nonsense. Nevertheless, from the modernist perspective, this explanation is unappealing. (145–146)

In postmodernist logic, the negativities, contraries, or problematics that critique modernist logic often have a playful quality to them, as the following lists (Table 6.2) serve to indicate.

Many of the similarities between this characterization of the differences between modernism and postmodernism and Clark's description of the difference between classic and postpositivist organizational paradigms described earlier in

TABLE 6.2   CRITIQUES OF POSTMODERNISM AS A THEORY

Modernist	Postmodernist
Form (conjunctive, closed)	Antiform (disjunctive, open)
Purpose	Play
Design	Chance
Hierarchy	Anarchy
Mastery/Logos	Exhaustion/Silence
Art Object/Finished Work	Process/Performance/Happening
Distance	Participation
Creation/Totalization	Decreation/Deconstruction
Synthesis	Antisynthesis
Presence	Absence
Centering	Dispersal
Signified	Signifier
Narrative	Antinarrative
God the Father	The Holy Ghost
Symptom	Desire
Origin/Cause	Difference-Difference/Trace
Metaphysics	Irony
Determinancy	Indeterminancy

SOURCE: Hassan 2001, pp. 121–122.

this chapter are worth noting. The question is, what does a public administration theory built on antiform, play, chance, anarchy, and so forth, look like?[3] The hardcore postmodernist would likely answer that question with a comment such as this: "You cannot either describe or understand the postmodern world by answering such a question." The soft-core postmodernist would likely answer thus: "Postmodern public administration theory looks rather like a combination of the sensemaking logic described in Chapter 7 on decision theory, many of the modern elements of institutional theory described in Chapter 4, and public management theory described in Chapter 5 of *The Public Administration Theory Primer*." To carry postmodern theory forward will most likely require adoption of the soft postmodernist perspective.

"Postmodern Public Administration researchers, then, have an interest in Public Administration practice. But they rarely engage in consulting practitioners, and particularly high-level civil servants, as their more traditional colleagues do" (Bogason 2005, 248).

Even though modernists or traditional public administration scholars would argue that postmodernists are less practical, an argument could also be made that they are more democratic. By engaging individuals often overlooked in modernist research, postmodernists provide a unique perspective on governance and policymaking.

Following Farmer, postmodern public administration theory can be understood to include the following traits: dialectic, a return to imagination, a deconstruction of meaning, deterritorialization, and alterity. As a postmodern perspective, dialectic has to do with distinctions and absence of distinctions. Postmodernity, for example, denies the distinction between appearance and reality. The postmodern state is therefore one of hyperreality, a merging of the real with appearances, stimulation, illusion. The dividing lines between objects and pictures, descriptions, impressions, or simulations of that object have imploded to such an extent that we no longer have a direct understanding of the object. In a state of hyperreality, everything is virtual and simulation becomes more real than real (Farmer 1995, 150). In its most extreme view, postmodernism argues that humans have dropped out of history and have left reality behind.

As this brief description of the postmodern dialect and the notion of hyperreality indicate, postmodern public administration has mostly to do with the definitions and understandings of such basic philosophical questions as these: What is real? What is reality? Deconstruction is central to this perspective. Not a methodology or a system of analysis, postmodern deconstruction

> can be used to dismantle narratives that constitute the underpinnings of modernist public administration theory and practices. Bureaucratic deconstruction can also be used to dismantle narratives constructed in postmodernity. Grand narratives

are the accounts that are thought to explain the development of history, and Hegel's and Marx's (the march of history being explained by the workings of, respectively, the Absolute Spirit and economic factors) are often given as examples. An Enlightenment grand narrative is that rationalization equals human progress. Public administration and practices are also underpinned by certain narratives. One narrative is that *the* goal for public administration theory should be objectivity. A second narrative is that efficiency is a viable goal for public administration practice. One narrative is illustrative of a modernist underpinning of theory, and the other is an example of a grounding of much practice. Certainly, alternative examples of narratives could have been selected. (Farmer 1995, 179)

The postmodernist might approach the subject of efficiency by taking efficiency to be a part of a master or grand narrative and then deconstructing that narrative, and, with it, both the concept of efficiency and the practical applications of efficiency, such as cost-benefit analysis or performance measurement. Doing this has a great deal to do with the so-called deep structure of a word, the word here being "efficiency," and its intended meanings. The point is that the word efficiency merely represents or simulates some actual phenomenon that we choose to describe as efficiency. Obviously, efficiency as a word not only describes something but also favorably represents it. Efficiency is good; inefficiency is bad. Although such deconstruction might be all dolled up in postmodern language, the end result would look very much like the standard critique of efficiency already found in the public administration literature. A good example of this is the emergence of NPM in public administration, a perspective resting on the logic of efficiency or the efficiency grand narrative. Whether the critique of efficiency is furthered by using postmodern logic or postmodern language depends on how one views postmodernity. In the postmodern dialectic, words and images come together more powerfully than the images of men and women in public administration.

There is a close connection between postmodern public administration theory and feminist perspectives on the field (Stivers 2002, 1990, 1992, 2000; Hendricks 1992; Haslinger 1996; Ferguson 1984; Cocks 1989; Ackelsberg and Shanley 1996; Morgan 1990). The problem begins, following Camilla Stivers, with this:

Public administration scholars overwhelmingly acknowledge that the field is an applied one and debate ways of making their research more useful to practitioners, one aspect of the real world of public administration has gone relatively unnoticed—the dynamics of gender in public organizational life. Since women first entered government work in the mid-19th century, their experience of life in public agencies has been fundamentally different from men's. Women have been paid less, done a disproportionate share of the routine work, struggled with the question of how to accommodate themselves to organizational practices defined by men, brooded over how to turn aside men's advances without losing their jobs, and fought to balance work demands with what was expected of them—what they expected of them—on the domestic front. Those who have made it to the middle ranks find themselves bumping up against a glass ceiling that keeps a disproportionate number of women from top positions. (2002, 37)

At the core of all of these challenges, based on the application of postmodern theory to feminist perspectives in public administration, is the matter of image. Again, following Stivers:

Public administration's stress on autonomy, on not simply taking orders but instead making discretionary decisions, is a culturally masculine concern in tension with the stereotypically feminine obligation to be responsive. One could argue that other aspects of public administration's political role are similarly feminine—for example, the norm of service. At the level of cultural ideology, it is women who serve others while men are served; women unselfishly devote themselves to helping the unfortunate while men pursue self-interest, albeit sometimes the enlightened variety. If what makes public administrators different from other experts is their responsibilities of service and responsiveness, then as a group they too, like women, do not fit the professional role very well. Professionalism is too masculine for the feminine aspects of public administration. In this context the effort to assert the worth of public administration in such terms as professional, helmsman, agent, objective scientist, and neutral expert is an effort to acquire masculinity and repress femininity or project it outward. In this sense, public administration is not only masculinist and patriarchal, it is in fundamental denial as to its own nature and conceptually and practically impoverished as a result. Women are not the only ones in public administration faced with the gender dilemma. Theorists may extol the virtues of the responsive, caring bureaucrat who serves the public interest, but the argument will face uphill sledding until we recognize that responsiveness, caring, and service are culturally feminine qualities and that, in public administration, we are ambivalent about them for that very reason. (2002, 57–58)

The feminist perspective in public administration probably traces to the work of Mary Parker Follett (1918, 1924). Parker Follett argued that administrative processes are more important than hierarchy and authority, that the exercise of power is a central feature of bureaucratic behavior, and that the analyst view of reality is more an interpreting function of practical experience than a pursuit of objective findings. All these theoretical perspectives are thought to be more feminine than masculine (Stivers 1996; Morton and Lindquist 1997).

Many of the elements of postpositivist public administration described earlier in this chapter could be thought of as inclined toward a feminist perspective in the field. In specific terms, the logic of bureaucratic neutrality is anything but neutral. Bureaucratic functioning tends to subordinate women. The logic of the hierarchy is also understood to be more masculine, but the service or helping perspective of process approaches to bureaucratic functioning is thought to be feminine (Stivers 2000).

Professions are important features in the evolution of the public service public—engineers being mostly men, teachers mostly women, for example. The feminist professional distinction has been brilliantly set out in the richly empirical *Bureau Men, Settlement Women: Constructing Public Administration in the Progressive Era* (Stivers 2000). The feminist perspective in the progressive era is captured in a study of settlement women (we would now probably call them social workers) who organized and operated large service programs for the poor. "Female reformers of the time developed their own understanding of science, one centered not around objectivity and rigor but around connectedness (313). The day-to-day work of the settlement involved an intimate understanding of the circumstances of others, sympathy and support, advocacy, and anything but disinterested neutrality.

Feminists see leadership differently. The masculine logic of taking charge, being the decisionmaker, executing authority, maximizing efficiency, and being goal oriented is challenged by a feminist leadership logic. The feminist perspective looks a lot like the logic of democratic administration found in postpositivist public administration—group decisionmaking, consensus, teamwork, deliberation, and discourse. In its most extreme form, this perspective favors the leaderless organization or the logic of leader rotation.

From the feminist perspective, images of the public administrator as guardian, hero, or high-profile leader are masculine. The application of fairness, compassion, benevolence, and civic-mindedness are thought to be more feminine. The administrator as citizen rather than leader is also associated with feminist logic:

> Women's perspective on the administrative state is much more likely to be developed sitting in the secretarial pool or on one side or the other of the caseworker's desk than it is as a member of the Senior Executive Service. A feminist approach to public administration means examining the material realities of women's place in the bureaucracy and the barriers they face to fuller participation, which as we have seen include both glass ceilings and glass walls.
>
> In addition, a feminist perspective on the administrative state would encourage theory to come to terms with depersonalized power. The claim to administrative discretion is the claim to power on the basis of technical, managerial, and moral expertise. The discretionary judgments of administrators are said to be justifiable because they make decisions on the basis of the more objective knowledge, clearer vision, higher principles, or deeper commitment to wrestling with the tough questions of public life than do other citizens. This claim to power is asserted on the

basis that the arena in which it is exercised is distinctive because it is public. But as we have seen, a discrete public sector maintains its boundaries (therefore its exceptionalism) at the expense of women. A feminist interpretation of administrative discretion and of the power inherent in it must therefore begin by calling into question the accepted model of discretionary judgment. (Stivers 2002, 141–142)

Many other dialectics appear in the postmodern perspective—image and reality, black and white, colonial and postcolonial, local and global, and so forth. Of these, the feminist perspective is probably the most developed.

It is worth noting a contradictory strand of feminist reasoning that has recently developed in the public management literature. Like Stivers and other feminist scholars, this research stream acknowledges the culturally masculine values embedded in organizations. However, it departs from traditional feminist approaches by emphasizing the aspects of bureaucracy that can empower rather than oppress women in public-sector organizations. From this perspective, organizational rules are viewed as potential levelers of the organizational playing field, tools of legitimacy for women who hold positions of power, and protectors of support staff autonomy (mostly women), whom managerial discretion could render servile (DeHart-Davis 2009). Accordingly, organizations with fewer rules and more administrative discretion—particularly within male-dominated hierarchies—are seen as potentially debilitating to the experiences of organizational women, particularly regarding career ascendency, exercise of authority, and differential performance expectations. These perspectives are supported by empirical evidence that women in city organizations tend to perceive bureaucracy more favorably than their male counterparts do and are slightly less likely to bend organizational rules, even as they ascend the hierarchy (Portillo and DeHart-Davis 2009). Even though this research is influenced by postmodern feminist thinking, it is pragmatic in its leanings and thus represents a hybrid form relatively new to the public administration literature.

The search for greater imagination in public administration is an enduring feature of both postpositivism and postmodernism. Indeed, because frustration with rigid unresponsive bureaucracy is probably as old as bureaucracy, the call for organizational creativity is equally as old. In postmodernity, this yearning has a somewhat different language and is more associated with rejecting old paradigms in search of new paradigms. Postmodernists base their quest for greater imagination in public administration on rejecting rationality and rationalization: "Modernity's rationalization extended more and more throughout society, bringing more and more under the domain of rationality. The basis of science, technology, and modernist interpretations is rationality. . . . Postmodernity's *imaginization,* in a parallel fashion, can be expected to spread through society. Individuals in society, and elements of society, might try to give imagination the central role in their interrelationships and in their lives that modernists previously give to rationality" (Farmer 1995, 158).

Imagination is important to postmodern public administration theory because of the view that the metaphor, images, allegory, stories, and parables play a central role in how people think. Our preoccupation with objective rationality, both in bureaucratic practice and in public administration theory, limits, it is claimed, our possible capacity for imagination or creativity. Gareth Morgan (1993) refers to *imaginization* as the art of creative management. This resembles the standard humanist management training/interventionist menu of improving abilities to see things differently, now popularly and tritely referred to as "thinking outside the box," finding new ways to organize, encouraging personal empowerment, and finding new ways to self-organize. When connected to theory and research methodology, creative management could be described as essentially an action-learning model or ethnographic research in which the analyst/interventionist not only engages in research but also presumes to help the organization learn to improve itself.

A second version of the postmodern imagination perspective is associated with leadership and strategic management. This is the call for public administrators to improve their capacities to see around the corner, to have greater vision, and to take risks. Again, this is a staple in the standard training/intervention manual.

Although imagination and vision are central to the postmodern argument, in many ways this dimension of the argument is premodern. It was, after all, the visions of those who presumed to speak for the deity that characterized the organizing forces and the exercise of power in much of the premodern world. And, too, it was those who held power by the mysteries of lineage who controlled the land and the armies of the premodern world. If the logic of rationality has weaknesses, and it does, and if organizing and managing the public sector through rationality result in less than entirely effective organizations, and they do, where will the vision and imagination of postmodern public administration theory take us? Referring to Plato, Farmer maintains, "The best government is lawless and the true statesman is one whose rule is adapted to each individual case. In postmodernity, this development will take place in a new context, one that Baudrillard calls the transpolitical" (1995, 177). The transpolitical is "the obscenity of all structures in a structureless universe . . . the obscenity of information in a defactualized universe . . . the obscenity of space in a promiscuity of networks" (Baudrillard 1990, 163). This brings us to that element of postmodern public administration that has tinges of either the antistate or the antijurisdiction, or is openly antistate.

Although it is a rather grand generalization, the overall postmodern perspective tends to be somewhat antiauthoritarian and antistate. It may seem curious, therefore, that the field of public administration, a field closely identified with the state and with the exercise of authority, would include several scholars who are attempting to build a postmodern theory of the subject. These scholars, many of them already cited in this chapter, tend toward a soft or modified postmodern perspective, a less shrill and dogmatic view of the state and the exercise of state authority. We chose here to use elements of the postmodern public administration perspective on the state and on authority that, in our view, make important contributions to understanding modern public administration. The postmodernists are most attuned to the weaknesses of the nation-state and to an open and direct criticism of the state. Because of this, postmodern public administration theory comes the closest to thoughtful perspectives on one of the most important contemporary issues facing the field: the declining salience of the state.

The modern nation-state is essential to the core logic of public administration because the field simply assumes the existence of the nation-state and assumes that public administrators are agents of the state and of the public interest. It is difficult for scholars working from the perspectives of institutional theory, decision theory, managerial theory, rational choice theory, political control-of-bureaucracy theory, and bureaucratic theory to assume away the polity, the jurisdiction, or the state. Only governance theory and postmodern theory are open to challenges to the assumption that practicing public administration is the representation of the nation-state and state sovereignty. In postmodern public administration theory, the particular form these challenges take include elements of deconstruction, imagination, deterritorialization, and alterity.

The emergence of the modern nation-state parallels in time the coming of the Enlightenment. Although bureaucratic theory came much later, the practices of bureaucracy preceded the emergence of the state and were simply patched into the modern state (Weber 1952; Gladden 1972). In modern democratic states, bureaucratic assumptions of legitimacy based on laws, constitutions, formal appointments, and tenure are all associated with the core assumption of jurisdiction and national sovereignty. The postmodern deconstruction of the state concept and the functioning of the state takes this form:

1. The state is a place, a physical territory with borders and boundaries.
2. The state is a particular history, social construction of reality, and usable past.
3. The state includes founding myths that take on great importance.
4. The state is often sustained by traditional or hereditary enemies.
5. The state is the exercise of authority in the form of sovereign-legitimated actions based on the exercise of authority in the name of the state.
6. The state rests on some capacity to tax its residents.
7. The state is expected by its residents or citizens to provide order, stability, predictability, and identity.

Postmodernists, and many others, argue that in the modern world all the characteristics of the state are in play. Borders are porous to people, money, disease, and pollution. People are increasingly mobile, less and less attached to one place and to one jurisdiction or nation. Business is increasingly global. Many modern transactions are now virtual, accomplished electronically and without respect to national boundaries; and, too, transactions are increasingly difficult to tax and regulate. Enemies of the state might be other nations; but they might be, as the United States learned on September 11, 2001, stateless movements or groups. Wealth has less and less to do with fixed property and the production of goods, and more and more to do with information and ideas, which are difficult to contain and manage by one state because they have nothing to do with borders or sovereignty. The modern nation-state is "too remote to manage the problems of our daily life . . . and too constrained to confront the global problems that affect us" (Guéhenno 1995, 12–13).

Politics in the modern nation-state is deeply challenged by postmodern circumstances.

> In the age of networks, the relationships of citizens to the body politic is in competition with the infinity of connections they establish outside of it. So, politics, far from being the organizing principle of life in society, appears as a secondary activity, if not an artificial construct poorly suited to the resolution of the practical problems of the modern world. Once there is no longer a natural place for solidarity and for the general good, the well-ordered hierarchy of a society organized in a pyramid of interlocking powers disappears. (Guéhenno 1995, 19)

In the postmodern perspective, legislative gridlock, the influence of money in politics, and the power possessed by interest groups have so polluted the political system that it has been drained of legitimacy. Modern politics has moved from the pursuit of the general good to the professionalization of interests. The litigious pursuit of individual rights coupled with exaggerated individualism weakens the possibility of a greater good. Finally, the common public understanding of politics is based on media coverage so shallow, so inclined to sensationalism, so preoccupied with personalities, and so disinclined to deal with issues that politics is reduced to sound bites and clichés.

If this postmodern critique of the nation-state is even partially correct, it has powerful implications for public administration. If sovereignty is in doubt, for whom do public administrators work? If the nation-state's constitutional order is altered by global influences, how shall public administration respond?

The generalized postmodern answer to these questions is somewhat like our descriptions of governance theory in Chapter 9:

As soon as the frontier is no longer a given, whether in the case of a corporation or a state, the function of management, and thus the nature of power, changes. The managers thus become "intermediaries" rather than bosses, constantly adjusting the organization of the relationships between the different units. . . . And even this management is efficient only if it is strongly decentralized. . . . The multidimensional model, based on so-called interlocking databases, succeeds the "natural" model, with straightforward, spreading branches. The hierarchical, pyramidal structure, in which to be powerful was to be in control and command, is succeeded by a structure of the diffusion of power with multiple connections, in which to be powerful is to be in contact, in communication, and in which power is defined by influence and no longer by mastery. (Guéhenno 1995, 61–62)

Following this argument, postmodern public administration will need to think in postnational terms. Public administration in the postnational world will move subtly away from the logic of state or nation building (to include cities) and the concentration of ever more economic capacity or sovereignty toward the search for multi-institutional compatibilities, attempts to find cross-jurisdictional convergence, and, above all, searches for procedures that will aid the development of generally acceptable decision processes and rules. Postmodern public administration will be "a network of agreements facilitating the compatibility between open units, rather than the architecture artificially built around a capital" (Guéhenno 1995, 65).

Postmodern public administration will be all about process, procedure, and the search for rules. One postmodernist describes the role of agents of the state as being engaged with the agents of other states in a collective search for the invisible chains that can bind people together:

When society is functioning, there is no time for conflict to appear, it is dissolved in a multitude of microdecisions and microadjustments, in which the weak test the strength of the strong and the strong make the weak feel the force of their strength, and in which everyone, in the last analysis, finds their place. We are thus also as far here from the institutional age of power, which institutionalizes conflict, as from the feudal age, in which the triumph of the strong leads to the absorption of the weak. In the imperial age (postmodern and postnational), the strong are sufficiently strong as soon as the weak have come to recognize their place. A certain social geography naturally imposes itself.

This peaceful tranquility of the imperial age is not that of the triumph of reason. It covers the muffled echoes of the thousand piecemeal battles that have prepared the way for the splitting off of great confrontations. In this respect, Japan is much more "modern" than litigious America. Decisionmaking in Japan takes much longer than in America, and its implementation is shorter. (Guéhenno 1995, 70–71)

The emphasis on networks is in line with what others view as the key to moving postmodern theory forward. To adequately address concerns across groups and networks within a society requires a focus on dialogue and participatory governance (Bogason 2005, 249). A focus on the interests of the individual citizen, rather than on bureaucratic structures or centralized bases of power, is best achieved through direct citizen participation. However, to make advances within the field will require working within existing theoretical frameworks. Thus, many postmodern scholars seem to recognize that to effectively move the field of postmodern public administration theory forward requires an approach that includes both traditional institutional factors and a strong emphasis on networks and relationships within the institution itself (Bogason 2005, 244–245).

Postmodern public administration theory emphasizes teamwork and, although it is seldom admitted, conformity. The objective is to reduce the need for structural hierarchy and the exercise of power, to put in their place a multitude of precautionary microadjustments. Because there will be no institutional center, the emphasis will be on the management of social, religious, ethnic, and cultural differences. When this is done well, there will be an emphasis on modesty and prudence in administrative action. Nation building as a goal will gradually diminish as the primary purpose of the nation-state, to be replaced by societies that find meaning in connections and associations. The network will become as important as the individual, and networks always extract some level of individual conformity for their functioning. Populations will continue to want to recognize each other as nations, but even the most powerful nations will not have the capacity in the postmodern global world to protect and serve their citizens. The declining comfort of geographical boundaries will stimulate the discovery of new forms of human community.

American approaches to postmodern public administration theory tend to be less bold, choosing to emphasize improved discourse and more humane and democratic administration (Fox and Miller 1995; Farmer 1995; Jung 2002). American public administration postmodernists have little interest in postnationalism, whereas European postmodernists tend to be more antistate and have clearly been influenced by the formation of the European Union. The breakup of the Soviet Union, continued social and political unrest in the Middle East, and a generalized political and economic turmoil in Africa have also influenced European postmodernists more than their American cousins.

Finally, the postmodern condition is described as increasingly fragmented jurisdictionally, with more and more small jurisdictions emerging. At the same time, vehicles for effective regional multistate polities are absent. In the absence of effective regional polities, there are no orderly patterns of regional politics. Instead, regional power and politics tend to be in the hands of networked technicians, public administrators, specialists representing states, and networked nonstate actors representing nongovernmental organizations and global business. The International Monetary Fund and the World Bank are the best current examples. Therefore, in the postmodern world, public administration is more rather than less powerful and important. Insofar as there is regional and even global governance, it is primarily the province of public administration (Frederickson 1999b).

One of the more interesting characteristics of postmodern public administration theory has to do with its approach to methodology. Although some associated with postmodernism reject empiricism and objectivity out of hand, most are empiricists in the qualitative methodology sense. The most complete description of this methodological perspective is naturalistic inquiry, an approach more identified with postpositivism than with postmodernism (Lincoln and Guba 1985). Nevertheless, from the perspective of empirically based theory, it captures what is now generally described as the postmodern approach to field research. The methodological approach in operational naturalistic inquiry is as follows:

1. Natural setting. Conduct research in the natural setting or context because, among other reasons, "realities are whole that cannot be understood in isolation from their context."

2. Human interest. Use humans as the primary data-gathering instruments, as opposed to, say, paper-and pencil instruments.

3. Utilization of tacit knowledge. Regard tacit (intuitive, felt) knowledge as legitimate, in addition to prepositional knowledge.

4. Qualitative methods. Choose "qualitative methods" over quantitative ones (although not exclusively) because the former are more adaptable to dealing with multiple (and less aggregatable) realities.

5. Purposive sampling. Avoid random or representative sampling because, among other reasons, the researcher thereby "increases the scope or range of data expressed."

6. Inductive data analysis. Use inductive data analysis because it "is more likely to identify the multiple realities to be found in those data."

7. Grounded theory. Allow "the guiding substantive theory [to] emerge from . . . the data."

8. Emergent design. Allow the research design "to emerge (flow, cascade, unfold) rather than construct it preordinately (a priori)."

9. Negotiated outcome. Negotiate "meanings and interpretations with the human sources from which the data have chiefly been drawn" because "it is their construction of reality that the inquirer seeks to reconstruct."

10. Case study reporting mode. Prefer the "case study reporting mode (over the scientific or technical report)."

11. Ideographic interpretation. Interpret data and conclusions "ideographically (in terms of the particulars of the case) rather than nomothetically (in terms of law-like generalizations)."

12. Tentative application. Be hesitant about applying the findings broadly.

13. Focused-determined boundaries. Set boundaries to the inquiry "on the basis of the emergent focus (problems for research, evaluands for evaluation and policy options for policy analysis)."

14. Special criteria for trustworthiness. Adopt special trustworthiness criteria because the "conventional trustworthiness criteria (internal and external validity, reliability, and objectivity) are inconsistent with the axioms and procedures of naturalistic inquiry." (Adapted from Lincoln and Guba 1985, 221–240, by Farmer 1995, 216)

An emerging body of impressive empirically based research uses essentially this methodological approach. One of the most highly acclaimed empirical analyses of the field-level behavior of bureaucrats and welfare claimants uses this methodological approach (Soss 2000). Two impressive studies of the street-level operations of the law and the legal system are clearly identified as methodologically postmodern (Ewick and Silbey 1998; Conley and O'Barr 1998). An especially important analysis of the street-level choice-making behavior of social case workers, disability case managers, and teachers uses a postmodern methodology (Maynard-Moody and Musheno 2003). At the methodological base of all of these studies are narratives and stories and their careful collection and interpretation (Maynard-Moody, Musheno, and Kelly 1995; Maynard-Moody and Leland 1999).

Bureaucratic sense making, as described earlier in this chapter and in Chapter 4, is at the logical core of the empirical findings in these studies. Stories and narratives recount in significant detail how public administrators interpret generalized laws and rules in their day-to-day application of those laws and rules to specific clients and citizens. Reconciling laws, regulations, and policies with specific client or citizen qualifications or needs is deeply interpretive and usefully understood as sense making. These, and other similar studies, come closer to accurate descriptions of how public services are provided, and why, than interviews or survey data. But such studies are difficult to replicate, and the theories they test are dense and inelegant.

Conclusions: Fading Away or Still Useful as a Theory?

A recent review of *Public Administration Review*, one of the leading journals of the discipline, indicates that the dominant methodological approach continues to be quantitative/statistical, more specifically "behavioral-empirical" (Raaddschelders and Lee 2011, 24). Very little journal space appears to be devoted to the dialectal/hermeneutic qualitative approaches advocated by postmodernists; from 2000 to 2009 less than 15 percent of articles were devoted to normative, descriptive, biographical, and historical methodologies combined. These reviewers are right to note however that the journal's addition of sections devoted to "Practitioner-Academic Exchange" and "Theory to Practice" open the door for more qualitative approaches; for postmodernists these sections provide valuable research avenues to reach a wide audience.

Using primarily logic, deduction, and philosophical reasoning, scholars working from the postmodern public administration theory perspective have provided thoughtful and provocative analyses of the problem of administrative responsibility (Harmon 1995), trust (Kass 2003), gender (Stivers 2002), legitimacy (McSwite 1997), and a wide range of other issues in the field. Although these studies might be criticized for lacking an empirical base, the same criticism can be leveled at assumption-based mathematical modeling used to test rational choice theory.

Postmodern research and theory, in addition to their central place in PATnet and its journal, *Administrative Theory and Praxis*, is highly influential among the members of the Law and Society Association. Of the leading scholarly publications associated with public administration, the prestigious *Law and Society Review*, the association's journal, is the leading example of the importance of postmodern research and theory in the field. Less directly associated with public administration, but strongly influenced by postmodern theory, are journals dealing with women in the public sector, such as *Woman and Politics*. It is probably a safe generalization that many of the public administration issues being considered in this literature have to do with race, gender, class, and inequality—all central themes in postmodern thought.

The postmodern methodological perspective described here is associated with deterritorialization, an analytic approach that seeks to break down the structural territories found in all organizations. These territories are reflected in rigid departmental and bureau categories, in reified accounting categories, in the special professions and educational processes that prepare people for public service, and in all the other ways that work is divided. Like virtually everyone in public administration, postmodernists seek to break down both the organizational silos and the fixed patterns of thought that come with categories and actual or intellectual territory. In postmodern lingo, the postmodern deterritorialization argument has long been a part of public administration, although postmodernists could claim that their approaches to ameliorating the structural deficits of organization promise to be more successful than earlier approaches.

The postmodern methodological perspective also includes the logic of alterity, or a forthright concern for the "moral other" on the part of public administrators.

Postmodernists rightly claim that all administrative acts directly or indirectly affect others and that traditional public administration hides, overlooks, generalizes, or rationalizes these effects. In public administration, according to postmodernists, the concern for others needs to be shifted from the abstract idea of nonspecific "others" to concrete, live, actual "others." Therefore, the postmodernist research agenda has often to do with ground-level considerations of bureaucratic functioning and the consequences of that functioning on others. It is the postmodernists who appear to have inherited the mantle of research on street-level bureaucracy, and to have considerably advanced that research (Lipsky 1980; Maynard-Moody and Musheno 2003). One interesting contemporary example is the issue of the "collateral damage" associated with war.

The critiques of postmodern theory have been well documented. For positivists, the question is about how to evaluate the methodology, particularly as it relates to foundational concepts such as efficiency. Democratic concepts such as equity and responsiveness become even more nuanced and problematic under a postmodern framework. More generally, public administration is plagued by a problem of a lack of a unifying theory; postmodern theory does nothing to resolve this debate, nor does it see this as necessary. Postmodern theory does add to the discussion and practice of public administration, but as yet offers little in the way of an agreed-upon methodology or means to determine the effectiveness of an institution. Postmodern public administration is perhaps best viewed as adding a tool to the public administration toolkit, but is not redefining the use of existing tools as will be suggested by recent work on decision theory and rational choice in Chapter 7 and Chapter 8. Finally, although postmodern research has certainly contributed to our understanding of public administration obligations to each citizen, it is only fair to point out that such issues have been a part of the subject and a part of the research agenda for many years.

Notes

1. Some theorists whose work is considered in this chapter might reject being categorized as postmodern.

2. We describe here only that part of the so-called New Public Administration that was, at the time, generally called the humanistic perspective. Other perspectives, concepts, and theories emerged from the subsequent meetings of Minnowbrook Conference, most notably the social equity argument (Frederickson 1980).

3. For a particularly interesting postmodern playful analysis of public administration theory, see McSwite 2002. For a less playful, but nevertheless interesting, use of contraries, negatives, and problematics in postmodern public administration, see Fox and Miller 1995.

7

Decision Theory

Introduction

Although now quite distinct, rational choice theory and decision theory in many ways trace to the same origins. Both are associated with the early work of Herbert Simon and particularly his *Administrative Behavior*, first published in 1947.

Rational choice theory, the subject of Chapter 8, is an application of decision theory that is heavily influenced by economics and the logic of markets; it tends to use mathematical models to test the relationships between preferences, or objectives, and alternative courses of action. The purpose is to determine the most efficient, or rational, decisions to achieve preferred objectives, ordinarily thought to be individual self-interest or organizational survival.

What has come to be called decision theory is the other important application of early decisionmaking logic, and it has evolved into arguably the most mature and fully developed body of empirically informed theory in public administration. Certainly, decision theory is the most obvious multidisciplinary body of theory in public administration, influenced as it is by economics, organizational sociology, social psychology, and political science. The relative maturity of decision theory is characterized by a generally agreed-upon set of conceptual categories and the use of a distinct language to explicate those categories. Finally, of the bodies of theory covered in this book, decision theory is the least contained and has the fuzziest borders. Because all theories of public administration describe decisions, key elements of decision theory are found in virtually all other theoretical perspectives. Nevertheless, for purposes of description we put borders around decision theory to contain it as a discrete body of theory.

We begin this chapter by reviewing the origins of decision theory. Simon's *Administrative Behavior* (1947/1997) argues that administration is a world of deciding and that decisions are as important as actions. Indeed, decisions are the predicates of actions, and actions are almost always based on accumulated decisions. The traditional study of administration was, Simon claimed, too preoccupied with action, and particularly with unsubstantiated "principles" of action, which he labeled "proverbs." The modern study of administration needed to be more scientific, and the science of administration needed to be based on a new and different unit of analysis—the decision. The scientific focus on this unit of analysis is still a hallmark of the conceptual framework theory, and contemporary scholarship is currently combining advances in several fields into a rapid new evolution of decision theory. Whereas in the late 1990s the edge of decision theory in public administration was defined by the tenets of bounded rationality, recent advances in psychology, sociology, and the relatively new field of behavioral economics have created a new concept of decisionmaking that might be described as "predictable irrationality."* In this newer framework, decisions are seen not simply as a product of humans whose rationality is bounded by cognitive and environmental limits, but also as a product of evolutionarily designed and predictable patterns of cognitive information processing. We discuss these advances later in the chapter.

Epistemologically, the firm scientific grounding of decision theory is hardly surprising given its intellectual origins. Certainly as conceived by Simon, a theory of decisionmaking has to be based on the logical positivist argument that there must be a primary distinction between facts, which can be tested and verified, and individual and collective preferences and values, which cannot be scientifically verified. At the base of Simon's decision theory is the concept of efficient administrative rationality: "The correctness of an administrative decision is a relative matter—it is correct if it selects appropriate means to reach designated ends. The rational administrator is concerned with the selection of these effective means" (1947/1997, 72). Rationality is based on means-ends logic, and assumes that the question at hand is selecting the best means to achieve agreed-upon ends. Facts and values "are related to means and ends. In the decision-making process those alternatives are chosen which are considered to be appropriate means for reaching desired ends. Ends themselves, however, are often merely instrumental to more final objectives" (61). We are thus led to Simon's conception of a series, or hierarchy, of ends: "Rationality has to do with the construction of means-ends chains of this kind" (62). He noted the limitations to the logic of means-ends analysis and the hierarchy of ends: Because means and ends can never be entirely separated, ends are often incomplete and unclear, and both means and ends are influenced by time and changing circumstances.

---

* This phrase is modified from Dan Ariely's book *Predictably Irrational: The Hidden Forces That Shape Our Decisions* (2009). As in Chapter 8, we use this term as a reference to an emerging field of decision theory that provides empirical evidence of how human decisionmaking departs (rather predictably) from rational choice theory and even bounded rationality.

Rationality is therefore limited (later called bounded or limited). Nevertheless, the science of administration should be based on the analysis of decisions, the decision being the proper unit of analysis for our research and theory. "In the first place, an administrative science, like any science, is concerned purely with factual statements. There is no place for ethical assertions in the body of science. Whenever ethical statements do occur, they can be separated into two parts, one factual and one ethical; and only the former has any relevance to science" (Simon 1947/1997, 253).

The boldness of Simon's assertions prompted one of the sharpest exchanges in the history of academic public administration, one that defined the two dominant scholarly perspectives in the field for the next fifty years. In 1952, Dwight Waldo published a long essay that reviewed much of the public administration literature of the time, including Simon's *Administrative Behavior*. Waldo wrote this (presented here in condensed form):

One major obstacle in the way of further development of democratic theory is the idea that efficiency is a value-neutral concept or, still worse, that it is antithetical to democracy. To hold that we should take efficiency as the central concept of our "science" but that we nevertheless must tolerate a certain amount of democracy because we "believe" in it, is to poison the taproot of American society. To maintain that efficiency is value-neutral and to propose at the same time that it be used as the central concept in a "science" of administration is to commit oneself to nihilism, so long as the prescription is actually followed.

Efficiency is, however, a tenet of orthodoxy that has refused to decline. No one now believes in a strict separation of politics and administration; but in the proposition that there are "value decisions" and "factual decisions" and that the latter can be made in terms of efficiency.

In this contention, the present "weight of authority" is against me. But I believe that there is no realm of "factual decisions" from which values are excluded. To decide is to choose between alternatives; to choose between alternatives is to introduce values. Herbert Simon has patently made outstanding contributions to administrative study. These contributions have been made, however, when he has worked free of the methodology he has asserted. (1952)

Simon's reply (again presented in condensed form):

Study of logic and empirical science has impressed on me the extreme care that must be exercised, in the search for truth, to avoid logical booby traps. For this reason the kind of prose I encounter in writings on political theory, decorated with assertion, invective, and metaphor, sometimes strikes me as esthetically pleasing, but seldom as convincing.

No one who has studied seriously the writings of logical positivists, or my own discussion of fact and value in *Administrative Behavior*, could attribute to us the "proposition that there are 'value decisions' and 'factual decisions.'" (1952b)

Quite apart from whether Mr. Waldo's premises are right or wrong, I do not see how we can progress in political philosophy if we continue to think and write in the loose, literary, metaphorical style that he and most other political theorists adopt. The standard of unrigor that is tolerated in political theory would not receive a passing grade in the elementary course in logic, Aristotelian or symbolic. (1952b)

To this, Waldo then replied (again in condensed form):

Professor Simon charges me with profaning the sacred places of Logical Positivism, and I am afraid I have. I use this figure of speech because Professor Simon seems to me that rare individual in our secular age, a man of deep faith. His convictions are monolithic and massive. His toleration of heresy and sin is nil. The Road to Salvation is straight, narrow, one-way, and privately owned.

Even if we should be inclined to elect salvation by logical positivism, the matter is not so simple as it is represented by Professor Simon.

May I state for the record, though I had hoped that I had made it clear, that I am not opposed to positivism and empiricism as whole bodies of thought or techniques of investigation or action.

The creative processes of the mind are still a mystery and at best are merely aided by training in logic, Professor Simon must know. Perhaps Professor Simon needs to examine whether the logical positivism of which he is enamored has become an obstacle in his pursuit of the science to which he is dedicated. To me, at least, logical positivism, empiricism, and science are far from being the nearly or wholly congruent things which they seem to be to Professor Simon. (1953)

These differing theoretical perspectives still frame the two primary bodies of scholarship in public administration. One public administration perspective is in the tradition of Waldo. This scholarship is philosophical, logical, deductive; it is a scholarship primarily associated with the tension between democratic values and bureaucratic behavior (Goodsell 1983; Wamsley and Wolf 1996). The other important perspective in the field is broadly represented by Simon's perspective, understood to be the scientific study of public administration. This study, however, has been significantly influenced by philosophical perspectives tracing to Waldo (Carroll and Frederickson 2001).

In the public sector, Simon argued, decisions are made in the context of organizations that tend to stability and equilibrium. In an organization, "the controlling group, regardless of its personal values, will be opportunistic—will appear to be motivated in large part at least by conservation objectives" (1947/1997, 119). In decision theory, therefore, it is rational for organizations to minimize risk and to regard collective institutional survival as an end or a value (Downs 1967). Simon also argued that the relationship between organizations and the individuals in them can be understood as an equilibrium between the personal goals and preferences of individuals and organizational needs. Both the effective individual and the rational organization will tend toward conserving efficiency; that is, they will make decisions that will achieve as much of extant organizational preferences and values as possible given resource and other contingencies.

We see here an important theoretical distinction between private or commercial organizations in markets and the concept of market equilibrium, on the one hand, and nonmarket public organizations and the rational conserving efficiency concept, on the other (Simon 2000). Decisions made under conditions of the rational conserving efficiency concept will be guided by preferences for institutional order, stability, predictability, and survival (Kaufman 1991; Smith 1988). Because the public institutional environment may be volatile, survival may depend on adaptations based on estimates of the need to change patterns of order, stability, and predictability. Public institutions that do not survive make the wrong guesses and their resources dry up. Public institutions that do survive routinely search for the balance between order and adaptation, a kind of institutional natural selection (Kaufman 1991). This understanding of decision-theoretic rational conserving efficiency, although generally descriptive of public-sector decision behavior, deemphasizes the shared values of decisionmakers and their collective commitments to organizational purposes.

In its rudimentary form, rational decision theory sought to (1) clarify and put in priority order organizational values and objectives; (2) consider the available alternative or alternatives that might achieve those objectives; and (3) analyze alternatives to find the alternative or group of alternatives most likely to achieve preferred objectives. In its most simplified form, rational decision theory describes goal-oriented behavior.

Rational decision theory was challenged early on because it was considered unrealistic and out of touch with actual patterns of organizational decisionmaking. Rather than make rational choices, organizations "muddle through" by making small incremental decisions that are based on mixed-together means and ends, that are made with limited knowledge, limited analytic capabilities, and limited time, and that are less likely to involve big risks (Lindblom 1959, 1965, 1979). These challenges were a characterization of Simon's claims because his initial decision theory anticipated the limits of rationality and described them. Nevertheless, the scientific and systematic study of decision rationality, however limited, was the key to understanding public administration. So, by the late 1950s, the stage was set for the transition from decision theory based on rationality to decision theory based on bounded rationality.

The Evolution of Decision Theory

From this description of the origins of decision theory, we fast-forward more than half a century for a consideration of contemporary decision theory and the logic of rationality. Since the 1990s, there has been a growing movement, backed largely by experimental research, to define how decisions are bounded, not by cognitive or environmental constraints, but instead by patterns or biases in individual information processing. As we discuss in the Conclusions, the notion of bounded rationality as an alternative to pure rationality potentially prevents theoretical advancement in decision theory.

Rationality

Rationality is still a central concept in decision theory, but modern conceptions of rationality account for key variations in describing and understanding rationality. Although rationality has many meanings (sane, intelligent, calculating), in decision theory rationality is more narrowly defined "as a particular and very familiar class of procedures for making choices" (March 1994, 2). This includes a rationality of process, usually called procedural rationality, which links choices to preferred outcomes, usually called substantive rationality. As we discuss later in the chapter and in Chapter 8 on rational choice theory, recent advances in decision theory suggest that this link is often disrupted or more malleable than originally postulated.

Two distinct patterns of rational logic also appear in decision theory. Both are based on Simon's initial logical-positivist means-ends description of rational decisionmaking, but they define ends differently. One is the rational decision logic of consequences; the other the rational decision logic of appropriateness. In the former, rational decisions are consequential because actions based on those choices anticipate preferred future consequences, results, or ends. The rational logic of consequences is most compatible with Simon's early conceptions of decision theory and with substantive rationality (Simon 1947/1997, 1960; March and Simon 1993). The decision logic of consequences is more suited to modeling, cost-benefit analysis, performance measurement, risk analysis, and quantitative methodologies. Decision theorists coming from the perspective of the logic of consequences tend to be associated with economics and political science. The modeling of Thomas H. Hammond and Jack H. Knott (1999) illustrates the decision logic of consequences.

The rational logic of appropriateness is much less connected to Simon. Decisions are thought to be appropriate when choices are based on shared understandings of the decision situation, the nature or "identity" of the organization, and accepted rules of what is expected in particular situations. The rational logic of appropriateness tends to emphasize procedural rationality. The decision logic of appropriateness is more suited to institutional analysis, historical analysis, contingency theory, population ecology, case analysis, and narrative-deductive methodologies. Decision theorists working from the appropriateness perspective are likely to be associated with sociology, organization theory, and social psychology. Public administration has excellent contemporary examples of both perspectives. The research of Todd R. LaPorte and Paula M. Consolini (1991) on tightly coupled high-reliability systems illustrates the decision logic of appropriateness.

Bounded Rationality

Rather than describing rationality, both forms of decision logic in fact describe limited or bounded rationality.

Pure rationality is an artifact of analysts' assumptions. Decision-theoretic modeling usually includes at least some assumptions, such as agreement regarding objectives or values; perfect or, at least, highly developed knowledge of alternatives; and the known consequences of applying alternatives. By using such assumptions, the prediction of either individual or institutional decision behavior and the results of that behavior tend to be highly generalized, usually described as modalities or tendencies. Such models are often tested in experimental settings in which variables can be controlled and manipulated and assumptions changed. The long series of prisoners' dilemma experiments and other field tests of game theory, subjects covered in more detail later in this chapter, illustrate this research (Milgrom and Roberts 1992; Rasmussen 1990). Ordinarily, rather than claiming to explain rational decision behavior in complex organizational settings, this research claims to provide insight or to have heuristic qualities. Perhaps the strongest results gained from experimental tests of "pure" rationality are found in the research on individual and institutional tendencies to cooperate (Axelrod 1984; Brown 1995) or compete (Hirschleifer and Riley 1992). The generalities and insights tracing to experimental tests of rational decision behavior under some "pure" assumptions are promising, particularly in the extent to which they explicate the bounds of rationality. But such models are less than satisfactory descriptions of how decisions actually happen (March 1994, 5). We turn, then, to limited or bounded rationality in decision theory.

In a rational decision theory framework, the key questions, problems, and challenges all have to do with the limits of rationality. How is decision rationality bounded? We suggest that the closer decision theorists come to measuring and describing the limits of rationality, the closer they come to credible representations of how decisions actually happen. More importantly, the closer decision theorists come to accurate descriptions of decision behavior, the more likely they are to improve the capabilities of decisionmakers and the results of their decisions. The recent emphasis in behavioral economics on using experiments to explicate patterns of boundedness or "irrationality" is a step in the right direction (Camerer, Lowenstein, and Rabin 2004). We return to this point in Chapter 8.

Those rational choice theorists inclined toward pure decision theory as well as to the logic of consequences now accept limited rationality and tend to refer to individuals and organizations as "intendedly rational." In spite of their best efforts to be rational, decisionmakers, individually and especially collectively, are constrained by limited cognitive capacity, incomplete information, and unclear linkages between decisions and outcomes. Others have shown that boundedly rational decisionmaking has led to the development of useful heuristics for making decisions in constrained environments, resulting in "good" decisions (Gigerenzer and Todd, 1999). Decision theorists working from the appropriateness perspective tend to focus heavily on the usually obvious points that not all alternatives can be known and considered, not all preferences or values can be reconciled, and not all alternatives can be considered. Instead of seeing the individual or the organization as intendedly rational, they emphasize Simon's "satisficing" concept that, rather than finding the best course of action, decisionmakers usually search for actions that are good enough. They somehow muddle through.

Depending on the logic of decision theory, rationality is differently bounded. We return to the two primary decision theory perspectives, the logic of consequences and the logic of appropriateness, to describe differing understandings of the limits and bounds of rationality.

Irrationality

At the time of the first edition of this text, modern decision theory was mostly about the limits and bounds of decision rationality. Rational choice theorists inclined toward pure decision theory conceived of individuals and organizations as, in effect, seeking to make rational decisions but falling short because of specific limits that made fully rational decisionmaking difficult for humans. Theorists of bounded rationality, then, were driven in large part by the need to explain decisions or choices that deviated from rational choice theory, and within the decision theory framework such deviations were explained as being the result of environmental and cognitive constraints.

Contemporary decisionmaking research, however, has begun to step further and further from the foundations of rational choice. Rather than comparing actual decisions to the baseline of fully rational decisionmaking, empirical research has increasingly tackled head-on widely demonstrated patterns of decisionmaking that are examples not just of humans falling short of perfect rationality, but of humans being perversely and consistently irrational. Amos Tversky and Daniel Kahneman's (1974) pioneering work laid the foundation for an increased interest in theorizing about alternatives to rational choice theory. A central issue highlighted by Tversky and Kahneman was the descriptive nature of bounded rationality; it could not predict decisionmaking, only describe post hoc how (and perhaps why) a decision deviated from a purely rational baseline. While largely accepting bounded rationality's notion of decisionmaking limits (be they cognitive, environmental, or informationally incomplete), Tversky and Kahneman showed that human decisionmaking can actually be highly predictive. They demonstrated that decisionmaking is consistently biased by certain environmental conditions or general human predispositions. Predictable biases empirically demonstrated by their work include "anchoring," the "availability bias," and "representativeness."

Anchoring simply means that past decisions disproportionately affect future decisions. Rather than approaching each problem as a blank slate, decisionmakers tend to evaluate new conditions in the context of past decisions. Anchoring has been shown to affect the baseline level for comparative judgments among even the brightest of college students (Ariely 2009). Related to this tendency is the availability bias, in which people will assess the pros and cons of any decision on the basis of the most readily available information, often recent experiences, particularly if such experiences were highly salient or traumatic. The representativeness bias simply states that individuals have a tendency to draw on existing stereotypes when attempting to discern patterns in others' behavior. Other prominent biases have also been well documented, including the status quo bias and what researchers have described as "loss aversion" (Kahneman, Knetsch, and Thaler 1991). In situations involving uncertainty, individuals will take fewer risks if the gains from the decision are perceived as being less than a potential loss. And, vice versa, the potential gains from any decision must be more than offset (often at least double) the potential loss; in short, the ratio of gains to losses is not a 1:1 relationship as would be predicted by a model of pure rationality. Kahneman and his colleagues have labeled these tendencies "anomalies," that is, persistent and predictable deviations from rational decisionmaking. Since the groundbreaking work of Kahneman, Tversky, and others, there has been an effort to use anomalies to build a broader theoretical framework, a point we return to later in the chapter and in Chapter 8.

Tversky and Kahneman spawned a new generation of researchers under the moniker of "heuristics and biases" (Thaler and Sunstein 2009, 23). In conditions of incomplete information, decisionmakers tend to demonstrate any or all of the heuristics or biases just noted. Such tendencies have been well documented since Tversky and Kahneman's original work, with scholars focusing on biases in information processing, developing the appropriate methodologies for testing such biases (mostly experimental), and devising a new theoretical framework for explaining such tendencies. Reviews of this emerging research agenda can be found in behavioral economics (Camerer, Lowenstein, and Rabin 2004), experimental economics (Kagel and Roth 1995), and political science (Ostrom, Gardner, and Walker 1994), as well as more general audience introductions (Ariely 2009; Brafman and Brafman 2008). Given the rich tradition in public administration on the psychology of decisionmaking (Barnard 1938; McGregor 1960; Simon 1947/1997), it seems only logical public administration scholars should look to this emerging field for new insights into how bureaucrats make decisions.

The basic premise of this new decision-theoretic framework is to move beyond "intendedly rational" as a description of decisionmaking. Bounded rationality implies that with complete information and lacking environmental constraints, decisions would resemble pure rationality. The irrationality framework emerging from Tversky and Kahneman's research suggests otherwise; even with complete information and absent external constraints, decisions follow a predictable, irrational pattern based on the way in which individuals process information. The irrationality framework also begins to explain why individuals are bounded and, as we discuss later in the chapter, allows for a more predictable theoretical framework. Irrationality would suggest that the logic of consequences is not possible, or at the very least subject to constant changes based on biases in information processing. The logic of appropriateness presents a more realistic framework for decisionmaking, but even here, more emphasis on the psychology of decisionmaking is required.

Revisiting the Logic of Consequences

It is with two arguments in mind that we now revisit the logic of consequences and the logic of appropriateness. The first argument contends decisions are limited by informational constraints (Bendor, Taylor, and van Gaalen 1987). To sum up the second argument, "People tend to be somewhat mindless, passive decision makers" (Thaler and Sunstein 2009, 37).

Information

First, the capacity of individuals and organizations to process information, particularly in an information-rich environment, is illustrated by the functioning of Internet search engines. Sorting and then processing information by preferences, priorities, and reliability are notoriously difficult; and even when well done, properly sorted information must still be interpreted. The capacity to summarize, comprehend, and use information has its limits. Inferred causal connections among information, actions, and outcomes are ordinarily weak. *Second*, individual and institutional memories are often faulty, compartmentalized, difficult to retrieve, and hard to connect to the problems at hand. *Third*, attention, in both time and capabilities, is limited. Often, an overload of problems needs attention, and not all problems can be treated at once. *Fourth*, especially in organizations with complex technologies, communication problems arise from compartmentalization, professional subculture, language, and information overload.

Under conditions of bounded rationality, decisionmakers cope with imperfect information by editing and sorting, a process guided by assumptions based on stereotypes and typologies that simplify what information is and is not considered. Problems tend to be unbundled and reduced to their parts. It is often easier to associate particular available information with the parts of a problem in the search for more comprehensive solutions; this unbundling is especially useful in the context of organizational specialization and departmentalization. Given available information, parts of problems can be managed in this disaggregative form.

Some information, such as budgets, balance sheets, and performance measures, is always given a special place in decisionmaking. This information has the authority of evident objectivity and certainty. Decisionmakers give careful guidance to organizing and developing this type of information source and thus manage the information upon which their future decisions are to be based.

Coping with imperfect information is bounded rationality and satisficing in action. Satisficing, or "good enough" rationality, has the very big advantage of moving an organization in the direction of preferred values while preserving institutional equilibrium. Indeed, recent work on the application of bounded rationality to decisions by street-level bureaucrats indicates decisionmaking is further shaped by information about what others within the organization will do (Keiser 2010). Bounded rationality, thus understood, is rational behavior that stabilizes and supports continuity and order while enabling at least some adaptation.

Even with perfect information, however, decisions will depart from pure rationality. Empirical evidence demonstrates that information processing is also shaped by cognitive biases and the behaviors of others. As noted earlier in the chapter, evidence from behavioral economics shows a strong tendency toward a status quo bias (Tversky and Kahneman 1974). Past information and previous decisions exert a powerful effect on future decisions. Although such evidence may appear at face value to be similar to incrementalism or bounded rationality, the underlying assumptions are different. Even in cases of complete information, the processing of information will in large part be shaped by previous decisions. This tendency toward relativity bias or an anchoring effect (Ariely 2009) shows that future decisions and, importantly, the evaluation of alternatives tend to be based on previous decisions, experiences, or outcomes. Bounded rationality is often linked with incrementalism, in which incomplete information prevents full consideration of alternatives, and thus the safe play is to make small, incremental adjustments (Jones and Baumgartner 2005a, 326). Cognitive biases such as anchoring effects or a "commitment bias" (Brafman and Brafman 2008, 26–39) can lead to decisions that result in no change in policy despite new information.

Attention

Attention, both individually and collectively, is a scarce resource, reflected in limitations of time, too much information, changing problems, and changing priorities. The study of agendas in political science describes the changing patterns both of the attention of the public and the attention of legislative bodies, and strategies for influencing that attention (Kingdon 1995). In public administration, the study of strategic planning and priority setting is a body of work that assumes limited attention and the need to bring order to attention by structuring agreements about which issues are most important (Bryson 1988; McGregor 1991). Systems of quality control and customer complaints in business management are techniques for searching for the organizational problem most deserving of attention. The logic of managing by exception and the logic of managing at the boundaries of the organization are ways to describe the subjects or problems most deserving of attention. Contemporary interests in reform, innovation, and change work from the assumption that improving institutional order, continuity, and predictability deserves less attention and that finding what to change deserves more attention.

Attention can be both failure and success driven. Rapid changes in air travel security systems illustrate failure-driven shifts in attention away from customer convenience and on-time service toward increased air travel safety. The failure to stop airplane hijacking as a form of terrorism has replaced the war on drugs as the focus of FBI attention. On the success side, the logic of benchmarking focuses decisionmakers' attention on the successes of other organizations in the same field, particularly prizewinners (the Baldridge Award, the Harvard Innovation Award, etc.), and a process of mimicking so-called best practices. This attention to copying the changes of others appears to have more to do with a rational search for legitimacy and acceptance than a rational search for productivity, because there is little evidence of improved institutional performance (DiMaggio and Powell 1983).

Such limited attention capabilities are an important component to building a new model of decision theory. Limits in attention, or what scholars have termed "attention-driven choice," can result in nonincremental policy change for an institution or political system (Jones and Baumgartner 2005a, 2005b). Policymakers do not have the time or cognitive resources to evaluate incoming information in a rational or "proportionate" way. Instead, unequal weight is given to certain pieces of information, resulting in a bias updating of beliefs regarding a particular policy (Jones and Baumgartner 2005a). The result is a decisionmaking process in which there may not be a logical connection between means and ends.

Risk Taking

From a decision-theoretic perspective, risks and risk taking can explain variations from equilibrium. The estimation of organizational risk is influenced by two simple features associated with equilibrium: first, the past success of key decisionmakers and second, the tendency to overestimate the salience of experiences based on stable environments.

Risk in decision theory is a function of the influence of uncertainty on rationality. Decision rationality is bounded by uncertainty regarding the consequences of present actions, and even greater uncertainty regarding the possible future consequences of possible future decisions. To accommodate the uncertainty of consequences when taking risk into account, decisionmakers tend to evaluate both the expected value of preferred consequences (will productivity be improved sharply or just a little by this risk?) and the degree of uncertainty involved (is this risk slight or great?). Decisions, then, are determined by these estimates and by the individual or organizational propensities to be risk averse or risk prone. Estimations of risk for the purpose of reducing uncertainty depend on perceptions of the context, assumptions regarding knowledge, and attempts to control the context of institutions (MacCrimmon and Wehrung 1986).

Uncertainty, and therefore risk, varies by the level of predictability in an institution's context. In settings in which decisionmakers have experience, they do rather well in predicting risk and in guiding institutions through unpredictable circumstances (March 1994, 37). Outside the range of their experiences, however, decisionmakers seem to deny uncertainty and underestimate the probability that rare or unexpected events will occur. If they are lucky, events will keep within the range of their experiences.

Decisionmakers tend to imagine greater control over the context of their institutions than they actually have, and they fail to imagine the possible effect of factors over which they have no control. When things go well and decisionmakers are successful, they tend to imagine it is because of their skill and leadership rather than luck, chance, or a friendly institutional context.

Uncertainties and decision risk associated with a turbulent context can be reduced by attempts to control that context. Systems of co-optation reduce uncertainty and risk (Selznick 1949). Partnerships and contracts, when coupled with contract deadlines and performance guarantees, may not reduce decision risk, but do broaden or spread the responsibility of risk.

Organizations use internal controls, procedures, and red tape to attempt to reduce risks and deal with uncertainty (Bozeman 2000). For example, some businesses and organizations routinely overcomply with governmental regulation to lower the risks of possible investigations and negative publicity (DeHart-Davis and Bozeman 2001). Overcompliance rationality is difficult to explain in terms of economic cost and benefits, but easy to explain in the likely overestimation of the possible risks of being caught undercomplying. Overcompliance can also be normative. Many universities, for example, essentially overcomply with affirmative action requirements simply because of ideological commitments to diversity. Institutional undercompliance is more often explained by ignorance rather than by risk-prone decisionmakers (DeHart-Davis and Bozeman 2001).

The propensity toward risk taking is associated with goals or targets. Less risk will be taken if goals are met or nearly met, whereas more risk will be taken if the individual or institution expects to fall well below expected goals. Goals and targets tend to be adjusted to adapt to risk. Successful risk taking opens the way for higher goals, and unsuccessful risk taking leads to lower aspirations (March 1994).

Success-inclined risk has to do with the prosperity of key decisionmakers to attribute success to their abilities and failure to their bad fortune. Persistent executive successes lead to an underestimation of risk because experiences have been based on successes. Successful executives are promoted and tend to have high confidence in their abilities. Because they know the secrets of success, they have such confidence that they can beat the odds that they may guess wrong or fail to anticipate changing circumstances. The remarkable success of the dot.coms in the 1980s and 1990s and the sharp reversal of dot.com fortunes at the turn of the century illustrate the success-induced underestimation of risk.

Risk underestimation based on experience is, at one level, rational, because most decisionmakers have not directly experienced unlikely events. On the other hand, experience with a particular decisionmaking context can cause decisionmakers to treat that decision as the "anchor" from which all future decisions are made (Ariely 2009). This tendency, coupled with a bias for the status quo and the overwhelming tendency toward loss aversion (Kahneman, Knetsch, and Thaler 1991), can create conservative institutions.

Because rare events are unlikely, the decision process is biased—first, in the direction of overlooking the very substantial consequences of some rare events, and second, in assuming that, if one rare event is unlikely (a flood, an earthquake, a depression), all possible rare events are unlikely. It is correct to assume that one rare event is highly unlikely, but it is incorrect to assume that all possible rare events are all highly unlikely. Organizational decisionmakers and planners tend to base their plans and decisions on essentially linear extrapolations of their direct experiences (Tuchman 1984; Roberts 1999; Conquest 2000).

High-reliability organizations (nuclear power systems, air traffic security systems, nuclear ships, space travel, etc.) are especially structured to reduce risk. High-reliability decision protocols include a much different logic when compared with trial-and-error, failure-tolerant systems. The incremental, mixed scanning, loose coupling, resource scarcity, and bounded rationality theories—theories that explain much of standard organizational behavior—are replaced in high-reliability theory, described in Chapter 4. Most persons associated with high-reliability systems and most institutions in tightly coupled high-reliability systems seldom or never experience unlikely events. When they do, they tend to attribute systems failure to such exogenous forces as weather or acts of God. Over time, those associated with such systems come to think of their systems as more reliable than they are; when this happens, they tend to relax decision protocols and engage in risk-prone behavior (Epstein and O'Halloran 1996).

The September 11, 2001, terrorist airplane hijackings, which destroyed the World Trade Center in New York City, damaged the Pentagon, and crashed an airplane into the ground in Pennsylvania, illustrate a kind of high-reliability rationality trap. To be sure, there have been airline accidents and criticisms of air travel reliability and security. And there have been accidents (Perrow 1999). But, however tragic these accidents have been, the magnitude of risk associated with each separate accident, particularly when there were substantial periods between separate accidents, was not enough to prevent substantial deviation from air travel security decision protocols. Significant deviations from tightly coupled high-reliability decision logic included little training of airport security screeners, poor management of ramp security, extended systems of contracts and subcontracts, lax management of these contracts, and disincentives for contractors to report error (Commonwealth of Massachusetts 2001). Finally, and most importantly, because the events of September 11, 2001, were well beyond anyone's experience, the possibility of such a tragedy was systematically discounted.

The popular literature in public administration in recent years has made much of the desirability of decisionmakers to be entrepreneurial and willing to take risks (Osborne and Gaebler 1992). The premise upon which risk-taking advice is based is that public organizations are bureaucratic, slow, wasteful, and unresponsive. Unsaid in this premise is that most public organizations are stable, predictable, and reliable—at equilibrium. Greater risk taking as a decision strategy trades institutional stability, predictability, and attention for the risk that decisionmakers will make the right guesses regarding how the organization can be made to change. Very often the risk-taking perspective is associated with calls for reform.

Formal Testing of Bounded Rationality

These bounded rationality generalizations, viewed from the logic of decision consequences, form the basis of testable assertions subject to modeling and to experimental field testing. Much of this scholarship is based on assumptions-based institutional models and upon choice-making experiments in controlled settings. This is a robust scholarship and a significant body of research, too large to cover here (Hirschleifer and Riley 1992; Krause 2003). Perhaps the most common combination of decision modeling and experiments uses the prisoners' dilemma, a contrived heuristic, as follows: Two prisoners are accused of the same crime. They are interviewed separately. Each is rational, rationality defined as self-interest, and each knows the range of choices available to the other. If prisoner Bill confesses, he will get a shorter sentence than prisoner Al, and vice versa. If both Bill and Al confess, they will both get long sentences. But if they cooperate and neither one nor the other confesses, then both may escape the charges. As Bill makes his rational decision, he takes into account the range of Al's possible rational decisions. Because Bill and Al are acting independently and simultaneously, each will tend to try to avoid the risk that the other will confess. So it is likely that they will not cooperate and remain silent (which is also a risk), and each will decide to confess in his rational self-interest. By failing to cooperate and to each pursue rational individual self-interest, both make suboptimal decisions.

The prisoners' dilemma and dozens of variations of it are a part of modern game theory (Rasmussen 1990; Radner 1985). This body of research has been very influential in settings in which a firm needs to make decisions regarding location. The pattern of cooperation-competition seen in modern shopping malls and auto plazas is an example. In the public sector, such models have been usefully applied to national defense policy and particularly to battlefield estimates of an enemy's actions. Such models have also been successfully used to describe bureaucratic politics (Bendor and Moe 1985; Hammond 1986; Hammond and Knott 1999; Hammond and Miller 1985; Moe 1984). As noted in the Conclusions, the field of public administration has much to gain by applying experimental methodology to the issue of governance. Although there are clear biases in the way in which information is processed, these patterns can be formalized in a manner that is typical of the logic of consequences framework. As we discuss in Chapter 8, what is required is a new theory, or for public administration, a new theoretical framework for explaining decisionmaking, one that is by necessity multidisciplinary.

Bounded Decision Rationality and the Logic of Appropriateness

Thus far we have described decisions as intendedly rational individual choice calculations and consequent institutional behavior. In this description, pure, model-based, and boundedly rational decisions are evaluated according to their results, the results being judged on the basis of values, objectives, and preferences. We turn now to an understanding of rational decision theory in terms of the logic of appropriateness. The logic of decision appropriateness traces to the work of James G. March and Johan P. Olsen (1984, 1989) and March (1994, 1988), a body of work that is both a convenient perspective on decisionmaking and a synthesis of understandings of bounded rationality found primarily in sociology, social psychology, and parts of business and public administration.

Following the logic of appropriateness, individuals and organizations are rationally goal oriented. But their rational behavior is oriented toward an understanding of goals that is less associated with assumptions of efficiency, marketlike competition, and self-interest and more associated with assumptions of rules, identities, situations, and actions (Wright 1984). In both the decision logic of consequences and the decision logic of appropriateness, rationality is bounded, but it is differently bounded. And in the decision logic of consequences and the decision logic of appropriateness there are patterns of analysis, systematic reasoning, and complicated choices. It is an error to assume that, because much of the decision-theoretic work using the logic of consequences is formal and mathematical, it deals with complexity, and that decision-theoretic work using the logic of appropriateness explains simple or less complex decision choices. Both patterns of reasoning can account for or explain simple or complex patterns of decisionmaking (Zey 1992).

Rules and identities are the stuff of formal organizations. "Most people in an organization execute their tasks most of the time by following a set of well-specified rules that they accept as part of their identity. This is true of doctors in hospitals, workers on assembly lines, sales representatives in the field, teachers in a classroom, and police officers on a beat. It is also true for those people in organizations whose tasks primarily involve making decisions. Organizational rules define what it means to be a decision maker" (March 1994, 60). There are rules of process and procedure that channel decision processes. There are rules regarding the factors to be considered in making decisions. There are rules limiting choices (who can be hired or promoted) and rules allowing choices. There are criteria for evaluating performance. There are formal and informal rules. Rules are not independent of the identities of those who work in organizations. Rules frame their identities, and their identities influence organizational rules.

Organizations select individuals who already have identities and tend to behave according to rules associated with those identities: professors, doctors, truck drivers, cops. And organizations socialize individuals to their unique rules. This is because organizations also have identities. Organizational identities are socially constructed on the understanding of how particular kinds of institutions should or ought to behave to have legitimacy and standing. Organizational identities can be highly defined—consider the US Marines—or mildly defined, such as a small business.

As can been seen by this description, decision theory following the logic of appropriateness is deeply contextual. Contexts can be highly complex and decision-making heavily informed by contextual rules and identities filled with ambiguity, uncertainty, risk, imperfect information, and limited attention. Organizations guide individual action by providing the content of identities and rules and cues about when and how to make rational decisions. These are the decision rules of appropriateness. Decisionmaking behavior studied from the vantage of appropriateness describes rational action and the processes that guide rational action quite differently from descriptions of the formal analysis of noncontextual decision experiments.

Because of the relative stability, order, and predictability of formal organizations, one might think that a perspective on rational decisionmaking so embedded in context might tend toward static descriptions of order. This is not so. Much of the decision-theoretic research using the logic of appropriateness deals with how organizations and the individuals in them cope, and especially how they cope with individual and institutional rules and identities given the dynamic environments in which institutions are embedded (Thompson 1967; Harmon and Mayer 1986). This is the study of institutional change and decisionmaking patterns of mediation between institutions and their environments.

Decision patterns of institutional change are history-dependent adaptations. This is the process of constructing a usable history, one that involves a mixture of experiences carried along in institutional narratives and stories, and the selective exploitation of particular institutional successes and failures (Bellow and Minow 1996). Individual identities and organizational identities and rules reflect this usable history and understand present rules to be residuals of this history. The processes of history-dependent adaptation involve forms of the collective imagining of a preferred future, imagining taking the form of strategic planning, visioning exercises, the aspirations of leaders, long-range budgeting, and so forth. This is an intentional process of capturing institutional preferences and desires and setting out to achieve them. In the decision logic of consequences, this process is the result of the preferences of decisionmakers and calculations of the likely future consequences of action. In the decision logic of appropriateness, decisionmakers create history-based rules as instruments of control, construct history-based identities and expectations of behavior, identify an attractive future, and go about enacting that future. This is understood to be not just a process by which the institution adapts to its environment, but also a process by which the institution and the environment adapt to each other. This process involves analysis, bargaining, patterns of imitation, and trial-and-error experiences of institutional learning (Schram and Neisser 1997).

March and Olsen (1995) describe an institutional learning cycle involving the selective recollection and interpretation of experiences (the usable history), understandings of the rules and identities derived from these experiences, interpretations of the nature of previous institutional actions and their consequences, and the adaptation of rules and identities based on these interpretations. This can be a noisy iterative process of competing institutional interpretations of its past and estimates of the consequences of previous actions and what the institution learned. Institutions may learn poorly because of misinterpretation of history, imperfect memory, and, above all, attribution of historical successes to effectiveness while discounting the influence of good fortune. Cycles of institutional learning, embodied in changing patterns of rules and identities, describe the processes by which institutions adapt to their environments and environments adapt to institutions.

Ambiguity, Uncertainty, and the Logic of Appropriateness

Easily the most interesting and provocative part of decision theory based on the logic of appropriateness is the treatment of the concepts of uncertainty and ambiguity. Classic conceptions of decisionmaking assume an objective reality, an understandable world amenable to description and understanding. This is the positivist assumption that there are knowable patterns of order, from DNA to the solar system, and that there are also knowable patterns of human behavior, including how we make decisions. In decision patterns, there is also the assumption of causality, a structure of connections between causes and effects, problems and solutions. The job of the decision theorist is to describe this causality. Finally, decisions are instrumental, choices designed to bring about or cause preferred states. These three assumptions, objective reality, causality, and intentionality, are all conditioned by the bounds of rationality. Much of the development of rational decision theory from the logic of consequences and the logic of appropriateness is based on these classic conceptions.

But some is not.

Ambiguity is at the center of an alternative understanding of rationality and of institutional decisionmaking. Ambiguity is a lack of clarity or consistency in interpretations of reality, causality, and intentionality. Ambiguous situations and purposes resist categorization and therefore systematic analysis. Ambiguous outcomes are fuzzy. In the ambiguous decision world, alternatives are hazy, objectives are contradictory, and reality is not so much to be discovered as it is to be invented.

How shall we understand this decision world?

In the alternative understanding of rationality, the institution is less understood as a world of decisionmaking and better understood as a world of sense making (Harmon 1989). Consider these differences.

In formal decision theories, preferences are assumed to be observable, consistent, stable, and exogenous. In the sense-making perspective, preferences may or may not be revealed, and, when they are revealed, are contradictory, volatile, ambivalent, and both exogenous and endogenous. Planning and visioning processes are designed to make sense of preferences and seek agreement regarding preferences, and such processes can do that. But planning and visioning processes are also symbols that signal messages to the environment about what the organization is doing or might do (Cohen and March 1976; Weick 1979; Harmon and Mayer 1986). Plans are also advertisements to attract support or investments, games to test levels of support, and excuses for interaction (Weick 1979). "In practice, decisionmakers often seem to take an active role in constructing and shaping their preferences. They make decisions by considering their effects on future preferences" (March 1994, 189–190).

In formal decision theories, individual and organizational identities are assumed to be knowable, rational, and self-interested. In the sense-making perspective, identities are ambiguous. Identities are multiple and driven by expectations. An identity, such as that of a police officer, is ambiguous because of imprecise, unstable, inconsistent, and exogenous expectations. How, then, do individuals make decisions in their institutional roles? Mostly they enact identities by observing others in the same role, by listening to stories, by following instructions and rules, and by uncoding what they understand others expect of them. Informal group norms have been shown to exert a powerful effect on individual behavior, particularly when behavior that is considered nonconforming is made public (Cialdini and Goldstein 2004). Institutions develop agreed-upon norms that, although informal, guide individual behavior. Over time, stories change, expectations shift, rules change, and identities evolve. This evolution is an ambiguity-driven constant interpretation and reinterpretation of the individual in the organization and the organization itself. To manage the fuzziness of identity, identity evolves (Bellow and Minow 1996).

In classic decision theory, reality is knowable, a direct application of the physical sciences and their logic to the social world. From the sense-making perspective, reality is socially constructed, at least that part of reality having to do with organizing and deciding (Berger and Luckmann 1967). In the social construction of reality, decisionmakers conserve belief by interpreting new experiences in ways that make them consistent with prior beliefs. Decisionmakers rely on experience; they overestimate the probability of events they have experienced and underestimate the probability of events that might occur (Frederickson 2000). Decisionmakers attribute events and actions to their own intentions and capabilities rather than to happenstance or good fortune. And successful decisionmakers are especially likely to see decisions as confirming their own beliefs and to refute contradictory evidence (March 1994, 183).

Because institutional reality is socially constructed, it is subject to multiple contradictory constructions. Constructions of institutional reality tend to be hegemonic, that is, a dominant interpretation of reality, usually based on a master narrative and winning arguments (Hood and Jackson 1991). In this way, the inherent ambiguity of social reality is reduced and replaced by a socially constructed, less ambiguous version of reality. Decisionmaking, in the context of socially constructed reality, is often a process of reconciling the socially constructed institutional hegemony with other understandings of reality.

"Neither rational theories of choice nor rule-following theories of identity fulfillment deal particularly well with ambiguity. The contradictions, inconsistencies, and fuzziness of reality, preferences and identities are largely ignored. The problems of ambiguous realities are either denied or treated as special cases of uncertainty" (March 1994, 192).

Decision theorists working from the logic of the appropriateness perspective and from the sense-making perspective suggest that institutions respond to all these ambiguities with decentralized patterns of decisionmaking. In the language of decision theory, the ambiguity challenges faced by decisionmakers are reduced by loose coupling.

Loose Coupling, Garbage Cans, and Attention

To deal with complex, confusing, inconsistent, and ambiguous environments, complex organizations decentralize, delegate, and contract out. In the language of decision theory, this is loose coupling. Under conditions of loose coupling, institutions trade central control, comparability, and standardization for semiautonomous groups of decisionmakers organized around specializations, clientele, or geography. And loose coupling trades high levels of overall institutional ambiguity for lower levels of subunit ambiguity (Cohen and March 1986). The initial description of loose coupling was based on a study of American universities and can be summed up with a now-famous saying: The university faculty is a group of people held together only by their shared need for parking. As the archetype of loose coupling, universities are made up of semiautonomous departments that control, within certain limits, departmental curriculum, hiring, promotion, and, at the graduate level, student admissions. Each department has constructed its own reality, its own usable history. It is far easier for departments to wrestle with disciplinary ambiguities, although such wrestling matches can be bloody, than it is for entire universities to sort through their ambiguities. Indeed, Michael Cohen and March state that "almost any educated person can deliver a lecture entitled 'The Goals of the University.' Almost no one will listen to the lecture voluntarily" (1986, 195). The same could be written about the speeches of corporate executives, mayors, governors, and leaders of other complex and decentralized institutions.

Under conditions of loose coupling, each semiautonomous group has a range of decision discretion that it will jealously guard. Think of the police or the US Marines. As it sorts through decision ambiguities and make decisions, a department will "discover preferences through action more often than it acts on the basis of preferences" (Cohen and March 1986, 3). Under conditions of loose coupling, semiautonomous subunits may appear to make decisions at odds with stated overall preferences. The reason for this is because it is true that an agreed-upon specific preference at the subunit level, sorted out through experience and action, will often trump an abstract preference at the institutional level, a preference filled with ambiguity and competing interpretations. In the words of Cohen, March, and Olsen, the institution "appears to operate on a variety of inconsistent and ill-defined preferences" (1972, 1).

Observations of decisionmaking in loosely coupled institutional settings would lead one to the opinion that there is little order to it. Decisionmaking appears to be chaos. Decision theorists working from the sense-making perspective suggest that conventional decision theories are able only to see chaos. This is because there is order in loosely coupled decisionmaking processes, but it is not conventional order.

The best-known alternative explanation of order in loosely coupled settings is garbage can theory. The famous Cohen, March, and Olsen description of organizations as decision garbage cans is this: "An organization is a collection of choices looking for problems, issues and feelings looking for decision situations in which they might be aired, solutions looking for issues to which they might be the answer, and decision makers looking for work" (1972, 2).

This is a distinctly process-oriented description of decision theory. In the "decision soup" there will be institutional competencies and social or political needs and preferences. Under the right circumstances, competencies and needs will find each other, bond, and thereby significantly modify or adapt institutional arrangements, preferences, and decision processes. In the conventional decision model, means are applied to ends. In the garbage can, it is just as likely that ends will be applied to means. It is important to note the relative unimportance of efficiency or rationality in this conception of decision theory. The garbage can theory of decisionmaking may not be rational in the traditional means-ends understanding of rationality, but under certain circumstances it "makes sense." Such sense making is retrospective, the sense derived from looking back. "Doing something requires such an active and immediate engagement with the objects of our attention that only afterwards are we able to stop and reflect on, to 'see,' what we have done" (Harmon and Mayer 1986, 355).

One might assume from this that decisions and actions are accidental, random, purposeless, and chaotic. Not so, argue decision theorists from the sense-making perspective. Decisionmaking is less a process of rational choices and more a process of the temporal mixing of decisions and actions and the attendant decision processes of enacting the future (Yanow 1996).

Perhaps the best-known application of garbage can theory in the public sector is John Kingdon's *Agendas, Alternatives, and Public Policies* (1995). He describes three essentially parallel but independent streams: the political stream, the policy stream, and the problem stream. Triggers can cause the streams to find each other in windows of opportunity. Triggers include changes in the collective understandings of problems, changes in political power, possible new ways of dealing with problems, or a focusing event. Using these streams and the garbage can metaphor, Kingdon describes a range of policy changes that resemble the patterns of attraction between decisionmakers, problems, and solutions, and the eventual "solution" to problems. As March suggests, garbage can theory is essentially a temporal sorting process under conditions of very loose coupling. At some point, the attention of decisionmakers may be uniquely focused on a particular problem; this is especially important because attention is scarce and carefully rationed. If a problem has achieved attention, the questions change to definitions of the problem and its possible solutions. If, however, a possible solution is already available and there is agreement regarding attaching the problem to the solution, questions of problem definition and possible better solutions fall away.

Temporal sorting describes the flows of solutions, problems, and decisionmakers. In their simulation of garbage can decision processes, March and Olsen (1976) describe choices made by oversight, problem resolution, and flight. Under conditions of oversight, in temporal sorting a choice opportunity arrives but no problems attach themselves to the choice. No problems are resolved. Consider the military, AmeriCorps, or community service as solutions and the opinion of some that the events of September 11, 2001, call for mandatory national service. Thus far, no problems have attached themselves to these proposed solutions. Under conditions of problem resolution, problems are associated with choices, and decisionmakers have the attention and energy to link them and thereby solve the problem. Consider the use of the Army Reserves and the National Guard to oversee airport security. Consider universities presenting themselves as choices for research and development, economic development, or moral leadership. Some universities tend to imagine they are the solutions to a wide range of problems.

March (1994, 205–206) groups those interested in garbage can theory as follows: (1) the critics who see garbage can processes as the enemy of proper decisionmaking; (2) the pragmatists who use garbage can processes to their own ends by attempting to have their solutions attached to every problem that comes along; and (3) the enthusiasts who see garbage can theory and temporal sorting as the future of decision theory.

Applications of the chaos metaphor to decision theory are rather similar to the logic of garbage can processes. What appear to be disorder, chaos, and highly unsystematic patterns of institutional decisionmaking can, in fact, hide deep patterns of order. These patterns of order have to do primarily with temporal sorting, the rhythms of time in work processes, group norms in work settings, budget cycles, reporting cycles, and so forth. The patterns reveal not only an underlying organizational symmetry but also primarily incremental patterns of contextual adaptation. For reasons rather similar to the explanations of garbage can processes, organizational decision symmetry will change nonincrementally as the result of relatively minor changes in key decision processes. Chaos theorists love the butterfly metaphor: Butterflies flapping their wings in Tokyo may cause a tornado in Oklahoma, an example of nonlinear, nonincremental, and mostly unrevealed orderly substructures in what appears to be chaos (Kiel 1994). As shown by Bryan D. Jones and Frank R. Baumgartner (2005b), disproportionate updating of beliefs can also produce nonincremental policy change that, while appearing unpredictable, is the logical outcome of limits in attention capabilities.

Despite the claims of chaos theory, decision processes are seldom as chaotic as claimed, and order is a good bit easier to find than claimed. That everything connects to everything else and that a seemingly small decision choice in one part of the organization can result, later in time, in a big consequence elsewhere, are interesting ideas. The problem is that most versions of chaos theory applied to institutional decisionmaking assume that such matters are more amenable to management than evidence would suggest.

Methodology

Studies of bounded decision rationality using the logic of appropriateness ordinarily use qualitative methods; cases studies based on observations, interviews, and surveys are staples. Cases also sometimes use quantitative data (Brehm, Gates, and Gomez 1998). Syntheses combined with modeling, using that word in the sociological sense, are common (Lipsky 1980; Yanow 1996). Stories and narratives are common (Bellow and Minow 1996; Maynard-Moody and Leland 1999; Schram and Neisser 1997).

To illustrate the application of methodology to the study of decision theory from the appropriateness perspective, we turn briefly to the work of Steven Maynard-Moody and Michael Musheno (2000). They studied street-level workers in police departments, vocational rehabilitation offices, and schools to discover how these workers made decisions, particularly from the perspective of the decision discretion available to them. Here is the description of their methodology:

> The research that informs this discussion is based on extensive on-site observation, in-depth entry and exit interviews, a questionnaire, and archival research. But street-level worker stories about fairness and unfairness are the primary source for observations about decision norms. Like all methods, story-based research has strengths and weaknesses. Stories reveal information that is rarely found in interviews or especially in other quantitative forms of social scientific information. Stories allow the simultaneous expression of multiple points of view because they sustain and suspend multiple voices and conflicting perspectives. They can also present highly textured depictions of practices and institutions. Rather than merely repeating the rules or beliefs, a story can show what situations call for cer-

tain routines and how the specifics of a case fit or do not fit standard practices. Stories illustrate the consequences of following, bending, or ignoring rules and practices. They bring institutions to life by giving us a glimpse of what it is like to work in a state bureaucracy or cruise a tough neighborhood in a patrol car. They give research a pungency and vitality because they give prominence to individual actions and motives. Stories are the textual embodiments of the storytellers', in this case street-level workers', perspectives. (2000, 336)

Using data gathered through a narrative methodology, they presented their findings in the form of contrasting models (they called them narratives). The two dominant models of decision discretion are (1) the state-agent model, which acknowledges the inevitability of street-level decision discretion but emphasizes self-interest as the guiding norm; or, (2) the street-level-worker model, which acknowledges discretion and assumes that it is exercised to make work easier, safer, and more rewarding. Maynard-Moody and Musheno did not find either of these models, but found instead the citizen-agent model (they call it a counternarrative).

Rather than discretionary state agents who act in response to rules, procedures, and law, street-level workers describe themselves as citizen agents who act in response to individuals and circumstances. They do not describe what they do as contributing to policymaking or even as carrying out policy. Moreover, street-level workers do not describe their decisions and actions as based on their views of the correctness of the rules, the wisdom of the policy, or accountability to a hierarchical authority or democratic principle. Instead, they base their decisions on their judgment of the individual citizen client's worth.

Street-level workers discount the importance of self-interest and will often make their work harder, more unpleasant, more dangerous, and less officially successful in an effort to respond to the needs of individuals. They describe themselves as decisionmakers, but they base their decisions on normative choices, not in response to rules, procedures, or policies. These normative choices are defined in terms of relationships to citizens, clients, coworkers, and the system. But in substituting their pragmatic judgments for the unrealistic views of those holding formal and legitimate authority, street-level workers are, in their own view, acting responsibly. Maynard-Moody and Musheno's findings are splendid examples of the decision rationality of appropriateness and the processes of sense making.

Conclusions

We can make several generalizations from this review of decision theory in public administration. First, there is an obvious close affinity between the decision logic of consequences and rational or public choice theory, the subject of Chapter 8.

The former tends to a greater emphasis on the bounds of rationality, the later to a greater emphasis on pure rationality. Both are grounded in economics and political science and tend to use the same methodologies. Second, there is also a close affinity between the decision logic of appropriateness and modern institutional theory, the subject of Chapter 4. Both are grounded in sociology, social psychology, and business and public administration, and both tend to use the same methodologies. Third, the level of theorizing, modeling, and categorizing about institutional choice making from either perspective is probably greater than the level of empirically based, theory-testing research (Simon 2000). Fourth, and most importantly, scholars using the decision logic of consequences and scholars using the decision logic of appropriateness are increasingly influenced by one another.

Consider theory and research on the prisoners' dilemma. The decision rationality of the two prisoners is increased when there are repeated trials. The point is that partnerships that endure introduce considerations of reputation, trust, retaliation, and learning into the rationality equation. Repeated trials aid mutually advantageous coordinated action. Under conditions of repeated trials, it matters whether the players can assume that each is completely rational, understands the situation, has complete knowledge, and acts consistently. If there is a small probability that the other player is not completely rational, outcomes change. The point is that the resolution of the prisoners' dilemma is based on trust, experience, and making sense of the situation. Experience and trust are expressions of appropriate decision behavior rather than purely rational self-interested behavior.

To complete this sketch of decision theory, we return to Simon. A few months before his death in November 2000, he gave the John Gaus Lecture at the annual meeting of the American Political Science Association (Simon 2000). He described a meeting of Nobel economists at which "I treasonably defected to my political science origins in order to defend our political institutions against the imperialism of utility maximization, competitive markets, and privatization" (2000, 750). He described contemporary economics as in a "productive state of disorganization" in its search for alternatives to the market model.

Simon suggested that we are moving from a market economy to an organizational economy. The bulk of modern economic activity now takes place within the walls of large corporations, not in markets. In the organizational economy, two organizational factors matter most. The first is the way the organization designs the coordination of specialized work; "organizational design focuses on balancing the gains from coordination against its costs" (2000, 752). This is another language for loose and tight coupling and the factors that influence organizational design choices. Those factors include measurable gains and costs, but they also include the management of ambiguity, risk, imperfect information, and uncertainty. The second factor is the contract between the organization and its participants: This is almost exactly the same thing as identity.

Near the end of his lecture, Simon turned to another explanation for the salience of organizations. Markets cannot handle either power or fairness well. Decisions regarding power and fairness are made best in nonmarket democratic institutions, and in such institutions the logic of rational self-interest is a poor guide for either power or fairness in decisionmaking.

We turn back to advice from Simon.

> It is not too fanciful to think of writing a history of human civilization in terms of progress in the means of human cooperation, that is, of organization. In that history, hierarchical and nearly decomposable systems would play a central role. Almost from the beginning, the division of work into component tasks and the assembly of the components into a hierarchy were discovered to be powerful means for achieving efficient coordination of effort. . . .
>
> Gradually, increases in the demands for, and in the advantages of, more coordination in economic activity, together with the accumulation of skills of organizing, brought into existence ever-larger corporations that begin to emulate in size the administrative organizations of the nation-states—and we were launched into our modern world.
>
> Both private and public organizations have played essential roles in these modern developments, complementing each other's functions, learning from each other, and, at the same time, competing for power to steer and manage the systems that have emerged. That process has not reached its end and political science and economics must continue their mutual education, with each discipline learning from the other. (2000, 756)

The principal-agent model of the logic of appropriateness perspective is no longer applicable. From the sense-making perspective, ambiguity and uncertainty are reduced in part by the norms of the institution and the level of trust between superiors and subordinates (Brehm and Gates 2004; Dirks and Skarlicki 2004). To accommodate this shift, decision theory will necessarily require a multidisciplinary approach (Pollitt 2010). However, the field still has a ways to go in terms of incorporating insights from other disciplines. A recent empirical investigation showed that public administration actually does a rather poor job of incorporating insights from disciplines considered the most germane to the field, namely, law, management, and political science (Wright 2011). A multidisciplinary approach will require a move away from traditional decision-theoretic frameworks—for example, the logic of consequences and the logic of appropriateness. To understand how cognitive structures affect information processing necessarily requires a broader theoretical approach than currently exists. We suggest that public administration scholars would be wise to engage both theoretically and empirically with other disciplines in order to gain a greater appreciation and understanding of the fundamentals of human decisionmaking.

As a prescription for the field, we believe more scholars should be engaged in experimental research, both in the field and in the lab. The greatest theoretical advances in decision theory, namely, from behavioral economics and experimental psychology, have been made since the late 1990s primarily through experimental methodology. Rather than having public administration scholars continue to borrow from other disciplines, which creates a lag in modifying existing theories, scholars engaging in similar research methods will allow for public administration to make a unique contribution. Although we are beginning to understand how individuals are "predictably irrational," little work has been done on how this affects institutions or the act of governance. The field of public administration is well positioned to contribute to our understanding of how irrationality shapes government decisionmaking. We agree with Simon that political science and economics must continue to learn from each another; a bridge for such learning may in fact be a common methodology—experimental. Such an opportunity also allows the discipline to be more visible to other fields, something that recent empirical evidence suggests is sorely needed (Wright 2011).

We began the chapter by rehashing the debate between Waldo and Simon on the issue of efficiency and "value-neutral" decisions. In public organizations, what is efficient may in fact be defined in terms of both fairness and costs and benefits. Understanding that what is fair is often socially defined, and that cost-benefit calculations are difficult to conceptualize owing to bias in information processing may help to resolve debates about what is "efficient." Whatever path public administration takes, we believe that in regard to decision theory, the field would be wise to lead rather than follow, and is in a unique position to do so.

8

Rational Choice Theory and Irrational Behavior

Introduction: What Is Rational Choice Theory?

For public administration scholars, rational choice can be simply thought of as neoclassical economic theory applied to the public sector. It seeks to build a bridge between microeconomics and politics by viewing the actions of citizens, politicians, and public servants as analogous to the actions of self-interested producers and consumers (Buchanan 1972). This analogy not only makes it possible to conceive of the public sector in market terms but also makes available to public administration scholars a well-developed set of theoretical tools from economics. The terminology for these tools varies (they are sometimes called political economy or welfare economics), but they are best known and most widely applied as rational or public choice.

The intellectual roots of rational choice date back at least to the work of Adam Smith, whose *The Wealth of Nations* (first published in 1776) is the intellectual rock on which neoclassical economic theory is constructed. Smith's great insight was that people acting in pursuit of their own self-interest could, through the mechanism of the "invisible hand," produce collective benefits that profited all society. For example, businessmen might be motivated only by a desire to enrich themselves, but their ability to turn a profit depends upon producing cheaper, better-quality goods than their competitors. Higher-quality goods at lower prices benefit everyone. If this is true, it implies that social order and collective benefits can be produced by market mechanisms rather than by the strong centralized hand of government. These basic elements—the self-interested actor, competition among producers, and a relatively unregulated market—are the hallmarks of neoclassical economic thought and central to rational choice theory. Although Smith did not construct a theory of public administration, he was fully cognizant of the

193

implications of his arguments for the public sector, and often supplied government with policy advice based on his intellectual labors (Buchholtz 1999, 10–41).[1]

Though rational choice's basic intellectual toolkit is centuries old, students of public administration largely ignored it until relatively recently. Public administration was intellectually cross-fertilized with business-oriented disciplines such as management and organization theory as early as the late nineteenth century, but it was another half century before economists began transferring the formal theories of their home discipline to politics. With Anthony Downs's *An Economic Theory of Democracy* (1957), and James Buchanan and Gordon Tullock's *The Calculus of Consent* (1962), the implications of economic theory for the public sector could be ignored no longer. These works presented an immediate challenge to orthodox thinking in public administration and political science (Buchanan and Tullock's work is widely considered to mark the formal founding of rational choice theory). The key characteristic separating these works from traditional approaches to political and public administration theory was their emphasis on the rational, self-interested actor. In these frameworks, the public-spirited citizen and the neutrally competent public servant were replaced with the rational utility maximizer. Following Smith's lead, citizens and civil servants in these frameworks were not presumed to engage in political behavior because of civic ideals or commitment to the common good; instead, it was assumed they engaged in political behavior for the same reasons they engaged in economic behavior, namely, they were motivated by a desire to benefit themselves.

Rational choice theory is thus anchored to the belief that the central behavioral assumption of the neoclassical economic paradigm is universal: Self-interest drives our decisions and actions, whether these are purchasing a car, voting, or formulating a public budget. From this starting point, it is a short step to the notion of markets for public services, a situation where citizen-consumers shop for the public goods and services they most prefer, and producers of these services are competitive organizations whose self-interest is coupled to the need for efficient response to consumer demand. This, needless to say, contradicts orthodox public administration notions of who should provide public services and how: bureaucracies in centralized jurisdictions that are responsive to representative democratic institutions rather than consumer demand.

This large-scale challenge to traditional thinking in public administration is fashioned from remarkably simple theoretical tools. As outlined by Buchanan and Tullock, there are only two key assumptions of rational choice theory. (1) The average individual is a self-interested utility maximizer. This means an individual knows her preferences or goals, can rank-order them, and when faced with a set of options to achieve those preferences will choose those expected to maximize individual benefits and minimize individual costs. This preferred mix of benefits and costs is referred to as an individual's utility function, and Buchanan and Tullock (1962, 32) argued that individuals will act to maximize that utility by choosing "more rather than less" of their preferences. (2) Only individuals, not collectives, make decisions. This is known as methodological individualism, and it presumes that collective decisions are aggregations of individual choices, not a unique property of the group. In laying down the foundations of rational choice theory, Buchanan and Tullock clearly stated the importance of methodological individualism to their project: "We start from the presumption that only the individual chooses, and that rational behavior . . . can only be discussed meaningfully in terms of individual action" (32).

From these simple premises, rational choice scholars have deductively constructed entire theories of individual and organizational behavior, and extended the implications deep into the administrative arrangements of government and the intellectual development of public administration. Indeed, it is difficult to underestimate the impact of rational choice on the applied and scholarly sides of public administration. This impact has been felt in three primary areas. (1) Organizational behavior. Rational choice theory offers a comprehensive framework to answer the question of why bureaucracies and bureaucrats do what they do. (2) Public service delivery. Rational choice theory offers an explanation of how public goods are produced and consumed, and from these insights favors a series of public-sector reforms that turn traditional public administration presumptions and prescriptions on their heads. (3) A claim for a new theoretical orthodoxy. Advocates of rational choice theory have argued that it is the natural successor to the Wilsonian/Weberian ideas that have dominated a century's worth of intellectual development in rational choice. Rational choice, some suggest, is not just a positive theory (an explanation of how the world *does* work), but also a normative theory (an explanation of how the world *should* work). As a normative theory, rational choice has been argued to be a way to fuse the economic theory formulated by Smith and the democratic theory formulated by James Madison and Alexander Hamilton. It thus has staked a claim to meet the challenges of Dwight Waldo and John Gaus, public administration scholars who argued the discipline could move forward only when administrative theory developed into political theory.

Yet despite the grandiose claims of early rational choice scholars, recent decades have seen a plethora of essays, articles, and books challenging the basic assumptions of rational choice theory. The basic premise behind this movement is that the individual acting as a self-interested utility maximizer is not easily defined in terms of costs and benefits. Rather, there are sharp deviations from what would be considered utility-maximizing behavior. Emerging research indicates utility maximization includes some sense of fairness where literally less may be preferred to more (Smith 2006). At the very least, this new group of scholars argues that utility is quite malleable and context-dependent. These arguments may have put a mortal wound in the tenets of rational choice theory, made all the more damaging by the fact that many of these scholars hail from economics (the discipline directly responsible for rational choice theory), notably behavioral and experimental economics.

In this chapter we briefly examine the impact of rational choice on the three areas mentioned earlier in this section. We also provide a discussion of how recent advances in behavioral economics, experimental economics, social psychology, and psychology are redefining the ways in which public administration scholars view the contribution of rational choice to these areas, and more generally are changing the way scholars theorize about utility.

The Rational, Self-Maximizing Bureaucrat

One of the earliest and most far-reaching impacts of rational choice theory was in explaining the actions of bureaucrats and bureaucracies. Picking up the intellectual foundation laid by Buchanan and Tullock, several scholars extended the rational choice framework into a model of organizational behavior that challenged traditional scholarly perspectives on bureaucracy. The best known of these works are Gordon Tullock's *The Politics of Bureaucracy* (1965), Anthony Downs's *Inside Bureaucracy* (1967), and William Niskanen's *Bureaucracy and Representative Government* (1971).

Following the core assumptions of rational choice theory, all these works begin with the presumption that what bureaucracies do can be understood by viewing bureaucrats as self-interested utility maximizers. They also borrow heavily from the Weberian picture of a mature bureaucracy, particularly in the sense that a bureaucracy is an organization that enjoys an information advantage over its supposed political masters. Given these starting presumptions, Tullock, Downs, and Niskanen presented a picture of public administrators far removed from the neutrally competent agents of implementation that populate traditional public administration folklore.

Tullock sought to explain what a bureaucracy would look like if bureaucrats were self-interested utility maximizers. He argued that a rational, self-interested bureaucrat maximizes utility through career advancement, and that advancement in the merit-based systems of public bureaucracies often depends upon the favorable recommendations of superiors. If this is so, Tullock reasoned, the rational bureaucrat will seek to please superiors and put himself in as favorable a light as possible. Thus, a rational bureaucrat will highlight information that reflects favorably upon himself and will repress (perhaps even suppress) information that does not. Distorting information in this way will create a host of problems. Lacking accurate and/or complete information, agency leaders and external political actors will form skewed expectations about an agency's performance and capabilities. The same lack of information will concurrently diminish their ability to hold the bureaucracy accountable. The net result is an agency prone to mistakes, difficult to manage, and hard to control.

Traditional managerial responses to these problems in public agencies emphasize replacing or restructuring the bureaucratic hierarchy. Tullock's argument suggests that such reforms will be ineffective because, although they may alter the institutional environment, they pay little attention to the individual incentives that are the real source of the problem. Tullock went so far as to suggest that in extreme situations, the external political control of bureaucracies will virtually evaporate as bureaucrats engage in "bureaucratic free enterprise," that is, pursue their own goals rather than the public missions associated with their agencies (1965, 167). This picture of unwieldy, self-interested agencies whose actions increasingly became divorced from public rhetoric seemed to offer intellectual confirmation for negative and widespread perceptions of public bureaucracies.

Downs's work is only slightly more optimistic. Building from the assumption of rational self-interest, Downs argued that a set of behavioral biases should be common to all bureaucrats: (1) Like Tullock, Downs (1967, 77) argued that bureaucrats will be motivated to distort information as it passes upward in the hierarchy to reflect favorably on themselves and their individual goals. (2) Bureaucrats will favor policies that fit with their own interests and goals. (3) How bureaucrats react to directives from superiors will depend on how those directives serve the bureaucrats' self-interest. If the directives favor individual interests, the degree of compliance will be high; if not, it will be low. (4) Individual goals will determine the extent to which bureaucrats seek out responsibility and also determine their risk tolerance in pursuit of responsibility and power.

Rather than concentrate on career advancement, Downs sought to accommodate a wider variety of individual goals in conceptualizing the motivations of the self-interested bureaucrat, and systematically ordered these goals into a typology of bureaucratic personalities. In Downs's classification (1967, 92), "climbers" are bureaucrats who want to maximize their power, income, or prestige. Climbers are likely to pursue responsibility aggressively, especially in the sense of creating new functions for their agencies. In contrast, "conservers" are bureaucrats who want to maximize security and convenience, and they will more likely defend existing prerogatives and functions rather than try to invent new ones. "Zealots" are bureaucrats motivated to pursue particular policies, even in the face of overwhelming obstacles. Downs suggested that because zealots are unlikely to make good administrators, they are unlikely to hold high organizational ranks. Other categories included "advocates," who, like zealots, aggressively pursue favored policies but are more open to influence from peers and superiors, and "statesmen," bureaucrats seeking to promote the public interest through the promotion of broad policy goals (102).

Working from this typology, the basic assumptions of self-interest and the likely impact from the structural characteristics found in the bureaucratic form of organization in shaping individual motivations, Downs proposed a series of general propositions about the behavior of bureaucrats and bureaucracies. These included the "Law of Increasing Conserverism," which posits that in the long run most bureaucrats become conservers; and the "Law of Imperfect Control," which posits the larger an organization, the weaker the control those at the top of the hierarchy have over the actions of those in the middle and at the bottom. Downs added to the picture portrayed by Tullock, but did not radically change the overall impression: The rational, self-maximizing bureaucrat led to public agencies that were unwieldy, difficult to manage, and, at best, only partially oriented toward the public-interest concerns embedded in their putative missions.

Although Downs and Tullock presented a radically alternative picture of bureaucratic behavior than that conveyed by previous research, it was Niskanen who really thrust rational choice theory into a central role in explaining bureaucratic behavior. Niskanen's great achievement was to create the first *formal* economic theory of bureaucratic behavior (i.e., his theory was based on mathematical derivations concerning the utility and productivity functions of bureaucrats and bureaucracies). Niskanen's starting points were similar to those of Tullock and Downs in that the central figure in his theory is the individual utility-maximizing bureaucrat. Niskanen, however, paid more detailed attention to what bureaucrats seek to maximize. The rational choice assumptions of economics argue that in making decisions and taking actions, an individual seeks to maximize personal utility.

In and of itself, however, this is not a particularly useful insight. What, after all, constitutes "personal utility"? In economics, utility is typically put into operation according to Buchanan and Tullock's "more rather than less" dictum. Decisions that yield more of something (wages, profits, consumption opportunities) are thus presumed to increase utility. Niskanen sought to extend this reasoning from the individual economic actor to the bureaucrat by suggesting several variables that might enter into the latter's utility functions: salary, perquisites, power, prestige, patronage, public reputation, and agency output. Niskanen argued that most of these variables are tied to the budget of a given agency. If such things as salary, power, and prestige are tied to the overall budget of an agency, the rational bureaucrat should therefore strive to make that budget as large as possible. Niskanen (1971, 38) thus suggested that budget maximization serves as a good proxy for the utility of the bureaucrat.

Niskanen recognized that not all bureaucrats are motivated by financial bottom lines or career advancement, and was willing to acknowledge that some bureaucrats genuinely seek to serve and advance the public interest. These bureaucrats, however, have a problem: "A bureaucrat . . . is neither omniscient nor sovereign. He cannot acquire all of the information on individual preferences and production opportunities that would be necessary to divine the public interests" (1971, 39). In other words, bureaucrats have different ideas about what constitutes the public interest, and no individual has all the information required to make a definitive claim that his or her conception of the civic good is the correct one. So although Niskanen recognized that some public servants might be public spirited, he believed they were unlikely to be particularly effective in advancing the public interest. In fact, argued Niskanen, "it is impossible for any one bureaucrat to act in the public interest, because of the limits on his information and the conflicting interests of others, regardless of his personal motivations" (39). In contrast, the rational bureaucrat is well positioned to act on behalf of his own interests. All he needs to know are his own preferences.

Niskanen thus viewed a bureaucracy as a rough equivalent of a business in which budget maximization substitutes for profit maximization. Niskanen created a market analogy where bureaucracies are monopoly producers of public services, and legislators are monopsonist buyers. Bureaucrats seek to maximize their budgets by "selling" a certain level of public services to legislators. For any given bureaucracy, a subgroup of legislators will have powerful incentives to secure high levels of the service produced. These incentives are largely electoral—bureaucracies provide contracts, jobs, and services that benefit constituents and for which legislators can claim credit. A market with monopoly producers and a handful of dominant buyers has predictable outcomes: inefficiency in production and supply outpacing demand (1971, 227). To combat this inherent dysfunction in public service production, Niskanen suggested that the financing of public services be restricted to the lowest level of government possible, and that budget decisions be required to muster a two-thirds vote in a legislature (227–229). The idea was to reduce the influence of monopoly buyers and to better connect the supply of public services to demand by putting producers as close as possible to consumers.

Coming as they did in the late 1960s and early 1970s, the work of scholars such as Tullock, Downs, and Niskanen struck a chord not just because their theoretical approach was novel (to public administration), but also because their conclusions fit with widely held conceptions of bureaucracy. As the public sector expanded in the decades after World War II, people began to question the cost and efficiency of public services. The ineffective, inefficient bureaucracy of popular perception gained intellectual confirmation in these works. The prescriptive conclusions—less bureaucracy, less centralization, and more competition in the production of public services—may have turned administrative orthodoxy on its head, but they found a ready audience in policy circles. Yet as public administration scholars from the more orthodox schools were quick to point out, these works were almost purely theoretical, and their prescriptive conclusions rested on untested assumptions and anecdotal evidence.

The work of Tullock, Downs, and Niskanen generated a good deal of research seeking to take rational choice beyond calculations of abstract utility functions. The more data-driven research helped support some of the theoretical underpinnings of rational choice, but it also made clear that economic theory had difficulties digesting the public sector. Empirical counters to works such as Niskanen's center on claims that the underlying assumptions about individual behavior and the institutional dysfunction deduced to follow from these premises bear only a passing relationship to the real world. In a wide-ranging examination of the empirical foundations of the budget-maximizing bureaucrat, for example, Andre Blais and Stephane Dion (1991) note that the evidence is mixed. Bureaucrats do seem to request larger budgets, but it is not clear they profit from them through better salaries, increased reputations, or any of the other elements Niskanen was trying to condense into an individual utility function. Though budget maximizing has become firmly entrenched as public administration folklore, it is not even clear that bureaucrats pursue these strategies as a general pattern. Some studies have found evidence that bureaucrats routinely pursue *minimizing* strategies, looking not for ever bigger budgets but "for solutions for problems within their agency through mandate clarification as well as organizational, planning, and information changes" (Campbell and Naulls 1991, 113).

Niskanen even acknowledged some of these problems, and suggested that the budget-maximizing model developed in *Bureaucracy and Representative Democracy* was incomplete. He added, "In an important sense, it was also wrong!" (Niskanen 1994, 269). The empirical evidence since the 1960s, Niskanen argued, suggests that what bureaucrats tend to maximize is their discretionary budgets rather than their overall budgets. The discretionary budget is defined as "the difference between the total budget and the minimum cost of producing the output expected by the political authorities" (274). This is a subtle but important difference from the budget-maximization standpoint. It means that bureaucrats are seeking to maximize control over their budgets rather than the absolute size of their budgets. In addition to this nuanced shift in the behavioral assumptions driving his model, Niskanen also suggested that his original work seriously underestimated the role of the political sponsors in monitoring bureaucracy, an issue having even more important implications for the conclusions of Tullock and Downs. These early rational choice theories of bureaucracy tended to paint pictures of politically powerful bureaucracies that, at least under certain conditions, could act almost unilaterally as bureaucratic self-interest displaced their public missions. To use Tullock's words, rather than agents of implementation for democratic institutions, a form of "bureaucratic free enterprise" could develop in which bureaucrats pursued their own goals. Since then, empirical work has provided considerable evidence that bureaucracies tend to be highly responsive both to their political principals and to public opinion generally (Wood and Waterman 1994; see Chapter 2 for a more thorough discussion of this topic). This does not necessarily mean that bureaucracies act altruistically in pursuit of the public interest. Nonetheless, it does suggests more constraints on the self-interested bureaucrat than are accounted for by rational choice theory.

Some of these constraints may even be willingly imposed by the individual. As various researchers have concluded, bureaucrats routinely espouse a commitment to the public interest. If Niskanen is correct, these worthy motives will cumulatively account for little because no one bureaucrat has the necessary information to divine the public interest. Perhaps so, but when it comes to information, bureaucrats are better equipped to create a reasonable approximation of the public interest and act in its pursuit than are most other social actors. Most career administrators at the Environmental Protection Agency are committed to environmental protection, and their counterparts in the Defense Department are committed to national defense. Such bureaucrats often evidence a willingness to shift policies and programs in pursuit of these goals, even if the benefits to themselves or their agency are hard to discern. For example, the senior career administrators in at least one major federal agency (the Civil Aeronautics Board) successfully worked to put their organization out of business (Meier 1994, 228). These sorts of findings do not necessarily disconfirm rational choice theory's explanation of bureaucratic behavior, but they do raise questions about the fundamental assumptions that supply the framework's explanatory power.

James L. Perry's seminal work (Perry, Mesch, and Paarlberg 2006) on public service motivation is also instructive here. Most notably for our purposes, the link between financial incentives and the motivations and behaviors of public-sector employees is more nuanced than would be predicted by a strict model of pure rationality. Variables relating to participation in organizational decisionmaking, the amount and quality of employee feedback, and the degree to which the job is challenging all affect public-sector employee motivations (Perry, Mesch, and Paarlberg 2006; Perry 2000). Rather than fixed preferences as assumed by strict rationality, the institutional environment can also shape individual preferences. More hierarchical organizations with less red tape can increase the level of public service motivation reported by employees (Moynihan and Pandey 2007). Niskanen's self-interested bureaucrat engages in predictable behavioral patterns; she will maximize salary when possible, shirk work in the absence of monitoring, and reliably respond in the face of financial incentives. Recent empirical evidence suggests that, even though bureaucrats are predictable, their behavior is not rational.

Trust and the Irrational Bureaucrat

Despite the ordered logic of rational choice theory as a model for explaining inefficiency in public organizations, recent work in organizational psychology suggests the basic assumptions of such a model are flawed. Bureaucrats may seek to maximize their own self-interest, but managers can improve efficiency. Tullock and Downs both presented a picture of a self-interested bureaucrat quite willing to distort information, and subsequently the public, in order to maximize individual self-interest, that is, career advancement. The solution that emerges from this framework is primarily institutional—-more rules, more rigid structure, more hierarchy. More recently, however, evidence exists suggesting that the solution depends less on the structure of the institution and more on the interrelationships between actors within the institution.

A growing body of literature suggests that bureaucrats' responses to the task environment often depend on psychological, nonmonetary assessments. For a leader, whether in an organization or in elected office, to be effective, he or she must possess a certain set of skills that encourage follower trust, thereby increasing follower productivity and a willingness to comply with authoritative requests. Scholars have classified these skills under the umbrella of "political skill," and they are characterized most prominently by an ability to form lasting social networks and the possession of a certain set of social skills that allow for interpersonal influence (Ammeter et al. 2002; Ferris et al. 2005; Hall et al. 2004). Leaders with high levels of political skill tend to be viewed as more effective leaders and are positively correlated with work unit performance (Douglas and Ammeter 2004). Leader political skill also tends to positively affect perceptions of organizational support among subordinates, in turn increasing job satisfaction and organizational commitment (Treadway et al. 2004). There is good reason to expect such findings to apply to both the private *and* the public sector.

The public management literature has a rich theoretical tradition focusing on the relationship between leaders and followers. Beginning with Chester Barnard's (1938) "acceptance theory," perceptions of bureaucratic authority have been critical to the study of public management theory. Barnard argued that the effectiveness of administrative authority depends on the willingness of others to accept and comply with such authority. Following Barnard, public administration scholars have long recognized the influence of individual personalities on organizational activity and performance (Simon 1947/1997; Downs 1957; McGregor 1960; more recently, Terry 1998; deLeon and Denhardt 2000). Recent empirical evidence shows that perceptions of a leader's characteristics influence whether a follower will engage in a particular behavior (Dirks and Skarlicki 2004; Kramer 1999; Kramer and Cook 2004; Kramer and Tyler 1996). Followers that attribute competence and trustworthiness to leaders are not only more likely to follow authoritative requests but are also more likely to engage in risky behavior on behalf of leaders/managers (Elsbach 2004), and are less likely to perceive a need to break the rules or "sabotage" the organization (Brehm and Gates 2004). Moreover, employees are more likely to identify with their organization and engage in voluntary compliance with organizational norms when they trust their superiors (Darley

2004; Dirks and Ferrin 2001; Podsakoff, MacKenzie, and Bommer 1996). This is a direct counter to one of Downs's behavioral biases that bureaucrats will shirk responsibility. Identity-based trust is important because it reduces the likelihood of betrayal within organizations and increases the probability that employees will seek to prevent organizational crises (Darley 2004). In short, subordinates respond favorably to leaders who exhibit trustworthiness (see Carnevale 1995; Ruscio 1997). This fits well with other scholarly research indicating that people are more likely to comply with a leader's requests if they perceive the leader to be trustworthy and the leader's motivations to be neutral (Tyler 2001, 1990; Tyler and DeGoey 1996).

The extension of rational choice into the realm of organizational behavior has thus created a long-running controversy within public administration over the motivations and explanations of bureaucratic behavior. In advocates such as Niskanen, rational choice developed into one of the most rigorous and theoretically elegant models applied to bureaucracy. It offers public administration a strong deductive basis for building general models of bureaucratic behavior that, at least internally, are logically consistent and produce a wide variety of empirically testable hypotheses. The critics of rational choice argue that its starting assumptions are too narrow and unreasonably downplay the possibility that bureaucrats might seek to maximize the public interest, professional or ethical norms, or a variety of group-based motivations that threaten methodological individualism. From this perspective, the analogy of monopoly producers and monopsonist buyers propping up the supply of public services shrinks to a metaphor that caricatures rather than characterizes public life.

The Niskanen model's emphasis on individual self-interest is not without merit; it is just that the definition of utility requires revision. For example, in instances of information asymmetry, as is often the case with bureaucrats and clients, the tendency to appear fair and unselfish dominates the tendency to engage in actual fair behavior (Smith 2006). This tendency, however, can actually lead to suboptimal behavior in that decisionmakers are willing to incur significant costs in order to appear fair. Even though in the early 1990s the empirical record seemed to declare no clear winner in this debate, the momentum has clearly shifted to a more diverse view of bureaucratic, and human, behavior. Nonetheless, it is clear that work in rational choice has stimulated public administration scholars to think about bureaucracies in different ways and will continue to do so into the foreseeable future.

The Self-Maximizing Citizen and the Tiebout Hypothesis

Although rational choice has had a considerable impact on the study of bureaucratic behavior, its greatest theoretical and applied implications arise from its application to citizens rather than to bureaucrats. Bureaucrats and bureaucracies represent a challenge to rational choice theory in that the market analogy sometimes seems forced. In works such as those of Tullock, Downs, and Niskanen, public servants have no clear, consistent role as "buyer" or "seller," and what is being exchanged, with whom, and by what mechanism is simply not as intuitively or empirically obvious as the market for, say, cars or soft drinks.

The market analogy becomes much sharper when rational choice turns its attention to citizens and the services produced by local governments through public agencies. In the rational choice framework, citizens consume public services; the patterns and motivations of their consumption can become the rough equivalents of consumption patterns in markets for cars or soft drinks. This analogy will not be perfect. By definition, a public good is indivisible, something that cannot be broken up and distributed individually. For example, an individual consumer can purchase a car or a can of soda based on personal preferences with relatively little input from or impact on anyone else. This is hard to do with public goods such as clean air or national defense because they require binding collective decisions rather than individual ones. Traditionally, such goods were considered to be subject to market failure, that is, left to themselves, free-exchange mechanisms would either underproduce these goods or not produce them at all. For this reason, the production of public goods traditionally is held to be appropriately concentrated under government control. From here it is but a short step to prescriptively embracing administration orthodoxy—public goods and services can be most effectively and efficiently provided by functionally organized agencies with centralized jurisdictions. Thus, one public bureaucracy should provide, say, law enforcement for a given area. This will ensure that a vital public service is available to all, avoid duplication of service, simplify command and control, and, in doing so, promote efficiency and accountability.

One problem with this line of reasoning is that some goods and services fall into a gray area between public and private. Education and garbage services, for example, are provided by both the public and the private sectors. Private contractors, and therefore the free market, play a role in providing even "pure" public goods such as national defense. The fuzzy line between public and private goods provides an intellectual leverage point for arguing that the mechanisms used to provide the latter might be able to handle a greater role in providing the former. When that lever is pulled, public administration orthodoxy crashes head-on into basic economic theory. What James Q. Wilson or Max Weber might call a well-run public bureaucracy, Adam Smith and Milton Friedman might call a monopoly. Monopolies are unresponsive and inefficient producers because, according to the axiom of self-interest, they have no reason to be otherwise. The consumer has no option but to buy the monopoly good at the monopolist's price, and the monopolist has all the advantages in the producer-consumer exchange. If, as Tullock, Downs and Niskanen argued, bureaucrats are self-interested, and public agencies are in effect monopoly producers of public goods and services, the citizen-consumer may be getting a very bad deal from the centralized bureaucracies advised by traditional public administration orthodoxy. A better arrangement would be a market for public services, where instead of one centralized agency in one jurisdiction, citizen-consumers have a broad variety of tax-service packages and could move to the location that best fit their preferences. Competition would force these multiple agencies to produce high-quality public services at low cost, their alternative being to face being abandoned by the public. This line of reasoning suggests that, rather than centralized bureaucracies providing public goods and services, they could be better supplied by a competitive market arrangement.

These arguments were first formally articulated in a seminal 1956 article by Charles Tiebout. Like Tullock, Downs, and Niskanen, Tiebout's work also rested on the twin assumptions of self-interest and methodological individualism. Tiebout's work, however, centered not on the internal workings of bureaucracy but on the relationship between citizens and public agencies as consumers and producers of public goods. Tiebout argued that a competitive market for public services could be created if mobile citizens could shop across local jurisdictions for the package of public services and attendant tax burden that best suited their preferences. As Tiebout put it, mobility would provide "the local public goods counterpart to the private market's shopping trip" (1956, 422). If citizen-consumers shopped around for preferred tax-service packages, competitive pressures would force producers—that is, local governments and public agencies—to respond to citizens' preferences. The result, at least in theory, would be efficiently produced public services that reflected public demand for those services.

Note that the Tiebout model prescriptively implies the exact opposite of orthodox approaches to supplying public services. The central hypothesis of the Tiebout model and its various extensions is that many agencies competing horizontally (across jurisdictions) and vertically (within jurisdictions) will provide a higher-quality service at a lower price, and be more attuned to citizens' preferences, than will large bureaucracies in centralized jurisdictions.

This hypothesis has stimulated an enormous amount of empirical and prescriptive research on the differences between polycentric (centralized, single-jurisdiction) and monocentric (fragmented, multijurisdiction) government. Much of this research has sought to assess the validity of the Tiebout model by examining the impact of fragmentation on spending for public services. According to public administration orthodoxy, highly fragmented institutional arrangements for public services results in inefficient duplication and thus should result in higher levels of spending. According to the Tiebout hypothesis, fragmentation stimulates competition, creates incentives for efficiency and responsiveness, and should therefore lower spending. In thirty years of research, no clear winner has emerged from these competing propositions. George Boyne (1998, 42–43) reviews fourteen studies examining the effects of fragmentation on spending by various forms of local government. Of the approximately twenty-five variables used to measure fragmentation in these studies, about half were associated with lower spending by local units of government, two-fifths were associated with higher levels of spending, and the remainder were statistically insignificant. These numbers give a slight edge to the Tiebout hypothesis, but not by much. In a similar review of fifteen studies seeking to assess the impact of vertical and horizontal fragmentation, Boyne (46–47) finds six of twenty-three measures of fragmentation clearly associated with lower spending, four with higher spending, with the rest reporting insignificant or unstable results based on level of analysis and form of measurement. At the macrolevel, Tiebout's work stimulated a good deal of empirical research that cumulatively neither confirmed nor rejected its key hypothesis.

Given the ambiguity of the empirical research at the macrolevel, advocates and critics of the Tiebout hypothesis in the 1990s began to pay serious attention to the foundations of the theory at the microlevel. To make his model work, Tiebout was required to make several assumptions about individual actors that went above rational utility maximization. First, Tiebout assumed that citizens are perfectly mobile, meaning they can easily move from community to community. Second, the model requires citizens to be highly informed about tax-service packages across several jurisdictions. Tiebout did not seriously propose that these conditions existed in reality, but he adopted them as necessary simplifying assumptions to make the model tractable. The more realistic microlevel expectations implied by the Tiebout model are that citizens in fragmented government settings will be more informed about public services than those in centralized government settings; will be more likely to exit if they are dissatisfied with those services; and, given that they can make choices about tax-service packages, will be more satisfied with the services they do receive.

These propositions were given their most thorough empirical examination in a study by David Lowery, William Lyons, and Ruth Hoogland DeHoog (1992), who used a survey based on matched samples of residents in polycentric and monocentric metropolitan settings. For the most part, their findings flatly contradicted the assumptions inherent in the Tiebout model. People in polycentric settings were not particularly well informed; in fact, most people in fragmented regions seemed to have only a vague idea of what government provided what service to them. Instead, "the residents in our consolidated-government sites were far better informed about their local government services than their fragmented-government counterparts" (104). There was no discernible difference in levels of satisfaction with public services between residents in consolidated and residents in fragmented government settings. There was some limited evidence that residents in fragmented settings were more likely to be mobile than those in consolidated settings. In all settings, however, the probability of moving was very low—an average of 2.66 percent in fragmented areas, and 1.32 percent in areas served by consolidated government. Lowery, Lyons, and DeHoog (99–114) were skeptical that such limited mobility was enough to create the competitive pressures envisioned by the Tiebout model.

In an effort to resurrect the microfoundations of the Tiebout model, Paul Teske et al. (1993) posited that a market for public services could be created by a few mobile, well-informed citizens. The markets for private goods such as automobiles and soda, after all, do not require that all consumers of these products be fully informed rational utility maximizers. All that's needed is a critical mass to make informed decisions and introduce the competitive pressures that deliver the market's benefits. Teske and his colleagues (709) mentioned Senator Paul Douglas's oft-quoted remark that a competitive market could exist if only 10 percent of consumers made rational, informed decisions. If this were so, where could that 10 percent be found in a local market for public services? Teske et al. recognized that for most citizens it is rational to be ignorant about public services simply because, at any given time, the average citizen is not making decisions based on issues related to local services and taxes. The exception might be actual movers. Teske and his colleagues accepted that most people do not move because of dissatisfaction with local tax-service packages but because of job or family considerations. Nonetheless, movers would still have a high incentive to gather information as they shopped for a house. If there were enough of these people, and if they gathered enough information to make reasonable choices about tax-service packages, these "marginal consumers" might be enough to create the competitive market conditions suggested in the Tiebout model.

Teske et al. tested this proposition through surveys of people who had recently purchased homes in Suffolk County, New York, and matched them with longtime residents of that area. To test levels of knowledge, the researchers asked citizens to rank their school district expenditures and taxes relative to other school districts in the county. The results indicated that overall levels of knowledge were very low, even though the study set a generous threshold for being considered informed. Respondents were asked whether school taxes and expenditures were above average, below average, or about average compared to other districts in the county. Those who responded "average" were judged to be informed if they were in one of the 50 percent of districts surrounding the mean. Using this criterion, 21 percent of residents were able to rank their schools accurately. Movers actually had less accurate information than nonmovers—24 percent of nonmovers accurately ranked school taxes and expenditures versus 19 percent of movers. When movers were separated into categories according to income, however, information levels in the high-income category jumped ahead of those of nonmovers. High-income movers were accurate 28 percent of the time (Teske et al. 1993, 707). Teske and his colleagues reasoned that this subgroup—wealthy movers with higher levels of information—might be enough to drive a market for public services, create the pressures for efficiency, and provide an empirical basis for the microfoundations of Tiebout's theory.

In a response to Teske et al.'s refinement of the theory underpinning the Tiebout model, Lowery, Lyons, and DeHoog (1995) argued that it provided marginal, and quite possibly contradictory, evidence for the potential of public service markets. They argued that the threshold used to judge a respondent informed was very low, the subset of "marginal consumers" small, and these results dealt with education—the local government service with the highest community profile. In the region used for the Teske et al. study, education was even higher profile than is typical. Lowery et al. noted that school districts on Long Island hold annual referendums on school spending, an unusual budgetary process that provides citizens with a cue to education taxing and spending issues that is not present in most districts. If more than 70 percent of the high-income movers were uninformed on a minimal measure of such a high-profile local service, the levels of information about, say, police services and sanitation were likely to be minuscule. Although stopping short of arguing that the Teske model was wrong, Lowery and his colleagues argue that the empirical evidence supporting it is very weak.

Although it is difficult to take anything definitive from the empirical research on market mechanisms on public services, these studies do bring into sharp relief the central disagreements over the Tiebout model. Advocates of rational choice argue that, if constructed with care, something approaching a competitive market for public services can be created that will produce benefits for all. The competitive pressures of the market can provide public agencies with the incentives to be responsive to consumer-citizen preferences and to become efficient producers of public goods. Opponents of rational choice argue that faith in markets is naïve and ignores the reality that competition produces losers as well as winners. Such losses are acceptable in the private sector, but when, say, a school goes out of business, the losers are not just the producers but the consumers, and what is lost is not just a consumption opportunity but a part of the common weal. Regardless of the theoretical payoffs to deregulating the public sector, critics of rational choice argue that in reality there are too few informed consumers to drive a competitive market for public services. The likely result of trying to create such a market is not more efficiency but less equality. The socioeconomically advantaged are simply better positioned in such markets to defend their dominant social position, an outcome at odds with the egalitarian values of democratic government.

While academics debate the pros and cons of the Tiebout model, its core arguments have entered mainstream political debates and helped drive numerous reforms in public agencies. The 1990s movement to "reinvent" government through decentralizing authority and encouraging competition, for example, popularized the key arguments underlying Tiebout's model and sparked a raft of organizational reform in the public sector (see Osborne and Gaebler 1992). School vouchers, Total Quality Management, privatization, and contracting out—many of the most controversial reforms attempted in the public sector since the early 1990s—spring from the arguments first formally articulated by Tiebout. Whether these reforms will expose the weakness or the wisdom of orthodox perspectives in public administration scholarship is still an open question.

Perhaps the most comprehensive and useful revision to the Tiebout model, and rational choice more generally, comes from the work of Nobel Laureate Elinor Ostrom. Ostrom and her colleagues have advanced a theoretical paradigm in which cooperation can be achieved in the absence of an external authority or explicitly stated rules and sanctions. The Hobbesian solution to a social dilemma is not supported by empirical reality. In a public goods setting, Ostrom has shown that, given the opportunity to communicate, people are quite capable of solving social dilemmas through cooperation (Ostrom, Gardner, and Walker 1994). In short, people are able to govern themselves. Reviewing the work on social dilemmas and public goods games since, Ostrom (2003, 27) argues there are distinct behavioral patterns that severely limit the applicability of rational choice as a predictable theory. In particular, the first move in a public good setting is cooperation, not defection, as would be suggested by rational choice theorists. Research from behavioral economics has demonstrated a strong tendency to abide by norms of fairness, even in the absence of an external authority or in cases of anonymity (Camerer, Lowenstein, and Rabin 2004). Also of note, communication increases the likelihood of cooperation, and individuals tend to voluntarily punish those who fail to cooperate (Fehr and Gachter 2000).

Rational choice theory and the logic of appropriateness discussed in Chapter 7 both depend heavily on the principal-agent model—that an external actor wielding sanctions or incentives is necessary to achieve optimal outcomes. Ostrom's work demonstrates this to be incorrect. Mutually beneficial relationships can develop so long as there is a medium to facilitate and improve trust between individuals. For Ostrom (2003, 49), the key factors are trust, reciprocity, and reputation. Trust and trustworthy reputations create opportunities for cooperation between individuals, cooperation that in turn tends to be reciprocated. A reputation as someone who is untrustworthy causes the breakdown of cooperation and ultimately suboptimal outcomes.

A clear implication of Ostrom's work is that institutions able to facilitate trust, either through more open communication or more transparency, are likely to lead to improvements in the organizational culture of the institution, and potentially more beneficial relationships. Communication, particularly face-to-face communication, provides a signal of trustworthiness. Although Ostrom's early work tended to come to a similar conclusion as Tiebout, emphasizing "polycentricity" (Toonen 2010, 194), her more recent work on common pool resources (CPRs) provides a fresh alternative for public service delivery. For small-scale jurisdictions, competition between providers is not necessary. The notion that most individuals lack perfect mobility is well accepted. However, this is not a limit to the establishment of efficient policymaking institutions. As Vincent Ostrom would later comment, Elinor's work was unique in that it placed an emphasis on "human (as over and against) bureaucratic management" (Toonen 2010, 195).

Rational Choice as the New Orthodoxy

Rational choice mounts a challenge to the prescriptive arguments taken from traditional public administration scholarship, some of its advocates argue, and it should be adopted as the core paradigm of the discipline. These advocates present rational choice not simply as an economic framework that can be adopted to help understand bureaucratic behavior and the production of public services but also as a normative, democratic theory of administration in its own right.

The most forceful and best-known articulation of this argument comes from Vincent Ostrom in his book *The Intellectual Crisis in American Public Administration* (1973). Ostrom's central thesis was that public administration scholarship was centered on a theoretical construct that was in the process of breaking down. Ostrom (24–25) argued that the intellectual foundations of public administration were built upon a set of seven theoretical propositions formulated by Woodrow Wilson. *First*, there is, and always will be, a dominant center of power in any system of government. *Second*, the more power is divided, the more irresponsible and difficult to control it becomes. *Third*, the structure of a constitution determines the composition of central power. *Fourth*, the process of government can be separated into two parts: determining the will of the state (politics) and executing the will of the state (administration). *Fifth*, although the institutions and processes of politics vary widely from government to government, all governments share strong structural similarities in administration. *Sixth*, "good" administration is achieved by the proper hierarchical ordering of a professional public service. *Seventh*, perfection of "good" administration is a necessary condition for advancement of human welfare.

These basic propositions, Ostrom (1973) argued, were used to construct the paradigm that constituted orthodox public administration theory; that is, administration could be considered separately from politics, and good administration was tied to the organizational form of Weberian bureaucracy. Ostrom noted, however, that this orthodox thinking ignored some of the lessons conveyed by Weber's conception of bureaucracy, even as it embraced others. Weber considered bureaucracy a technically superior form of organization in the sense that it favored merit, professional expertise, rational division of labor, and standardized decisionmaking processes. These seemed a worthy alternative to patronage, partisan fealty, and political expediency as a basis for carrying out the will of the state. Yet, as Ostrom (25–28) pointed out, Weber's theory also suggested that mature bureaucracies would become central political institutions, not just technically superior agents of implementation. The fully developed bureaucracy would enjoy a huge informational advantage over their political masters, and there was no reason to expect that advantage would be deployed to advance the public interest over the bureaucracy's interest.

Ostrom argued that public administration scholars had concentrated on the technical superiority of the bureaucratic organization—its purported abilities to produce public goods efficiently—while ignoring the potential implications for the democratic process. Weber, Ostrom noted, also described a democratic alternative to the hierarchical and authoritarian basis for administration inherent in bureaucracy. Weber said that a democratic administration would have four characteristics. (1) Everyone is assumed to be qualified to participate in the conduct of public affairs. All citizens, not just technocrats, are assumed to have the necessary expertise to become involved in deciding what policies to pursue and how to pursue them. (2) Important decisions are opened up to all members of a community and their elected representatives. (3) Power is broadly diffused, not concentrated in a dominant center. (4) Administrative functionaries are public servants, not a technocratic elite of "public masters." Under these conditions, a democratic administration will be concentrated by polycentric government—one with multiple power centers in multiple layers (Ostrom 1973, 65–86).

Following Weber, public administration as a discipline rejected the concept of a democratic administration as theoretically and empirically untenable. Democratic administration placed unrealistically high knowledge and participation demands on citizens, and in diffusing power also weakened accountability over public agencies. Accordingly, public administration cast its intellectual lot with Wilson's assumption that power needs to be concentrated if it is to be controlled, and that efficient administration is more likely to come from technical experts functionally organized into bureaucracies than from multiple, contradictory, and poorly informed signals from the masses. Ostrom responded to this reasoning by arguing that its intellectual props had already crashed down. Scholars such as Dwight Waldo (1948) and Herbert Simon (1947/1997) had bored so thoroughly into the Wilsonian assumptions (especially the public-administration dichotomy) that they were simply incapable of supporting the orthodox perspective. Thus, Ostrom argued, public administration was left in a volatile and dangerous position: Its intellectual rudder ripped away, it was drifting and in danger of being consumed by other disciplines.

Ostrom argued that rational choice could not only provide an intellectual lifeboat but also provide the discipline with its theoretical ship of state. Ostrom suggested that a democratic theory of administration along the lines considered and dismissed by Weber is, in fact, possible, and that rational choice provides the obvious means to achieve it. If markets can efficiently match supply and demand for private goods and services with little in the way of centralized power centers or jurisdictional consolidation, why can they not do the same for public goods and services? After all, we have little difficulty in presuming that those who buy cars and soft drinks are informed enough to match their purchases to their preferences. Similarly, we expect consumers to know enough to abandon producers who fail to satisfy those preferences, thus allowing the market to weed out those who are inefficient or fail to respond to consumer demand. Why are these minimal assumptions about information and individual behavior not transferable to public services? Although not using the terms common to microeconomists, the writings of James Madison and Alexander Hamilton in the *Federalist* embraced the notion of individual determinism, and their conception of divided power fit with the polycentric nature of democratic administration. As Buchanan and Tullock put it, "Madisonian theory, either that which is explicitly contained in Madison's writings or that which is embodied in the American constitutional system, may be compared with the normative theory that emerges from the economic approach" (1962, 24). Given such a theoretical connection, Ostrom argued that rebuilding the intellectual enterprise of public administration on rational choice foundations was compatible with the democratic principles articulated in the Constitution.

Critics of the Ostrom perspective not only reject rational choice as the basis for a normative democratic theory of administration but also argue that its underlying principles lead to fundamentally undemocratic processes and outcomes. Indeed, some argue that rational choice has created rather than solved an intellectual crisis, one considerably more severe than the lack of a central disciplinary paradigm alluded to by Ostrom. M. Shamsul Haque (1996) argues that the pro-market values unavoidably embedded in rational choice theory threaten the credibility and the very existence of public administration as an independent scholarly discipline.

Haque further argues that the movement to introduce market mechanisms into the public administration has advanced by denigrating the performance of the public sector and extolling the excellence of private enterprise. The negative image of the public service threatens its legitimacy in the popular mind and creates the incentive to think of public administration as a slightly modified branch of business administration. The problem with this, Haque suggests, is that the public and private sectors are different and, at least in democratic systems, operate on different principles. What gets lost when viewing the public sector through the lens of rational choice is that market values and democratic values are not just different but probably incompatible. For example, markets may efficiently distribute goods and services, but they do not distribute them equitably, and markets may strive to connect supply to demand, even if the good or service is patently offensive to democratic ideals.

Consider education, a public service about which rational choice arguments have spread from academic matters to policy debates in the forms of proposals for vouchers, charters, and other marketlike mechanisms. One of the earliest calls for a system of school choice, that is, to create a competitive market within public education, was by southern whites in the wake of the *Brown v. Board of Education* desegregation orders. Going unmet was the demand for racial segregation, and the creation of a market for public education was seen as a way to persuade schools to pay less attention to external political institutions and more to local consumers. Most accept that a market for public education services could produce pockets of excellence and higher levels of consumer satisfaction among "marginal consumers," but widespread disagreement remains about whether markets will equitably distribute those benefits to everyone or concentrate them in the hands of a socioeconomically advantaged few (Henig 1994). Such outcomes may represent the technical advantages of the market in efficiency, but contradict the egalitarian values of democracy. In Madisonian terms, markets may unleash rather than constrain the corrosive power of factions.

Haque (1996) argues that the contradictions between markets and democracy have important implications for the practice as well as the study of public administration. The basic ethics of public service as established by the American Society of Public Administrators emphasize norms such as legality, responsibility, accountability, commitment, responsiveness, equality, and public disclosure (Mertins and Hennigan 1982). As rational choice becomes the epistemological standard in public administration courses, Haque (1996, 518) suggests, it has to redefine "public" in market terms if it is to preserve its internal theoretical consistency. As the concept of "public" atrophies under the paradigmatic insistence of rational choice, students, teachers, and scholars of public administration are left with an identity crisis. The likely result is that public administration morphs into business administration, where efficiency and productivity are prized and equity and representativeness are relegated to secondary concerns. This, Haque suggests, is not a concept of administration that is compatible with the democratic theorizing of Madison or Hamilton.

Other critics also argue that rational choice's focus on methodological individualism has blinded it to the core purpose of public administration. Ronald Moe and Robert Gilmore (1995) argue that from the standpoint of representative democracy, the mission of any public bureaucracy has to be top-down, not bottom-up. A public agency is ultimately responsible to the representative legislature and the law that authorizes its existence, its purpose, and its mission. The job of a public agency is not to divine the preferences of its clientele and then satisfy them. A public agency, in other words, is just that: public. It is not the equivalent of a private-sector producer serving a market niche by satisfying the preferences of a certain set of customers. A public agency's job is to serve the collective institutions of the democratic system and, ultimately, the Constitution. An agency's clientele might not like some of the actions when they are responsive to such top-down considerations, but public administration is supposed to serve the will of the state, not the selfish wants of the individual. There are any number of conceivable instances in which an agency might serve its clientele well, but, in doing so, harm the common good. A school in a competitive education market, for example, may offer religious indoctrination as part of the curriculum. Parents who find this attractive can take their children, along with their tax dollars, to such a school and be highly satisfied. From an individual and market perspective, all is well—supply is efficiently matched with demand through the mechanisms of competition among producers and choice among consumers. From a group-level democratic perspective, the result is less pleasing. The central legal justification for public schooling—to teach the imperatives of democratic citizenship—is subordinated to market demand, if not lost altogether (Rebell 1998).

Democracy is ultimately a set of guarantees about process—a person's rights to participate in collective decisions—not about outcomes. The market delivers what the individual wants; democracy delivers what we can all agree upon and live with. The two, as critics of rational choice take some pains to point out, are not the same thing in practice or in theory (Callan 1997). For such reasons, critics argue that rational choice is a poor choice for the central paradigm of public administration. Market values and democratic values are not interchangeable equivalents, and rational choice favors the latter over the former. The decades since the seminal contributions of Waldo (1948) and Simon (1947/1997) may have been marked by an intellectual crisis in the study of public administration, and the discipline's difficulty in intellectually accommodating its scholarly underpinnings with democratic values is by now well known.

Conclusions

Rational choice theory has provoked some of the most contentious and controversial debates in public administration scholarship, but it has also provided the discipline with a little-rivaled intellectual stimulant. Regardless of whether the purpose has been to advocate the theory or to expose its faults, some of the most original and valuable contributions to public administration knowledge come from those working from a rational choice foundation.

The attractions of rational choice theory (especially its formal applications) are not only its internal consistency but also its ability to generate logically deduced, empirically testable propositions. As long as its founding premises hold, it is capable of parsimoniously and comprehensively explaining a broad range of phenomena of interest to public administration scholars. In addition to presenting a formidable challenge to public administration orthodoxy, the central ideas of rational choice theory have become popularized and were foundational to the attempts by many Western democracies to "reinvent" their administrative apparatus in the 1980s and 1990s.

The problem with rational choice is that significant questions remain about the validity of its starting premises. If these are incorrect, or valid only under limited circumstances, the broad claims of rational choice—and its widely adopted prescriptive implications—immediately become suspect. As a deductive theoretical framework, rational choice stands and falls on the twin pillars of rational self-interest and methodological individualism. As Buchanan and Tullock argue, "The ultimate defense of the economic-individualist behavioral assumption must be empirical" (1962, 28). Thus far, the empirical record has not definitively rejected these assumptions, but neither has it done much to confirm them. One of the persistent criticisms of rational choice theory is that its conception of human nature is too narrow to be of much use. Consider the firefighters who died while trying to fight their way into the World Trade Center towers during the terrorist attacks of 2001. Undoubtedly, these men were doing a job they were being compensated for, and job performance undoubtedly plays a role in the career prospects of any civil servant. Yet to describe their actions as "self-interested" requires a very broad interpretation of that concept. Countless more mundane examples of public-sector behavior support the contention that whatever comprises the average civil servant or citizen utility function, it is not adequately accounted for by the traditional portrait of a rational utility maximizer.

Some of these criticisms are built from the same intellectual tools that rational choice proponents use to expose the weaknesses of orthodox public administration theory. For example, rational choice advocates are quick to cite Simon's work as a mortal blow to the orthodox intellectual tradition, but Simon also explicitly rejected the economic concept of the rational utility maximizer. Simon's administrator was a satisficer, not a maximizer; that is, a decisionmaker equipped with limited information, driven by habit and values, who settled for decisions that were "good enough" to deal with the situation at hand, not those that maximized individual utility (Simon 1947/1997). Simon drew his concept of bounded rationality out of psychology rather than economics, and his portrait of administrators was more psychologically complex than the cost-benefit calculator that shows up in Niskanen's formal models. Simon argued that the economic concept of human rationality at the heart of rational choice theory fails the empirical acid test set by Buchanan and Tullock (Simon 1985). Simon may well have helped undermine the Wilsonian/Weberian theoretical tradition, but his arguments are no less corrosive to the core assumptions of rational choice.

This mixed empirical and theoretical record is discomforting because there is another side to Smith's insight that the pursuit of individual self-interest can produce collective benefits. Scholars have also long known that individuals who pursue self-interest can impose collective costs. This is known as the "tragedy of the commons" problem, and was most famously articulated in a 1968 essay by biologist Garrett Hardin. Imagine a public pasture, open to any cattle owner who wants to put his herd out to graze. A rational herdsman will seek to maximize his gain from this public resource by putting as many cattle out to graze as he can. The problem is that if every herdsman does this, the grazing of the cattle will quickly exceed the carrying capacity of the pasture. When the common resource has been exhausted, all the herdsmen will face ruin because they rationally sought to maximize self-interest.

Hardin took some pains to point out that the tragedy of the commons was more than a cautionary parable; indeed, numerous real-world examples range from the exhaustion of certain fishing stocks to the overuse of national parks. The tragedy of the commons is, in fact, a problem as old as man, and all societies are forced to create mechanisms to preserve the common good from the corrosive effects of individual self-interest. Adam Smith recognized that self-interest could be harnessed for the collective good, but even he made no claims that this was a universal possibility. If market mechanisms driven by self-interested actors cannot protect the common interest, what can? As Hardin pointed out, modern industrialized democracies tend to converge on a single answer to this question: administrative agencies with the power to "legislate temperance." As Hardin put it, "Since it is practically impossible to spell out all the conditions under which it is safe to burn trash in the back yard or to run an automobile without smog-control, by law we delegate the details to bureaus" (1968, 1245).

This solution may fit easily with the Wilson/Weberian perspective, but does little to solve its inherent problems, especially its difficulty in reconciling the hierarchical, authoritarian nature of bureaucracy with democratic values and the inevitable political role Weber assigned to mature bureaucracies. Rational choice has played an important role in determining the limits of this orthodox perspective, but has thus far met only limited success in establishing itself as its intellectual successor. If there are unbridgeable differences between markets for cars or soft drinks and markets for public goods such as library, education, and law enforcement services, economic theory may have limited use for scholars of the public sector. To become the central paradigm of public administration, rational choice requires markets to be somehow made synonymous with democracy. Ostrom showed that this is not necessarily impossible, though subsequent work raises doubts about whether it is probable.

There are signs of an emerging synthesis between the orthodox perspective and the challenge from rational choice. Rational choice scholars have expanded and refined the concept of utility maximization since the 1970s in ways that allow the committed public servant a place in formal models of bureaucracy (Ostrom 1998). Relaxing the assumptions that define rational utility maximization to allow a greater role for altruistic or group-oriented goals—for example, the desire to help others or serve the public interest—considerably tempers the portraits of bureaucracy created in early rational choice works such as those of Downs and Tullock. Teske and his colleagues show that, at least in theory, competitive markets can exist under considerably less-than-optimal market conditions, though these markets may require a strong regulatory role for public bureaucracies to mitigate the social-democratic downside of market excess. Perhaps rational choice's lasting contribution will be to redefine intellectually rather than to replace the role of bureaucracy in public administration theory.

Cleary, as indicated in this and the previous chapter, research being conducted in other disciplines is changing the theoretical framework surrounding decision theory and rational choice. David Brooks (2011), political columnist for the *New York Times*, has labeled the need for a broader look at human nature as the "new humanism." In order to fully understand the political process, how people respond to incentives, and the human decisionmaking process, a more interdisciplinary approach is needed. Others have also called for combining the natural and social sciences through a process of "consilience" (Wilson 1998). A brief review of the number of journal articles, and even journals (e.g. *Organizational Psychology* founded in 2011), attests to the strength of this movement. Some of the discipline's most well-respected figures, Simon and Ostrom, were strong advocates of the need to draw on theory and evidence from other disciplines, primarily psychology and economics. To date, however, the field at large has been reluctant to more directly situate itself as interdisciplinary (Wright 2011). Some, such as Elinor Ostrom, have even explored and utilized theoretical insights from beyond the social sciences, to include biology and environmental science. The notion that communication within CPRs can facilitate trust and prevent hoarding illustrates an important distinction between maximizing short-term and long-term self-interest. People are willing and able to avoid maximizing short-term self-interest (e.g., overgrazing) in order to maximize long-term self-interest (e.g., the longevity of the pasture). Although still a form of utility maximization, rational choice theory, as currently conceptualized within public administration, does not distinguish between the two, or when one or the other will be pursued.

Despite such shortcomings, there is hope for public administration and the potential for the development of a dominant paradigm as advocated by Vincent Ostrom. As discussed earlier in this and the previous chapter, early attempts to apply rational choice theory to the behavior of bureaucrats and citizens break down in light of recent evidence on human decisionmaking. A brief web search on Amazon or Barnes and Noble using the keyword "irrational" will reveal that since the mid-1990s there has been a tremendous increase in the attention devoted to patterns of decisionmaking that depart from the rational actor model described in the first part of this chapter. Common to most of these texts is the notion that rationality is rarely defined in terms of maximizing economic utility. Rather, humans tend to engage in behavior that, although less than financially maximizing, is in large part predictable. The title of Dan Ariely's book *Predictably Irrational* (2009) is an appropriate moniker for this emerging line of research.

Beyond Vincent Ostrom and Simon, perhaps few have shaped decision theory and rational choice theory more than Elinor Ostrom. To rein in self-interested bureaucrats, orthodox public administration advised a top-down, centralized management structure. Revisions from Tullock, Downs, Niskanen, and Tiebout suggested that competition and market forces were a more practical alternative to achieving efficiency. Ostrom's work on common pool resources suggests that the solution may in fact be endogenous—within-group communication allows for the establishment of self-regulating institutions. Coordination, and thus efficiency, can be achieved without competition and without centralized control. Even though Ostrom's work on CPR dilemmas is consistent and robust, the implications for large-scale bureaucracies are less clear. Nonetheless, institutions able to facilitate open communication and participatory decisionmaking processes are most likely to engender trust and the accompanying organizational benefits that it provides.

Whatever its weaknesses, rational choice has few equals in public administration theory for internal rigor and the ability to explain complex phenomena with clarity and parsimony. There are, however, clear alternatives emerging within the social sciences. Indeed, as discussed earlier in the chapter, when applying insights from organizational psychology, the theoretical and practical utility of Tullock and Downs is questionable at best. A new behavioral theory is emerging, one that is by necessity interdisciplinary. Yet the insular nature of public administration raises concern as to whether the field will be able to efficiently incorporate insights from other disciplines in this regard (Wright 2011). Thus, it is likely that for years to come, rational choice will continue to be employed (both gainfully and perilously) as a way of organizing and studying public bureaucracies and public service provision.

Notes

1. Although Adam Smith is best known as a founding father of economics, his ties to public administration are considerable. Smith never held a position as a professional economist, but he undoubtedly was a public administrator—he enjoyed something of a second career as a government tax collector.

9

Theories of Governance

Introduction: Public Administration's Need for a Theory of Governance

During the last quarter century, industrialized democracies have witnessed a fundamental shift in the purposes and methods of government. Various elements combined to produce this change: increasing deficits, economic stagnation, disenchantment with the intermittently met promises of the welfare state, and a general sense that government was encroaching on individual liberty. Reversing a trend characteristic of post–World War II development, governments in the 1970s, 1980s, and 1990s became less hierarchical, more decentralized, and increasingly willing to cede their role as dominant policy actor to the private sector (Kettl 2000).

These changes raise questions about the scope and nature of public administration, both as a profession and as a scholarly discipline. For virtually all of the twentieth century, public administration was synonymous with bureaucracy, hierarchy, and accountability. Though the golden age of theoretical hegemony in public administration collapsed in the 1950s under the combined assault of Dwight Waldo, Herbert Simon, and others, the retreat of the politics-administration dichotomy as the discipline's core organizing principle did not alter the constitutional or institutional nature of government. The collapse of orthodox theory meant that bureaucracies within centralized policy jurisdictions could no longer be considered outside or above politics, but they remained the central suppliers of public goods and services and continued to define what administration theory was called upon to explain. The theoretical pluralism that followed struggled with mixed success to explain bureaucracy's newly acknowledged relationship with legislatures, executives, and the rest of the polity, but those relationships, the technical arrangements underpinning them, and the role of civil servants in maintaining them remained more or less untouched. The theoretical landscape of public administration changed, but its professional and empirical reality remained stable.

That stability was irretrievably upset by the worldwide movement to develop and adopt alternate methods of carrying out policy and providing public service. Although this movement was not centrally directed or planned and varied widely in specifics, it was characterized by common core elements. These included adoption of market-based management and resource allocation techniques, an increased reliance on private-sector organizations to deliver public services, and a deliberate and sustained effort to downsize and decentralize government's role as the central policy actor in society.

These changes amount to more than just another administration reform fad. Not only is the nature of government itself being questioned and changed, but also the powers and responsibilities of the city, the state, and the nation-state are becoming less defined and increasingly merged with other jurisdictions and the private sector. The administrative state is now less bureaucratic, less hierarchical, and less reliant on central authority to mandate action. Accountability for conducting the public's business is increasingly about performance rather than about discharging a specific policy goal within the confines of the law (Moe and Gilmour 1995). Since the 1980s, the scholarly record has seen increased attention devoted to the "hollow state," a metaphor for government that contracts public service provision out to networks of (mostly) nonprofit organizations and reduces its role as a direct supplier of public goods (Milward and Provan 2000b, 240). Increasingly, "public policies and programs in the United States and elsewhere are being administered . . . through complicated webs of states, regions, special districts, service delivery areas, local offices, nonprofit organizations, collaborations, networks, partnerships and other means for the control and coordination of dispersed activities" (Lynn, Heinrich, and Hill 2001, 1). Scholars have labeled this development "hybridity" (Skelcher 2005) or "mixed" institutions (Koppell 2011), requiring different theoretical frameworks and methodological techniques—a point we return to later in the chapter.

These changes challenge a good deal of existing public administration theory because they reshape the concept at the heart of the discipline. Traditionally, the "public" in public administration meant government. As the traditional role of government changes, and with it expectations about how that role is to be fulfilled, public administration is being forced to redefine and reposition itself both in applied practice and as a field of scholarship. To keep up with the new reality, public administration scholars are being forced to rethink their discipline and its theoretical foundations. The hollow state literally redefines what the "public" in public administration means. At a minimum, the definition of public must now include a broad variety of institutions and organizations traditionally considered outside the realm of government, as well as the relationships these organizations have with each other and with policymaking authorities. This new definition dramatically increases the number and complexity of the explanatory targets public administration theory must account for.

This expansion of public administration's scholarly arena is reflected in an increasing interest in the concept of governance, both as an idea and as a general description of what public administration scholars study. Indeed, the term "governance" is increasingly a surrogate or proxy for "public administration" or "public management" in the discipline's leading literature (Kettl 2000; Salamon 1989; Garvey 1997; Peters and Pierre 1998). The linguistic morphing of public administration into the study of governance acknowledges the new realities of the administrative state and is argued by some to herald a new and theoretical orientation for the discipline. Gerald Garvey (1997), for example, uses governance as a way to distinguish between the public administration orthodoxy built upon the principles of politics-administration dichotomy (defined as expertise, merit selection, specialization, institution building, and a science of management) and a new theory of public administration based on understanding the diffuse networks increasingly responsible for providing public service. Such concepts of governance expand and complicate the challenge of developing public administration theory. They are also argued to be a more empirically valid way of understanding how government programs actually operate; of providing a more realistic way to teach those preparing for careers in the public sector; and of offering more useful construction materials for theory-building than the worn and increasingly irrelevant planks of orthodoxy.

Although the need for public administration theory to account for the changes in the role and practices of government during the last few decades is widely recognized, it is not clear that a theory of governance exists to meet this challenge. The Weberian model of bureaucracy and management is undoubtedly less relevant to public administration than it once was, yet it remains a sharper set of intellectual tools than the still-fuzzy concept of governance. Though governance is now virtually a synonym for public administration, much of the literature putatively about "governance" does not even bother to define the term, apparently on the assumption that it is understood naturally and intuitively (Osborne and Gaebler 1992). As a substitute for theory, intuition is unlikely to provide much lasting use for the discipline.

Lacking a universal definition, governance is currently more an acknowledgement of the empirical reality of changing times than it is a body of coherent theory. According to H. George Frederickson (2005), the inchoate state of governance theory can be traced to how it is currently operationalized among public administration scholars. Frederickson argues there are five main problems with the state of the governance framework. *First*, it is fashionable; governance has become a catchall phrase. *Second*, as we discuss later, governance, in its current form, is imprecise. *Third*, governance is "freighted with values" (289). Those employing the term governance tend to have preexisting negative views of government institutions and orthodox bureaucratic structures. *Fourth*, "governance is primarily about change" (290). Governance does not have to be a prescriptive framework, emphasizing reform and the restructuring of institutions. Governance can also be used as a descriptive term for interjurisdictional relationships between public and private actors. As Frederickson writes, "Most descriptions of governance—networks, inter-organizational and inter-jurisdictional cooperation, power-sharing federations, public-private partnerships, and contracting out—are forms of institutional adaptation in the face of increasing interdependence" (290).

Fifth, governance theory tends to give disproportionate weight to "non-state institutions" (Frederickson 2005, 290). Rarely are services provided in the complete absence of public or governmental institutions. Instead, public service delivery is often characterized by "public-private partnerships" (Skelcher 2005).

Nonetheless, the debate on governance is well under way, and its potential to reshape public administration as a scholarly discipline is seen by some as inevitable. Numerous scholars are painstakingly trying to capture the purpose and process of the new realities of government in theory. This project is undertaken from a variety of viewpoints and intellectual traditions. Here in the emerging field of governance theory, public administration scholars wrestle with the key questions created by the growth of the fragmented state: What is government's role in society? How should this role be fulfilled? Are the new realities of providing public service sufficiently accountable to the democratic process? This chapter explores some of the dominant themes in the governance debate and their potential for providing the discipline with the theoretical tools necessary to understand and explain public administration in the twenty-first century.

A New Model of Governance

Among the most important contributions to the emerging governance literature is the work of Laurence E. Lynn Jr., Carolyn J. Heinrich, and Carolyn J. Hill (1999, 2001; Heinrich and Lynn 2000). Their work represents an ambitious synthesis of the field that attempts to articulate a broad-reaching research agenda and provide the framework necessary to carry this agenda forward. They suggest that governance is a concept that has the potential to unify the sprawling public management and public policy literature, investing it with common explanatory objectives and highlighting a critical contribution of a huge body of research. Lynn and his colleagues argue that the basic question at the heart of all governance-related research is this: "How can public-sector regimes, agencies, programs and activities be organized and managed to achieve public purposes?" (2001, 1).

Given the complex administrative arrangements that characterize the hollow state, answering this question is an extraordinarily difficult challenge. There is an enormous amount of variation in rules, procedures, organization, and performance among the dispersed and decentralized entities now involved in public service provision. This variation occurs both within and across the jurisdiction of cities, states, and nations. What accounts for this variation? Is it systematic? Will understanding this variation help fashion better public administration and management strategies? A theory of governance may help provide answers to such questions and provide public administration with an intellectual handle on the hollow state. Lynn, Heinrich, and Hill do not claim to create such a theory, but they do seek to lay a systematic foundation for the study of governance. Their goal is advisory rather than prescriptive; it is to suggest approaches to research design and interpretation that "will promote the creation of a body of knowledge whose value equals or exceeds the sum of its numerous parts" (2001, 15).

Although Lynn et al.'s objectives do not include the construction of a comprehensive explanatory framework, they do offer several planks necessary to construct such a full-blown theory. These begin with a definition of governance as the "regimes of laws, administrative rules, judicial rulings, and practices that constrain, prescribe, and enable government activity, where such activity is broadly defined as the production and delivery of publicly supported goods and services" (Lynn, Heinrich, and Hill 2000, 3). This definition implies that governance consists of separate but interrelated elements. These elements include organizational, financial and programmatic structures; statutes and laws; policy mandates; available resources; administrative rules; and institutionalized rules and norms. The definition also implies that governance is inherently political, that it involves bargaining and compromise between actors with different interests, and that it comprises both formal structures and informal influence, either of which may characterize the relationship between formal authority and the actual conduct of government-mandated operations (10).

The combined elements that make up Lynn et al.'s concept of governance are argued to describe the ends and means of governmental activity and how these ends and means connect. A particular configuration of these elements is termed a "governance regime," with each regime encompassing the broad array of components that determine public service provision in a particular area. These components include policy domain (e.g., environmental protection), type of government activity (e.g., regulation), particular jurisdiction (e.g., a state), and particular organization (e.g., a state department of natural resources). The formation of these regimes is a product of a dynamic process they call the "logic of governance." This process links the values and interest of citizens with the actions of legislatures, executives, and the courts (Lynn, Heinrich, and Hill 1999). Lynn and his colleagues argue that the key to the study of governance is coming to some systematic understanding of this process and its relationship to performance: "The central theoretical problem in governance research is applying theories that impose a causal ordering or a priori structure on the logic that links contexts, governance, and consequences or outcomes" (2001, 17).

Lynn et al. suggest that the study of governance has two primary intellectual antecedents. The first is institutionalism, especially as practiced by public choice scholars. This body of literature has repeatedly confirmed that structural arrangements shape behavior within an organization, determine the performance of an organization, and structure its relationships with external actors. The second is the study of networks. The research literature on networks emphasizes "the role of multiple social actors in arrays of negotiation, implementation and service delivery" (O'Toole 2000, 276). Given these underpinnings, it is unsurprising that many of the elements of governance as described by Lynn et al. resemble elements of traditional public administration. But governance is a broader idea that synthesizes and pushes forward key ideas from the institutional and network literatures while also drawing on several other theoretical traditions familiar to public administration scholars.

Like network theory, Lynn et al.'s concept of governance operates on at least three distinct levels: the institutional, the organizational, and the technical. At the institutional level, there are stable formal and informal rules, hierarchies, boundaries, procedures, regime values, and authority. Understanding institutions draws on several bodies of thought, including public choice, theories concerning the control of the bureaucracy, and the broader theories or philosophies of government. The institutional level of governance is aimed at understanding the formation, adoption, and implementation of public policy (especially the latter). At the organizational, or managerial, level of governance are the hierarchical bureaus, departments, commissions, all the other executive agencies, and various nongovernmental organizations linked to public authority by contract or by other incentives or mandates. Understanding this level of governance draws on agency theory, theories of leadership, and network theory. The primary concern at this level is understanding incentives, administrative discretion, performance measures, and civil service (or nongovernmental agency) functioning. The technical level of governance represents the task environment, where public policy is carried out at the street level. Issues of professionalism, technical competence, motivation, accountability, and performance are the main interests at the technical level, which draws on analytical techniques (and theories) of efficiency, management, organizational leadership, accountability, incentives, and performance measurement.

In reduced form, Lynn, Heinrich, and Hill (2000, 15) present their logic of governance as a model that takes the following form:

$$O = f [E, C, T, S, M]$$

Where:

O = Outputs/outcomes. The end product of a governance regime.
E = Environmental factors. These can include political structures, levels of authority, economic performance, the presence or absence of competition

among suppliers, resource levels and dependencies, legal frameworks, and the characteristics of a target population.

C = Client characteristics. The attributes, characteristics, and behavior of clients.

T = Treatments. These are the primary work or core processes of the organizations within the governance regime. They include organizational missions and objectives, recruitment and eligibility criteria, methods for determining eligibility, and program treatments or technologies.

S = Structures. These include organizational type, level of coordination and integration among the organizations in the governance regime, relative degree of centralized control, functional differentiation, administrative rules or incentives, budgetary allocations, contractual arrangements or relationships, and institutional culture and values.

M = Managerial roles and actions. These include leadership characteristics, staff-management relations, communications, methods of decisionmaking, professionalism/career concerns, and mechanisms of monitoring, control, and accountability.

The reduced form model is intended as a starting point for empirical research on governance. Lynn and colleagues (2000, 15) deliberately seek to make the model flexible, and recognize that alternate theoretical starting points or particular research objectives may call for the inclusion of other variables. They also recognize that explanatory variables in the model are not wholly independent of each other, and exploring the interrelationships among them is another fruitful avenue for governance scholars.

Though their concept and model are obviously not axiomatic theory, Lynn et al.'s approach to governance immediately clarifies some important issues for governance research. Critically, their approach highlights the multilevel nature of governance, something that is not particularly well reflected in scholarly research or completely recognized by the advocates of decentralization. The outcome of any large-scale reform, be it good or bad, depends on the decisions made at various levels of administration and the context in which these decisions are carried out. These implications are clear in Lynn et al.'s presentation of governance, though they are largely ignored by the architects of reform. Lynn et al. are calling for studies that attend to the hierarchical system of government organizations, studies that use data from multiple sources and multiple levels of analysis and that employ methodologies capable of employing these multiple data inputs (Roderick, Jacob, and Bryk 2000).

Lynn et al.'s concept and model of governance underpin their call for an ambitious research agenda to help explain and improve the performance of the decentralized administrative state. As a motivation and guide to research, their work is yielding some dividends, but its potential to mature into a full-blown theory is questionable. As preface to theory, their arguments have two central problems.

First, and most importantly, neither their concept nor their model is particularly parsimonious. Their model "comes close to the economist's criticisms of political science: by including everything, one runs the danger of explaining nothing" (Ellwood 2000, 329). Even as a heuristic, their model is so all encompassing that its use as a systematic guide is questionable. Rather than imposing a causal order on governance, the model may do nothing more than provide a handy list of broad conceptual elements that can be selectively mined to fit a particular case. This is a useful service, but it does not provide the heavy explanatory lifting required for theory. Indeed, the comprehensiveness of Lynn et al.'s model creates difficulties in terms of drawing distinct disciplinary boundaries because "there appears to be little difference between studying the whole of government and politics and studying public administration" (Frederickson 2005, 287).

The second problem is that even if a more parsimonious and general model could be constructed from these elements, it would probably be unable to generate general conclusions. Governance regimes seem to be shaped by their policy domains, and different types of policies lead to different sorts of governance problems. What works for, say, welfare, may not work for environmental protection. The basic problem of public policy is that it is inherently a political process. Its design, implementation, and administration involve multiple actors with multiple objectives and multiple agendas. Governance as outlined by Lynn et al. acknowledges this reality rather than explains it systematically (Ellwood 2000, 329–330).

Lynn et al.'s model has other, more technical difficulties. These include persuading scholars to adopt more complex research methodologies and overcoming some difficult measurement issues. For example, it is one thing to include an abstract and loosely defined concept such as management in a heuristic model, but empirically capturing that concept in a study seeking to assess its impact on agency performance is quite another matter. Some of the difficulties of corralling a large and amorphous explanatory target into a research agenda characterized by conceptual and methodological coherence seem to be at least implicitly recognized by Lynn et al. Almost out of necessity, their call to action narrows as it moves from its broad conceptual ambitions toward dealing with the difficult details of putting that vision into practice. Operationally, their model devolves into a proposal for creative econometric models of agency performance or outputs (Lowery 2002).

Although we do not discount these problems, the criticisms may turn out to be premature. Lynn et al. never claimed to have a fully functional theory of governance; their goal was simply to foster a research program that theoretically and empirically addressed the governance of public policies and contributed to improving their creation, implementation, and administration. That research program has already attracted scholars to its standard (Lynn et al. 2000). For example, recent work on the response to Hurricane Katrina employs a governance framework based on network analysis that is similar to the multilevel model presented by Lynn et al. (Koliba, Mills, and Zia 2011).

Governance as the New Public Management

The largest criticism of Lynn et al.'s approach is that it is predicated on a definition of governance so broad and inclusive that it loses specific meaning. An alternate approach sets firmer conceptual boundaries by equating governance with New Public Management (NPM), sometimes referred to as the "new managerialism." NPM characterizes a global public management reform movement that has redefined the relationships between government and society.

Although this management reform movement has numerous variations across and even within nation-states, it has several universal themes. In a wide-ranging overview of this reform movement, Donald Kettl (2000, 1–2) argues that it is predicated on six core issues. (1) Productivity. The reform effort is a serious attempt to assess how governments can do "more with less" by sustaining, or even expanding, public services with lower resource investments. (2) Marketization. The reform movement is predicated on government leveraging market mechanisms to overcome the pathologies of traditional bureaucracy. (3) Service orientation. One of the common objects of reforms is to better connect government with citizens and to improve customer satisfaction with public services. (4) Decentralization. This is not just a mindless devolution of decisionmaking power to lower levels in the political or bureaucratic hierarchy but also a conscious effort to put those who make policy decisions as close as possible to the people who are going to be affected by those decisions. The goal is to put government closer to citizens and make it more sensitive and responsive to their preferences. (5) Policy. The reform movement seeks to improve government's capacities to create, to implement, and to administer public policy. (6) Accountability. The reform movement is an effort to make government deliver on what it promises.

Kettl contends that at its heart, the management reform movement represents a debate about governance: "What should government do? How can it best accomplish these goals? What capacity does it need to do it well? . . . The management reform movement builds on the notion that good governance—a sorting out of mission, role, capacity, and relationships—is a necessary (if insufficient) condition for economic prosperity and social stability" (2000, 5–6). Governance in the management reform context thus refers to the "core issues of the relationship between government and society," and the reevaluation and reformation of this relationship at the core of NPM represent a fundamental shift in the politics of the administrative state (36).

Kettl argues that there are various reasons for the timing and motivations of the grand governance debate at the heart of the public management movement. These include the economic stagnation faced by many democracies in the 1970s and early 1980s and its association with overregulation by government, the erosion of trust in government in many democratic polities during the same period, and the end of the cold war, which left some countries building public administration infrastructures around newly formed democratic polities and forced democracies in the West to seriously rethink their models of governance for the first time in fifty years.

All these elements combined to create a global push to reshape the formal and informal connections between government and society. The net result of the governance debate was the emergence of NPM. Though there are many variants of NPM, the majority of these are predicated on two models. The first is the Westminster model, which originated in New Zealand in the late 1970s and quickly spread to other parliamentary democracies, such as Australia, Canada, and (especially) the United Kingdom. The second is the reinventing government model, which came much later and is unique to the United States.

These two models share a basic underlying philosophy. Both, for example, are characterized by the six issues Kettl identifies at the core of the management reform movement. Primarily, it is the institutional and political differences and histories between parliamentary or Westminster-style democracies and the federal system of the United States that give each model its unique flavor. New Zealand and the United Kingdom, for example, have strong, centralized governments that in the 1970s directly controlled key parts of their economies, including transportation and telecommunications. Characteristic of the Westminster model are sweeping privatization of these state-controlled industries, separation of government operations into functional units, and delegation of decisionmaking power to actors within those functional areas. In contrast, as there was never any enthusiasm for nationalizing large sectors of the economy in the United States, there is less to privatize. And because local, state, and national governments in the United States share responsibility in most policy arenas and are subject to different political motivation, there is no central agent powerful enough to force functional reorganizations on the scale pursued by the Westminster model.

One of the results of these differences is that the Westminster model is characterized by a more fundamental and systematic effort to identify what government should and should not be responsible for, to shed the operations deemed better handled by the private sector, and to concentrate on finding better ways to carry out the operation deemed appropriate for the public sector. This does not mean the reinventing government model is somehow "Westminster lite." Indeed, in some ways it represents a more radical effort to reshape governance. Although the Westminster reforms retained a powerful role for administrators in the public sector—sometimes bureaucrats got sweeping decisionmaking authority—they were more oriented toward creating cooperative arrangements in creating networks of public service provision. Reinventing government tended to emphasize competition to a greater degree, and to fundamentally alter the regulatory role of government (Kettl 2000, 7).

Despite the variations, it is the underlying similarities that make the NPM movement a debate about governance. As Kettl puts it, in both the private and public sectors administration is centered on the need for social coordination: "It is how leaders pull together widely disparate resources—money, people, expertise, and technology—to get things done" (2000, 31). The "intricate dance" of implementing public policy and programs represents the connection between government and society, and governance is a term that describes that connection. Because NPM represents a serious effort to describe, rethink, and improve upon that link, it therefore represents a coherent model of governance.

Equating governance with NPM avoids the key criticism of the Lynn et al. approach by putting clear boundaries on the concept and focusing it on a reasonably well-defined model of public management. Some, however, argue that, although the overlap between NPM and governance is undeniable, there are fundamental differences between the two. Among the scholars who have given the most serious efforts to intellectually unpack NPM and governance as two separate concepts are B. Guy Peters and John Pierre (1998, 2000b). Peters and Pierre begin by accepting the reality that government's role as the central public policy actor and the major influence on the economy fundamentally altered during the last twenty years of the twentieth century. This change has precipitated a fundamental shift in the relationship between the public and private sectors and their relative roles and responsibilities in providing public service. This relationship is at the core of the debate on governance.

Peters and Pierre (1998) argue that four basic elements characterize discussions of governance. (1) The dominance of networks. Instead of formal policymaking institutions, governance is dominated by an amorphous collection of actors having influence over what and how public goods and services are to be produced. (2) The state's declining capacity for direct control. Although governments no longer exercise centralized control over public policy, they still have the power to influence it. The power of the state is now tied to its ability to negotiate and bargain with actors in policy networks. The members of these networks are increasingly accepted as equal partners in the policy process. (3) The blending of public and private resources. Public and private actors use each other to obtain resources they cannot access independently. For example, using private companies for policy implementation allows government to sidestep some expensive and time-consuming procedural and accountability issues. Private companies can persuade the state to bankroll projects that benefit the public interest but are unlikely to be funded by the private sector. (4) Use of multiple instruments. This means an increasing will-ingness to develop and employ nontraditional methods of making and imple-menting public policy. These are often indirect instruments, such as using tax incentives to influence behavior rather than command-and-control regulations to mandate behavior.

If these elements define governance, Peters and Pierre (1998) observe that NPM and governance obviously share a good deal of common ground. Both mod-els shrink the traditional roles and responsibilities of elected officials. Representa-tives are still expected to set long-term goals, develop networks, and help pool public and private resources, but they are no longer the dominant policy actors. Essentially, NPM and the general thrust of the governance debate propose shifting power from public office or legal mandates to "entrepreneurial activity" in policy networks. This shift in power not only characterizes NPM and governance but also creates a shared problem of accountability. If public officials have less power and responsibility, is it fair or even possible to hold them accountable for public policy? If the answer is no, who or what should be held accountable for public policy? NPM tackles the accountability issue by leveraging the powers of supply and demand. Public service providers should compete with each other to satisfy clientele demand. This, however, redefines rather than solves the accountability problem (Peters and Pierre 1998). A homogenous clientele group does not neces-sarily represent the wishes and wants of the broader pool of taxpayers who foot the bill for the public services this group consumes. If public service providers are held accountable to their clientele, the problem of regulatory capture is raised, that is, the service providers seek to benefit the clientele rather than serve the pub-lic interest.

Another similarity between NPM and governance is that both are predicated on an assumption that government is too distant from citizens and society, and that its agents have become inefficient and discourteous as a result (Peters and Pierre 2000b). Although the forces of a globalizing economy forced private-sector operations to become leaner, to be more attentive and responsive to their cus-tomers, and to develop and adopt more sophisticated management tools, govern-ment operations were insulated from these changes because of government monopolies over public service production. Both models seek to use competition to correct the inefficiencies held to be inherent in the traditional bureaucratic model and to force public service providers to become more responsive to the cit-izens they serve. NPM and governance are also both results oriented. In contrast to traditional models of public administration, they are oriented toward the con-trol of outputs rather than inputs. The focus is on producing what will increase efficiency and satisfy the customer rather than on the resources available to a pub-lic agency.

Finally, both governance and NPM embrace the concept of steering. David Osborne and Ted Gaebler (1992) are generally credited with coining the phase that governments should "steer rather than row," where steering means setting broad policy objectives and rowing means actually taking the actions that fulfill those objectives. Like others who make little distinction between NPM and governance, Osborne and Gaebler argue that rowing is best left to entrepreneurial activity in relevant policy networks rather than to direct, centrally micromanaged government action. In the abstract, this retains for elected officials and their bureaucratic agents a strong role in policymaking, but in practice it aggravates the accountability problems inherent in NPM and creates a new set of management problems for government. If, as NPM advocates Osborne and Gaebler suggest, governments did a poor job of steering when they had central control over policy and public service provision, how are they going to do a better job of steering when much of their power has been diffused into amorphous policy networks? Peters and Pierre (1998) suggest that this question is critically important to the governance debate and that NPM has not thus far provided a satisfactory answer.

The list of similarities may show a good deal of overlap in the conceptual arguments supporting NPM and governance, but this does not mean the former is a synonym for the latter. Peters and Pierre (1998) argue that, although these differences constitute more than a set of questions raised in governance debates to which NPM has no universal answer, they are fundamental enough to treat governance and NPM as distinct and separate intellectual frameworks. First, governance represents a concept—a relationship between government and the rest of society—that has always been part and parcel of a democratic polity. Western democracies, for example, have always engaged in partnerships with the private sector. NPM, in contrast, is more ideological; it constitutes a specific normative view of how that relationship should be structured. At its core, NPM is an attempt to inject corporate values into the public sector. It sees no sacrosanct cultural or societal role for the public sector, and separates it from the private sector only by the type of product being produced. In contrast, most visions of governance recognize that the public sector serves a unique role in securing and promoting the commonweal of a democratic polity. Accordingly, most visions of government recognize the fundamental difference between the public and private sectors and that corporatizing the latter has broad implications for the underpinnings of a democratic polity.

Second, the substantive focus of the two models is different: Governance is about process, whereas NPM is about outcomes. Governance is concerned with understanding the process by which public policy is created, implemented, and managed. Its explanatory goal is to identify the actors and their role in this process, and to illuminate how their behavior and interrelationships shape public service provision. NPM is considerably less interested in process. It is more concerned with the how much rather than the how of policy. Its explanatory targets are efficiency and customer satisfaction—that is, it seeks to illuminate how public goods that are prized by the citizens who consume them can be produced with minimal input. Process is obviously a part of this explanatory mission, but only as a means to the ends of explaining efficient production.

Third, according to Peters and Pierre (1998), governance and NPM occupy different philosophical ground. NPM is essentially an organization theory. Building on the institutional literature, especially that anchored in public choice theory, its explanatory orientation and its prescriptive conclusions are focused on organizational structure. Those such as Osborne and Gaebler (1992) who have shaped and popularized NPM owe much to scholars such as James Buchanan and Gordon Tullock (1962), William Niskanen (1971), and Vincent Ostrom (1973). In public choice, NPM advocates find a highly developed set of intellectual tools that offer a comprehensive alternative to organizing public service provision using the orthodox Weberian model. They have borrowed from this toolkit freely, and in doing so, they have constructed a model that is focused on organizational and institutional reform. In contrast, governance is less concerned with institutions than with understanding the relationship between government and society. Clearly, there is an institutional component to any such understanding, but governance is considerably less hostile to the Weberian model and is perfectly willing to prescriptively incorporate it when and where it is deemed appropriate. Governance is essentially a theory of politics, or at least a political theory in the making. It targets the "authoritative allocation of values" (David Easton's famous definition of politics) as its ultimate objective, seeking to explain why government does what it does and to discover how it can do that better. Equating governance with NPM risks perceiving the former as a wholesale rejection of the public sector. Governance and modern policymaking are often described in terms of public-private partnerships (PPPs) or "hybridity," organizations with both public and private characteristics (Skelcher 2005).

Empirical evidence regarding the utility of complete privatization under NPM is also lacking. Suzanne Leland and Olga Smirnova (2009) reexamine the work of James L. Perry and Timlynn Babitsky (1986) on the privatization of transit services. Contrary to the original findings, Leland and Smirnova demonstrate that, in terms of efficiency, there is no difference between privately and government-owned transit services. This presents a distinct challenge to the NPM framework, which rejects the structure of and need for government institutions. In fact, for privatization to be successful in terms of improving efficiency over the public sector, the empirical record suggests there must be identifiable means for measuring performance and evaluating outcomes, substantial competition between private providers, and the task must be specific enough to allow direct implementation

(Leland and Smirnova 2009), which is unlikely for many large-scale public goods. In fact, privatization tends to be the most effective when "the task is not central to the agency's mission" (856).

Fourth, as a theory that encompasses government and society, governance recognizes the unique cultural and political role of public goods and the public sector. Because of this, those working within a governance framework are interested in keeping public service provision under government control. The form of control may be altered to push government closer to society, and this may mean delegating a greater public policy role to the private sector. Ultimately, however, governance seeks to keep a clear line of responsibility and control between public services and public officials. In contrast, NPM is focused on bringing about a sweeping change of the public sector. Although governance seeks to develop strategies that retain the government's capacity to control public-sector resources, NPM is interested in public management models primarily as a way to replace the Weberian organizational orthodoxy of traditional public administration.

Yet again, the empirical evidence supporting this argument is lacking. Most notably, Hill and Lynn (2005) conducted a meta-analysis of the governance and management literature from 1990 to 2001. Examining over 800 articles in 70 journals, the authors found that the Weberian notion of hierarchical bureaucratic structure is actually quite persistent. Despite the claim by NPM that hierarchy and centralization are detrimental to "good" governance, Hill and Lynn's research clearly demonstrates that "the American political scheme remains hierarchical and jurisdictional" (189). As Hill and Lynn write, the "shift away from hierarchical government and toward horizontal governing (hence the increasing preference for 'governance' as an organizing concept) is less fundamental than it is tactical" (189). Analysis of emergency management following Hurricane Katrina in 2005 demonstrated there is a strong need for stable networks and cooperative relationships between public and private actors (Koliba, Mills, and Zia 2011).

Fifth, and perhaps this is most important, Peters and Pierre argue that governance does not have the ideological baggage as NPM. At its root, governance does not share the same ideals or the core motivation to bring about a market-based cultural revolution in the public sector that characterizes NPM. NPM is an attempt to unilaterally impose corporate values, objectives, and practices on public service provision, a project that finds strong favor and support in conservative circles. Governance does not share these ideological goals. It poses serious questions about what government should do and how it can do this better, but governance does not unilaterally reply with market-based institutional reform. Governance is as likely to give public-sector agencies more power and force them to engage in greater cooperative arrangements with the private sector as to strip those agencies of their power and force the creation of a competitive market for public goods and services.

Indeed, as states and localities face fiscal stress, we are seeing more examples of such partnerships. For example, the state of Iowa has recently proposed changing the name and function of the Department of Economic Development to the "Iowa Partnership for Economic Progress." This new agency would consist of both a public nonprofit element and a private economic corporation that would encourage private donations and investments on behalf of the state (Clayworth 2011). In the United Kingdom, the British government is experimenting with "pay for success bonds" or "social impact bonds." In such cases, nonprofit groups invest in public programs traditionally provided by the state. If, after several years, the program is successful, the government will reimburse the nonprofit entity (Leonhardt 2011). Both examples expand and build upon the notion of governance as a series of collaborative networks and relationships among public, private, and nonprofit sectors.

Peters and Pierre (1998) make a strong case for separating governance and NPM as distinct intellectual frameworks, but in doing so, they leave governance in something of an undefined status as a theory. Despite its ideological stripes, NPM rests on solid theoretical foundations supplied by public choice and the broader literature of organizational theory. In Peters and Pierre's conception, governance borrows from this, too, but it also draws from the much broader well of democratic theory. The result is enough to make a strong case that governance is different from NPM, but although NPM emerges as a sharply defined public management model (albeit one sporting clear ideological stripes), the same cannot be said of governance. Governance is more encompassing, is less hostile to orthodox models of public administration, and is wedded to no particular point of the ideological spectrum, but as a theory it is left rather vague.

Governance as a Unifying Framework for Public Administration?

If governance is not NPM, then what is it? Peters and Pierre (1998) conclude that in many ways the governance debate simply shows that academics are catching up to the reality of changed times. The rise of the fragmented state and the growing obsolescence of existing public administration frameworks have forced the discipline to undertake a sometimes painful search for new intellectual foundations.

H. George Frederickson (1999b) refers to this search as the repositioning of public administration. This process, in the making since the late 1970s, is producing a new form of public administration that has a new language and a unique voice. The repositioning of public administration, Frederickson suggests, represents something of a watershed era for public administration. A half century after the collapse of theoretical hegemony in public administration, after decades of colonization by theories originating in other disciplines (especially economics, policy analysis, and organization theory), the repositioning movement is fostering a line of theoretical thinking that is indigenous to public administration. These original contributions directly tackle the problem of governance in a fragmented state.

The core of Frederickson's repositioning argument can be best described by comparing its theoretical orientation to that of political science, the discipline most closely associated with public administration (the latter is considered by many to be a subcategory of the former). In political science, theory is directed toward the clash of interests, electoral competition, strategic games, and winners and losers. Given this orientation, it is unsurprising to find rational choice, market theory, game theory, and their various offshoots as popular, perhaps even dominant, intellectual frameworks in political science. Yet public administration, prompted by the fragmentation of the state, is steadily moving away from these frameworks and toward theories of cooperation, networking, and institution building and maintenance. In practice and theory, public administration is repositioning itself to deal with the enormous challenges of the fragmented state. Frederickson calls this challenge "the political science of making the fragmented and disarticulated state work" (1999b, 702).

The latter is essentially how Frederickson defines governance. Governance refers to the lateral and interinstitutional relations in administration in the context of the decline of sovereignty, the decreasing importance of jurisdictional borders, and a general institutional fragmentation. Of these basic elements, the most important to the practice and theory of public administration is the declining relationship between political jurisdiction and public management. The weakening of this bond "disarticulates" the traditionally centralized link between government and the agents of public service provision.

In the disarticulated state, borders are less meaningful in political jurisdictions of all types—special districts, cities, counties, states, and nation-states (Strange 1995). Economic activity and social activity are increasingly multijurisdictional, a trend encouraged by the development of new technologies, the globalization of the marketplace, increased residential mobility, and immigration. Someone employed by a company physically headquartered in Atlanta, Georgia, can consult with clients on both coasts while telecommuting from home in Lincoln, Nebraska. A suburban crime problem may originate in the economic conditions of a neighboring city. Polluted water in one country may be a product of economic activity in another. The benefits and the problems of public policy and public management are increasingly harder to confine within the borders of one political jurisdiction because so many relevant policy issues are multijurisdictional.

Administrative Conjunction

This trend presents considerable challenges for the practice and theory of public administration. How do you define and understand public management when political jurisdictions are less relevant? How do you define and understand public management when sovereignty is in considerable doubt? How do you conceptualize a representative democracy where decisions that affect the represented are not controlled, perhaps not even influenced, by those who represent them? How does public administration, traditionally the agent of government that linked the decisions of the representatives to the preferences of the represented, reposition itself to deal with this growing gap between government and the governed?

These are questions of governance; they cut to the heart of the relationship between government and society and focus the theoretical concerns of public administration upon the problems of public management in the disarticulated state. Frederickson (1999b) suggests a theory of administration conjunction to help explain and understand the vexing problems of governance created by the rise of the disarticulated state.

The theory of administration conjunction arises from two observations. The first is attributed to Matthew Holden Jr. (1964), who noted that in the United States intergovernmental relationships in metropolitan areas could be viewed as problems in diplomacy. In a fragmented metropolitan area, the actions of one agency or government are likely to affect actors in other jurisdictions. With no centralized authority, how can these actions be coordinated to ensure effective representation and public service provision? Holden argued that systems or networks of cooperation evolve across jurisdictions that serve essentially the same purpose as diplomacy in nation-states. They result in agreements and understandings that synchronize governmental activities across jurisdictions and allow for the smooth functioning of policy and public service provision.

The second observation is that political jurisdictions are still important to politics (in a narrow sense), even as they hold less importance for administration. Politics in the sense of campaigns, elections, offices, and titles is still jurisdictional. These elements are mostly autonomous and only marginally interdependent (the campaign for a mayor in one city, for example, only rarely has repercussions for the campaign of a mayor in an adjacent suburb). This stands in fairly stark contrast with administration, which is highly interdependent, increasingly less jurisdictional, and characterized by organized patterns of "conjunctions"—systematic patterns of cooperation and coordination among and between administrative operations. As Frederickson describes it, "Administration conjunction is the array and character of horizontal formal and informal association between actors representing units in a networked public and the administrative behavior of those actors" (1999b, 708).

The power to carry out this interagency conjunction is based upon the professional expert's authoritative claim to knowledge rather than on some basis of formal authority. Conjunction is thus primarily an activity undertaken by like-minded professionals, specifically functional specialists dealing with a particular issue or policy domain. This connection between functional specialists serves to couple or link together administrative units across jurisdictions and coordinate government operations within the disarticulated state.

Frederickson suggests that the ability of administration conjunctions to impose order and coherence on public service provision depends upon several factors. These factors include the scope, strength, and duration of formal and informal agreements among interjurisdictional executive actors. Formally negotiated agreements tend to produce tight coupling; informal agreements result in looser links between jurisdictions. Yet regardless of whether the cooperation is formally mandated or informally agreed upon, most forms of administration are organized, maintained, and operated voluntarily by public service professionals. This latter point is important because it implies that the world of conjunction has little hierarchy, few transaction costs, and no apparent need to restructure the public sector when introducing marketlike behavioral incentives. Central authority in conjunction is simply replaced by voluntary cooperation and networks that evolve out of professional interests and values.

Frederickson argues that, although conjunction itself is nonhierarchical, hierarchy is necessary for conjunction to exist. Administration conjunction will not happen without the institutional structure that is still tied to political jurisdictions, namely, the formal, hierarchical structure that still characterizes most governments. If these hierarchical structures are thought of as buildings that house the politics of a given jurisdiction, then administrative conjunction can be thought of as a series of pedestrian bridges that connect these buildings. The bridges will not stay up if the buildings come down. And although any given bridge gives the impression of a small carrying capacity, considered as a whole the bridges constitute a strong and capable network for coordination and cooperation.

With its motivational force coming from values and professional interests, and cooperation between institutional actors as its objective, administration conjunction is a theory that stands in fairly stark contrast with NPM. NPM draws heavily from market theory, emphasizing self-interest and competition, neither of which is particularly good at explaining the interjurisdictional behavior of actors in conjunctions. Conjunction seems to be driven by the values and beliefs of public service professionals, and by the innate and learned instinct to cooperate shared by all humans. Underlying conjunctions are professional concepts of the public interest and an obligation among public servants to represent an inchoate public outside of a particular jurisdiction. The end result is not just coordination among the various units of the disarticulated state, but also the reappearance of the meaningful representation that has leaked steadily from elected offices as jurisdictional borders become less relevant to policy problems.

The theory of administration conjunction is not just the abstract musing of academics. It also has considerable backing from various empirical studies (Frederickson 1999b). In studying the metropolitan Kansas City area through the prism of administration conjunction, Frederickson (1999b, 708) reports that high-ranking government appointees (department heads and above) spend approximately 15 percent of their time engaged in conjunction activities. There are, of course, limits to administration conjunction and a regime theory of governance. Politics in any given jurisdiction may produce powerful forces opposing cooperation. Given the highly personal nature of the interactions between administrative units, something as trivial as a personality clash between two department heads could potentially narrow the scope and the success of a conjunction. Empirically, studies supporting the theory of administration conjunction are, at least so far, largely limited to urban areas. Conjunction's ability to usefully explain and help us understand government-society relationships at higher levels such as the state or nation has yet to be fully explored.

Regime Theory of Governance

Despite the work of Lynn et al. (2001), a general theory of governance is still lacking. For Frederickson, governance is more of a unique and emerging subfield within public administration than a distinct stand-alone discipline. To encourage growth of governance as a theory, Frederickson (2005) suggests that scholars would be wise to look to international relations, specifically regime theory.

Theoretical developments regarding the emergence, structure, stability, and legitimacy of regimes have direct application to governance theory where the unit of analysis is organizations (of all types) and how they collaborate to produce a desirable public good. Regime theory is the study of how entities (in this case, states) adapt to changes in in the environment and relations with other entities (states). Changing "states" to "agencies" shifts the focus to how agencies (across multiple sectors) adapt and form relationships with each other. As such, Frederickson uses regime theory from international relations to develop a three-part theory of governance:

1. "inter-jurisdictional governance," defined as "vertical and horizontal inter-jurisdictional and inter-organizational cooperation"
2. "third-party governance," or the "extension of the state or jurisdiction by contracts or grants to third parties, including subgovernments"
3. "public nongovernmental governance," including "forms of public non-jurisdictional or nongovernmental policy making and implementation" (2005, 294–295)

The purpose of this three-part theory is not only to provide scholars with a working definition of governance, but also to aptly couch governance within the field of public administration. "It is suggested that there be a fundamental distinction between public administration as the internal day-to-day management of an agency or organization on one hand, and public administration as governance, the management of the extended state, on the other" (Frederickson 2005, 300).

As such, the three parts of Frederickson's theory can be thought of as follows:

> First, inter-jurisdictional governance is policy-area specific formalized or voluntary patterns of interorganizational or interjurisdictional cooperation. Second, third-party governance extends the function of the state by exporting them by contract to policy-area specific nonprofit, for-profit, or sub-governmental third parties. Third, public nongovernmental governance accounts for those activities of non-governmental organizations that bear on the interests of citizens in the same way as governmental agencies. (Frederickson 2005, 301)

The regime theory of governance is an attempt to place distinct boundaries around the concept of governance. Moving beyond the work of Lynn et al., it provides an organizing theme and direction for public administration and governance scholars. The regime theory of governance further identifies specific institutional definitions, characteristics, and relationships between actors that should allow for theory development. Nonetheless, two key democratic elements are absent from such a theory: accountability and legitimacy.

Accountability and Global Governance

The basic concept of democratic accountability becomes muddied when examining hybrid or interjurisdictional organizations. The problem therein lies with identifying the appropriate stakeholder. For government, this role rests with citizens. For public-private partnerships or governance networks, the type and number of stakeholders become more numerous and less obvious. For some government agencies, the advantage of partnering with a private organization is in fact "reduced public accountability" (Skelcher 2005, 361). For governance theory to move forward, however, requires an examination and development of an accountability framework appropriate for twenty-first-century governance.

Chris Skelcher writes that the new face of governance, particularly PPPs, will require public managers to answer a new set of questions:

1. Does the rhetoric of common interest between the parties occlude important differences of value and motivation?
2. With what do the partners trust each other?
3. To what extent do governments have the capacity to engage in PPPs?
4. How do PPPs articulate with democratic institutions and processes? (2005, 363–364)

Questions 2 and 4 deal directly with issues pertaining to accountability and governance. Governance theory, based on public-private partnerships, hybrid organizations, or interjurisdictional organizations, clearly faces an accountability dilemma. How do you hold public and private actors accountable? Can they be held accountable in the same fashion? Should accountability be considered jointly or separately for partnerships?

The fundamental goal of any governance network should be to provide for the quality delivery of some public service or good. Christopher J. Koliba, Russell M. Mills, and Assim Zia (2011, 212) present an accountability framework for governance networks that extends across three different frames (Democratic, Market, and Administrative) and eight different accountability types. Within the Democratic frame, accountability is "rendered" to elected officials, citizens, and the courts. In the Market frame, shareholders/owners and consumers are the two targets for accountability. Finally, in the Administrative frame, accountability is left to principals, experts and professionals, and collaborating peers or partners. The framework is based on an examination of emergency management responses following Hurricane Katrina, and is viewed as the most appropriate system for avoiding the "blame game" among government actors and fostering a collective sense of the public interest. Underlying this theory of accountability, however, is the assumption that all relevant actors can agree on basic notions of accountability and legitimacy. As others have shown, when the organization becomes transnational and/or lacks strong sanctioning mechanisms, that assumption is easily violated.

Jonathan Koppell (2008) brings the issue of accountability to governance in international, or what he describes as global governance organizations (GGOs). Organizations such as the United Nations, the World Trade Organization, and the European Union all are "suffer[ing] from an accountability shortage" (177). GGOs tend to lack formal or enforceable sanctioning mechanisms, making compliance with authoritative requests difficult. Legitimacy takes on many forms, but "cognitive legitimacy," a focus on "the degree to which an institution is accepted," imposes the fewest costs on an organization in terms of the amount of resources required to ensure compliance. Most GGOs, however, are unable to achieve such legitimacy and instead focus on "normative legitimacy . . . a function of beliefs about what entitles an individual or institution to wield power" (182). As Koppell writes, "Legitimacy is essentially a psychological source of authority" (187), but this psychological source tends to vary widely across peoples and cultures. By defining legitimacy, and ultimately the source of power for GGOs, Koppell is able to provide a foundation upon which global organizations should be held accountable. Indeed, out of this focus on normative legitimacy comes a set of six principles to which GGOs should adhere in order to retain some level of legitimacy: representation, participation, equality (fairness or neutrality), constitutional basis (rules and order), transparency, and a rational basis for decisions (191).

The dilemma, of course, is that perceptions regarding adherence to such principles are likely to vary widely among actors in global governance systems. Because perceptions of legitimacy vary across governmental and private actors, perceptions of accountability also vary. For governance theory, the problem thus becomes identifying the components, whether rules or structures, that provide enough accountability to an adequate number of actors in a governance network so as to ensure compliance. For PPPs or governance networks, it is difficult to apply democratic ideals such as transparency and a code of ethics. Private actors, as well as nonprofit actors, bring different sets of values and ethics to the governing network.

Koppell's work on global governance presents a new challenge to the governance framework. Most notably, differences exist in terms of the perceptions of the nature of relationships between institutions, and between institutions and citizens (Koppell 2010, 2008). GGOs lack formal and uniform accountability standards. Moreover, identifying the relevant actors is less obvious for more traditional public-private partnerships. With GGOs, authority is granted without an agreed-upon sense of legitimacy; GGOs "are structured to manage the tension" between authority and legitimacy (Koppell 2008, 199). Traditional notions of democratic accountability based on the preferences of citizens and elected representatives are likely to be inadequate when studying GGOs. Koliba, Mills, and Zia's theory (2011) of accountability includes eight different actors to whom governance networks should be held accountable. Questions remain, however, as to whether all eight actors can agree upon the sources of accountability. In at least one instance, to resolve "accountability gaps" between the public and private sector over local public finance, what was advocated were *more* government and *more* bureaucracy (Howell-Moroney and Hall 2011). Contrary to NPM, government maintains a prominent role in this governance network. The challenge for governance scholars is to build a theory that allows for empirical testing of the appropriate balance between public and private involvement (which will most likely be policy specific), as well as the implications of increasing (decreasing) public-sector accountability and decreasing (increasing) private-sector accountability.

Yet, even when we recognize the limits and preliminary nature of empirical support, Frederickson's work on governance theory and Koppell's analysis of global governance organizations provide solid theoretical and practical foundations for future research on governance. The confusing jumble of the increasingly fragmented state is proving to be fertile ground for original thinking in public administration, and shows how frameworks indigenous to and outside of mainstream public administration can be formulated to help explain and address the rapidly changing relationship between state and society.

Conclusions

The theories and concepts associated with the word "governance" are increasingly important for public administration scholars. Yet even as governance becomes a virtual synonym for public management and public administration, it is not exactly clear what governance is. Certainly, governance is centered on the need to account for the changing relationship between government and society. The growth of the fragmented or hollow state has brought about a fundamental shift in the process and nature of public administration, a change that has altered conceptions of what government should do and how government should go about doing it. These changes have forced public administration scholars to account for the new realities in their intellectual frameworks, and varied attempts to do this are being carried out under the loose umbrella of governance.

Among these efforts, it is possible to identify at least three distinct conceptions of governance. (1) Governance is simply a surrogate word for public administration and policy implementation. Thus, governance theory is an intellectual project attempting to unify the various intellectual threads running through a multidisciplinary literature into a framework that covers this broad area of government activity. This, essentially, is the position staked by Lynn et al. (2000, 2001). (2) Governance equates to the managerialist, or NPM, movement. This is particularly evident in nations associated with the Westminster model, where NPM followed from serious attempts to reform the public sector by defining and justifying what government should and should not do, and to reshape public service provision by attacking the pathologies of bureaucracy (Kettl 2000). (3) Governance is a body of theory that comprehends lateral relations, interinstitutional relations, the decline of sovereignty, the diminishing importance of jurisdictional borders, and a general institutional fragmentation.

Of these three approaches, the first is the most ambitious. Unifying a large literature spread across several disciplines by distilling its central objectives and methodologies into a well-defined research agenda is a project grand in scope and of enormous complexity. If successful, the payoff is sure to be considerable. The all-encompassing objective, however, is also the largest weakness of this approach to governance. The target is so large that trying to fit everything within its intellectual confines causes the framework to lose parsimony and clarity. The definition of governance is so broad and inclusive that it runs the risk of losing any specific meaning, a problem Lynn et al. implicitly acknowledge. As one reviewer has pointed out (Lowery 2002), as they move from their sweeping definition to grappling with the specifics of model building, Lynn et al. drastically narrow the scope of governance. In operation, their model boils down to focusing on one dependent variable (agency performance or outcomes) and is heavily predicated on econometric models employing a specific set of input factors. Regarding its conceptual utility, "the application of governance to public administration would be improved by narrowing the scope of the subject" (Frederickson 2005, 300).

Others, however, disagree with the notion of repositioning governance within the field of public administration. Drawing on the writings of Luther Gulick (1937), Kenneth Meier (2011, S285) calls for complete embrace of governance as the defining concept for the field. Interest groups, nonprofit organizations, political institutions, and both formal and "informal organizations" play critical roles in the way government provides for its citizens. Frederickson's regime theory of governance does not deny the role of such actors; in fact, regime theory, specifically public nongovernmental governance, places particular emphasis on "informal" institutions and institutional development. The apparent disagreement between Frederickson and Meier is not so much a debate as two sides of the same coin; both agree that the role of governmental and nongovernmental institutions is critical, and that the future of public service delivery will be characterized by collaborative relationships between both types of institutions. Instead, Frederickson is attempting to define the limits of governance theory, whereas Meier is describing the key explanatory variables that will be needed. The challenge for scholars is to merge these two conversations in such a way as to produce a viable theoretical framework of governance.

Koppell's work on global governance perhaps provides an important step in this direction. Like Frederickson, Meier, and many contemporary public administration scholars, Koppell (2011) recognizes that the way in which services are delivered and individual public interests are met is rapidly changing; citizens interact with both public and private institutions that are both domestic and foreign. Unfortunately, "the pages of our journals feature limited discussion of the distinctive administrative issues associated with transnational boundaries" (S51). As a way forward, Koppell proposes that public administration move away from the notion that only government can provide public goods. Instead, scholars should discuss the "publicness" of the good being provided without any regard to the "governmentalness" of how it is delivered (S52). Koppell directly states that such a conception of governance moves beyond Frederickson's notion of the "extended state." The more general argument, however, challenges scholars and practitioners to examine the type of good being provided, not the source. This most likely will lead to "a more expansive conceptualization of public administration—one that is empirically and historically grounded—that accommodates the varied forms and approaches to the implementation of public policy" (S53).

As the line between the public sector and the private sector becomes increasingly blurred and traditional policymaking roles and processes are rearranged or abandoned altogether, questions naturally arise about the purposes of government and the methods used to accomplish those purposes. It is difficult, however, to see how a specific management reform approach—even one with as many variations as

NPM—can position itself as a comprehensive answer to those questions. This seems to entail a drift from theory-building into something approaching ideological advocacy: governance as the embrace of corporate values and practices by the public sector. Whatever its original motivations, Kettl points out that the global management reform movement has advanced only where it served the ends of political expediency: "Few if any government leaders launched management reforms to improve administration and service delivery" (2000, 51). Lynn et al.'s concept may be too intellectually broad, but the NPM conception of governance may be too politically narrow. As Peters and Pierre argue, NPM and governance overlap, but this does not mean they are the same thing. The work of Hill and Lynn and the work of Koliba, Mills, and Zia demonstrate that the assumptions of NPM regarding government structure and service delivery are lacking in empirical support.

This leaves governance as the attempt to comprehend the lateral and institutional relations in administration in the context of the disarticulated state. Like the other approaches, this is an explicit attempt to put the facts of the fragmented state into a coherent explanatory picture. Its strength is its empirical basis—governance is largely predicated on trying to identify systematic patterns in observations of what administrators are actually doing. This contrasts with the search for the unifying thread in what strikes some as a research literature characterized by theoretical pluralism (Lynn et al.) or the imposition of what strikes others as an ideological framework on the public sector (NPM). Although progress is increasing on this front, this approach to governance remains underdeveloped. In times of fiscal stress, governments are increasingly likely to look to cost-saving alternatives for public service delivery. Bringing in nonpublic actors, whether privately owned enterprises or nonprofit organizations, is a viable alternative and increasingly being used in the United States and Europe (Skelcher 2005). However, as we have discussed throughout the chapter, even though this is changing the face of governance, the basic structure, as advocated in the Weberian model, remains the same. Public institutions in public-private partnerships, or the networks in governance systems, are likely to have some hierarchical component. Privatization and the shadow bureaucracy will remain constants in the years to come, but the size and shape of the shadow are expanding and changing rapidly. The theories of administration conjunction, regime theory of governance, and global governance show the possibilities for building theories indigenous to public administration that tackle the important questions of governance. These approaches seem to hold a good deal of promise, but a good deal of work remains to be done if that promise is to be fulfilled.

10

Conclusion: A Bright Future for Theory?

Does theory have a useful role in a field as fragmented and applied as public administration? The primary purpose of this book was to answer this question with a definitive *yes*. The broad and multidimensional nature of public administration increases rather than decreases the need for reliable theoretical frameworks. In such a field, the primary purpose of theory is to assemble facts into a comprehensive explanatory picture and to use this comprehension to usefully inform policy-making and guide public policy implementation. If the complex undertaking of public service provision is to evolve more effective forms of public administration that remain accountable to fundamental democratic values, then there is a considerable need for intellectual tools designed with these purposes in mind.

The underlying utility of any theory is its capacity to describe, explain, and predict. A theory should parsimoniously and systematically describe the phenomenon under study and logically connect its elements into a clear understanding of the actors, institutions, and processes involved. By doing so, it should provide a platform to make probabilistic assessments about the likely consequences or outcomes of specific actions (or nonactions) that reflect a more accurate understanding and a greater predictive power than arguments reliant upon intuition, common sense, political expediency, ideological preference, or individual experience.

Public administration theory takes various distinct forms reflecting these objectives. (1) Theory in the positivist, scientific sense. This is theory that is premised upon generating universal axioms that can be empirically confirmed. (2) Theory that orders factual material to convey a systematic understanding of the complex and various dimensions of public administration. (3) Theory as a normative argument, a philosophical case for what constitutes "good" or "best" or "just" in administrative practice.

Regardless of an intellectual framework's particular theoretical purpose, in public administration the ultimate test of any theory is how useful it is—does it increase our general understanding of public administration, and/or can it improve the applied practice of public administration? Some scholars (e.g., Wilson 1989) have suggested that comprehensive, useful, and reliable theories are not possible in the arena of public administration. Others have suggested that the fragmented nature of the field, coupled with the tendency of public administration scholars (and academics generally) to "work in their silos," potentially threatens useful practical and theoretical developments (Pollitt 2010, S293). The field is too broad, too disjointed, too multidisciplinary, too undefined for any intellectual framework to usefully achieve any of the purposes of theory. Our object was to lay before the reader evidence that counters these claims. The goal in describing in some detail a series of intellectual frameworks and analytical approaches was to present a convincing brief that in public administration there is a body of work that is worth taking seriously as theory.

By examining whether the theoretical frameworks in the previous chapters fit with our general characterization of theory in this concluding chapter, we assess to what extent that objective has been achieved. A tabular summation of our assessments can be found in Table 10.1. Each framework is evaluated through the process assigning it a score of high, low, or mixed on six dimensions related to the core purposes of theory as we have described them. (1) Parsimony/elegance refers to a theory's ability to account concisely for the phenomenon under study by using tightly ordered internal logic. (2) Explanatory capacity refers to a theory's ability to explain real-world phenomena. (3) Replicability refers to a theory's ability to generalize beyond the confines of one case or a handful of cases. (4) Descriptive capacity refers to a theory's ability to portray the real world accurately as it is observed. (5) Predictive capacity refers to a theory's ability to generate testable hypotheses and make probabilistic assessments about the future. (6) Empirical warrant refers to the relative success of a theory in gaining empirical confirmation for the hypotheses and probabilistic assessments it generates. These criteria form the basis of our overall assessments of the theories examined in earlier chapters.

Theories of Political Control of Bureaucracy

Theories of political control of bureaucracy have at their heart a simple question: Does bureaucracy comply with the law and the preferences of lawmakers? The importance of this question in public administration reflects the distrust for concentrations of power underpinning the American philosophy of government. That specific philosophy, not to mention more general principles of democratic government, is contradicted if the nonelected element of the executive branch—insulated from the ballot box and protected by civil service mechanisms—is allowed to accumulate and exercise political power independently.

TABLE 10.1   THE PERFORMANCE OF
PUBLIC ADMINISTRATION THEORIES

Theory	Parsimony/ Elegance	Explanatory Capacity	Replicability	Descriptive Capacity	Predictive Capacity	Empirical Warrant
Political Control of Bureaucracy	high	high	mixed	mixed	mixed	high
Bureaucratic Politics	mixed	high	mixed	high	mixed	high
Institutional	low	mixed	mixed	high	low	mixed
Public Management	low	mixed	low	mixed	low	mixed
Postmodern	low	mixed	low	high	low	mixed
Decision	mixed	low-mixed	mixed	mixed	mixed	mixed
Rational	high	low-mixed	high	low	mixed	low
Governance	mixed	mixed	mixed	mixed	mixed	mixed

Theories of political control of bureaucracy, then, have a basic objective to explain and ensure how administration can be accountable and subordinate to the formally designated institutions of democratic decisionmaking. This objective implies the key challenge in this project: conceptually and empirically separating administration from politics. The explanatory orientation and the underlying logic in theories of political control virtually require a conceptual distinction between politics and administration, and it is this distinction that provides such frameworks with their strength—and with their key weakness.

The imposition of the dichotomy provides theories of bureaucratic politics, at least in their traditional form, with considerable parsimony and elegance. This is accomplished through the expedience of ignoring the messy implications of politics for administration and clearing the way to conceptualize administration in technical terms with less worry about how these fit within the values of a democratic polity. As long as the dichotomy holds, these theories have high explanatory capacity—they provide a comprehensive, well-ordered explanation of administration that serves as a solid guide for action. The problem, of course, is that from the theory's beginnings as an organizing construct in public administration, there has been wide recognition that reality inconveniently contradicts the keystone assumption of the dichotomy.

From a purely theoretical standpoint, systematic thinking about public administration is aided enormously by sticking with the politics-administration dichotomy. This tractability comes at a price: The inaccurate portrayal of the real world represented by the dichotomy lessens the replicative, descriptive, and predictive capacities of the theory. Since Dwight Waldo (1948) and Herbert Simon (1947/1997), assuming away the salience of politics has become virtually impossible for anyone engaged in the serious study of administration. Waldo, especially, made a persuasive argument that at a fundamental level administration *is* a powerful form of politics and that any attempt to separate the two is likely to fail. Rebuilding a firewall between politics and administration that can withstand the battering ram of Waldo's critique is an extraordinarily difficult challenge.

In answering that challenge, scholars have avoided the orthodox mistake of simply assuming a clean separation between administration and politics, seeking instead a realistic accounting of the working relationship between administration and politics. Scholars such as James Svara (1994) convincingly demonstrate that administration clearly treads within the political arena, and vice versa. Yet Svara also shows that decisionmaking areas are dominated by administration or politics. This mixed relationship and the relative influence of the administrative or the political sphere seems to be determined, at least in part, by organizational structure and the formal and informal roles and responsibilities it imparts to administrative actors.

Numerous frameworks have been constructed to describe and explain the elements of this varied relationship between the administrative and political functions of government. Capture theory explains the political role of the bureaucracy by suggesting that public agencies "go native," that is, they become advocates of those they purportedly regulate. Although logically sound, capture theory has never had much empirical support. The theory of client responsiveness explains how structure can determine bureaucracy's political role—as bureaucracy is split into functional specializations, each distinct administrative operation becomes an advocate for its clientele. The most promising work to come out of the theory of client responsiveness is Michael Lipsky's (1980) examination of the street-level bureaucracy. He found that rather than being advocates for their clients, bureaucrats are more realistically described as people who deal with difficult social situations but who have limited resources and little guidance from political authority.

In this situation, Lipsky concluded, bureaucrats in effect are forced to make policy decisions.

The most promising framework in which to coherently distinguish and link the administrative and political elements of government is agency theory. This theory is grounded in economics and describes a contractual relationship between elected and appointed government actors. Elected officials are the principals in this relationship—they seek to persuade bureaucracy (the agents) to follow through on their policy preferences. Key to agency theory is the assumption that principals are interested in compliance and that bureaucracy feels some obligation to respond to the interests of elected actors. Empirical support for this argument is fairly extensive. Dan Wood and Richard Waterman (1994) convincingly demonstrate that bureaucracy is highly responsive to changes in political environment and direction. Bureaucratic agents do occasionally resist the control of their political principals, but when this happens, it is as likely to be resistance in the name of the public interest as it is an attempt to undermine the superior policy role of principals.

One method that had been gaining traction was the use of formal performance assessments required by principals of the agents. The George W. Bush administration developed the Program Assessment Rating Tool (PART) as a way to force the bureaucracy to be cognizant of and respond to the requests of elected officials. Other attempts, such as organizational, and even state-level, report cards, have been or are being used. Such mechanisms clearly inject a high degree of politics into the issue of democratic accountability. Although PART was discontinued by the Obama administration, pressure from the public to hold all institutions accountable (both elected and unelected) will force elected officials to continue to consider such options. What remains in question is whether PART, or any other assessment tool, improves or impedes the quality of public service provision.

Although these subsequent frameworks have avoided the primary flaw of the original politics-administration dichotomy, tradeoffs are involved. It is probably fair to say that theories of political control of the bureaucracy have not completely reestablished a clear division between politics and administration, but it is also accurate to say they have contributed to a much deeper and more realistic understanding of the symbiotic relationship between these two. By continuing to unpack administration and politics into distinguishable operations, theories of political control of the bureaucracy have helped us understand how the two mix and combine to produce public policy. The later evolution of theories of political control is somewhat less parsimonious and elegant, but they have improved dramatically the replicability, descriptive qualities, and predictive capacities of theories of political control of bureaucracies. As much of this work is highly empirical (and often largely inductive), the empirical warrant of the theories of political control has to be rated as fairly high.

Theories of Bureaucratic Politics

Theories of bureaucratic politics stake their claim to utility on a convincing demonstration of the intellectual poverty of the politics-administration dichotomy. This demonstration was something of a demolition project. In rejecting the politics-administration dichotomy, advocates of theories of bureaucratic politics were deliberately removing the keystone supporting the intellectual edifice of traditional public administration. As the latter came crashing down, so did public administration's unifying paradigm. This left public administration groping for a framework to define itself and cleared the way for efforts at theoretical colonization from other disciplines.

There is a payoff to this seismic shaking of public administration's intellectual foundations: Politics gets recognized as a fundamental component of administration, and vice versa. Even though this recognition may have sounded the death knell of theoretical hegemony in public administration, it also recognized some of the long-ignored (at least in a theoretical sense) realities of administration in practice. The architect of the bureaucratic politics movement was, of course, Waldo (1948). His devastating critique of the first half century of public administration scholarship not only exposed the suspect theoretical assumptions underpinning public administration theory but also convincingly demonstrated the fundamentally political role of administration. Indeed, Waldo made a supportable claim that public administration's intellectual framework was a normative political philosophy. This claim—and Waldo made it extraordinarily hard to challenge— made it virtually impossible for scholars of administration to continue assuming away the bewildering complexities of politics. After Waldo, a central challenge of the discipline was to square a theoretical circle by reconciling the authoritative and hierarchical nature of bureaucracy with the egalitarian values of democracy. Any theory of administration, as Waldo (1952) famously put it, *has* to be a theory of politics.

Theoretically integrating the political role of bureaucracy has proven to be extraordinarily difficult. The basic approach to accomplishing this task is to treat bureaucracy and bureaucrats as political actors in their own right, actors with identifiable agendas who engage in the push and pull of bargaining and compromise that results in policy decisions. This characterizes both Graham Allison's (1971) model of bureaucratic politics and the theory of representative bureaucracy. Both of these approaches have enjoyed mixed success in fulfilling the three purposes of theory listed previously.

Allison's project is notable because it was the first truly comprehensive attempt to answer Waldo's challenge to create a theory of politics with administration at its center. Model III, in Allison's taxonomy, had ambitions of universality but turned out to have significant weaknesses. So much was included in this framework that, in seeking to explain everything, it explained not much at all. As originally presented by Allison, Model III groaned under the weight of an extraneous clutter that belies the hallmark of comprehensive theory. As scholars began trimming this clutter back in an effort to apply Model III as a guide to empirical study, they quickly discovered its limits—its field of application turned out to be relatively narrow, and its explanatory powers weak.

The theory of representative bureaucracy has a sharper explanatory target than Allison's Model III. Rather than explain the entire process of policymaking, representative bureaucracy scholarship attempts to explain how bureaucratic decision-making can be considered democratic. Although bureaucracy is well insulated from the pressures of the democratic process, the ranks of the civil service can represent a broad demographic cross-section of society. If varied enough, this cross-section is enough to ensure that the major interests of the various groups within society are included in bureaucratic decisionmaking. Through diversity in the civil service ranks, bureaucratic policymaking can be considered representative, and as such, can stake a legitimate claim to abiding by and upholding democratic values.

The basic claims of representative bureaucracy have received considerable empirical support, and shown themselves to be capable of limited predictive as well as descriptive and explanatory power (Selden 1997). Once again, however, there are limits. It is not clear that some interests are embodied in demographics, and at least some civil servants seem to be highly capable of representing interests that are not associated with their demographic profiles. A further weakness of the representative bureaucracy literature is the surprising lopsidedness of its empirical focus—there is a considerable body of literature examining the demographic makeup of the bureaucracy, and a comparative paucity of studies examining the link between this demographic variation and a given agency's policy outputs. Work by Nick Theobald and Donald Haider-Markel (2009) has further demonstrated that even when representative bureaucracy fails to produce tangible policy benefits, shared demographic representation between citizens and bureaucrats can produce attitudinal benefits.

Beginning with Waldo, the bureaucratic politics movement has thus far been much more successful in demonstrating the need for political theories of bureaucracy than in actually creating comprehensive frameworks to fill that need. In the scientific sense, then, theories of representative bureaucracy are still immature. They tend to be considerably less parsimonious and elegant than the positivist ideal (a not-unusual characteristic of inductivism), and their focus on contextual detail has presented difficulties for replicability and predictive capacity.

Where bureaucratic politics theories shine is in their ability to make systematic sense of the often confusing arena of public administration as we find it in the real world. As a path to ordering the facts of administration coherently, the bureaucratic politics movement has yielded important dividends. Work such as

Harold Seidman's (1998), for example, represents an important leap in creating a more realistic portrayal and understanding of administration. In practice, administration is not about efficiency, or even effectiveness. It is about politics, and once that basic fact is grasped, the confusing jumble of agencies and their roles and relations to the rest of the polity becomes much easier to understand.

In the latter sense, theories of bureaucratic politics have served the discipline well. In highlighting bureaucracy's political role, they have forged a greater understanding of why public agencies do what they do. If there is one area in which such theories may fall short, it is in elegance or parsimony of the models. As the number of actors, institutions, and sectors involved in policymaking expands, theories of bureaucratic politics will have to adapt for such complexity. The framework and tools for such an adaptation are in place. It will be up to future public administration scholars to accept such complexity and the accompanying political jumble.

Public Institutional Theory

Institutional theory in public administration is concerned with the organization and management of contained and bounded public institutions. Its explanatory target covers the relationship among organizational structure, its associated rules and norms, and the organizational process, behaviors, outcomes, and accountability of public agencies. In public administration, the term "institution" typically refers to a public organization that can invoke the authority of the state to enforce its decisions. In this context, institutions are generically defined as the social constructs of rules and norms that constrain individual and group behavior. Institutionalism also incorporates ideas of performance, outcomes, and purposefulness.

Following this general conceptual orientation, the big themes of institutional theory tend to focus on how structure and organization shape the behavior of public actors, particularly how variation in structure affects decisionmaking, program implementation, and outcomes. If there is such a thing as a general conclusion from institutional research, it is this: Change an institution, alter its rules or norms, and you change behavioral predispositions and agency outcomes.

Institutional theory is premised on the assumption that collective outcomes and individual behavior are structured by institutions. Institutional theory encompasses several cross-disciplinary literatures, including branches in economics, sociology, and political science. The contemporary tone and general orientation of institutional theory in public administration were set by two key 1989 publications: James Q. Wilson's classic *Bureaucracy: What Government Agencies Do and Why They Do It*, and James G. March and Johan P. Olsen's *Rediscovering Institutions*. The key contribution of both these works was a convincing demonstration of the limits of economic and market theory in explaining institutional behavior. Although these scholars did not reject outright all the elements of economic and market theory, they resurrected the traditional disciplinary theme of hierarchy and grafted on the important insights of scholarship on organizational culture. In doing so, they created a more realistic portrayal of how public institutions shape the interaction of individuals and organizations in their political, social, and economic contexts.

Institutional theory in various forms guides several research literatures important in public administration. For example, institutional theory is of particular importance in guiding scholarship on the decentralization of the state. This is because institutional theory is not predicated on assumptions of sovereignty and jurisdiction and thus continues to function as a useful way to organize thinking about public actors as both these concepts become less meaningful. As the importance of sovereignty and jurisdiction erode in an increasingly fragmented state, institutional theory retains the capacity to explain relationships between and within the various administrative units that make up the decentralized whole, and so continues to provide a coherent understanding of their success and effectiveness (or lack thereof) as suppliers of public goods and services.

Although institutional theory undoubtedly performs yeoman's service to a wide range of scholarship, its strength is also its key weakness. Perhaps more than any other branch of public administration theory, institutionalism is doggedly pluralistic. Institutional theory shares a loose understanding of definitions and terminology (though even here differences are not difficult to detect), and a general conclusion that institutions matter. These are characteristics broad enough to describe and include a good deal of public administration scholarship ranging from new public management to theories of democratic control of bureaucracy. But although we may all be institutionalists under its generous terms of inclusion, we are obviously not all relying on a single easily identifiable theoretical framework. Institutional theory lacks a center, a core conceptual framework that provides some universal comprehension of public agencies, a frustration Wilson (1989) gave voice to in his claim that useful theory in public administration was unattainable. Although institutional theory provides rich contextual detail to the descriptive capacity of organization behavior, its extreme pluralism robs it of any claim to parsimony and makes it difficult to assess the theory's explanatory and replicative capacities, as well as its empirical warrant. The fact that most public organizations operate as low-reliability systems, subject to constant trial and error, and that that such systems are ever expanding to include nongovernmental actors, creates further problems for its predictive capacities.

Because institutional theory (singular) lacks a conceptual core, it is probably more accurate to use the plural, institutional theories. Taken individually, the contributions of the many frameworks traveling under the umbrella of institutional theory are significant. Considered as a whole, however, institutional theory gets more mixed reviews.

Theories of Public Management

About a century ago, the scientific management movement created what is probably the most enduring set of intellectual tools in public administration (Taylor 1911/2010). Frederick W. Taylor's purpose was to take the "science" of scientific management literally, that is, to reduce management to its most elemental operations and reassemble it on the basis of universal principles discovered and confirmed by the scientific method. Discovering those universal management principles was a project that occupied a good deal of effort in the first fifty years of public administration scholarship; indeed, famous and enduring offerings came from people such as Luther Gulick (1937), Henri Fayol (1949), and Chester Barnard (1938).

These principles were exposed as proverbs by Simon (1947/1997), who stripped scientific management of its claim to "science." Although Simon demolished the principles approach, he shared its basic objective—to lay the foundations for a science of administration within a positivist framework. Simon's devastating critique not only discredited the principles approach but also led to a general loss of interest in public management theory. Following the positivist grail, public administration scholarship in the 1950s followed Simon's lead into rational choice and decision theory. This left the public management field open to colonization by sociologists, who took full advantage of the opportunity by constructing various creative intellectual frameworks for studying management, many of them centered on group theory.

Ironically, Simon's positivist agenda has suffered a fate somewhat similar to Taylor's scientific management movement. Neither Taylor's agenda nor Simon's has mustered a convincing record to support a claim to theory in the positivist sense—the universal axioms necessary for a true science of administration still seem beyond our grasp. The principles approach has been remarkably resilient and useful in fulfilling the second and third purposes of theory listed earlier in the chapter. Fayol, Gulick, or McGregor may not have distilled universal axioms of management, but their frameworks proved to be practical in the applied sense. In variants too numerous to cite comprehensively, the principles approach shows up as a useful heuristic for formulating management objectives and providing a guide for action. Such frameworks are not theories in the strict sense—as Table 10.1 indicates, public management theory has a mixed record when it comes to descriptive capacities, but is relatively weak when considered as anything other than a systematic guide to action.

This contribution, however, should not be underestimated. Public management theory is where scholarly work in public administration has arguably found its greatest applied impact. And if anything, since the early 1990s the principles approach seems to have entered something of a new golden age. Much of this newfound attention is associated with the rise of New Public Management (NPM). NPM recycles the principles project—most famously in David Osborne and Ted Gaebler's (1992) "ten arrows in the quiver" of public management—while repackaging it in a broadly appealing political philosophy. These normative elements do raise some concerns; NPM is closely associated with conservative political ideology and tends to equate corporate values with democratic values. Yet regardless of its deep historical roots or its contemporary ideological appeal, NPM has some clear drawbacks as a comprehensive conceptual framework for public administration. Not the least of these is NPM's shaky empirical warrant. The work of Kenneth Meier and Laurence O'Toole (2009), for example, indicates that the key assumptions of NPM, at least in some cases, lack empirical support—most notably, the notion of contracting out for efficiency and a change-oriented management style. Yet, even when we acknowledge these concerns, there is little doubt that the principles approach is continually recycled, relabeled, and adopted by public administrators as a useful guide to action. If nothing else, this longevity suggests that theories of public management have a supportable claim to meet the ultimate test of theory: Many find them to be useful.

Postmodern Theory

Postmodern theory in many ways is the culmination of the theoretical fragmentation in public administration that began with the assault on the politics-administration dichotomy. Certainly the balkanized frameworks that appeared after the "golden age" of theoretical hegemony (though this was perhaps more imagined than real) give the foundations of postmodernism in public administration a measure of face validity. This is because postmodern theory rejects the possibility that any given paradigm is capable of producing universal truths about any social phenomena. Postmodernists are not surprised that, having decisively rejected the politics-administration dichotomy as its theoretical touchstone, public administration has failed to generate a universal replacement. Postmodernists would suggest that no universal replacement, at least in the positivist sense, is really possible.

Postmodern theory is a subjective approach to studying social phenomena that focuses heavily on language, the context of human interactions, and the social construction of reality. Postmodernists believe that there are no absolute truths and therefore that any given question will have several possible answers, all of which may be equally valid. As authors such as David John Farmer (1995) and Charles J. Fox and Hugh T. Miller (1995) apply the postmodern lens to the study of public administration, what emerges is the belief that there is no "best" or "universal" method of organization or of understanding administrative processes. Moreover, and despite the theory's theoretical pluralism, postmodernists in public administration see the existing choices of intellectual frameworks as too constraining; that is, too confined not only by geography (there being a particular concentration in the United States) but also by the boundaries of the scientific method. Postmodernists question the scientific method's claim to produce a steady accumulation of knowledge, and with these doubts come questions about the research that underpins empirical research in public administration.

Given this perspective, postmodern theory is not particularly supportive of the traditional cornerstones of applied public administration, especially the authority and legitimacy of hierarchical bureaucratic organizations and their reliance on technocratic experts. Questioning these traditional approaches provides postmodern theory a set of unique vantage points for examining administration. These have created opportunities for a wide range of new scholarly directions in public administration—feminism and the push for more interactive forms of administration being notable examples. For example, Shannon Portillo and Leisha De-Hart-Davis (2009) have shown that support for administrative hierarchy is in fact gendered. Although their methodology (surveys) is positivist in nature, the theoretical arguments have a postmodern, if not feminist, basis.

Given postmodern theory's explicit doubts about some of the core purposes of theory as they have been defined here, it is hard, and perhaps unfair, to judge this theory using the same yardsticks as the other frameworks examined by this book. For example, in Table 10.1's summary assessment, postmodern theory's replicability is judged as low. But should this be viewed as a weakness in an intellectual framework that emphasizes the importance of individual contexts and explicitly rejects the notion that any theory can universally transcend these contexts? Perhaps the biggest problem with postmodern theory is that its attachment to relativism makes it more a way of thinking about the world than a tool to explain it. Scholars attracted to more positivist goals—for example, finding systematic explanations of human and institutional behavior across a variety of empirical cases—view postmodernism as a disorienting intellectual gyroscope and an unreliable explanatory compass.

Although postmodern theory is unlikely to ever rest comfortably in frameworks with explicit or implicit positivist goals, its service to public administration is considerable. At a minimum, it has provided a forceful critique about how to conceptualize and think about the core elements of the discipline.

Decision Theory

Decision theory is probably the most mature and empirically informed formal theory in public administration. This may be a result of its origins, which, like those of rational choice theory, are clearly anchored in the well-developed concepts of rationality associated with neoclassical economics. Decision theory, however, is not simply an economic framework applied to the public sector but a distinct model indigenous to public administration.

The father of decision theory is Simon, who laid down the basic concepts and logic in his classic work *Administrative Behavior* (1947/1997). At the heart of Simon's argument was the proposition that the basic objective of any purposive organization was to discover or define those purposes and take the necessary actions to fulfill them. Decisionmaking describes the process that links an organization's means to its ends, and thus decisionmaking is the core administrative activity and the appropriate explanatory target for any truly scientific theory of administration.

Simon drew heavily from the concept of rationality to explain the process of making choices that link means to ends. Crucially, however, he rejected the orthodox concept of rationality and recognized that the human capability for making rational decisions was limited, or bounded. Instead of utility maximizers, Simon described humans as satisficers—actors who adopt behaviors that are "good enough" to have a reasonable probability of achieving a desired end. Perfectly rational decisions would require information, attention, and other resources that simply are not available to the average human being. A satisficer needs just enough of these resources to make a reasonable connection between action and the desired objectives.

Simon's concept of bounded rationality presented a much more realistic portrait of how administrators made decisions. Simon did not assume that decisionmakers had perfect information or made decisions independent of institutional context, historical experience, or individual values. Instead, he portrayed administrators as decisionmakers dealing with ambiguity, the limits of attention and time, the constraints of their own values, and any number of the other elements that separate the messy reality of human behavior from the cleanly logical cost-benefit calculations of the purely rational utility maximizer.

The concept of bounded rationality allowed decision theory to escape the confining orbit of traditional rational choice theory and move in directions that clearly offered more realistic descriptions of administrative behavior. Bounded rationality underpins the "science of muddling through," Charles Lindblom's (1959) description of bureaucracy's pattern of incremental decisionmaking. In muddling through, bureaucracy always starts with its immediate history as a baseline for decisionmaking. Creating and justifying a budget from scratch every year, for example, would be a very resource-intensive exercise. Beginning with last year's budget and making minor adjustments to fit new priorities or altered circumstances are considerably less resource intensive and make budgetary decisionmaking a more manageable undertaking. Such incremental decisionmaking, of course, means that some information is not gathered and some options are not considered, so in one sense it is not a purely rational exercise. For one thing, means and ends tend to get mixed up. In practice, however, incrementalism is usually good enough to ensure that means are indeed connected to ends and, most of the time, provides a reasonable description of what bureaucracies actually do.

The multidisciplinary nature of decision theory opens the field to changes in all directions. As we discussed in Chapter 7, now even the tenets of bounded rationality are being challenged on the basis of recent work in psychology, social psychology, and even neuroscience. Whereas bounded rationality would predict policy change owing to new information, the tenets of "predictable irrationality" suggest that biases in information processing can also prevent change in such instances.

Garbage can theory (March and Olsen 1986) also owes a considerable debt to the concept of bounded rationality, even though in some sense it reverses the causal assumptions embraced by Simon. The "organized anarchy" is the context in which ends and means are not tightly coupled and decisionmaking is often ad hoc. In organized anarchy, goals can be discovered during the process of taking action, or even after an action is completed. This veers from the purposive, means-ends process Simon put at the heart of administration, but takes seriously the ambiguity a satisficer has to face in reality. As a realistic description of how universities and other public institutions actually operate, the organized anarchy of the garbage can seems uncomfortably close to the truth.

Decision theory has clearly succeeded in categorizing the confusing internal processes that determine the behavior of public agencies into something approaching a coherent and understandable framework. Bits and pieces of decision theory have also been grafted onto management theory and employed as useful heuristics to guide administrative action. Thus far, however, it has not fulfilled the positivist promise Simon saw in its initial development. The emerging field of predictable irrationality or "new decision theory" reduces the predictive capacity and empirical warrant of decision theory as displayed in Table 10.1. The explanatory capacity is also mixed to low given the limitations of bounded rationality as a framework for not only predicting human decisionmaking, but also explaining the actual biological and cognitive processes involved in decisionmaking. The source of this mixed performance can be traced to Waldo's primary criticism of *Administrative Behavior*. The theory it proposed relied on separating facts from values. This, Waldo suggested, was a project doomed to repeat the failure of the administration-politics dichotomy. Bounded rationality might be employed to create a more realistic description and understanding of administrative behavior, but its predictive power and its ability to generate universal axioms are always going to be weakened by the caprice of human unpredictability. Thus far, even though decision theory has struggled to prove Waldo incorrect, there is hope pending in the ability of the field to adopt a more interdisciplinary theoretical approach, as well as greater use of experimental methodology.

Rational Choice Theory and Irrational Behavior

Rational choice (also known as public choice) is premised on the belief that the central behavioral assumption of neoclassical economics is universal, that is, that rational self-interest is the primary motivator of purposive action. More specifically, rational choice has two central assumptions: (1) individual utility maximization, which assumes that individuals know their preferences, can rank those preferences, and, where choices are available, will pick the option that fulfills their preferences at the least cost; and (2) methodological individualism, which assumes that all collective decisions and actions are the aggregation of individual decisions and actions, that collectives have no unique properties of their own.

From these remarkably simple premises, rational choice scholars have constructed deductive portraits of bureaucratic behavior that are unparalleled in public administration for their internal logical consistency and formal theoretical elegance. Through its prescriptive implications, rational choice theory has also had an enormous applied impact on the practice of public administration.

This impact stems from how rational choice perceives bureaucrats and bureaucracy. Gordon Tullock (1965), Anthony Downs (1967), and William Niskanen (1971) introduced the discipline to the self-maximizing bureaucrat rather than the neutrally competent civil servants that populate traditional scholarship. The self-maximizing bureaucrat is an actor driven by self-interested motivations, and because he lacks complete information, he is largely incapable of effectively pursuing the public interest even if these selfish motivations include an altruistic streak. The implications for bureaucracy are alarming—organizations will be more interested in aggrandizing themselves than in serving the public interest. Rational choice portrays the traditional executive branch agency as a monopoly public service provider bidding its wares to monopsonist buyers in the legislature and suffering from all the pathologies and inefficiencies associated with private-sector monopolies.

The explanatory impact of this movement is fading quickly, however. Evidence now abounds that bureaucrats, and human beings more generally, are not in fact selfish utility maximizers, but instead actors who are extremely sensitive to their social surroundings. The behavioral manifestations of this sensitivity, as documented in Chapter 8, pose serious challenges to the rational choice framework. As examples, empirical evidence shows that people are quite willing to incur costs in order to appear fair in cases of information asymmetry (Smith 2006), and, if an organizational leader is perceived as trustworthy, will engage in number of organizationally beneficial behaviors, including extra effort (Dirks and Skarlicki 2004), risky behavior (Elsbach 2004), and a reduced likelihood of sabotaging the organization (Brehm and Gates 2004). Although pure rational choice theorists may describe such behavior as "irrational," the evidence discussed in Chapter 7 and Chapter 8 suggests these departures from the strict rational choice model are actually quite rational from a noneconomic point of view, and quite predictable.

The rational choice conception of bureaucracy also suggests the need for sweeping reforms in the public sector to avoid concentrating power in nonelected institutions, to forge a stronger link between citizen preference and government action, and to bring the political system generally into a closer embrace of democratic values (Ostrom 1973). Rational choice argues that such reforms should rely on the introduction of market forces into the arena of public service provision. Competition and choice in a market for public services, according to rational choice theory, should improve the quality of public goods, reduce their costs, and increase citizen satisfaction. This prescriptive vision has a normative cast that was recognized and amplified by rational choice scholars. Elinor Ostrom (1998) and others argued that rational choice represented a truly democratic theory of public administration, one that offered a better way to realize the republican form of government envisioned by James Madison. Ostrom's work has also shown that the path to more efficient organizations may not always flow through the use of market mechanisms such as competition. Organizations, through open communication and transparency, can be self-regulating and produce optimal outcomes (Ostrom, Gardner, and Walker 1994; Ostrom, Schroeder, and Wayne 1993).

Although the scope and impact of rational choice are hard to underestimate, its lofty ambitions to provide a central positive and normative theoretical paradigm for public administration remain unrealized. As a theory in the positivist sense, rational choice is hampered by doubts about its core assumptions and the mixed empirical confirmation of the hypotheses generated by these assumptions. Rational choice is deductively tied to the concepts of rational utility maximization and methodological individualism. These core assumptions provide the theory with its parsimony and predictive capacities. If either of these is wrong or (more likely) incomplete when applied to a public-sector phenomena, the conclusions and prescriptions of rational choice stand on soft foundations. The mixed empirical record of rational choice scholarship has done little to ease such concerns.

Rational choice is criticized as a normative theory because it equates market values with democratic values, even though these clearly conflict in specifics. For example, an agency may satisfy its clientele, but in doing so it does not necessarily serve the public interest. Public agencies are supposed to be accountable to the collective, not to the individual, and their duty is to serve the law rather than seek customer satisfaction. To serve the egalitarian purposes of democracy, they cannot subordinate process to outcomes, or accountability to efficiency (Moe and Gilmour 1995). Critics of rational choice argue not only that it is incompatible with fundamental democratic values but also that it is fundamentally hostile to them.

Even though rational choice theory has clearly sought to fulfill all the purposes of theory, there are clear problems regarding explanatory and predictive capacity, as well as empirical warrant. As such, rational choice theory receives a low to mixed rating across all three categories. The increasingly obvious inability to describe real-world phenomena accurately also leads to a low rating for descriptive capacity. Thus, the empirical record points to a strong need for a new theory of human behavior that overcomes the increasingly clear limitations of rational choice. The problem for practicing scholars is that such a theory does not yet exist; instead, scholars are left to gather evidence piecemeal from multiple disciplines using multiple methodologies. The evidence, both theoretical and empirical, is available for the field to move away from strict rational choice theory to a more interdisciplinary and theoretically useful approach. The direction and pace at which this transition occurs, however, are up to practicing scholars.

Theories of Governance

During the past three or four decades, governments in industrialized democracies have subjected themselves to a rigorous and sometimes painful self-examination by questioning their purposes and the methods used to achieve them. Governments have become less hierarchical, less centralized, and more willing to delegate considerable grants of policymaking power to the private sector (Kettl 2000). These changes have forced public administration to rethink and begin repositioning its intellectual foundations. In a disarticulated state where public service provision is increasingly carried out by networks with little central direction, the intellectual planks the discipline traditionally relies upon—especially Weberian-based models of bureaucracy and management—lose much of their ability to help public administration scholars build a coherent explanatory picture of the world they study. The rise of the hollow or fragmented state has created a need for new intellectual tools in public administration. Governance has stealthily crept into the discipline's language and established itself as a virtual synonym for public administration. Faced with a new reality of government, where cooperative networks and competitive market forces are as likely to describe the means of public service provision as bureaucracy and hierarchy, public administration seems to be evolving into the study of governance. Governance, however, implies a different definition of public administration than its customary understanding, one that incorporates a variety of nontraditional policy processes and actors. Currently, "governance" is more a term describing a changing public administration than it is a coherent theory itself. Faced with significant change in the focus of its study, public administration needs to create new intellectual frameworks to explain and understand this change and to help assess how these changes affect public service provision.

Governance is the label used to comprehend these changes and describe nascent theoretical frameworks.

The clear need for theories of governance has prompted at least three identifiable responses. The first of these is to treat governance as a project to corral a broad multidisciplinary literature on government activity into a coherent intellectual whole (Lynn, Heinrich, and Hill 1999, 2000, 2001). Here governance is a proxy for a public administration of expanded scope, a study of public service operations that include public, private, and nonprofit sectors. The attempt to impose a core set of goals and intellectual consistency on such a pluralistic enterprise raises questions about the ability of this approach to generate a useful theory. It is exceedingly difficult to extract a parsimonious and universally applicable logic of governance given such a broad target, though the attempt is usefully driving public administration scholars to adopt new concepts and apply them in creative ways.

The second approach equates governance with the NPM movement (Peters and Pierre 1998). This approach provides an intellectual handle on governance that is easier to grasp, but its ability to carry all that is implied by governance is questionable. All the variants of NPM are, at their core, attempts to persuade the public sector to adopt corporate values and practices. Differentiating the public sector and private sector only by the type of goods or services they produce requires adopting a distinct ideological conception of government, one where government is largely reduced to being a contractual agent for various groups of citizens. This conception challenges the cultural and philosophical role of democracy (McCabe and Vinzant 1999; Box, Reed, and Reed 2001). As B. Guy Peters and John Pierre (1998) argue, NPM and governance may share common ground, but this does not make them conceptual equivalents. NPM carries too much ideological baggage, is too much an attempt to realize a particular political vision of what the world *should* look like to function as a general scholarly theory of governance. Although these normative components are not formally captured in Table 10.1, the bottom line is that equating NPM with governance theory mischaracterizes both frameworks. For example, despite the claims of the NPM movement, there is substantial evidence showing that the Weberian structure of bureaucracies justifiably remains prevalent in public institutions (Hill and Lynn 2005), because such structural arrangements can actually increase, rather than decrease, organizational efficiency (Leland and Smirnova 2009). Governance theories can quite comfortably absorb such empirical findings; for NPM, they come dangerously close to falsifying central theoretical (or at least ideological) assumptions.

The third approach, and the one we believe most promising, is to treat governance as the attempt to understand the lateral and institutional relations in administrative agencies in the context of the disarticulated state (Frederickson 1999b). This approach is bounded by and anchored to the recognition that jurisdictional boundaries are less meaningful to the practical necessities of effective policy implementation. Although not a comprehensive theory of governance, the theory of administrative conjunction demonstrates the promise of intellectual frameworks built from this particular starting point. In administrative conjunction, appointed public officials and civil service professionals make effective policy possible through voluntary, multijurisdictional cooperation. As the state becomes increasingly fragmented and the importance of political boundaries erodes, conjunctions connect the various units of government and make coherent patterns of policy implementation possible in the absence of a central authority. Frederickson builds upon this notion by offering a theory of governance as the "management of the extended state" (2005, 300). As a framework for theory-building, Frederickson's extended state advises scholars to look to international relations, specifically regime theory. The regime theory of governance embraces the notion of the disarticulated or extended state, but attempts to place boundaries around the concept of governance. These boundaries are not exclusionary, recognizing the importance of interjurisdictional, third-party, and public nongovernmental governance.

What is particularly striking about the rapidly developing field of governance theory is that it is primarily an intellectual project indigenous to public administration. After decades of colonization by economics, sociology, and other disciplines, governance theory is still borrowing what it finds useful, but is increasingly showing signs of a confident originality in its theoretical development. Currently, it is difficult to award governance theory anything but mixed marks as a theory—the project is simply too immature for sweeping judgments to be made with any degree of confidence. Frederickson's regime theory of governance attempts to resolve the issue of what fits in the framework of governance theory, but key questions remain unresolved. For example, to what end do democratic concepts such as accountability fit within the governance theoretical framework, and to what degree should governance scholars concern themselves with such questions? Given the increasing fiscal constraints faced by governments at all levels, and the accompanying volume and complexity of social problems, the number of actors and networks necessary for successful policy provision will continue to expand. But can all actors and networks, both public and private, as well as "hybrid" organizations, be held accountable? Public institutions derive their power from the public. What, then, should be done about private organizations that contribute to a public good? What should be done about organizations in which accountability mechanisms are lacking? Jonathan Koppell's (2010) work on global governance organizations, discussed in more depth in Chapter 9, is instructive on this point. For transnational organizations, or even complex governance networks, the key is identifying a sufficient number of actors in order to secure legitimacy and compliance. The scholarly record that is emerging on this point indicates mixed results by policy type (Koliba, Mills, and Zia 2011; Howell-Moroney and Hall 2011).

Much in the way of governance theory has been written since the first edition of this text. Yet the early signs are encouraging. And despite all the controversy over the role of governance theory within or over the field of public administration (see Frederickson 2005 and Meier 2011 for opposing views), there is universal agreement that advancements in governance theory, perhaps more so than in any other theoretical framework, provide the best opportunity for improving public service provision. As a message to young public administration scholars, governance theory is the wave of the future that by necessity is here to stay—offering both a fruitful scholarly exercise and a chance to provide tangible policy benefits by improving the way in which services are provided. Although the payoff from the governance effort is not yet fully realized, its potential to clear the fog of confusion that settles quickly after sweeping decentralization and to usefully inform the practice of public administration is considerable.

Theory in Public Administration

This brief summary of the frameworks considered in this book should make clear that theory in public administration has primarily served two basic purposes: (1) to assemble facts into a coherent and explanatory whole and (2) to provide perspectives on what "should" be done and to create guides for action. Virtually all the major contributions covered in the *Primer* help provide a clearer understanding of the complex world of public administration in explaining both what it does and why. Indeed, even though rational choice scores low in descriptive capacity and empirical warrant and both decision theory and rational choice score low/mixed in explanatory capacity in Table 10.1, these conceptual platforms are driving some of the most promising empirical work relevant to public administration. Empirical advances are being made in all directions regarding decision-making processes, at both the institutional and individual levels, and scholars are increasingly gaining a firmer grasp on what constitutes utility given various social constraints. At least a substantial minority of these contributions has also contributed to the applied practice of public administration (see the work of Elinor Ostrom as a prime example). The extraordinary persistence of the principles of management approach as guides for administrative action is perhaps the best example of this claim. NPM, Total Quality Management, management by objectives, and any number of other administrative movements with their own acronyms testify to the theoretical fecundity and applied utility of intellectual frameworks pioneered by the likes of Taylor, Barnard, Fayol, and Gulick.

Public administration has been less successful in creating theories in the positivist, scientific sense. This failure cannot be attributed to lack of effort, not with sustained projects such as decision theory, rational choice theory, and newly developing behavioral theories explicitly aimed at this objective. As Table 10.1 indicates, public administration theory struggles with a predictable series of tradeoffs. Parsimonious theories, for example, tend to have comparatively weak descriptive capacities; theories with strong descriptive capacities struggle to match such strengths in parsimony and predictive capacity. Needless to say, despite the persistent search for a science of administration, we still lack administrative equivalents to the laws of motion or gravity. Postmodern theory argues that such universals are beyond the reach of any explanation of social phenomena and casts a skeptical eye on all theory-building projects having positivist aspirations.

Given this background, there are two views of theory in public administration. The first, given an intellectual anchor by postmodernism, is of a discipline in difficulty, struggling to define itself and repeatedly failing to find much traction. This lack of forward movement comes despite increasingly desperate attempts to catch a ride with whatever extradisciplinary intellectual vehicle is currently fashionable in other social sciences. The second, and the one favored here, is of an intellectual field engaged in a healthy introspection, not tied to any paradigmatic dogma, constantly experimenting with fresh approaches, and beginning to formulate original ways of thinking about its arena of study. At a minimum, the projects covered in this book shaped the scholarly and applied worlds in important ways even when they fell short of their ambitious theoretical goals. For example, rational choice concepts are central to NPM, and management gurus seem to be in a continual process of rediscovering the applied benefits of the insights Simon first codified in *Administrative Behavior* (1947/1997). Given this track record, we suggest there is ample evidence that public administration theory has repeatedly met its ultimate test: It has been found useful in an applied or practical sense.

Public administration theory is not always as fragmented as it seems. Though we have presented a series of in-depth examinations of various intellectual movements as independent theoretical projects, this is to some extent misleading. The astute reader will surely have noticed the recurrence of themes and arguments throughout this tour of public administration thinking. Theory here consists of a persistent mixing of the established and (at least to public administration) the new into creative and original perspectives. Any linear process of theory in public administration, any semblance of a steady incremental march toward a central paradigm or disciplinary objective—these disappeared long ago. The loss of theoretical hegemony gave public administration an identity crisis and made it vulnerable to colonization from other disciplines, but it also caused an evolution in theory that has successfully branched out into many directions. Pick any two of these branches, and it's possible to recognize common building blocks—for example, NPM with rational choice, theories of bureaucratic politics with theories of political control—even though their differences are equally clear. Even the foundations of decision theory and rational choice, which have been seriously challenged, now seem to be moving in similar directions.

In conclusion, we should also point out not only the interconnectedness of theory in public administration but also the limited sample of frameworks that any one volume can carefully consider. Network theory, for example, is arguably an intellectual framework important enough to warrant separate treatments on its merits, rather than be assigned to the supporting role it played here. Similar arguments can be made for numerous other frameworks distinct enough to claim their own labels. Our goal, however, was not to present a comprehensive guide to all the theories successfully employed by public administration scholars. The goal was to present what we believe to be the key contemporary theories and to use them to demonstrate the importance of theory to scholarship and to the shaping of applied practice. Whatever its failures, public administration theory can count among its successes its numerous contributions to increasing our systematic understanding of the public sector and to repeatedly providing public service professionals (albeit sometimes in a diluted, popularized form) useful guides for action.

References

Aberbach, Joel, and Bert Rockman. 2000. *In the Web of Politics*. Washington, DC: Brookings Institution.

Ackelsberg, Martha A., and Mary Lyndon Shanley. 1996. "Privacy, Publicity, and Power: A Feminist Rethinking of the Public-Private Distinction." In *Revisioning the Political: Feminist Reconstructions of Traditional Concepts in Western Political Theory*, edited by Nancy J. Hirschman and Cristine DiStefano. Boulder, CO: Westview Press.

Adams, Guy, and Jay White. 1994. "Dissertation Research in Public Administration and Cognate Fields: An Assessment of Methods and Quality." *Public Administration Review* 6:565–576.

Adrian, Charles. 1955. *Governing Urban America*. New York: McGraw-Hill.

Allison, Graham. 1971. *Essence of Decision*. Boston: Little, Brown.

Allison, Graham, and Morton Halperin. 1972. "Bureaucratic Politics: A Paradigm and Some Policy Implications." *World Politics* 24:40–79.

American Political Science Association. 1950. *On Divided Government*. Washington, DC: American Political Science Association.

Ammeter, Anthony P., Ceasar Douglas, William L. Gardner, Wayne A. Hochwarter, and Gerald R. Ferris. 2002. "Toward a Political Theory of Leadership." *The Leadership Quarterly* 13:751–796.

Argyris, Chris. 1962. *Interpersonal Competence and Organizational Effectiveness*. Homewood, IL: Dorsey Press.

Argyris, Chris, and Donald Schon. 1978. *Organizational Learning: A Theory of Action Perspective*. Reading, MA: Addison-Wesley.

Ariely, Dan. 2009. *Predictably Irrational: The Hidden Forces That Shape Our Decisions*. Rev. and expanded ed. New York: Harper-Perennial.

Aristotle. 1932. *Rhetoric*. Translated by L. Cooper. New York: Appleton-Century, Croft.

Axelrod, Robert. 1984. *The Evolution of Cooperation*. New York: Basic Books.

Balazs, Etienne. 1964. *Chinese Civilization and Bureaucracy*. New Haven, CT: Yale University Press.

Bardach, Eugene. 1977. *The Implementation Game: What Happens After a Bill Becomes a Law*. Cambridge, MA: MIT Press.

Barnard, Chester. 1938. *The Function of the Executive*. Cambridge, MA: Harvard University Press.

———. 1948. *Organization and Management*. Cambridge, MA: Harvard University Press.

Barzelay, Michael. 1992. *Breaking Through Bureaucracy*. Berkeley and Los Angeles: University of California Press.

Baudrillard, Jean. 1984. "Games with Vestiges." *On the Beach* 5:24.

267

————. 1990. *Revenue of the Crystal: Selected Writings, on the Modern Object and Its Destiny.* Translated by Paul Foss and Julian Pefanis. London: Pluto Press.

Behn, Robert D. 1991. *Leadership Counts: Lessons for Public Managers from the Massachusetts Welfare, Training, and Employment Program.* Cambridge, MA: Harvard University Press.

————. 2000. *Rethinking Democratic Accountability.* Washington, DC: Brookings Institution.

Bellow, Gary, and Martha Minow, eds. 1996. *Law Stories.* Ann Arbor: University of Michigan Press.

Bendor, Jonathan, and Thomas Hammond. 1992. "Rethinking Allison's Models." *American Political Science Review* 86:301–322.

Bendor, Jonathan, and Terry Moe. 1985. "An Adaptive Model of Bureaucratic Politics." *American Political Science Review* 79:755–774.

Bendor, Jonathan, Terry Moe, and Kenneth Shotts. 2001. "Recycling the Garbage Can: An Assessment of the Research Program." *American Political Science Review* 95:169–190.

Bendor, Jonathan, Serge Taylor, and Roland van Gaalen. 1987. "Politicians, Bureaucrats, and Asymmetric Information." *American Journal of Political Science* 31:796–828.

Bennis, Warren. 2003. *On Becoming a Leader.* New York: Basic Books.

Berger, Peter L., and Thomas Luckmann. 1967. *The Social Construction of Reality.* New York: Doubleday.

Berry, Francis, Richard Chackerian, and Barton Wechsler. 1995. "Reinventing Government: Lessons from a State Capitol." In *Public Management Reform and Innovation: Research, Theory, and Application,* edited by H. George Frederickson and Jocelyn Johnston. Tuscaloosa: University of Alabama Press.

Blais, Andre, and Sephane Dion. 1991. "Are Bureaucrats Budget Maximizers?" In *The Budget-Maximizing Bureaucrat: Appraisals and Evidence,* edited by Andre Blais and Stephane Dione. Pittsburgh: University of Pittsburgh Press.

Bledsoe, Timothy. 1993. *Careers in City Politics: The Case for Urban Democracy.* Pittsburgh: University of Pittsburgh Press.

Bogason, Peter. 2005. "Postmodern Public Administration." In *The Oxford Handbook of Public Management,* edited by Ewan Ferle, Laurence Lynn Jr., and Christopher Pollitt. New York: Oxford University Press.

Boisot, Max. 1986. "Markets and Hierarchies in a Cultural Perspective." *Organizational Studies* 2:135–158.

Bourrier, Mathilde. 2011. "The Legacy of the High-Reliability Organization Project." *Journal of Contingencies and Crisis Management* 19:9–13.

Box, Richard, Gary Marshall, B. J. Reed, and Christine Reed. 2001. "New Public Management and Substantive Democracy." *Public Administration Review* 61:608–619.

Boyne, George. 1998. *Public Choice Theory and Local Government.* New York: St. Martin's Press.

Bozeman, Barry. 2000. *Bureaucracy and Red Tape.* Upper Saddle River, NJ: Prentice-Hall.

Bozeman, Barry, and Jeffrey D. Straussman. 1991. *Public Management Strategies: Guidelines for Managerial Effectiveness.* San Francisco: Jossey-Bass.

Brafman, Ori, and Rom Brafman. 2008. *Sway: The Irresistible Pull of Irrational Behavior.* New York: Broadway Books.

Brehm, John, and Scott Gates. 1997. *Working, Shirking, and Sabotage: Bureaucratic Response to a Democratic Republic.* Ann Arbor: University of Michigan Press.

————. 2004. "Supervisors as Trust Brokers in Social-Work Bureaucracies." In *Trust and Distrust in Organizations: Dilemmas and Approaches,* edited by Roderick M. Kramer and Karen S. Cook. New York: Russell Sage.

Brehm, John, Scott Gates, and Brad Gomez. 1998. "Donut Shops, Speed Traps, and Paperwork: Supervision and the Allocation of Time to Bureaucratic Tasks." Paper presented at the annual meeting of the Midwest Political Science Association, Chicago, Illinois, April 23–25.

Brooks, David. 2011. "The New Humanism." *New York Times*, March 8, A23.

Brown, Brack, and Richard Stillman Jr. 1986. *The Search for Public Administration: The Ideas and Career of Dwight Waldo.* College Station: Texas A&M University Press.

Brown, David. 1995. *When Strangers Cooperate.* New York: The Free Press.

Bryson, John M. 1988. *Strategic Planning for Public and Nonprofit Organizations: A Guide to Strengthening and Sustaining Organizational Achievement.* San Francisco: Jossey-Bass.

Bryson, John M., and Barbara Crosby. 1992. *Leadership for the Common Good: Tackling Public Problems in a Shared-Power World.* San Francisco: Jossey-Bass.

Buchanan, James. 1972. "Towards Analysis of Closed Behavioral Systems." In *Theory of Public Choice: Political Applications of Economics*, edited by James M. Buchanan and Robert D. Tollison. Ann Arbor: University of Michigan Press.

Buchanan, James, Robert Tollison, and Gordon Tullock, eds. 1980. *Toward a Theory of the Rent-Seeking Society.* College Station: Texas A&M University Press.

Buchanan, James, and Gordon Tullock. 1962. *The Calculus of Consent.* Ann Arbor: University of Michigan Press.

Buchholtz, Todd. 1999. *New Ideas from Dead Economists.* New York: Plume.

Burns, Tom, and Helena Flam. 1987. *The Shaping of Social Organization: Social Rule System Theory with Applications.* Beverly Hills, CA: Sage.

Callan, Eamonn. 1997. *Creating Citizens.* New York: Oxford University Press.

Camerer, Colin F., George Lowenstein, and Matthew Rabin, eds. 2004. *Advances in Behavioral Economics.* Princeton, NJ: Princeton University Press.

Campbell, Colin, and Donald Nauls. 1991. "The Limits of the Budget-Maximizing Theory: Some Evidence from Officials' Views of Their Roles and Careers." In *The Budget-Maximizing Bureaucrat: Appraisals and Evidence*, edited by Andre Blais and Stephane Dione. Pittsburgh: University of Pittsburgh Press.

Carnevale, David G. 1995. *Trustworthy Government: Leadership and Management Strategies for Building Trust and High Performance.* San Francisco: Jossey-Bass.

Carroll, James, and H. George Frederickson. 2001. "Dwight Waldo, 1913–2000." *Public Administration Review* 61:2–8.

Chi, Keon, Kevin Devlin, and Wayne Masterman. 1989. "The Use of the Private Sector in the Delivery of Human Services." In *The Private Sector in State Service Delivery*, edited by Joan Allen et al. Washington, DC: Urban Institute Press.

Chisholm, Donald. 1995. "Problem Solving and Institutional Design." *Journal of Public Administration Research and Theory* 6:25–47.

Chrimes, Stanley B. 1952. *An Introduction to the Administrative History of Medieval England.* Oxford: Oxford University Press.

Cialdini, Robert B., and Noah J. Goldstein. 2004. "Social Influence: Compliance and Conformity." *Annual Review of Psychology* 55:591–621.

Cigler, Beverly. 1990. "County Contracting: Reconciling the Accountability and Information Paradoxes." *Public Administration Quarterly* 3:285–301.

Clark, David L. 1985. "Emerging Paradigms in Organizational Theory and Research." In *Organization Theory and Inquiry: The Paradigm Revolution*, edited by Yvonne S. Lincoln. Beverly Hills, CA: Sage.

Clayworth, Jason. 2011. "Debate on Economic Development Bill Likely This Week." *Des Moines Register*, March 22, 5A.

Cleary, Robert. 1992. "Revisiting the Doctoral Dissertation in Public Administration: An Examination of the Dissertations of 1990." *Public Administration Review* 52:55–61.

Cleary, Robert, and Nicholas Henry, eds. 1989. *Managing Public Programs: Balancing Politics, Administration, and Public Needs.* San Francisco: Jossey-Bass.

Cocks, Joan. 1989. *The Oppositional Imagination: Feminism, Critique, and Political Theory.* London: Routledge.

Cohen, Michael, and James March. 1986. *Leadership and Ambiguity: The American College President.* Boston: Howard Business School Press.

Cohen, Michael, James March, and Johan Olsen. 1972. "A Garbage Can Model of Organizational Choice." *Administrative Science Quarterly* 17:1–25.

Cohen, Steven, and William Eimicke. 1995. *The New Effective Public Manager: Achieving Success in a Changing Government.* San Francisco: Jossey-Bass.

Commonwealth of Massachusetts. 2001. *Report of the Special Advisory Task Force on Massport.* December 4. Boston: Commonwealth of Massachusetts.

Conley, John M., and William M. O'Barr. 1998. *Just Words: Law, Language, and Power.* Chicago: University of Chicago Press.

Conquest, Robert. 2000. *Reflections on a Ravaged Century.* New York: Norton.

Considine, Mark, and Martin Painter. 1997. *Managerialism: The Great Debate.* Melbourne, Australia: Melbourne University Press.

Cooper, Terry L., and N. Dale Wright, eds. 1992. *Exemplary Public Administrators: Character and Leadership in Government.* San Francisco: Jossey-Bass.

Dahl, Robert. 1947. "The Science of Public Administration." *Public Administration Review* 7:1–11.

Darley, John M. 2004. "Commitment, Trust, and Worker Effort Expenditure in Organizations." In *Trust and Distrust in Organizations: Dilemmas and Approaches*, edited by Roderick M. Kramer and Karen S. Cook. New York: Russell Sage.

Davis, James H., Lex Donaldson, and F. David Schoorman. 1997. "Toward a Stewardship Theory of Management." *Academy of Management Review* 22:20–47.

Davis, Stanley, and Paul Laurence. 1977. *Matrix.* Reading, MA: Addison-Wesley.

DeHart-Davis, Leisha. 2009. "Can Bureaucracy Benefit Organizational Women? An Exploratory Study." *Administration and Society* 41:340–363.

DeHart-Davis, Leisha, and Barry Bozeman. 2001. "Regulatory Compliance and Air Quality Permitting: Why Do Firms Overcomply?" *Journal of Public Administration Research and Theory* 4:471–508.

DeHoog, Ruth Hoogland. 1984. *Contracting for Human Services: Economic, Political, and Organizational Perspectives.* Albany: State University of New York Press.

deLeon, Linda, and Robert B. Denhardt. 2000. "The Political Theory of Reinvention." *Public Administration Review* 60:89–97.

deLeon, Peter, and Linda deLeon. 2002. "What Ever Happened to Policy Implementation? An Alternative Approach." *Journal of Public Administration Research and Theory* 12:467–492.

Denhardt, Robert. 1993. *Theories of Public Organization.* Belmont, CA: Wadsworth.

Dias, Janice, and Steven Maynard-Moody. 2007. "For-Profit Welfare: Contracts, Conflicts, and the Performance Paradox." *Journal of Public Administration Research and Theory* 17:189–211.

DiIulio, John Jr. 1987. *Governing Prisons: A Comparative Study of Correctional Management.* New York: The Free Press.

————. 1994. "Principled Agents: The Cultural Bases of Behavior in a Federal Government Bureaucracy." *Journal of Public Administration Research and Theory* 4:277–320.

DiIulio, John Jr., Gerald Garvey, and Donald Kettl. 1993. *Improving Government Performance: An Owner's Manual*. Washington, DC: Brookings Institution.

DiMaggio, Paul, and Walter Powell. 1983. "The Iron Cage Revisited: Institutional Isomorphism and Collective Rationality in Organizational Fields." *American Sociological Review* 48:149–160.

Dirks, Kurt T., and Donald L. Ferrin. 2001. "The Role of Trust in Organizational Settings." *Organizational Science* 12:450–467.

Dirks, Kurt T., and Daniel P. Skarlicki. 2004. "Trust in Leaders: Existing Research and Emerging Issues." In *Trust and Distrust in Organizations: Dilemmas and Approaches*, edited by Roderick M. Kramer and Karen S. Cook. New York: Russell Sage.

Donahue, John. 1989. *The Privatization Decision*. New York: Basic Books.

Douglas, Ceasar, and Anthony P. Ammeter. 2004. "An Examination of Leader Political Skill and Its Effect on Ratings of Leader Effectiveness." *Leadership Quarterly* 15:537–550.

Douglas, Mary, and Aaron Wildavsky. 1982. *Risk and Culture*. Berkeley and Los Angeles: University of California Press.

Downs, Anthony. 1957. *An Economic Theory of Democracy*. New York: Harper.

————. 1967. *Inside Bureaucracy*. Boston: Little, Brown.

Drucker, Peter. 1952. "Development of Theory of Democratic Administration: Replies and Comments." *American Political Science Review* 46:496–500.

Dubnick, Melvin. 2005. "Accountability and the Promise of Performance: In Search of the Mechanisms." *Public Performance and Management Review* 28:376–417.

Easton, David. 1965. *A Systems Analysis of Political Life*. New York: Wiley.

Egger, Robert. 2006. "Casting Light on Shadow Government: A Typological Approach." *Journal of Public Administration Research and Theory* 16:125–137.

Eggertsson, Thrainn. 1990. *Economic Behavior and Institutions*. Cambridge: Cambridge University Press.

Eisenhardt, Kathleen. 1989. "Agency Theory: An Assessment and Review." *Academy of Management Review* 14:57–74.

Eisinger, Peter K. 1989. *The Rise of the Entreprenuerial State*. Madison: University of Wisconsin Press.

Ellul, Jacques. 1955. *Histoire des Institutions*. Paris: Presses Universitaires de France.

Ellwood, John. 2000. "Prospects for the Study of the Governance of Public Organizations and Policies." In *Governance and Performance: New Perspectives*, edited by Carolyn Heinrich and Laurence Lynn Jr. Washington, DC: Georgetown University Press.

Elsbach, Kimberly D. 2004. "Managing Images of Trustworthiness in Organizations." In *Trust and Distrust in Organizations: Dilemmas and Approaches*, edited by Roderick M. Kramer and Karen S. Cook. New York: Russell Sage.

Epstein, David, and Sharyn O'Halloran. 1996. "Divided Government and the Design of Administration Procedures: A Formal Model and Empirical Test." *Journal of Politics* 58:373–397.

Ewick, Patricia, and Susan S. Silbey. 1998. *The Common Place of Law: Stories from Everyday Life*. Chicago: University of Chicago Press.

Farmer, David John. 1995. *The Language of Public Administration: Bureaucracy, Modernity, and Postmodernity*. Tuscaloosa: University of Alabama Press.

Fayol, Henri. 1949. *General and Industrial Management.* London: Pitman.

Fehr, Ernst, and Simon Gachter. 2000. "Cooperation and Punishment in Public Goods Experiments." *American Economic Review* 90:980–994.

Felbinger, Clare, and Robert Whitehead. 1991a. "Development and Redevelopment of Infrastructure." In *Managing Local Government*, edited by Richard Bingman and others. Newbury Park, CA: Sage.

———. 1991b. "Management of Solid Waste Disposal." In *Managing Local Government*, edited by Richard Bingman and others. Newbury Park, CA: Sage.

Ferguson, Kathy E. 1984. *The Feminist Case Against Bureaucracy.* Philadelphia: Temple University Press.

Ferris, Gerald R., Darren C. Treadway, Robert W. Kolodinsky, Wayne A. Hochwarte, Charles J. Kacmar, Ceasar Douglas, and Dwight D. Frink. 2005. "Development and Validation of the Political Skill Inventory." *Journal of Management* 31:126–152.

Ferris, James, and Shui-Yan Tang. 1993. "The New Institutionalism and Public Administration: An Overview." *Journal of Public Administration Research and Theory* 3:4–10.

Fesler, James, and Donald Kettl. 1996. *The Politics of the Administrative Process.* Chatham, NJ: Chatham House.

Finer, Herman. 1941. "Administrative Responsibility in Democratic Government." *Public Administration Review* 1:335–350.

Fiorina, Morris. 1996. *Divided Government.* New York: Macmillan.

Flentje, H. Edward Jr. 1993. *Selected Solely on the Basis of Administrative Ability.* Wichita, KS: Wichita State University.

Follet, Mary Parker. 1918. *The New State.* London: Longmans, Green.

———. 1924. *Creative Experience.* New York: Longmans, Green.

Forrester, John, and Sheilah Watson. 1994. "An Assessment of Public Administration Journals: The Perspective of Editors and Editorial Board Members." *Public Administration Review* 54:56–68.

Forsythe, Dall W. 2001. *Quick Better Cheaper? Managing Performance in American Government.* Albany, NY: Rockefeller Institute Press.

Fox, Charles J., and Hugh T. Miller. 1995. *Postmodern Public Administration: Toward Discourse.* Thousand Oaks, CA: Sage.

Frederich, Carl. 1940. "Public Policy and the Nature of Administrative Responsibility." In *Public Policy*, edited by Carl Frederich and E. S. Mason. Cambridge, MA: Harvard University Press.

Frederickson, H. George. 1980. *New Public Administration.* Tuscaloosa: University of Alabama Press.

———. 1991. "Toward a Theory of the Public for Public Administration." *Administration and Society* 22:395.

———. 1997a. "Beyond the City: Finding Metropolitan Governance in America." Paper presented at the annual meeting of the National Academy of Public Administration, Durham, North Carolina.

———. 1997b. *The Spirit of Public Administration.* San Francisco: Jossey-Bass.

———. 1999a. "Public Ethics and the New Managerialism." *Public Integrity* 1:265–278.

———. 1999b. "The Repositioning of American Public Administration." *PS: Political Science and Politics* 32:701–711.

———. 2000. "The Wisdom of History and the Folly of Experience." Unpublished.

———. 2005. "Whatever Happened to Public Administration? Governance, Governance, Everywhere." In *The Oxford Handbook of Public Management*, edited by Ewan Ferle, Laurence Lynn Jr., and Christopher Pollitt. New York: Oxford University Press.

Frederickson, H. George, and Gary Johnson. 2001. "The Adapted American City: A Study of Institutional Dynamics." *Urban Affairs Review* 36:872–884.

Frederickson, H. George, Gary Johnson, and Curtis Wood. 2003. *The Adapted City: Institutional Dynamics and Structural Change*. New York: M. E. Sharpe.

———. 2004. "The Changing Structure of American Cities: A Study of the Diffusion of Innovation." *Public Administration Review* 64:320–330.

Frederickson, H. George, and Todd LaPorte. 2002. "Airport Security, High Reliability, and the Problem of Rationality." *Public Administration Review* 62:33–43.

Furubotn, Eirik, and Rudolph Richter, eds. 1984. "The New Institutional Economics: A Symposium." *Zeitschrift fur die Gesamte Staatswissenschaft* (special issue):140.

———. 1993. "The New Institutional Economics: Recent Progress, Expanding Frontiers." *Zeitschrift fur die Gesamte Staatswissenschaf* (special issue):149.

Garnett, James. 1992. *Communicating for Results in Government: A Strategic Approach for Public Managers*. San Francisco: Jossey-Bass.

Garvey, Gerald. 1992. *Facing the Bureaucracy: Living and Dying in a Public Agency*. San Francisco: Jossey-Bass.

———. 1997. *Public Administration: The Profession and the Practice*. New York: St. Martin's Press.

Gaus, John. 1931. "Note on Administration." *American Political Science Review* 25:123–134.

———. 1950. "Trends in the Theory of Public Administration." *Public Administration Review* 3:161–168.

Gigerenzer, Gerd, Peter M. Todd, and the ABC Research Group. 1999. *Simple Heuristics That Make Us Smart*. New York: Oxford University Press.

Gilmour, Robert, and Alexis Halley. 1994. *Who Makes Public Policy: The Struggle for Control Between Congress and the Executive*. New York: Seven Bridges Press.

Gladden, Edgar. 1972. *A History of Public Administration*. Vol. 2. London: Frank Cass.

Golden, Marissa Martino. 1992. "Exit, Voice, Loyalty, and Neglect: Bureaucratic Responses to Presidential Control During the Reagan Administration." *Journal of Public Administration Research and Theory* 2:29–62.

Golembiewski, Robert T. 1972. *Renewing Organizations*. Ithaca, IL: Peacock.

Goodnow, Frank. 1900. *Politics and Administration: A Study in Government*. New York: Russell and Russell.

Goodsell, Charles. 1983. *The Case for Bureaucracy: A Public Administration Polemic*. Chatham, NJ: Chatham House.

———. 1988. *The Social Meaning of Civic Space*. Lawrence: University Press of Kansas.

Gormley, William. 1989. *Taming the Bureaucracy*. Princeton, NJ: Princeton University Press.

Gormley, William, and Steven Balla. 2008. *Bureaucracy and Democracy: Accountability and Performance*. Washington, DC: CQ Press.

Gormley, William, and David Weimer. 1999. *Organizational Report Cards*. Cambridge, MA: Harvard University Press.

Gortner, Harold, Julianne Mahler, and Jeanne Bell Nicholson. 1997. *Organizational Theory: A Public Perspective*. Fort Worth, TX: Harcourt Brace College.

Graham, Cole Blease Jr., and Steven Hays. 1993. *Managing the Public Organization*. Washington, DC: CQ Press.

Greenwood, Ronald, and Charles Wrege. 1986. "The Hawthorne Studies." In *Papers Dedicated to the Development of Modern Management*, edited by Daniel Wren and John Pearce II. Washington, DC: Academy of Management.

Gross, Neal, Ward Mason, and Alexander McEachern. 1958. *Explorations in Role Analysis.* New York: Wiley.

Gruber, Judith. 1987. *Controlling Bureaucracies.* Berkeley and Los Angeles: University of California Press.

Guba, Egon G. 1985. "The Context of Emerging Paradigm Research." In *Organization Theory and Inquiry: A Paradigm Revolution*, edited by Yvonna S. Lincoln. Beverly Hills, CA: Sage

Guéhenno, Jean-Marie. 1995. *The End of the Nation-State.* Minneapolis: University of Minnesota Press.

Gulick, Luther. 1937. "Notes on the Theory of Organization." In *Papers on the Science of Administration*, edited by Luther Gulick and Lyndon Urwick. New York: Institute of Public Administration.

———. 1984. "The Metaphors of Public Administration." *Public Administration Quarterly* 44:714–723.

Gulick, Luther, and Lyndon Urwick, eds. 1937. *Papers on the Science of Administration.* New York: Institute of Public Administration.

Habermas, Jürgen. 1970. *Toward a Rational Society.* Translated by Jeremy J. Shapiro. Boston: Beacon Press.

———. 1971. *Knowledge and Human Interests.* Translated by Jeremy J. Shapiro. Boston: Beacon Press.

Hall, Angela, Fred R. Bass, Gerald R. Ferris, and Randy Massengale. 2004. "Leader Reputation and Accountability in Organization: Implications for Dysfunctional Leader Behavior." *Leadership Quarterly* 15:515–536.

Hammond, Thomas H. 1986. "Agenda Control, Organizational Structure, and Bureaucratic Politics." *American Journal of Political Science* 30:379–420.

———. 1993. "Toward a General Theory of Hierarchy: Books, Bureaucrats, Basketball Tournaments, and the Administrative Structure of the Nation-State." *Journal of Public Administration Research and Theory* 3:120–144.

Hammond, Thomas H., and Jack H. Knott. 1999. "Political Institutions, Public Management, and Policy Choice." *Journal of Public Administration Research and Theory* 9:33–85.

Hammond, Thomas H., and Gary Miller. 1985. "A Social Choice Perspective on Authority and Expertise in Bureaucracy." *American Journal of Political Science* 29:1–28.

Handler, Joel. 1996. *Down from Bureaucracy: The Ambiguity of Privatization and Empowerment.* Princeton, NJ: Princeton University Press.

Haque, M. Shamsul. 1996. "The Intellectual Crisis in Public Administration in the Current Epoch of Privatization." *Administration and Society* 27:510–536.

Hardin, Garrett. 1968. "The Tragedy of the Commons." *Science* 162:1243–1248.

Harmon, Michael M. 1981. *Action Theory for Public Administration.* New York: Longman.

———. 1989. "'Decision' and 'Action' as Contrasting Perspectives in Organizational Theory." *Public Administration Review* 49:144–149.

———. 1995. *Responsibility as Paradox: A Critique of Rational Discourse on Government.* Thousand Oaks, CA: Sage.

Harmon, Michael M., and Richard Mayer. 1986. *Organization Theory for Public Administration.* Boston: Little, Brown.

Haslinger, S. 1996. "Objective Reality, Male Reality, and Social Construction." In *Women, Knowledge, and Reality: Explorations in Feminist Philosophy*, edited by Ann Garry and Marilyn Pearsall. New York: Routledge.

Hassan, Ihab. 2001. *The Postmodern Turn: Essays in Postmodern Theory and Culture.* Christchurch, New Zealand: Cybereditions Corporations.

Heclo, Hugh. 1977. *A Government of Strangers: Executive Politics in Washington.* Washington, DC: Brookings Institution.

———. 1978. "Issue Networks and the Executive Establishment." In *The New American Political System*, edited by Anthony King. Washington, DC: American Enterprise Institute.

Hefetz, Amir, and Mildred Warner. 2004. "Privatization and Its Reverse: Explaining the Dynamics of the Government Contracting Process." *Journal of Public Administration Research and Theory* 14:171–190.

Heifetz, Ronald. 1994. *Leadership Without Easy Answers.* Cambridge, MA: Harvard University Press.

Heinrich, Carolyn, and Laurence Lynn Jr., eds. 2000. *Governance and Performance: New Perspectives.* Washington, DC: Georgetown University Press.

Hendricks, J. J. 1992. "Women-Centered Reality and Rational Legalism." *Administration and Society* 23:455–470.

Henig, Jeffrey. 1994. *Rethinking School Choice: Limits of the Market Metaphor.* Princeton, NJ: Princeton University Press.

Herz, John. 1962. *International Politics in the Atomic Age.* New York: Columbia University Press.

Herzlinger, Regina, and William Krasker. 1987. "Who Profits from Nonprofits?" *Harvard Business Review* (January–February):93–106.

Hill, Carolyn J., and Laurence E. Lynn Jr. 2005. "Is Hierarchical Governance in Decline? Evidence from Empirical Research." *Journal of Public Administration Research and Theory* 15:173–195.

Hindera, John. 1993a. "Representative Bureaucracy: Further Evidence of Active Representation in EEOC District Offices." *Journal of Public Administration Research and Theory* 3:415–429.

———. 1993b. "Representative Bureaucracy: Imprimis Evidence of Active Representation in EEOC District Offices." *Social Science Quarterly* 74:95–108.

Hirschleifer, Jack, and John Riley. 1992. *The Analytics of Uncertainty and Information.* Cambridge: Cambridge University Press.

Hirschman, Albert O. 1970. *Exit, Voice, and Loyalty: Responses to Declines in Firms, Organizations, and States.* Cambridge, MA: Harvard University Press.

———. 1982. *Shifting Involvements: Private Interest and Public Action.* Princeton, NJ: Princeton University Press.

Holden, Mathew Jr. 1964. "The Governance of the Metropolis as a Problem in Diplomacy." *Journal of Politics* 26:627–647.

Homans, George. 1950. *The Human Group.* New York: Harcourt, Brace.

Hood, Christopher, and Michael Jackson. 1991. *Administrative Argument.* Brookfield, VT: Dartmouth Publishing.

Howell-Moroney, Michael E., and Jeremy L. Hall. 2011. "Waste in the Sewer: The Collapse of Accountability and Transparency in Public Finance in Jefferson County, Alabama." *Public Administration Review* 71:232–242.

Hummel, Ralph P. 1994. *The Bureaucratic Experience.* 4th ed. New York: St. Martin's Press.

Huntington, Samuel P. 1952. "The Marasmus of the ICC: The Commission, the Railroads, and the Public Interest." *Yale Law Journal* 62:467–509.

———. 1961. *The Common Defense*. New York: Columbia University Press.

Jacob, Herbert. 1988. *Silent Revolution: The Transformation of Divorce Law in the United States*. Chicago: University of Chicago Press.

Jacobson, Gary. 1990. *The Electoral Originals of the Divided Government: Competition in U.S. House Elections: 1946, 1988*. Boulder, CO: Westview Press.

Jaques, Elliott. 1990. "In Praise of Hierarchy." *Harvard Business Review* (January–February): 127–133.

Johnson, J. 1976. "Recent Administrative Reform in Britain." In *The Management of Change in Government*, edited by A. F. Leemans. The Hague, the Netherlands: Martinus Nijhoff.

Jones, Bryan D., and Frank R. Baumgartner. 2005a. "A Model of Choice for Public Policy." *Journal of Public Administration Research and Theory* 15:325–351.

———. 2005b. *The Politics of Attention: How Government Prioritizes Problems*. Chicago: University of Chicago Press.

Jung, Jun S. 2002. *Rethinking Administrative Theory: The Challenge of a New Century*. Westport, CT: Praeger.

Kagel, John H., and Alvin E. Roth. 1995. *The Handbook of Experimental Economics*. Princeton, NJ: Princeton University Press.

Kahneman, Daniel, Jack L. Knetsch, and Richard H. Thaler. 1991. "Anomalies: The Endowment Effect, Loss Aversion, and the Status Quo Bias." *Journal of Economic Perspectives* 5:193–206.

Kass, Henry D. 2003. "Is Trust Enough? The Issue of Reliance and Reliability in Public Administration." Unpublished manuscript. Portland, OR: Hartfield School of Government, Portland State University.

Kaufman, Herbert. 1969. "Administrative Decentralization and Political Power." *Public Administration Review* 29:72–102.

———. 1991. *Time, Chance, and Organizations: Natural Selection in a Perilous Environment*. Chatham, NJ: Chatham House.

Keiser, Lael R. 2010. "Understanding Street-Level Bureaucrats' Decision Making: Determining Eligibility in the Social Security Disability Program." *Public Administration Review* 70:247–257.

Keiser, Lael R., Vicki Wilkins, Kenneth Meier, and Catherine Holland. 2002. "Lipstick and Logarithms: Gender, Institutional Context, and Representative Bureaucracy." *American Political Science Review* 96:553–564.

Kelleher, Christine, and Susan Webb Yackee. 2009. "A Political Consequence of Contracting: Organized Interests and State Agency Decision Making." *Journal of Public Administration Research and Theory* 19:579–602.

Kernaghan, Kenneth, Brian Marson, and Sanford Borins. 2000. *The New Public Organization*. Toronto: Institute of Public Administration of Canada.

Kettl, Donald F. 1988. *Government by Proxy: (Mis) Managing Federal Programs*. Washington, DC: CQ Press.

———. 1993a. "Public Administration: The State of the Field." In *Political Science: The State of the Discipline*, edited by Ada Finfter. Washington, DC: American Political Science Association.

———. 1993b. *Sharing Power: Public Governance and Private Markets*. Washington, DC: Brookings Institution.

———. 2000. *The Global Public Management Revolution: A Report on the Transformation of Governance.* Washington, DC: Brookings Institution.

———. 2002. *The Transformation of Governance: Public Administration for Twenty-first Century America.* Baltimore, MD: Johns Hopkins University Press.

———. 2007. *System Under Stress: Homeland Security and American Politics.* 2nd ed. Washington, DC: CQ Press.

Kiel, L. Douglas. 1994. *Managing Chaos and Complexity in Government.* San Francisco: Jossey-Bass.

Kingdon, John. 1995. *Agendas, Alternatives, and Public Policies.* New York: HarperCollins.

Kingsley, J. Donald. 1944. *Representative Bureaucracy.* Yellow Springs, OH: Antioch Press.

Knott, Jack. 1993. "Comparing Public and Private Management: Cooperative Effort and Principal-Agent Relationships." *Journal of Public Administration Research and Theory* 3:93–119.

Koliba, Christopher J., Russell M. Mills, and Asim Zia. 2011. "Accountability in Governance Networks: An Assessment of Public, Private, and Nonprofit Emergency Management Practices Following Hurricane Katrina." *Public Administration Review* 71:210–220.

Koppell, Jonathan. 2008. "Global Governance Organizations: Legitimacy and Authority in Conflict." *Journal of Public Administration Research and Theory* 18:177–203.

———. 2010. *World Rule: Accountability, Legitimacy, and the Design of Global Governance.* Chicago: University of Chicago Press.

———. 2011. "Administration Without Borders." *Public Administration Review* 70 (supplement s1):S46–S55.

Kramer, Roderick M. 1999. "Trust and Distrust in Organizations: Emerging Perspectives, Enduring Questions." *Annual Review of Psychology* 50: 569–598.

Kramer, Roderick M., and Karen S. Cook, eds. 2004. *Trust and Distrust in Organizations: Dilemmas and Approaches.* New York: Russell Sage.

Kramer, Roderick M., and Tom R. Tyler, eds. 1996. *Trust in Organizations: Frontiers of Theory and Research.* Thousand Oaks, CA: Sage.

Krause, George. 2003. "Agency Risk Propensities Involving the Demand for Bureaucratic Discretion." In *Politics, Policy, and Organizations: Essays in the Scientific Study of Bureaucracy*, edited by George Krause and Kenneth Meier. Ann Arbor: University of Michigan Press.

Krislov, Samuel. 1974. *Representative Bureaucracy.* Englewood Cliffs, NJ: Prentice-Hall.

Kuhn, Thomas S. 1962. *The Structure of Scientific Revolutions.* Chicago: University of Chicago Press.

Landau, Martin. 1991. "On Multiorganizational Systems in Public Administration." *Journal of Public Administration Research and Theory* 1:5–18.

LaPorte, Todd R., and Paula M. Consolini. 1991. "Working in Practice but Not in Theory: Theoretical Challenges to High-Reliability Organizations." *Journal of Public Administration Research and Theory* 1:19–47.

LaPorte, Todd R., and Ann Keller. 1996. "Assuring Institutional Constancy: Requisite for Managing Long-Lived Hazards." *Public Administration Review* 56:535–544.

Lasswell, Harold. 1936. *Politics: Who Gets What, When, How?* New York: McGraw-Hill.

Leland, Suzanne, and Olga Smirnova. 2009. "Reassessing Privatization Strategies 25 Years Later: Revisiting Perry and Babitsky's Comparative Performance Study of Urban Bus Transit Services." *Public Administration Review* 69:855–867.

Leonhardt, David. 2011. "For Federal Programs, a Taste of Market Discipline." *New York Times*, February 9, B1.

Levitan, David. 1946. "The Responsibility of Administrative Officials in Democratic Society." *Political Science Quarterly* 61:562–598.

Light, Paul. 1999. *The True Size of Government*. Washington, DC: Brookings Institution.

Lijphart, Arend. 1984. *Democracies: Pottering Majoritarian and Consensus Government*. New Haven, CT: Yale University Press.

Likert, Rensis. 1961. *New Patterns of Management*. New York: McGraw-Hill.

———. 1967. *The Human Organization: Its Management and Value*. New York: McGraw-Hill.

Lim, Hong-Hai. 2006. "Representative Bureaucracy: Rethinking Substantive Effects and Active Representation." *Public Administration Review* 66:193–204.

Lincoln, Yvonna S., and Egon G. Guba. 1985. *Naturalistic Inquiry*. Beverly Hills, CA: Sage.

Lindblom, Charles. 1959. "The Science of Muddling Through." *Public Administration Review* 19:79–88.

———. 1965. *The Intelligence of Democracy: Decision Making Through Mutual Adjustment*. New York: The Free Press.

———. 1979. "Still Muddling, Not Yet Through." *Public Administration Review* 39:517–526.

Lindblom, Charles, and David K. Cohen. 1979. *Usable Knowledge*. New Haven, CT: Yale University Press.

Lipsky, Michael. 1980. *Street-Level Bureaucracy: Dilemmas of the Individual in Public Services*. New York: Russell Sage.

Litchfield, Edward. 1956. "Notes on a General Theory of Administration." *Administrative Science Quarterly* 1:3–29.

Loewe, Michael. 1966. *Imperial China*. New York: Praeger.

Long, Norton. 1949. "Power and Administration." *Public Administration Review* 9:257–264.

———. 1952. "Bureaucracy and Constitutionalism." *American Political Science Review* 46:808–818.

Lowery, David. 2000. "A Transactions Costs Model of Metropolitan Governance: Allocation Versus Redistribution in Urban America." *Journal of Public Administration Research and Theory* 10:49–78.

———. 2002. "Improving Governance." Review of *Improving Governance: A New Logic for Empirical Research* by Laurence E. Lynn, Carolyn J. Heinrich, and Carolyn J. Hill. *Journal of Public Administration Research and Theory* 12:293–298.

Lowery, David, and William Lyons. 1989. "The Impact of Jurisdictional Boundaries: An Individual-Level Test of the Tiebout Model." *Journal of Politics* 51:73–97.

Lowery, David, William Lyons, and Ruth Hoogland DeHoog. 1992. *The Politics of Dissatisfaction: Citizens, Services, and Urban Institutions*. Armonk, NY: M. E. Sharpe.

———. 1995. "The Empirical Evidence for Citizen Information and a Market for Public Goods." *American Political Science Review* 89:705–707.

Lowi, Theodore. 1979. *The End of Liberalism*. New York: Norton.

Lynn, Laurence Jr. 1996. *Public Management on Art, Science, and Profession*. Chatham, NJ: Chatham House.

———. 2001. "The Myth of the Bureaucratic Paradigm: What Traditional Public Administration Really Stood For." *Public Administration Review* 61:144–157.

Lynn, Laurence Jr., Carolyn Heinrich, and Carolyn Hill. 1999. "The Empirical Study of Governance: Theories, Models, Methods." Presented at the Workshop on Models and

Methods for the Empirical Study of Governance, University of Arizona, Tucson, Arizona, April 23–May 1.

———. 2000. "Studying Governance and Public Management: Why? How?" In *Governance and Performance: New Perspectives*, edited by Carolyn Heinrich and Laurence E. Lynn Jr. Washington, DC: Georgetown University Press.

———. 2001. *Improving Governance: A New Logic for Empirical Research*. Washington, DC: Georgetown University Press.

Lyons, William, and David Lowery. 1989. "Governmental Fragmentation Versus Consolidation: Five Public Choice Myths About How to Create Informed, Involved, and Happy Citizens." *Public Administration Review* 6:533–543.

MacCrimmon, Kenneth, and Donald Wehrung. 1986. *Taking Risks: The Management of Uncertainty*. New York: The Free Press.

MacIntyre, Alasdair. 1984. *After Virtue*. Notre Dame, IN: University of Notre Dame Press.

Majone, Giandomenico. 1984. "Professionalism and Nonprofit Organizations." *Journal of Health Politics, Policy, and Law* 8:639–659.

———. 1989. *Evidence, Argument, and Persuasion in the Policy Process*. New Haven, CT: Yale University Press.

Mansbridge, Jane. 1980. *Beyond Adversary Democracy*. New York: Basic Books.

March, James G. 1988. *Decisions and Organizations*. Oxford: Basil Blackwell.

———. 1994. *A Primer on Decision Making: How Decisions Happen*. New York: The Free Press.

March, James G., and Johan P. Olsen, eds. 1976. *Ambiguity and Choice in Organizations*. Bergen, Norway: Universitetsforlaget.

———. 1984. "The New Institutionalism: Organizational Factors in Political Life." *American Political Science Review* 78:734–749.

———. 1986. "Garbage Can Models of Decision Making in Organizations." In *Ambiguity and Command*, edited by James March and Roger Weissinger-Baylon. Cambridge, MA: Ballinger.

———. 1989. *Rediscovering Institutions*. New York: The Free Press.

———. 1995. *Democratic Governance*. New York: The Free Press.

March, James G., and Herbert Simon. 1993. *Organizations*. Oxford: Basil Blackwell.

Marini, Frank. 1971. *Toward a New Public Administration: The Minnowbrook Perspective*. Scranton, PA: Chandler.

Martin, Roscoe C. 1965. *Public Administration and Democracy: Essays in Honor of Paul H. Appleby*. Syracuse, NY: Syracuse University Press.

Marx, Fritz Morstein, ed. 1946. *Elements of Public Administration*. New York: Prentice-Hall.

Mason, J. Alden. 1957. *The Ancient Civilizations of Peru*. New York: Penguin.

Mayhew, David. 1991. *Divided We Govern: Party Control, Law Making, and Investigation, 1946–1990*. Tuscaloosa: University of Alabama Press.

Maynard-Moody, Steven, and Suzanne Leland. 1999. "Stories from the Front-Lines of Public Management: Street-Level Workers as Responsible Actors." In *Advancing Public Management: New Developments in Theory, Methods, and Practice*, edited by Hal Rainey and Jeff Brudney. Washington, DC: Georgetown University Press.

Maynard-Moody, Steven, and Michael Musheno. 2000. "State Agent or Citizen Agent: Two Narratives of Discretion." *Journal of Public Administration Research and Theory* 10:329–358.

———. 2003. *Streetwise Workers: Enacting Identities and Making Moral Judgment*. Ann Arbor: University of Michigan Press.

———. 2009. *Cops, Teachers, Counselors: Stories from the Front Lines of Public Service.* Ann Arbor: University of Michigan Press.

Maynard-Moody, Steven, Michael Musheno, and Marisa Kelly. 1995. "Justice in the Delivery of Government Services: Decision Norms of Street-Level Bureaucrats." Unpublished proposal to the Law and Science Program, National Science Foundation.

Mazmanian, Daniel, and Jeanne Neinaber. 1979. *Can Organizations Change? Environmental Protection, Citizen Participation, and the Corps of Engineers.* Washington, DC: Brookings Institution.

McCabe, Barbara Coyle, and Janet Coble Vinzant. 1999. "Governance Lessons: The Case of Charter Schools." *Administration and Society* 31:361–377.

McCloskey, Donald N. 1985. *The Rhetoric of Economics.* Madison: University of Wisconsin Press.

McCoy, Edgar. 1940. "Patterns of Diffusion in the United States." *American Sociological Review* 5:219–227.

McGregor, Douglas. 1960. *The Human Side of Enterprise.* New York: McGraw-Hill.

McGregor, Eugene Jr. 1991. *Strategic Management of Human Knowledge, Skills, and Abilities: Workforce Decision Making in the Post-Industrial Era.* San Francisco: Jossey-Bass.

McKay, David. 1994. "Divided and Governed? Recent Research on Divided Government in the United States." *British Journal of Political Science* 24:517–534.

McKinney, Jerome, and Lawrence Howard. 1998. *Public Administration: Balancing Power and Accountability.* New York: Praeger.

McSwite, O. C. 1997. *Legitimacy in Public Administration: A Discourse Analysis.* Thousand Oaks, CA: Sage.

———. 2002. *Invitation to Public Administration.* Armonk, NY: M. E. Sharpe.

Meier, Kenneth. 1975. "Representative Bureaucracy: An Empirical Analysis." *American Political Science Review* 69:526–542.

———. 1980. "Executive Reorganization of Government: Impact on Employment and Expenditures." *American Journal of Political Science* 24:396–412.

———. 1993. *Politics and the Bureaucracy: Policymaking in the Fourth Branch of Government.* Pacific Grove, CA: Brooks/Cole.

———. 1994. *The Politics of Sin: Drugs, Alcohol, and Public Policy.* Armonk, NY: M. E. Sharpe.

———. 1997. "Bureaucracy and Democracy: The Case for More Bureaucracy and Less Democracy." *Public Administration Review* 57:193–199.

———. 2011. "Governance, Structure, and Democracy: Luther Gulick and the Future of Public Administration." *Public Administration Review* 70 (supplement s1):S284–S291.

Meier, Kenneth, and John Bohte. 2000. "Ode to Luther Gulick: Span of Control and Organizational Performance." *Administration and Society* 32:115–137.

———. 2003. "Span of Control and Public Organizations: Implementing Luther Gulick's Research Design." *Public Administration Review* 63:61–70.

Meier, Kenneth, and Jill Nicholson-Crotty. 2006. "Gender, Representative Bureaucracy, and Law Enforcement: The Case of Sexual Assault." *Public Administration Review* 66:850–860.

Meier, Kenneth, and Laurence O'Toole. 2009. "The Proverbs of New Public Management: Lessons from an Evidence-Based Research Agenda." *American Review of Public Administration* 39:4–22.

Meier, Kenneth, and Joseph Stewart Jr. 1992. "The Impact of Representative Bureaucracies: Educational Systems and Public Policies." *American Review of Public Administration* 22:157–151.

Meier, Kenneth, Joseph Stewart Jr., and Robert England. 1989. *Race, Class, and Education*. Madison: University of Wisconsin Press.

———. 1991. "The Politics of Bureaucratic Discretion: Educational Access as an Urban Service." *American Journal of Political Science* 35:155–177.

Meier, Kenneth, Robert Wrinkle, and J. L. Polinard. 1999. "Representative Bureaucracy and Distributional Equity: Addressing the Hard Question." *Journal of Politics* 61:1025–1039.

Mertins, Herman, and Patrick Hennigan. 1982. *Applying Professional Standards and Ethics in the '80s: A Workbook and Study Guide for Public Administrators*. Washington, DC: American Society for Public Administration.

Merton, Robert K. 1957. "Bureaucratic Structure and Personality." In *Social Theory and Social Structure*, edited by Robert Merton. New York: The Free Press.

Milgrom, Paul, and John Roberts. 1992. *Economics, Organization, and Management*. Englewood Cliffs, NJ: Prentice-Hall.

Milward, H. Brinton. 1994. "Implications of Contracting Out: New Roles for the Hollow State." In *New Paradigms for Government: Issues for the Changing Public Service*, edited by Patricia Ingraham and Barbara Romzek. San Francisco: Jossey-Bass.

———, ed. 1996. "Symposium on the Hollow State: Capacity, Control, and Performance in Interorganizational Settings." Including Eugene Bardach and Cara Lesser, "Accountability in Human Service Collaboratives: For What? and to Whom?"; Laurence O'Toole Jr., "Hollowing the Infrastructure: Revolving Loan Programs and Network Dynamics in the American States"; William Gormley Jr., "Regulatory Privatization: A Case Study"; H. Brinton Milward and Louise Ogilvie Snyder, "Electronic Government: Linking Citizens to Public Organizations Through Technology"; Steven Rathgeb Smith and Judith Smyth, "Contracting for Services in a Deregulated System"; and Laurence Lynn Jr., "Assume a Network: Reforming Mental Health Services in Illinois." *Journal of Public Administration Research and Theory* 6:193–314.

Milward, H. Brinton, and Keith Provan. 2000a. "Governing the Hollow State." *Journal of Public Administration Research and Theory* 10:359–379.

———. 2000b. "How Networks Are Governed." In *Governance and Performance: New Perspectives*, edited by Carolyn Heinrich and Laurence Lynn Jr. Washington, DC: Georgetown University Press.

Mintzberg, Henry. 1979. *The Structuring of Organizations*. Englewood Cliffs, NJ: Prentice-Hall.

———. 1992. *Structure in Fives: Designing Effective Organizations*. Englewood Cliffs, NJ: Prentice-Hall.

Moe, Ronald, and Robert Gilmour. 1995. "Rediscovering Principles of Public Administration: The Neglected Foundation of Public Law." *Public Administration Review* 55:135–146.

Moe, Terry. 1980. *The Organization of Interests*. Chicago: University of Chicago Press.

———. 1984. "The New Economics of Organization." *American Journal of Political Science* 28:739–777.

———. 1989. "The Politics of Bureaucratic Structure." In *Can the Government Govern?* edited by John Chubb and Paul Peterson. Washington, DC: Brookings Institution.

———. 1990. "Political Institutions: The Neglected Side of the Story." *Journal of Law, Economics, and Organization* 6:213–266.

Moore, Mark H. 1995. *Creating Public Value: Strategic Management in Government*. Cambridge, MA: Harvard University Press.

Morgan, Douglas F. 1990. "Administrative *Phronesis*: Discretion and the Problem of Administrative Legitimacy in Our Constitutional System." In *Images and Identities in Public Administration*, edited by Henry D. Kass and Bayard L. Catron. Newbury Park, CA: Sage.

Morgan, Gareth. 1993. *Imaginization: The Art of Creative Management.* Newbury Park, CA: Sage.

Morley, Sylvanus. 1956. *The Ancient Maya.* Stanford, CA: Stanford University Press.

Morton, N. O., and S. A. Lindquist. 1997. "Revealing the Feminist in Mary Parker Follett." *Administration and Society* 29:348–371.

Mosher, Frederick. 1982. *Democracy and the Public Service.* New York: Oxford University Press.

Moynihan, Donald P., and Sanjay K. Pandey. 2007. "The Role of Organizations in Fostering Public Service Motivation." *Public Administration Review* 67:40–53.

Nalbandian, John. 1995. "Politics, Administration, and the City Manager." In *Ideal and Practice in Council-Manager Government*, edited by H. George Frederickson. Washington, DC: ICMA Press.

Nathan, Richard. 1993. *Turning Promise into Performance: The Management Challenge in Implementing Workforce.* New York: Columbia University Press.

National Commission for Employment Policy. 1988. *Privatization and Public Employees: The Impact of City and County Contracting Out on Government Workers.* Washington, DC: National Commission for Employment Policy.

Neustadt, Richard. 1960. *Presidential Power.* New York: Wiley.

Newland, Chester. 1994. "Managing for the Future in Council-Manager Government." In *Ideal and Practice in Council-Manager Government*, edited by H. George Frederickson. Washington, DC: International City/County Management Association.

Niskanen, William. 1971. *Bureaucracy and Representative Government.* Hawthorne, NY: Aldine de Gruyter.

———. 1994. *Bureaucracy and Economics.* Brookfield, VT: Edward Elgar.

North, Douglass. 1990. *Institutions, Institutional Change, and Economic Performance.* Cambridge: Cambridge University Press.

Olsen, Johan. 2001. "Garbage Cans, New Institutionalism, and the Study of Politics." *American Political Science Review* 95:191–198.

Osborne, David, and Ted Gaebler. 1992. *Reinventing Government.* Reading, MA: Addison-Wesley.

Ostrom, Elinor. 1998. "A Behavioral Approach to the Rational Choice Theory of Collective Action: Presidential Address, American Political Science Association, 1997." *American Political Science Review* 92:1–22.

———. 2003. "Toward a Behavioral Theory Linking Trust, Reciprocity, and Reputation." In *Trust and Reciprocity: Interdisciplinary Lessons from Experimental Research*, edited by Elinor Ostrom and James Walker. New York: Russell Sage.

Ostrom, Elinor, Roy Gardner, and James Walker. 1994. *Rules, Games, and Common-Pool Resources.* Ann Arbor: University of Michigan Press.

Ostrom, Elinor, Larry Schroeder, and Susan Wayne. 1993. "Analyzing the Performance of Alternative Institutional Arrangements for Sustaining Rural Infrastructure in Developing Countries." *Journal of Public Communication Research and Theory* 3:11–45.

Ostrom, Vincent. 1973. *The Intellectual Crisis in American Public Administration.* Tuscaloosa: University of Alabama Press.

Ostrom, Vincent, Charles M. Tiebout, and Robert Warren. 1961. "The Organization of Government in Metropolitan Areas: A Theoretical Inquiry." *American Political Science Review* 55:831–842.

O'Toole, Laurence J. 1997a. "The Implications for Democracy in a Networked Bureaucratic World." *Journal of Public Administration Research and Theory* 7:443–459.

———. 1997b. "Treating Networks Seriously: Practical and Research-Based Agendas in Public Administration." *Public Administration Review* 57:45–52.

———. 2000. "Research on Policy Implementation: Assessment and Prospects." *Journal of Public Administration Research and Theory* 20:263–288.

O'Toole, Laurence, and Kenneth Meier. 2004. "Desperately Seeking Selznick: Cooptation and the Dark Side of Public Management in Networks." *Public Administration Review* 64:681–693.

Overman, E. Sam, and Kathy J. Boyd. 1994. "Best Practices Research and Postbureaucratic Reform." *Journal of Public Administration Research and Theory* 4:67–84.

Palumbo, Dennis. 1987. *The Politics of Program Evaluation.* Newbury Park, CA: Sage.

Perrow, Charles. 1999. *Normal Accidents: Living with the High-Risk Technologies.* Princeton, NJ: Princeton University Press.

Perry, James L. 2000. "Bringing Society In: Toward a Theory of Public Service Motivation." *Journal of Public Administration Research and Theory* 10:471–488.

Perry, James L., and Timlynn Babitsky. 1986. "Comparative Performance in Urban Bus Transit: Assessing Privatization Strategies." *Public Administration Review* 46:57–66.

Perry, James L., Debra Mesch, and Laurie E. Paarlberg. 2006. "Motivating Employees in a New Governance Era: The Performance Paradigm Revisited." *Public Administration Review* 66:505–514.

Peters, B. Guy. 2000. "Policy Instruments and Public Management: Bridging the Gap." *Journal of Public Administration Research and Theory* 10:35–47.

Peters, B. Guy, and John Pierre. 1998. "Governance Without Government? Rethinking Public Administration." *Journal of Public Administration Research and Theory* 8:223–244.

———. 2000. "Citizens Versus the New Public Manager: The Problem of Mutual Empowerment." *Administration and Society* 32:9–28.

Peterson, Paul, and Mark Rom. 1990. *Welfare Magnets.* Washington, DC: Brookings Institution.

Pfiffner, John, and Frank P. Sherwood. 1960. *Administrative Organization.* Englewood Cliffs, NJ: Prentice-Hall.

Podsakoff, Philip M., Scott B. MacKenzie, and William H. Bommer. 1996. "Transformational Leader Behaviors and Substitutes for Leadership as Determinants of Employee Satisfaction, Commitment, Trust, and Organizational Citizenship Behaviors." *Journal of Management* 22:259–298.

Pollitt, Christopher. 1990. *Managerialism and the Public Services: The Anglo-American Experience.* Oxford: Basil Blackwell.

———. 2010. "Envisioning Public Administration as a Scholarly Field in 2020." *Public Administration Review* 70(supplement s1):S292–S294.

Portillo, Shannon, and Leisha DeHart-Davis. 2009. "Gender and Organizational Rule Abidance." *Public Administration Review* 69:339–347.

Powell, Walter, and Paul DiMaggio, eds. 1991. *The New Institutionalism in Organizational Analysis.* Chicago: University of Chicago Press.

Prescott, William. 1908. *History of the Conquest of Peru.* New York: Dutton.

Protasel, Greg J. 1994. "Leadership in Council-Manager Cities: The Institutional Implications." In *Ideal and Practice in Council-Manager Government,* edited by H. George Frederickson. Washington, DC: International City/County Management Association.

Provan, Keith, and H. Brinton Milward. 1995. "A Preliminary Theory of Network Effectiveness: A Comparative Study of Four Community Mental Health Systems." *Administrative Science Quarterly* 40:1–33.

Raadschelders, Jos C. N., and Kwang-Hoon Lee. 2011. "Trends in the Study of Public Administration: Empirical and Qualitative Observations from Public Administration Review, 2000–2009." *Public Administration Review* 71:19–33.

Radin, Beryl. 2000. "The Government Performance and Results Act and the Tradition of Federal Management Reform: Square Pegs in Round Holes?" *Journal of Public Administration Research and Theory* 11:111–136.

Radner, Roy. 1985. "Repeated Principal-Agent Games with Discounting." *Econometrica* 53:1173–1198.

Rainey, Hal. 1997. *Understanding and Managing Public Organizations.* San Francisco: Jossey-Bass.

Rainey, Hal, and Paula Steinbauer. 1999. "Galloping Elephants: Developing Elements of a Theory of Effective Government Organizations." *Journal of Public Administration Research and Theory* 9:1–32.

Ranney, Austin. 1954. *The Doctrine of Responsible Party Government: Its Origins and Present State.* Urbana: University of Illinois Press.

Rasmussen, Eric. 1990. *Games and Information: An Introduction to Game Theory.* Oxford: Basil Blackwell.

Rebell, Michael. 1998. "Fiscal Equity Litigation and the Democratic Imperative." *Journal of Education Finance* 24:23–50.

Rehfuss, John. 1989. *Contracting Out in Government: A Guide for Working with Outside Contractors to Supply Public Services.* San Francisco: Jossey-Bass.

Renner, Tari, and Victor DeSantis. 1993. "Contemporary Patterns and Trends in Government Structures." In *The Municipal Year Book.* Washington, DC: International City/County Management Association.

Rhodes, Edward. 1994. "Do Bureaucratic Politics Matter? Some Disconfirming Findings from the Case of the U.S. Navy." *World Politics* 47:1–41.

Rhodes, Rod. 1994. "The Hollowing Out of the State." *Political Quarterly* 65:138–151.

Ringquist, Evan. 1995. "Political Control and Policy Impact in EPA's Office of Water Quality." *American Journal of Political Science* 39:336–364.

Rittel, Horst, and Melvin Webber. 1973. "Dilemmas in a General Theory of Planning." *Policy Sciences* 4:155–169.

Roberts, John. 1999. *Twentieth Century: The History of the World, 1901–2000.* New York: Viking.

Robinson, Scott. 2006. "A Decade of Treating Networks Seriously." *Policy Studies Journal* 34:589–598.

Roderick, Melissa, Brian Jacob, and Anthony Bryk. 2000. "Evaluating Chicago's Efforts to End Social Promotion." In *Governance and Performance: New Perspectives,* edited by Carolyn Heinrich and Laurence Lynn Jr. Washington, DC: Georgetown University Press.

Roethlisberger, Fritz J., and William J. Dickson. 1939. *Management and the Worker.* Cambridge, MA: Harvard University Press.

Rogers, Everett M. 1995. *Diffusion of Innovations.* New York: The Free Press.

Rohr, John. 1986. *To Run a Constitution: The Legitimacy of the Administrative State.* Lawrence: University Press of Kansas.

Romzek, Barbara, and Melvin Dubnick. 1987. "Accountability in the Public Sector: Lessons from the Challenger Tragedy." *Public Administration Review* 47:227–238.

Romzek, Barbara, and Patricia Ingraham. 2000. "Cross Pressures of Accountability: Initiative, Command, and Failure in the Ron Brown Plane Crash." *Public Administration Review* 60:240–253.

Rosati, Jerel. 1981. "Developing a Systematic Decision-Making Framework: Bureaucratic Politics in Perspective." *World Politics* 33:234–252.

Rosen, Bernard. 1989. *Holding Government Bureaucracies Accountable.* New York: Praeger.

Ruscio, Kenneth P. 1997. "Trust in the Administrative State." *Public Administration Review* 57:454–458.

Rusk, David. 1995. *Cities Without Suburbs.* Washington, DC: Woodrow Wilson Center Press.

Salamon, Lester. 1989. *Beyond Privatization: The Tasks of Government Action.* Washington, DC: Urban Institute Press.

Sarbin, Theodore, and Vernon Allen. 1968. *Role Theory.* In *Handbook of Social Psychology,* edited by Gardner Lindzey and Elliot Aronson. Reading, MA: Addison-Wesley.

Sayer, Wallace. 1958. "Premises of Public Administration: Past and Emerging." *Public Administration Review* 18:102–105.

Schilling, Warner. 1962. "The Politics of National Defense: Fiscal 1950." In *Strategy, Politics, and Defense Budgets,* edited by Warner Schilling, Paul Hammond, and Glenn Snyder. New York: Columbia University Press.

Schram, Sanford, and Philip Neisser, eds. 1997. *Tales of the State: Narrative in U.S. Politics and Public Policy.* Lanham, MD: Rowman and Littlefield.

Scott, W. Richard. 1995. *Institutions and Organizations.* Thousand Oaks, CA: Sage.

Seidman, Harold. 1970. *Politics, Position, and Power: The Dynamics of Federal Organization.* New York: Oxford University Press.

———. 1980. *Politics, Position, and Power: The Dynamics of Federal Organization.* 3rd ed. New York: Oxford University Press.

———. 1998. *Politics, Position, and Power: The Dynamics of Federal Organizations.* 5th ed. New York: Oxford University Press.

Selden, Sally. 1997. *The Promise of Representative Bureaucracy: Diversity and Responsiveness in a Government Agency.* Armonk, NY: M. E. Sharpe.

Selznick, Phillip, 1949. *TVA and the Grass Roots.* Berkeley and Los Angeles: University of California Press.

Shafritz, Jay, and E. W. Russell. 1997. *Introducing Public Administration.* New York: Longman.

Shaw, Marvin. 1981. *Group Dynamics: The Psychology of Small Group Behavior.* New York: McGraw-Hill.

Shepsle, Kenneth. 1989. "Studying Institutions: Some Lessons from the Rational Choice Approach." *Journal of Theoretical Politics* 1:131–147.

Shepsle, Kenneth, and Barry Weingast. 1987. "The Institutional Foundations of Committee Power." *American Political Science Review* 81:85–104.

Simon, Herbert. 1946. "The Proverbs of Administration." *Public Administration Review* 4:16–30.

———. 1947/1997. *Administrative Behavior.* New York: The Free Press.

———. 1952a. "Development of Theory of Democratic Administration: Replies and Comments." *American Political Science Review* 46:494–503.

———. 1952b. "Reply to Waldo." *American Political Science Review* 46:494–496.

———. 1960. *The New Science of Management Decision.* New York: HarperCollins.

———. 1969. *The Sciences of the Artificial.* Cambridge, MA: MIT Press.

———. 1985. "Human Nature in Politics: The Dialogue of Psychology with Political Science." *American Political Science Review* 79:293–304.

———. 1991. "Preface to the Reissue of Simon, Smithburg, and Thompson's Public Administration." *Journal of Public Administration Research and Theory* 1:79–88.

————. 2000. "Public Administration in Today's World of Organizations and Markets." *P.S.: Political Science and Politics* 33:749–756.

Simon, Herbert, Donald Smithburg, and Victor Thompson. 1950. *Public Administration*. New York: Knopf.

Singer, J. David. 1966. "The Behavioral Science Approach to International Relations: Payoff and Prospect." *SAIS Review* 10:12–20.

Skelcher, Chris. 2005. "Public-Private Partnerships and Hybridity." In *The Oxford Handbook of Public Management*, edited by Ewan Ferle, Laurence Lynn Jr., and Christopher Pollitt. New York: Oxford University Press.

Skowronek, Stephan. 1982. *Building a New American State*. Cambridge: Cambridge University Press.

Smith, Adam. 1776/2004. *The Wealth of Nations*. New York: Barnes & Noble.

Smith, Kevin B. 2006. "Representational Altruism: The Wary Cooperator as Authoritative Decision Maker." *American Journal of Political Science* 50:1013–1022.

Smith, Rogers. 1988. "Political Jurisprudence, the 'New Institutionalism,' and the Future of Public Law." *American Political Science Review* 82:89–108.

Smith, Steven, and Michael Lipsky. 1993. *Nonprofits for Hire: The Welfare State in the Age of Contracting*. Cambridge, MA: Harvard University Press.

Soss, Joe. 2000. *Unwanted Claims: The Politics of Participation in the U.S. Welfare System*. Ann Arbor: University of Michigan Press.

Stein, Robert. 1993. "Arranging City Services." *Journal of Public Administration Research and Theory* 3:66–92.

Stephens, G. Ross, and Nelson Wikstrom. 2000. *Metropolitan Government and Governance: New Perspectives, Empirical Analysis, and the Future*. New York: Oxford University Press.

Stivers, Camilla. 1990. "Toward a Feminist Theory of Public Administration." *Women and Politics* 10:49–65.

————. 1992. "A Wild Patience: A Feminist Critique of Ameliorative Public Administration." In *Public Management in an Interconnected World: Essays in the Minnowbrook Tradition*, edited by Mary T. Bailey and Richard T. Mayer. Westport, CT: Greenwood Press.

————. 1996. "Mary Parker Follett and the Question of Gender." *Organization* 3:161–166.

————. 2000. *Bureau Men, Settlement Women: Constructing Public Administration in the Progressive Era*. Lawrence: University Press of Kansas.

————. 2002. *Gender Images in Public Administration: Legitimacy and the Administrative State*. Thousand Oaks, CA: Sage.

Stone, Deborah. 2002. *Policy Paradox: The Art of Political Decision Making*. New York: Norton.

Strang, David, and Sarah Soule. 1998. "Diffusion in Organizations and Social Movements: From Hybrid Corn to Power Pills." *Annual Review of Sociology* 24:265–290.

Strange, Susan. 1995. *The Retreat of the State: The Diffusion of Power in the World Economy*. Cambridge: Cambridge University Press.

Svara, James. 1994. "Dichotomy and Duality: Reconceptualizing the Relationships Between Policy and Administration in Council-Manager Cities." In *Ideal and Practice in Council-Manager Government*, edited by H. George Frederickson. Washington, DC: International City/County Management Association.

Szanton, Peter L. 1981. *Not Well Advised*. New York: Russell Sage Foundation.

Taylor, Frederick W. 1911/2010. *The Principles of Scientific Management*. Lawrence, KS: DigiRead.

Terry, Larry D. 1998. "Administrative Leadership, Neo-Managerialism, and the Public Management Movement." *Public Administration Review* 58:194–200.

Teske, Paul, Mark Schneider, Michael Mintrom, and Samuel Best. 1993. "Establishing the Micro Foundations of a Macro Theory: Information, Movers, and the Competitive Local Market for Public Goods." *American Political Science Review* 87:702–713.

Thaler, Richard H., and Cass R. Sunstein. 2009. *Nudge: Improving Decisions About Health, Wealth, and Happiness.* New York: Penguin.

Theobald, Nick, and Donald Haider-Markel. 2009. "Race Bureaucracy, and Symbolic Representation: Interactions Between Citizens and Police." *Journal of Public Administration Research and Theory* 19:409–426.

Thompson, James D. 1967. *Organizations in Action.* New York: McGraw-Hill.

Tiebout, Charles. 1956. "A Pure Theory of Local Expenditures." *Journal of Political Economy* 44:416–424.

Toonen, Theo. 2010. "Resilience in Public Administration: The Work of Elinor and Vincent Ostrom from a Public Administration Perspective." *Public Administration Review* 70:193–202.

Tout, T. F. 1937. *Chapters in Medieval Administrative History.* Vol. 2. Manchester, England: Manchester University Press.

Treadway, Darren C., Wayne A. Hochwater, Gerald R. Ferris, Charles J. Kacmar, Ceasar Douglas, Anthony P. Ammeter, and M. Ronald Buckley. 2004. "Leader Political Skill and Employee Reactions." *Leadership Quarterly* 15:493–513.

Tuchman, Barbara. 1984. *The March of Folly: From Troy to Vietnam.* New York: Knopf.

Tullock, Gordon. 1965. *The Politics of Bureaucracy.* Washington, DC: Public Affairs Press.

Tversky, Amos, and Daniel Kahneman. 1974. "Judgment Under Uncertainty: Heuristics and Biases." *Science* 185:1124–1131.

Tyler, Tom R. 1990. *Why People Obey the Law.* New Haven, CT: Yale University Press.

———. 2001. "The Psychology of Public Dissatisfaction with Government." In *What Is It About Government That Americans Dislike?* edited by John R. Hibbing and Elizabeth Theiss-Morse. New York: Cambridge University Press.

Tyler, Tom R., and Peter DeGoey. 1996. "Trust in Organizational Authorities: The Influence of Motive Attributions on Willingness to Accept Decisions." In *Trust in Organizations: Frontiers of Theory and Research*, edited by Roderick M. Kramer and Tom R. Tyler. Thousand Oaks, CA: Sage.

Uphoff, Norman. 1994. "Revisiting Institution Building: How Organizations Become Institutions." In *Puzzles of Predictability in Public Organizations*, edited by Norman Uphoff. Oakland, CA: Institute of Contemporary Societies.

Van Slyke, David. 2007. "Agents or Stewards: Using Theory to Understand the Government-Nonprofit Social Service Contracting Relationship." *Journal of Public Administration Research and Theory* 17:157–187.

Von Hagen, Victor. 1962. *The Ancient Sun Kingdoms.* London: Thames and Hudson.

Waldo, Dwight. 1946. *The Administrative State.* San Francisco: Chandler.

———. 1948. *The Administrative State.* New York: Ronald Press.

———. 1952. "Development of Theory of Democratic Administration." *American Political Science Review* 46:81–103.

———. 1953. "Reply to Simon." *American Political Science Review* 47:500–503.

———. 1956. *Perspectives on Administration.* Tuscaloosa: University of Alabama Press.

Wamsley, Gary, and James Wolf, eds. 1996. *Refounding Democratic Public Administration: Modern Paradoxes and Post Modern Challenges.* Thousand Oaks, CA: Sage.

Weaver, Kent, and Bert Rockman, eds. 1993. *Do Institutions Matter?* Washington, DC: Brookings Institution.

Weber, Max. 1947. "The Chinese Literati." In *From Max Weber*, edited by H. H. Gerth and C. Wright Mills. New York: Oxford University Press.

———. 1952. "The Essentials of Bureaucratic Organization: An Ideal-Type Construction." In *Reader in Bureaucracy*, edited by Robert K. Merton, Ailsa P. Gray, Barbara Hockey, and Hanan C. Selvin. Glencoe, IL: The Free Press.

Weick, Karl. 1979. *The Social Psychology of Organizing.* Menlo Park, CA: Addison-Wesley.

———. 1995. *Sensemaking in Organizations.* Thousand Oaks, CA: Sage.

Weick, Karl, Kathleen Sutcliffe, and David Obstfeld. 2008. "Organizing for High Reliability: Processes of Collective Mindfulness." In *Crisis Management*, Vol. III, edited by Arjen Boin. London: Sage.

Weimer, David, and Aidan Vining. 1989. *Policy Analysis: Concepts and Practice.* Englewood Cliffs, NJ: Prentice-Hall.

West, William. 1995. *Controlling Bureaucracy: The Theory and Practice of Institutional Constraints.* Armonk, NY: M. E. Sharpe.

———. 1997. "Searching for a Theory of Bureaucratic Structure." *Journal of Public Administration Research and Theory* 7:591–613.

White, Jay, and Guy Adams. 1994. *Research in Public Administration: Reflections on Theory and Practice.* Newbury Park, CA: Sage.

White, Leonard. 1929. *Introduction to the Study of Public Administration.* New York: Macmillan.

Whyte, William Jr. 1956. *The Organization Man.* New York: Doubleday.

Wildavsky, Aaron. 1984. *The Budgetary Process.* Boston: Little, Brown.

———. 1987. "Choosing Preferences and Constructing Institutions: A Cultural Theory of Preference Formation." *American Political Science Association* 81:3–22.

———. 1988. *Searching for Safety.* New Brunswick, NJ: Transaction.

Wilkins, Vicki, and Lael Keiser. 2006. "Linking Passive and Active Representation by Gender: The Case of Child Support Agencies." *Journal of Public Administration Research and Theory* 16:87–102.

Wilson, Edward O. 1998. *Consilience: The Unity of Knowledge.* New York: Vintage.

Wilson, James Q. 1989. *Bureaucracy: What Government Agencies Do and Why They Do It.* New York: Basic Books.

Wilson, Woodrow. 1887/1941. "The Study of Public Administration." *Political Science Quarterly* 56:197–222.

Winch, Peter. 1995. *The Idea of a Social Science and Its Relation to Philosophy.* London: Routledge.

Wood, Dan. 1993. "The Politics of Antitrust Regulation." *American Journal of Political Science* 37:1–39.

Wood, Dan, and Richard Waterman. 1994. *Bureaucratic Dynamics: The Role of Bureaucracy in a Democracy.* Boulder, CO: Westview Press.

Wright, Bradley E. 2011. "Public Administration as an Interdisciplinary Field: Assessing Its Relationship with the Fields of Law, Management, and Political Science." *Public Administration Review* 71:96–101.

Wright, George. 1984. *Behavioral Decision Theory.* Beverly Hills, CA: Sage.

Yanow, Dvora. 1996. *How Does a Policy Mean? Interpreting Policy and Organizational Actions.* Washington, DC: Georgetown University Press.

Yutang, Lin. 1947. *The Gay Genius.* New York: John Day.

Zey, Mary, ed. 1992. *Decisionmaking: Alternatives to Rational Choice Models.* Newbury Park, CA: Sage.

INDEX

CPSIA information can be obtained at www.ICGtesting.com
Printed in the USA
LVOW13s0637271113

362929LV00002B/96/P